The Archaeology of Etruscan Society

The late sixth century was a period of considerable change in Etruria; this change is traditionally seen as the adoption of superior models from Greece. In a radical realignment of agency, this book examines a wide range of Etruscan material culture – mirrors, tombs, sanctuaries, houses, cities, and landscape – in order to demonstrate the importance of local concerns in the formation of Etruscan material culture. Drawing on recent theoretical developments, the book emphasises the deliberate nature of the smallest of changes in material culture form, and develops the concept of surface as a unifying key to understanding the changes in the ways Etruscans represented themselves in life and death. This concept allows a uniquely holistic approach to the archaeology of Etruscan society and has potential for other archaeological investigations. The book will interest scholars and students of archaeology and classical archaeology.

VEDIA IZZET is a Lecturer in Archaeology at the University of Southampton. She was a Fellow of Christ's College, Cambridge, and a Rome Scholar at the British School at Rome. She directed the British excavations of the Etruscan sanctuary at Sant' Antonio in Cerveteri. She is a co-editor of *Greece and Rome*.

The Archaeology of Etruscan Society

VEDIA IZZET

University of Southampton

CAMBRIDGE
UNIVERSITY PRESS

CAMBRIDGE UNIVERSITY PRESS

Cambridge, New York, Melbourne, Madrid, Cape Town, Singapore, São Paulo

Cambridge University Press
The Edinburgh Building, Cambridge CB2 8RU, UK

Published in the United States of America by Cambridge University Press, New York

www.cambridge.org
Information on this title: www.cambridge.org/9780521858779

First published 2007

Printed in the United Kingdom at the University Press, Cambridge

A catalogue record for this publication is available from the British Library

ISBN 978-0-521-85877-9 hardback

Contents

Illustrations

Acknowledgements

During the writing of this book, I have incurred debts to many people and institutions. The book had its origins as a PhD thesis submitted to the University of Cambridge, which was supervised by Nigel Spivey and examined by Simon Stoddart and Tom Rasmussen. I am very grateful for their help and suggestions. Parts of the book have origins in other places (Chapter 2 in R. Whitehouse (ed.) (1998) *Gender and Italian Archaeology: Challenging the Stereotypes*, London; Chapter 3 in J. B. Wilkins (ed.) (1996) *Approaches to the Study of Ritual: Italy and the Ancient Mediterranean*, London; Chapter 4 in *Cambridge Archaeological Journal* 11.2 (2001): 185–200; and Chapter 5 in J. R. Brandt and L. Karlsson (eds.) (2001) *From Huts to Houses: Transformations of Ancient Societies*, Stockholm). I am grateful to the editors of these volumes and to the Swedish Institute of Classical Studies in Rome for permission to revise some of this earlier material here. Many others read and commented on individual chapters of the thesis, and later the book, at preliminary or draft stages. This group of people overlaps with an ever-growing group of colleagues and friends who have helped in less direct, though no less important ways, ranging from informal discussion of ideas, participation in seminars, technical help, or 'mere' friendship. Most notable among these are Sara Aguilar, Graeme Barker, Mary Beard, Halid Izzet, Carl Knappett, Tamsin O'Connell, Rosanna Omitowoju, Roman Roth, Anthony Snodgrass and Kate Spence. I have received significant financial support from the British Academy, the British School at Rome and Christ's College, Cambridge, which it is a pleasure to acknowledge. The three readers for Cambridge University Press made extremely apposite and helpful suggestions, and Michael Sharp has been a considerate and thoughtful editor throughout. My debt to Rob Shorrock is inexpressible. The book is dedicated to the memory of my father, Ahmed Izzet.

Abbreviations

Abbreviations for the works of Classical authors follow those of S. Hornblower and A. Spawforth (eds.) (1996) *The Oxford Classical Dictionary*, 3rd edn, Oxford.

ABSA	*Annual of the British School at Athens*
AC	*Antiquité Classique*
AION	*Annali dell'Instituto Orientale Università di Napoli*
AION ArchStAnt	*Annali Archeologiae Storia Antica*
AIRRS	*Acta Instituti Romani Regni Sueciae* (supplement to ORom)
AJA	*American Journal of Archaeology*
AJAH	*American Journal of Ancient History*
AJPh	*American Journal of Philology*
A&R	*Atene e Roma*
AR	*Archaeological Reports*
ARC	*Archaeological Review from Cambridge*
ArchClass	*Archeologia Classica*
ARID	*Analecta Romana Instituti Danici*
ARP	*Accordia Research Papers*
BA	*Bollettino d'Arte*
BABesch	*Bulletin Anticke Beschaving*
BAR	British Archaeological Reports
BCAR	*Bullettino della Commissione Archeologica Comunale di Roma*
BCH	*Bulletin de Correspondance Hellénique*
BEFAR	*Bibliothèque des Écoles Françaises de Athènes et de Rome*
BIBR	*Bulletin de l'Institut Historique Belge de Rome*
CArchJ	*Cambridge Archaeological Journal*
CQ	*Classical Quarterly*
CSE	*Corpus Speculorum Etruscorum*
CVA	*Corpus Vasorum Antiquorum*
DArch	*Dialoghi di Archeologia*
EAA	*Encicopedia dell'Arte Antica*

JHS	*Journal of Hellenic Studies*
JRA	*Journal of Roman Archaeology*
JRGZ	*Jahrbuch des Römisch-Germanischen Zentralmuseums*
JRS	*Journal of Roman Studies*
LIMC	*Lexicon Iconographicum Mythologiae Classicae*
MAAR	*Memoirs of the American Academy in Rome*
MDAI(R)	*Mitteilungen des Deutschen Archäologischen Instituts (Römische Abteilung)*
MEFRA	*Mélanges d'Archéologie et d'Histoire de l'École Française de Rome, Antiquité*
MonAL	*Monumenti Antichi dall'Accademia dei Lincei*
NSA	*Notizie degli Scavi di Antichità*
OJA	*Oxford Journal of Archaeology*
ORom	*Opuscula Romana*
PBA	*Proceedings of the British Academy*
PBSR	*Papers of the British School at Rome*
PCPS	*Proceedings of the Cambridge Philological Society*
PP	*La Parola del Passato*
RIA	*Rivista dell'Istituto Nazionale di Archeologia e Storia dell'Arte*
SE	*Studi Etruschi*
TLE	*Thesaurus Linguae Etruscae*

Introduction

The late sixth century was a crucial period in Etruscan history: it witnessed the first monumental sanctuaries, the beginnings of planned cities, and the radical reorganisation of cemeteries. More widely, it was a period of intense contact with other cultures, notably those of Greece, Phoenicia and Central Italy; and it marked a dramatic and irreversible transformation of the agricultural and political landscapes of Etruria. Such changes came at the end of several centuries of internal development within Etruria, the beginnings of which can be traced back at least to the early first millennium BC. This book aims to examine these changes in Etruscan material culture. It brings together different aspects of Etruscan archaeology within a single analytical framework. While doing so it develops a new approach to Etruscan material and an integrated perspective on a society that is usually separated by intra-disciplinary boundaries. As such, it aims to provide a coherent explanation for change in Etruscan society.

Changes in Etruscan material culture (artefacts, images and standing structures) are traditionally explained in two main ways. The first sees the changes as a logical progression from primitive to modern; the second describes how the cultural world of Etruria falls under the influence of the Greeks. According to most accounts of Etrusco-Greek interaction, as Ridgway has so accurately put it, 'it was the proper business (and privilege) of the barbarians to be Hellenised, e basta!' (Ridgway 2000: 181). The material culture of the Etruscans is perceived as a pale imitation of that of their culturally 'superior' Hellenic neighbours. By contrast, the proposition of this book is that the making and transformation of Etruscan culture constitute an active process on the part of the Etruscan producers and consumers of that culture. Explanations of the major, macro-scale, transformations have thus to be sought in the detail of Etruscan approaches to making material culture on the micro level. Such an examination reveals that roughly contemporary changes across a range of Etruscan artefact types are linked by a common concern with the articulation of difference through the manipulation of surface. An increasing emphasis on the actual surfaces of the body, the tomb, the city and so forth is explored in the individual chapters and is concomitant with changing attitudes to the metaphorical distinctions these surfaces separate – such as the individual, the dead and the urban. These in turn were linked to changing attitudes towards cultural distinctions and differences.

In the following discussions of the material and social articulation of such differences, these concepts do not represent discrete or absolute states, and even less binary oppositions; rather, they are extreme points around which Etruscan culture negotiated its position in relation to these extremes. Over time, formal changes in Etruscan material culture were implicated in, and constituted, changing positions in relation to these categories.

The emphasis on surface in the following analysis stems from the nature of the changes in Etruscan material culture, and from a desire to explain these changes. Surface is a particularly helpful analytical tool for an archaeological study as it allows the close inspection of the formal characteristics of individual objects, while admitting broader cultural explanations for those characteristics. The concept is both object-specific and common to all objects, just as its use is important for Etruscan society and potentially others. Although the concept may be criticised for being a catch-all – all objects have surfaces – it remains grounded by paying attention to the particular characteristics of the individual surface under scrutiny. At the same time, its potential inclusivity provides a mechanism and focus for studying change between object types, over time and across space, as meaningful parallels can be traced across these distinctions. The differing treatment of the surfaces of people, objects and spaces over time and between regions has a bearing on their perception and definition. The dramatic changes that characterised the later sixth century in Etruria are both a symptom and a cause of the increased attention to surface at this time.

Of course, the analysis of surface is not the only key to understanding Etruscan material culture change – the importance of social, political, and economic factors has been amply demonstrated in recent studies. However, though these explanations operate convincingly within object types, the overarching quality of the concept of surface allows examination of change on a much broader level. Furthermore, though there are potentially other such concepts that could help our understanding of Etruscan archaeology, such as volume, scale, temperature, quality of light, movement, etc., the importance of visibility associated with the creation and manipulation of surface makes the concept more appropriate to the study of a period of political, social and ontological reordering. Without pre-empting later discussion, the important factors here are that viewing is a way of placing, or ordering the object being viewed, and that viewing is an activity that can be undertaken without active participation in the cultural, religious and social activities that are being viewed.

In its investigation of surface and (material) culture change, this book takes five types of object: respectively, mirrors, tombs, sanctuaries, houses and cities, and traces changing treatments of surface within them. The structure of the book reflects the nesting categories of social life that these objects represent – moving out from the individual to the wider urban community, and finally to the rural landscape, and by extension, beyond into the Mediterranean world. In doing so, it leaves aside potential parallel discussions that operate at these levels – for example, mirrors are discussed, while toilette boxes are not. This is not to suggest that the latter are not suitable for such analysis, but rather that they would not contribute significantly more to the discussion of the creation of individual identities than the discussion of mirrors. Thus, although it is an essential principle of this book that material culture is all-embracing, and that the concept of surface is equally instructive across that range, there are many categories of material culture that are not included here. Mirrors in particular were chosen as a starting point because of their explicit link (due to their function) with the creation of personal identity through the manipulation of the surface of the body. Other artefacts (such as ceramics, ceramic decoration, votive bronze sculpture and even funerary sculpture, where the representations are directly linked to individual Etruscans) are not implicated in the same way (though a recent analysis has shown the potential of such a line of inquiry: Roth 2001–3). For the same reasons, componential analysis of domestic or funerary contexts (a significant lack in Etruscan studies) has not been carried out for this study.

While the approach of this book is open to the criticism that much is left out, it is also susceptible, in considering different artefact types together, to charges of being too inclusive. The importance of overarching comparisons has been stressed for some time, and the resulting generalisation has been exploited for its potential to reveal more than the individual case study (for instance, Finley 1977: 314; more recently Hölscher 2004: 2–5). Inevitable results of such an approach are a lack of detail or resolution, and the conjouring of exceptions that do not 'fit' the overall pattern; nonetheless, the new patterns that emerge from broad comparisons can provide alternative perspectives to long-studied material. Continuing to study single areas or artefact types would be to perpetuate the particularistic studies of individual objects that are already well represented in Etruscan studies.

A significant consideration of wide-ranging comparisons across material types is chronological robustness – how closely can we reasonably expect parallel developments in complementary areas of culture to correspond?

Problems with chronology that lie at the materially specific level of investigation are addressed in the chapters on individual material. More importantly, the different dating bands applied to different material pose problems of comparability: a mirror can be dated to within twenty-five years, a house to two centuries. This means that changes that are noted can be dated only with varying precision according to the type of material under study. In terms of a wider study of material change, this means that change can appear to take place at different times or at different rates in different types of object.

Of course, it may be the case that change did take place at different times, or not at all in some areas. However, in the case of the Etruscan material culture examined in this book, I do not believe this to be the case. Instead of trying to see change occurring at exactly the same time in all kinds of material, it is important to bear in mind two considerations. The first is that not all aspects of social life change at the same rate, and that not all kinds of material production are as versatile as each other: for instance, it is far easier to make a mirror in a new way than to rebuild the walls of a city in a new way – mirror production would thus respond more quickly than city-wall construction to any cultural changes that may affect them. Second, changes in cultural or social behaviour are cumulative and progressive, taking place over time, and in relation to previous changes. This has been acknowledged most notably in the work of Italian prehistorians and proto-historians who, in their examination of the emergence of urban identities in the peninsula, take a far longer perspective than that traditionally taken by Etruscologists, pushing the origins of urbanism back into the Bronze Age. (For a summary and bibliography see Vanzetti 2002.) Therefore the changes that culminate in the late sixth century have long tails stretching back into previous generations. The length of these tails varies both because of the nature of archaeological dating and because of the differential receptivity of different areas of social life to change. This means that change of the kind discussed in this book is unlikely to occur according to excessively neat chronological coincidence; rather the changes are more gradual and the interlinked spheres of social life will be influenced by changes across a range of material. Such a change is also unlikely to have a single moment of inception or origin. For the material in this book, I hope to show that such an approach to change has greater potential for integrating the gradual increase in contact with foreigners, as well as the local long-term developments in central Italy.

The attempt to make connections between parallel spheres of Etruscan cultural activity is validated by the Etruscans themselves, who provide striking evidence that they thought in an analogical manner, in other words across categories. In the nineteenth century, in a field on the outskirts of what is now modern Piacenza, a farmer found an extraordinary bronze object while ploughing his fields: a solid-cast, life-size model of a sheep's liver (van der Meer 1987). Though stylised, it is nonetheless anatomically accurate. The surface of the liver has been divided up into different zones or regions, and each region contains the inscribed name of an Etruscan divinity. It is thought to be a teaching model for trainee augurs, or an *aide memoire* for more forgetful ones. As Rykwert was quick to point out, what is remarkable about the Piacenza liver is the evidence it provides of the deeply cosmological view that the Etruscans must have had of their built and natural environments: a view of their universe as a unified, ordered whole in which different spheres of human and natural life bore direct and coherent relationships to each other (Rykwert 1976). As a microcosm, the liver represents the division of the skies into regions, and the deities associated with each region. Thus, all natural phenomena observed within a particular sphere, for example the sphere of the sky, could be interpreted, through the microcosm of the liver, according to the will of the particular divinity associated with that region. The liver functioned as a refracting lens through which observed natural phenomena were viewed and interpreted.

The Piacenza liver, and similar surviving terracotta models, provide unique insight into the Etruscan conception of the world around them. Such evidence testifies to a culture with a particularly refined sense of the relationships between different ontological and spatial spheres. In the following analysis emphasis will be placed on the process by which ontological differences and categories were mapped on to the human material world. Whether we see this in terms of Tilley's 'metaphor', Shore's 'analogical schematisation', or Bourdieu's 'scheme transfers', it is important to acknowledge the central role of cognitive structures in the binding together of Etruscan culture. By focusing on changes in the treatment of surface in Etruscan material culture, this book will attempt to cast light on the cognitive structures according to which the Etruscan cultural environment was ordered. It will examine the process and impact of surface change in five main areas of Etruscan material culture.

Chapter 1 establishes the theoretical foundations upon which the following chapters are based. It is divided into four main sections. The first outlines the characteristics of previous approaches to the study of cultural change in Etruria. It identifies six major influences on the study of Etruscan culture and assesses them in the light of recent developments in other areas of archaeology. This section is not intended to reject all the findings of these approaches; it aims, rather, to draw attention to certain biases and assumptions that have been implicit in some past studies of Etruscan material culture. The work of the following chapters is based to a very large extent on the conclusions of the work discussed in Chapter 1.

The second section outlines the theoretical position taken in the rest of the book. Drawing on a wide range of disciplines and archaeological sub-disciplines, it presents a theoretical approach that emphasises the importance of social and cultural knowledge in the making of material culture, and argues for the existence of a culturally informed framework within which material culture was created. This stresses the deliberate nature of all decisions that go into the making of objects and spaces, thereby accounting for their social resonance and justifying a detailed study of change in material culture form. The formal aspects of material culture take on a new significance when viewed as the physical manifestation of the cognitive and ideological processes that shaped their creation and determined their use. This is not, however, to mark a return to an outdated model of material determinism; rather, this approach seeks to restore to material culture its active role in shaping the world in which individuals live. In a study so intimately and inherently concerned with culture change and contact, this approach affords us a unique opportunity to study the hitherto unacknowledged role of the Etruscans in the making of their own culture.

The chapter ends with a discussion of the importance of boundaries and surface in negotiating physical, social, cultural and ontological difference. As the visibility of boundaries and surface is such an important part of the argument of this book, the section also considers the concept of the viewer in Etruscan culture and the extent to which visual concerns may have impacted on changes in the treatment of surface.

Chapter 2 has two aims: first, to emphasise the growing importance of personal identity in the late sixth century; second, to explore changes in one aspect of that identity, namely gender identity. Both these inquiries derive from an analysis of bronze hand mirrors from the late sixth century onwards, and take as their starting point the importance of mirrors in the process of bodily adornment. Men and women used the reflective surface of mirrors as part of a process of adornment that was designed to alter the surface appearance of their bodies. This manipulation of bodily surface through the process and practice of adornment is deeply rooted in a society's concepts of beauty and desirability. Put another way, a society's concepts of beauty are inscribed on the surface of the bodies of men and women through adornment. It goes without saying that we do not have the products of adornment, the beautified bodies of Etruscans, left to study. However, on the backs of the mirrors, Etruscan craftsmen engraved images depicting a wide range of mythological and non-mythological scenes, and these images provide representations of the cultural and social norms and values in which the process of adornment was embedded. The chapter argues first that the sudden emergence and proliferation of this type of object in the late sixth century indicates a growing stress on the creation, through adornment, of an image of the body and self, and thus of personal identity. Second, it uses the scenes on the backs of the mirrors to explore the similarities and differences between male and female adornment in the creation of gender identity from the late sixth century onwards. It is argued that the deposition of mirrors in burial is a symptom of the wider cultural concern with surface, in this instance with the human body.

Tomb architecture forms the subject of Chapter 3. During the course of the sixth century, funerary monuments saw a radical decrease in scale. In place of the monumental, round burial mounds of the preceding century, smaller mounds were constructed, and by the end of the sixth century the decrease in scale was accompanied by a change in shape, resulting in rows of small, square, cube-tombs. Such changes in tomb architecture should be seen in relation to other changes in Etruscan material culture, and as part of a broader cultural transformation in Etruria. Surface functions as an important means of articulating and mediating distinctions. This chapter examines the changing treatment of the surface of Etruscan tombs and the role it plays as the interface between the living and the dead. Three specific areas of differentiation within the tomb will be considered: the treatment of the boundary between the inside and the outside of the tomb, the structure of the tomb itself, and the location and deployment of tomb decoration.

Chapter 4 examines the process of surface change through another form of ritual space: that of sanctuaries. More specifically, it examines the changing locations for communal ritual activity in Etruria from the Iron Age until the fifth century BC. During the early phases of Etruscan archaeology, cultic activity took place in locations in the landscape that were not marked architecturally. Although during the seventh and sixth centuries it is possible to argue for the ritual use of certain buildings and complexes, most notably at Roselle and Murlo, ritual is only one of many possible functions that have been attributed to these buildings. In fact, this ambiguity in the archaeological evidence suggests that such buildings had multiple uses and that ritual activity took place alongside other activities in the same physical space. This apparent heterogeneity of use changes dramatically in the sixth century. By the end of the sixth century there emerged the highly codified architecture of the Etruscan temple and sanctuary space; it was to remain in use, little changed, for at least two centuries. Chapter 4 takes two aspects of Etruscan temple architecture in order to examine changes in surface form and the material marking of difference. The first is the appearance of temples in the archaeological record: it is argued that the development of a codified, formal architecture that is specifically identifiable as a temple reflects the need to remove the ambiguity of the former centuries. This is then emphasised by the creation of a sanctuary space around the temple, bounded by a wall, and containing other temples or associated sacred structures. In this way, the activity of ritual was given a visible boundary and surface, with its own distinct architectural identity separated from the other activities with which it had co-existed in the former buildings. The second aspect of the chapter is to examine in detail those elements of Etruscan temple architecture that make it stand out from what went before, from contemporary Greek temple forms and, most importantly, from other types of spaces and structures. It examines the location and deployment of temple decoration, the architectural details set within the Etruscan rural and urban landscape, and the formal composition of sanctuary structures.

Chapter 5, on domestic architecture, is the first of two chapters that deal with non-sacred space. The archaeology of Etruscan houses is traced from the Iron Age to the fifth century BC, in order to examine the changing treatment of domestic space. The divisions marked here are those between the public sphere, outside the domestic unit, and the private sphere housed within it. The formal elements of individual houses are implicated both in marking the difference, and in allowing passage, between these spheres. The elements examined in the chapter include the form of the house, the materials used in its construction, the use of open spaces within domestic complexes, and the treatment of entrances. In a similar way to earlier chapters, the changing treatment of the externally visible surface of domestic architecture is seen as part of a wider process of the negotiation and articulation of difference in late sixth-century Etruria.

The larger urban context for domestic architecture forms the subject of Chapter 6. Urban form will be examined from the hut settlements of the Iron Age to the masonry cities of the sixth and fifth centuries. The malleability of the built environment is central to this chapter, as is the conception of urban form as a distinct entity, or an object in itself. As such, mutations and transformations in different elements of urban form will be considered as indicative of changing attitudes towards the city itself. Just as Chapter 5 focused on the negotiation of public and private space, the examination of urban elements focuses on the difference between concepts of urban and rural, and on different kinds of urban space. In other words it will examine the definition of the city in relation to the individual inhabitant, and also to the area outside the city. The material manifestation of changing attitudes to house form, street networks, craft or industrial production areas and city limits will form the main part of the chapter. Such surface change highlights an increasing awareness of the distinction between the urban sphere and the non-urban sphere.

The book concludes with an examination of the wider Mediterranean context in which the changes in Etruscan material culture took place. As already mentioned, these changes have often been ascribed to Hellenic agency. This concluding chapter examines the premises behind such 'colonialist' interpretations of cultural contact, and rejects them both on theoretical grounds and on the evidence of the Etruscan material culture. It then attempts to develop for the Etruscans a model of ancient Mediterranean interaction that more closely reflects the complexity and heterogeneity that characterise the conclusions of recent work on Greek activity in the central Mediterranean, much of it done in the light of post-colonial theory. The importance of surface in marking the boundaries of cultural identity is brought to the fore in considering the explanations for Etruscan material culture change within this more dynamic picture of Mediterranean and Italian interaction.

The increased emphasis on surface and the manipulation of surface in the different areas of material culture examined in this book is closely linked to wider cultural concerns about a need to articulate difference. It is the desire to express difference that is a key to our understanding of changing Etruscan attitudes to their identity within the Mediterranean world. Changes in attitudes to the surface of the body are analogically related to changes in tomb architecture, and both are related in a similar manner to a wider sense of cultural identity, or the difference between Etruscan and non-Etruscan.

1 | Models of change in Etruria

Introduction

This chapter sets out the theoretical basis on which the analysis of the following chapters takes place. First it considers some of the approaches that have underpinned and characterised previous studies of Etruscan material culture change; next it draws on recent developments in the wider discipline of archaeology and beyond in order to establish a theoretical model for the following chapters.

Models of change in Etruria

This section examines the characteristics of previous treatments of Etruscan material with particular emphasis on how change in material culture has been approached. Its aim is to open discussion about certain assumptions that have been implicit in previous treatments, and to highlight the limitations of such approaches for our understanding of Etruscan culture more widely. Though this section may often seem critical of these approaches, much of the work of the following chapters is based on their conclusions. The analyses in the rest of the book take for granted the chronological and cultural framework established by such work; they aim not to contradict them, but to push their conclusions further.

Classical studies

One of the most important factors affecting the study of the Etruscans has been the closeness of the subject to the discipline of Classics. Both within and outside Italy, the study of the Etruscans has proceeded concurrently with the study of Greece and Rome and this has had a significant influence on the way in which Etruscan culture has been studied. It is not surprising therefore that many inquiries into the Etruscan past have begun with the consultation of Greek and Roman writers.

Ancient sources

An area in which the influence of ancient writers has been particularly significant is in the study of Etruscan women. Ancient authors were the first to note what seems to have been the unique position held by Etruscan women in the ancient world. Athenaeus, writing in the late second / early third century AD and drawing on the fourth-century *Histories* of Theopompus, elucidates several aspects of the lives of Etruscan women that would have been truly shocking to a Greek, mentioning, among other things, their sexual licence, their extraordinary beauty, their luxuriousness and their practice of exercising and dining with men (Athenaeus 12.517–5; M. A. Fowler 1994; Shrimpton 1991).

In Roman literature, the Augustan historian Livy provides a similarly shocking image of Etruscan women. (For a comprehensive review of the Roman literature see Sordi 1981.) In the famous episode of the rape of Lucretia, the Roman heroine who sits spinning wool 'late into the night' with her serving women around her, is drawn into sharp contrast with the Etruscan princesses, who spend their time at an extravagant banquet (Livy 1.57.6–9).

The use of ancient writers as sources for Etruscan culture is not limited to representations of women. In discussions of Etruscan temple architecture, reference to the first-century AD Vitruvius is frequent (*De arch.*4.7; for instance, Andrén 1940: xxxv; Barker and Rasmussen 1998: 219; Boëthius 1955–6; 1978; Colonna (ed.) 1985: 60; Knell 1983; Lake 1935, esp. 89–92; Pfiffig 1975: 55; Prayon 1986: 104; Spivey 1997: 62). Etruscan religious practices, which form part of the so-called '*disciplina etrusca*', are also derived from later Roman sources that stress the Etruscan origins of the practices they themselves employed (Plutarch, *Rom.* 11.1; Varro, *Ling.* 5.143). This evidence has formed the basis for the understanding of Etruscan ritual: for example, the skill of the Etruscans in divination (Cicero, *Div.* 1.41.92; Plutarch, *Rom.* 11.1; Seneca, *Q Nat.* 2.32.2; Vitruvius 1.4.1–7.1); bird flight (Seneca, *Q Nat.* 2.32.3–5; see Grenier 1948: 19, 23–4; Pallottino 1975: 143; Pfiffig 1975: 150–2), the path of lightning (Pliny *HN* 2.51.138–44; see Dumézil 1970: 643; Weinstock 1951) and the ritual foundation of cities (Boëthius 1978: 21; Rykwert 1976; for the latter see Pfiffig 1975: 112; Grenier 1948: 21–4; Dumézil 1970: 663–4). Such literary references have formed the basis upon which archaeological objects have been interpreted. Perhaps the most famous example of this is the so-called 'Piacenza liver', a bronze model of a liver, the surface of which is divided into areas said to correspond to the sixteen regions of the sky, described in detail by the fifth-century AD writer

Martianus Capella and others (Martianus Capella, *De nuptiis Philologiae et Mercurii* 1.41–61, esp. 45; Pliny, *HN* 2.51.143; see Colonna 1994; Grenier 1948: 18; Maggiani 1982: 66–8; Pallottino 1975: 145; van der Meer 1987: 22–6; Weinstock 1946).

These examples serve to illustrate the extensive use of Greek and Roman writers within Etruscological inquiry. However, the Greek-ness or Roman-ness of these authors is a fact to which Etruscologists and those studying Etruscan culture have paid insufficient attention. An early criticism of this approach was that of Dumézil, who cautions that Roman authors would have emphasised elements of Etruscan ritual that were important in their own practice, such as divination (Dumézil 1970: 626), and that the Romans may have been archaising their own practices, and attributing them to the Etruscans for other motives: 'The Romans . . . were inclined to stamp their practices with the respectable Etruscan label, which gave them the prestige of antiquity and a kind of intellectual warranty' (Dumézil 1970: 661).

More recently, cultural historians of Ancient Greece and Rome have echoed the scepticism of Dumézil. For Roman religion, Beard, North and Price have shown the specifically Augustan agendas at work in the creation of these texts; more widely, Edwards has demonstrated the way in which such texts were part of a discourse in the construction of the Roman past, both literary and physical (Beard *et al.* 1998, esp. 20; Edwards 1996).

In Greek literature, ancient sources writing about 'other' cultures have received considerable attention, following Lloyd's celebrated analysis of 1966 (Cartledge 1993; E. Hall 1989; J. M. Hall 1997; Hartog 1988; J. Henderson 1994; Hölscher (ed.) 2000; M. C. Miller 1997). For example, the role of women, principally Amazons, in these 'ethnographic discourses' has been seen as an act of Greek construction of the self via contrast with others. Similarly, the passages from Athenaeus and Livy about women, like all discussions of Etruscan life in Greek and Roman sources, should be interpreted not as accurate and impartial accounts of Etruscan life, but as reaffirmations of what it was to be 'Greek' or 'Roman' through display of the mirror image of the classical ideal.

Accounts of the Etruscans have not hitherto received such treatment, despite a notable exception in Spivey and Stoddart's brief treatment of Livy (Spivey and Stoddart 1990: 14–17), and interesting precedents set for other Italic cultures (Ampolo 1996; G. Bradley 2000a; Dench 1995; for a Roman perspective see also Torelli 1999: 165–83). Most recently, Rathje has been explicit in pointing the way towards a more critical treatment of the 'rather vague' descriptions of ancient authors in discussions of Etruscan domestic architecture (Rathje 2001–3: 57).

While calling for a more critical approach to these Greek and Roman writers, several authors have emphasised the primacy of archaeological material in investigations of Etruscan culture, a trail blazed by Pallottino and recently continued by Rathje and by Spivey and Stoddart (Pallottino 1975: 139; Rathje 2001–3; Spivey and Stoddart 1990; see also Barker and Rasmussen 1998: 180; for other Italic cultures see for instance Bietti-Sestieri 1992, 2000). This position is not a blind following of a processualist rejection of literary sources, as the names of the scholars cited above testify; instead it is in line with recent revisionist emphasis on the cultural specificity of cultural artefacts, including texts. This is not to argue that archaeological material is intrinsically more useful than textual sources (a debate that is more often a matter of the questions researchers want answered (Snodgrass 1983)); rather, the point is that the textual sources of one culture are inappropriate for investigating the other societies about which they write. Thus, for the Etruscans, it is not the texts of Greece and Rome but the Etruscan material record that must be taken as the starting point for an investigation of their culture. The biases and agendas implicit in the Greek and Roman accounts of the Etruscans must be considered critically before they are brought to such a study.

Greek and Latin terminology

In addition to providing written accounts of the Etruscans and their practices, Greek and Roman authors have provided Etruscology with a large Greek and Latin vocabulary for Etruscan artefacts. In accounts of funerary architecture, the large mound covering a tomb is known by the Latin *tumulus*, while the entrance corridor into the tomb is referred to by the Greek term *dromos* (Izzet 1996). In domestic architecture, Greek terminology dominates the early period: the *megaron*, *pastàs* or *oikos* (Colonna 1986: 400, 425; Drews 1981: 146–7; Karlsson 1996: 265), while Latin is used to describe the later period: Boëthius compares Etruscan tombs to the Roman *atrium* house (Boëthius 1960: 47, 55; see also Prayon 1986: 192. According to Varro (*Ling.* 5. 161), the Latin *atrium* is derived from the Etruscan town of Atria (modern Adria), ascribing the form to the houses of the town), and he refers to *tabernae*, De Albentiis to the *fauces*, *tablina*, *cubiculi* and *tabernae* of the *domus*, and Donati to the *impluvium* and *conpluvium* (Boëthius 1978: 75; De Albentiis 1990: 68–9; Donati (ed.) 1994). It is not only Greek and Roman architectural terms that have been imported into Etruscan archaeology; words used to describe Greek cultural institutions, such as the *symposium* or *hoplite* warfare, have been applied to scenes depicted in Etruscan tomb paintings, or armour found in Etruscan graves.

The problems of using foreign terminology in discussions of the Etruscans are similar to those described by Goldhill and Osborne in the identification of figures in Classical imagery: once a figure has been identified, it is readily associated with existing knowledge about that figure, thus hampering an examination of the specificity of the particular representation (Goldhill and Osborne 1994: 9). Future readings are then informed by the original identification. The same is true for any labels or identifications, whether they are for figures in a representation, cultural practices or archaeological features (Piggott 1972: 948–9). Perhaps the best-illustrated case of archaeo-logical identification is in the assignation of functions to excavated spaces in buildings: once a room has been identified as, say, a dining room, then all the activity that took place in the room is likely to be understood in terms of that label alone. The restrictions to our understanding which result from such a narrow reading are summed up by Bailey citing Adams: a space labelled 'bedroom' can be used as a space in which 'to sleep, rest, get well, die, have sex, procreate, watch TV, read, nurse babies, wrap presents, lay coats' (Bailey 1990: 27 n. 1; see also Allison 1997: 119, 141; 1999; R. J. Lawrence 1987: 103–10; Nevett 1999: 25–6).

In their migration from Classical to Etruscan culture, such words carry with them a web of cultural associations from their original contexts that may well be inapplicable in their new ones. The ethnocentrism, and thus inappropriateness, of such transferred terminology has been pointed out by several authors, such as Spivey in a discussion of the use of space in Etruscan houses, Small in the use of the word *symposium* in describing Etruscan banquets, and d'Agostino and Snodgrass in questioning hoplite warfare in Etruria (d'Agostino 1990; Small 1994; Snodgrass 1965; Spivey 1991).

Cultural intersticiality

A final effect of the proximity between Etruscan and Classical studies has been a tendency to locate the Etruscans both culturally and chronologically as existing somewhere between the Greeks and the Romans. The 'value' of the Etruscans for study lies either in their transmission of features of Greek culture to the West, such as brick design or town planning, or in their nurturing of the seeds of later Roman growth, such as hydraulics or ritual. The vocabulary used to describe Etruscan domestic architecture illustrates the position occupied by Etruscan material culture between the worlds of Greece and Rome. As already mentioned, earlier houses (of roughly the seventh and sixth centuries) are described in Greek words, whereas later ones (fifth to third century) are described using Latin terms. Etruscan domestic architecture thus seems to be situated somewhere between Greek and Roman, moving from an imitation of the former to an archaic rendition of the latter.

Similarly, while in discussions of town planning it is argued that the Etruscans adhered to Greek theoretical principles of orthogonality (Owens 1991: 105), at the same time they are seen as providing a precedent for Roman developments. In Gros and Torelli's *Storia dell'urbanistica: Il mondo romano*, the first chapter is on Etruscan cities – an incidental prolegomenon to the interesting and historically important world of Roman urbanism. The Etruscan seeds of later Roman achievements are seen strongly in the field of engineering and hydraulics (Bergamini (ed.) 1991; Owens 1991: 98; Ward-Perkins 1962: 1637).

The Etruscan influence on the city of Rome itself is more contested: while some argue that the period of the 'Etruscan kings' of Rome (from the late seventh to sixth centuries BC; for chronology see Cornell 1995a: 122–7) saw the construction of the Temple of Capitoline Jupiter and other public buildings, the clear demarcation of open spaces, the regulation and control of the water supply and the construction of the *Cloaca Maxima* (contributions to Cristofani (ed.) 1990, esp. Quilici 1990: 37–8; C. J. Smith 1996: 183), others argue that the idea of Etruscan influence on Rome was a highly politicised reaction against 'the fascist cult of *romanità*' (Cornell 1995a: 153, 164, 165). Whatever the ancient reality, it is nevertheless clear that in academic discourse the Etruscans sit in an uneasy position between the Greeks and the Romans.

The long history of the proximity between Etruscology and Classical archaeology has had profound effects on the ways in which the Etruscans have been conceived. The relationship between the Etruscans and the Greeks and Romans has been a fraught and contentious one. The primacy given to ancient sources has, in some instances, led to uncritical acceptance of these texts as definitive narratives for the Etruscans; the lack of an Etruscan language has led to the borrowing of terms that are foreign to Etruscan cultural forms and that may not describe them adequately; and the dominant position of Greece and Rome in modern studies has tended to marginalise Etruscan culture to the extent that the Etruscans appear to exist only as a bridge between two superior cultures. As a result, Etruscan material culture has largely been viewed from the perspective of other cultures, and changes in Etruscan archaeological remains are considered within that light. Etruscan archaeology has been, in short, the handmaid to someone else's history (Finley 1968a; Snodgrass 1983).

Funerary bias

The second major influence on the way in which Etruscan culture has been studied results from the kind of archaeological evidence that has been available. Until very recently, funerary data formed the vast majority of material: it was not until the mid-twentieth century that interest in settlements and other non-funerary contexts began to develop and led to systematic excavation. Before that, funerary evidence was all that was available, and it was exploited to the full: objects and paintings from tombs as well as the architectural details of the structures and the layout of cemeteries were used in order to cast light on any and every aspect of Etruscan life and afterlife. This tradition of funerary archaeology has persisted, partly due to the enormous volume of such material in relation to that from non-funerary contexts. The effect on the objects studied, however, is that they are often methodologically removed from their original contexts.

Decontextualisation

Etruscan hand mirrors, which are found exclusively in funerary contexts, are an excellent example of such decontextualisation. These objects have been used to illuminate a variety of aspects of Etruscan life, including the clothes Etruscans wore (L. Bonfante 1975) or what furniture they used (L. Bonfante 1982; Steingräber 1979: 257–70), how they conducted ritual (Pfiffig 1975: 117–18), the influence of Greek myth (Francesco De Angelis 2001; Fiesel 1936: 130–6; Hampe and Simon 1964; Krauskopf 1974; Pfiffig 1980; Salskov Roberts 1993: 287–317; van der Meer 1995), and the details of temple architecture (Bendinelli 1920). Few of these instances bear any relation to the original use of the mirror in Etruscan society, or to its archaeological context. In many of these studies, the images engraved on to the non-reflective side of the mirrors have been taken as straightforward representations of the 'real' or 'everyday' existence of the Etruscans; there has been little acknowledgement of the culturally constructed nature of these images, or of the problems of interpretation that arise when using funerary material to understand non-funerary spheres of life. Similarly, paintings of dining scenes are routinely considered to be representations of dining scenes without any reference to their original funerary context.

In a similar way, Etruscan tombs have been used as an important source for the reconstruction of non-funerary architecture. In the funerary architecture of the eighth century onwards, details of roof construction, or the long, narrow ridge-pole of early tombs such as the Tomba della Capanna at Cerveteri, are seen as directly reflecting those of the houses of the living

(Colonna 1986: 395; Cristofani 1978: 68; Prayon 1975: 180, 182). Such comparisons extend beyond the details of architectural form to include the layout of settlements and cemeteries. The most famous and frequently cited example of this is the regular plan of the Crocifisso del Tufo cemetery at Orvieto, which is, according to Mansuelli, 'in realtà una riproduzione in miniatura di una sistemazione urbana in pianta e in alzato' (Mansuelli 1985: 111; 1970b; 1979: 363; see also Drews 1981: 148; Gros and Torelli 1988, who also refer to the Banditaccia at Cerveteri). The layout of the cemetery is thought to mirror that of the city, and in the absence of remains of the latter, the former is used. However, the implication that the funerary is a direct and accurate reflection of the quotidian sphere is at best optimistic, and ignores significant differences in the ways that ritual and non-ritual contexts were created (Barker and Rasmussen 1998: 181; Damgaard Andersen 1997: 344; Rathje 2001–3: 58, 61).

The relationship between the living and the dead in archaeological contexts is a rich and intimate one (see, for instance, Hodder 1990b), and funerary material cannot but form a central role in understandings of Etruscan culture and society. Recent developments in the archaeology of death have shown, on the one hand, the problems that beset simplistic readings of such material (R. Chapman *et al.* (eds.) 1981; I. Morris 1987, 1992; Parker Pearson 1982). On the other hand, they have shown the potential of a more sensitive approach to funerary data, and they point the way to future areas of investigation (as acknowledged, for example, by Spivey and Stoddart 1990: 141–51; Thoden van Velzen 1992).

Art-historical and single-object-based approach

The decontextualisation of objects that has resulted from ignoring the funerary origins of most Etruscan material culture has gone hand in hand with an art-historical and particularising tradition. This is evident in the frequency of single-object studies in the field. These studies take one object, or class of object (for example, mirrors or tombs), and examine it alone, in isolation from its original archaeological and cultural context. The most extreme version of this is in the form of the catalogue, such as the *Corpus Speculorum Etruscorum*. This multi-volume catalogue of mirrors (still in progress), arranged according to the museum collection in which they are housed, serves as an invaluable resource for Etruscologists, providing accurate drawings and a detailed examination of the objects and the images engraved on them, together with provenance and a comprehensive bibliography. Yet nowhere in the authoritative volumes is the function of a mirror or its funerary significance examined. Such a discussion would be out of place in a publication so embedded in the 'positivist tradition', but it is precisely this kind of issue that must be raised if we are to move from description to interpretation, and thus ultimately towards a more meaningful understanding of these objects and their ancient uses (Ridgway 1992: 282).

A similarly object-based approach has characterised many other areas of Etruscan archaeology. In discussions of ritual and sanctuaries, the focus on the objects found in votive deposits, or on the decoration of the temple, has led to the original ritual context of the objects being sidelined (for example Haynes 1985; Richardson 1983; though for a notable exception see Zamarchi Grassi (ed.) 1995). In these studies, sanctuaries and votive deposits are seen largely in terms of the 'art' that was contained within them. These objects are discussed in terms of their art-historical merit (or lack of it – for instance Spivey (1997: 66) on the 'Apollo' of Veii, Brendel (1978: 237–8) on the 'School of Vulca'; cf. Beasley 1942, 1956; Whitley 1987). Even recent socio-political readings of Etruscan 'art', while acknowledging the social context, largely ignore the religious nature of these objects (Pairault Massa 1992: 72–5; Torelli 1990: 170). In such approaches, the ritual function of sanctuaries and of the objects they contained is subsumed beneath an art-historical desire to study the objects that they have yielded. These inquiries have the potential to tell us a great deal about the objects themselves, though they make no claim to explain the emergence of the contexts in which the objects were used and found.

A related phenomenon to single-object studies is the highly particularistic nature of Etruscan scholarship. Alongside studies of single object types run those of single sites or single monuments within sites (for instance, Blanck and Proietti 1982). While the need for detailed reports of excavations and material is obvious, there are very few studies that draw connections between monuments or object types. The result is that few wide-ranging analyses of Etruscan material culture exist, leaving the objects and monuments cut off from the cultural context in which they were produced and in which they operated.

So far, this section has considered some general characteristics of Etruscan scholarship and the influences that have brought them about. The rest of this section will examine some approaches that have been explicitly concerned with explaining material culture change in Etruscology. Frequently, more than one of these are developed simultaneously within a single account, so that, for instance, an observed change in form is attributed at the same time to foreign influence and the superiority of a new technique. For the purpose of this study, however, it will be useful to consider these changes separately.

Evolutionary models of change

An aspect of the decontextualisation of Etruscan artefacts and buildings that was not considered above is an emphasis on the chronological development or spatial distribution of these objects. Each object is seen in relation to a developmental sequence within that object class, rather than as one of many interrelated objects, enmeshed in assemblages with both chronological, spatial and cultural connotations. As a result, the 'histories' of types of objects, buildings or complexes of buildings tend to focus on their origins and subsequent evolution. This is particularly true of architectural histories. In the case of the development of sanctuaries, the origins of Etruscan temples are sought in indigenous domestic architecture, and the history of sanctuary architecture follows as if it were a continuous development from the mudbrick house at Roselle, and the complexes at Murlo and Acquarossa, to the monumental sanctuary (Colonna (ed.) 1985: 53; 1986: 433; though this is now in need of revision in the light of the recent excavations at Tarquinia: Bonghi Jovino and Chiaramente Treré (eds.) 1997). At a wider level objects and buildings have been woven into evolutionary models of Etruscan social development. For instance, the presence of a sanctuary has been seen as an important component of an emerging city-state (Colonna 1986: 433). Similarly, the history of Etruscan domestic architecture has been written as though it were an inevitable march of progress from the hut to the house, and thence to the *insula*.

While such approaches mark a significant move away from the typological descriptions common in Etruscology, they still leave many questions unanswered, such as why cultural institutions, such as the city or domestic residences, developed in the forms that they did. Recent theoretical work on the built environment has shown that there is nothing natural or inevitable in house- or urban form (Parker Pearson and Richards 1994; Rapoport 1969); and Giddens has criticised 'unfolding models of change' more generally (Giddens 1979: 222–5; Samson 1990: 4). Instead of seeing Etruscan material culture as 'progressing', inevitably, through various stages of its history, we must ask why Etruscan artefacts took the forms that they did when they did.

Models of technological advantage

The superiority of new techniques or materials is a particularly common theme in accounts of Etruscan domestic architecture and urbanism. For example, Drews has argued that the durability that accompanied new techniques of masonry and terracotta tiling was the reason that such techniques were adopted by the Etruscans (Drews 1981: 148, 155). Although the advantages of durability are clearly important considerations in the history of Etruscan domestic architecture, such accounts have not tackled the question of why durability is, in itself, an advantage. Why did the people of Central Italy need more durable houses, or, similarly, planned cities, at the time that they started to build them?

A similar argument is followed for changes in house shape: the move from curvilinear to rectilinear residences has been seen as a result of technical advantage: the rectilinear structure could support a far larger (and heavier) roof than a curvilinear structure, and so larger houses are possible (H. W. M. Hodges 1972: 528–9). Again, the increased house-size is assumed to be so obviously advantageous that it does not require further explanation within an Etruscan framework.

Models of foreign influence

According to this, local developments in Etruria are explained in terms of foreign influences. This embraces developments in funerary and domestic architecture, as well as in urban form. In the area of funerary architecture, the late eighth- or early seventh-century circular arrangement of blocks enclosing a rectilinear chamber is thought to originate in the East, as is the arched door that appears from the beginning of the seventh century (both Colonna 1986: 395). Recently, Naso has emphasised the debt owed to central Anatolia by the large burial mounds of the Central Italian Orientalising period (Naso 1996a, 1996b). In domestic architecture, too, the stimulus for change is often sought outside Etruria, in Greece or in the East (Boëthius 1978: 28, 29, 34; Owens 1991: 103). This included elements such as the eastern '*liwan*' house type, as argued for in the case of the late sixth-century houses at Acquarossa (Torelli 1985: 27), or moulded and painted terracotta tiles from Greece, with some asserting that the practice of painting tiles was brought to Etruria by the Corinthian exile Demaratus (Torelli 1985: 24, 25, who uses Pliny the Elder (*HN* 35.152) as a source; see also Colonna 1986: 433; Spivey 1997: 60).

For urban form, Drews argues that the masonry city was a 'cultural borrowing' (Drews 1981: 154–5). Greek influence is argued for in urban planning: the layout of Marzabotto 'è chiaramente influenzato dalla dottrina urbanistica greca' (Colonna 1986: 464; see also Owens 1991: 96; Torelli 1985: 75, 83). According to Mansuelli, the Etruscans 'absorbed elements from the Greek experience before the Greeks had formulated their own theory' (Mansuelli 1979: 362).

Relationships between the Etruscans and the other cultures of the Mediterranean, and striking similarities in their material cultures, cannot be denied, and many of the arguments, such as those developed by Naso, are particularly convincing. An early critique of such a position emphasised the indigenous explanations for cultural change (Stoddart 1989). Yet what these discussions omit is an analysis of why it was that imports were desirable to Etruscan craftsmen and patrons. The reasons for the adoption of foreign elements are not obvious; rather, they need elaboration. Even a claim of the exoticism of Greek and eastern objects needs to be grounded in a model that explains why exoticism itself was desirable (such as, for example, in elite display). In explaining changes in material culture in relation to a foreign culture, it is essential to examine what benefit such changes brought to the importing culture, rather than assuming that their foreignness is enough. This is particularly the case when considering Greek imports because the hellenocentrism of many scholars makes it difficult to consider the possibility that Greek is not automatically best.

The need for such care is highlighted by a detailed examination of the processes of importation (see Appadurai 1986; Gosden and Marcus 1991; N. Thomas 1991; Stewart and Shaw 1994). These authors have shown the very specific and deliberate choices on the part of importers when acquiring ideas, techniques and objects, and have demonstrated that exposure to a different method will not lead to its adoption unless it is relevant for the importing culture (see for instance Sahlins 1988: 5–9, on the adoption of tea-drinking in England). This is backed up in the Etruscan context by the fact that only certain objects were imported, while others were obviously (by their absence in the material record) rejected (see for example d'Agostino 1990; Small 1994; Spivey 1991; see also chapter 7, below). In accounts of changes in Etruscan archaeology, we must ask why imported forms were pertinent to the Etruscan context.

Models of socio-cultural change

Over the last twenty years, one scholar in particular has been associated with the application of a socio-political approach to Etruscan archaeology. Followed by his students and others, Torelli has set an example of applying socio-political models to a wide range of Etruscan material culture, and has done so with considerable success (for example Torelli 1983, 1990, 1992a,

1992b; see also Menichetti 1994; Pairault Massa 1992). However, this 'school of Torelli' has not been alone in such endeavours. In funerary architecture, for instance, the large burial mounds of the seventh century have been interpreted by Colonna as 'indubbiamente la massima espressione delle elites aristocratiche' (Colonna 1986: 395; see also Cristofani 1978: 68), and the unity in style of the tombs from the late sixth century on, together with their increased number and decreased size, is interpreted as the rise of a 'ceto medio', at the expense of the old *gentilizi* (Colonna 1986: 398). Similarly the parity between iron-age dwellings has been interpreted as reflecting an egalitarian social structure, whereas the seventh-century change in technique and materials is seen to indicate a 'livello più elevato' (Torelli 1985: 23).

Torelli also introduces a socio-political explanation for the emergence of sanctuary complexes: he sees the building of these complexes as an anti-aristocratic impulse on the part of so-called 'tyrants' (Torelli 1990: 181; see also Pairault Massa 1992: 60–7). More recently, less historically focused socio-political models have been imported from outside the discipline. For instance, in his study of the emergence of sanctuaries, Rendeli has deployed the notion of peer-polity interaction (Renfrew and Cherry (eds.) 1986) in order to account for the construction of temples (Rendeli 1990); and Zifferero has developed de Polignac's concept of sanctuaries acting as a 'zona franca' between different territories and communities (de Polignac 1995; Zifferero 1995).

Such socio-political approaches share a desire to explain archaeological changes in terms of prevailing social and cultural needs. Developments in architectural form are understood as the result of the changing socio-political environment. The real value of these studies lies is the examination of the relationships between objects, buildings and places within a unified framework for exploring social change. However, although such accounts give very convincing explanations of, for example, the parity in the sizes of sixth-century houses or tombs, or the increased size of temples in the early fifth century, they nonetheless underplay the specific material form that they took. Concern with, say, the size of a temple or its location overrides formal details of its construction, such as decoration or architectural details.

Summary

In order to conclude this section on the ways in which changes in the archaeological record of Etruria have been explained in the past, it will be useful to examine the characteristics they share. My aim so far has not been to deny the conclusions reached by these approaches; in fact, in many instances, it is hard to see alternative interpretations, and what is more, these conclusions form an important starting point for the inquiries in the following chapters. However, it is possible to add a new dimension to each of these approaches by taking careful account of the active role of material culture in structuring, and being structured by, social and cultural factors.

Most of the approaches mentioned so far implicitly accept the fact that material culture is structured by societal needs. If objects from the past can tell us anything about that past, it must be because of the relationship between those objects and the society that created them. However, it is insufficient to see objects, buildings or individuals as merely reflecting the society that created them, in the sense that, for instance, it is possible to talk about changes in house shape reflecting increased wealth, or similarities between tombs indicating the rise of a middle class. The next step must be to acknowledge the deliberate selection, rather than inevitability, of the forms these units take. The form of an object or building is selected because of its efficacy in embodying the cultural and social imperatives that led to the creation of the object or building in the first place. At the same time, the ability of tomb form to embody the rise of a middle class must be seen as playing an important part in the creation of that middle class. It is in this way that material culture structures society.

Material culture form: an alternative model

The form, materials and scale chosen in the production of Etruscan material culture is the starting point of the analysis in the following chapters. The specifics of an object's physical form will be seen as deeply implicated in the creation and transference of that object's meaning. Form and decoration, usually the domain of the architectural or art historian, will be integrated into a broader cultural understanding of Etruscan culture.

The relationship between material culture and the social norms that produce it has been the focus much recent debate in archaeology. It is impossible to prioritise one over the other, and only possible to discuss them separately in a hypothetical sense. In reality, the two are inseparable. Until now, the bias in Etruscan archaeology has been towards extrapolating the social norms from the material culture. This book aims to examine the details of Etruscan material form in order to show the mutual dependence of the two. In doing so, it draws heavily on recent developments in material culture studies that emphasise the materiality of objects, and the power of objects to embody and transmit cultural meaning.

In this section, aspects of this body of theory that are most relevant to the following discussions of Etruscan material culture will be discussed. The purpose is to show the link between culture and material culture, and that this link empowers archaeological material to materialise cultural meaning. This has two important implications for Etruscan archaeology: the first is that a detailed examination of Etruscan material culture, because it is the result of cultural action, can tell us about past Etruscan societies that produced it; more importantly, its second implication is that in acknowledging the power of objects to embody meaning for us as archaeologists, we must also acknowledge the power it would have had for Etruscans. Etruscan behaviour, attitudes and ideas would have been shaped by the material world that surrounded them. Material culture form is thus not only the product of social or cultural change, but also one of its determinants.

The socially informed body

Before examining the workings of Etruscan material culture form in detail, it is important to examine more closely the links between material culture and the society that produced it. Here it is useful to take the human body as a starting point (see also Dobres 2000; Gell 1993; Gosden 1994: 119). The cognisant, 'socially informed body' (Bourdieu 1977: 124) not only shapes the material world that it inhabits, but is, in turn, shaped by material culture. The human body is the point of interaction between the material and cognitive worlds. The work of two scholars has been particularly influential in exploring this relationship. Bourdieu's concept of *habitus*, and Giddens' structuration theory, with its stress on *locale*, have been instrumental in establishing the importance of the everyday experiences of individuals (*praxis*) in the creation of social structures, both in archaeological inquiry and beyond (Bourdieu 1977; Giddens 1979, 1984). According to both, the quotidian actions, feelings and gestures of individuals are informed by knowledge that is socially based. From infancy, children are exposed to, and incorporated within, the daily enactment of codes of permissible or forbidden actions and responses in given social situations. From these repeated behavioural experiences an individual develops his or her sense of the world and the relationships between the different elements of that world. It is within this epistemological framework that the individual acts in the future. In a similar way, Strathern's concept of 'distributed personhood' elaborates the ways in which individual actions are the outcomes of socially mediated practices (Strathern 1988). More recently, the somewhat earlier concept of Heidegger's 'being in the world' has been cited alongside Giddens and Bourdieu in emphasising the importance of social knowledge being created through the material experiences of individuals (most notably in J. Thomas 1996).

Both Bourdieu and Giddens are at pains to stress, however, that though social structures and norms may inform the behaviour of individuals, human behaviour is by no means dictated by such structures. At every point, the individual is faced with the choice between challenging or reaffirming the social framework that he or she has learned. Rather than being a super-imposed set of rules to which individuals have no choice but to conform, social structure has been conceived as a web of socially acceptable behaviour patterns to which the individual can choose to adhere or to react. The importance of this approach for ritual contexts has been explored extensively (in classical archaeology see, for example, I. Morris 1987, 1992), though the small-scale, everyday, non-ritual, and non-prestige aspects of material culture are equally significant (and perhaps most rewarding for archaeologists in that they allow investigation of a range of objects that would otherwise be neglected). By choosing to act in a way different from that of the prevailing social norms, individuals reconfigure the social and cultural structures within which they exist. According to this model, social change takes place as a result of the sum of individuals acting against social norms; and in this way they alter the wider social structure (Gosden 1994; Silverblatt 1988).

The social production of objects

One of the results of this premise is that, because individuals behave in relation to existing social structures (reacting either according to or in defiance of them), all human actions are socially informed. For archaeologists the importance of this observation lies in its applicability to the creation of material culture as a form of human action. The socially knowledgeable body cannot help but embody that cognitive and social knowledge within the objects that it creates. If the way of enacting all human actions is bounded by social parameters, then so too must be the ways in which individuals choose to make objects. There is thus a clear inferential route from the object, through the individual, to the society in which both were formed (Dobres 2000: 110–11; Gell 1992: 55).

Because the maker of an object is a social being, the process of making is informed by social structures, and importantly, that very process materialises those structures and representations of the world (Gosselain 1998; Ingold 1993a, 1993b; Lemonnier 1986, 1989a). The resulting objects, in turn, play a role in shaping the social concepts and interpretations that surround them (H. Moore 1994: 74). However, just as individuals can choose whether or not to act according to the social parameters of conventional behaviour, they can also choose whether or not to make objects according to the norms and expectations that surround the production of those objects (Gosselain 1998).

The concept of the *chaîne opératorie* has been deployed as a means of analysing the processes of object production (in particular by Lemonnier 1986, 1989b, 1990, 1992. See also Karlin and Julien 1994; Schlanger 1994; the concept owes much to Mauss 1990). By highlighting the sequential nature of object production, the *chaîne opératorie* places particular emphasis on the many choices that take place along the way. As such it makes all aspects of material culture appropriate for study because all material culture is the result of a series of decisions taken with social knowledge. Accordingly, the social, cultural, and symbolic potential of all aspects of object production, from the choice of raw materials to the selection of mythical figures for representation, is marshalled and deployed in object production, use, repair or discard. It must be borne in mind, however, that just as *habitus* or *locale* is not binding or restrictive of individual actions, neither are the structures or mental templates according to which objects are fashioned (S. E. van der Leeuw 1993; 1994: 138–9). The *chaîne opératorie* allows for the dissent of individual makers at any stage in the *chaîne*, and, just as social change is brought about by the sum of individual actions, material culture change ensues from repeated diversions from the template.

Two anthropological examples serve to demonstrate the importance of the decisions made by producers of material culture. The first is the rejection by the Western Desert Aborigines of Australia of locally available and harder (and thus seemingly better quality) chert in adze production. Instead, a poorer, softer stone from further away is favoured. The reasons for this seemingly counter-intuitive behaviour are linked to ancestral ties (and associated prestige) with these more distant areas, and with the stone that comes from them (Gould 1980). These social and cultural considerations override the apparently more 'practical' considerations of the quality of the stone.

The second example is the extensive work of Lechtman in the metallurgy of the Moche in Peru (Lechtman 1977, 1984a, 1984b, 1993). Lechtman shows that the physical and chemical properties of the metals were overridden by complex technological procedures in the 'desire to achieve culturally valued colour effects . . . played out in the alloy systems they developed or invented' (Lechtman 1984a: 21). These examples show clearly the way in which production techniques and choices of materials are driven by cultural considerations of the anticipated product: the techniques deployed are those which produced the socially desired colour effect, regardless of the potentially off-putting complexity of achieving them (Gosselain 1998: 78). The production of every new artefact involves a number of decisions on the part of the maker (Dietler and Herbich 1998; Gell 1988: 219–21; Sackett 1985; 1990: 33–4; though see Hodder 1990a). These stylistic decisions range from the seemingly trivial and inconsequential to the more obviously impressive and deliberate (Gosselain 1998, 2000). We must acknowledge that the choice of any one action over another is informed by the social circumstances surrounding the maker, the object and those actions. In this way, all objects are shaped within a matrix that simultaneously comprises social tradition (Gell's axis of coherence or Bourdieu's structuring principle) and individual agency (aims, goals, desires of the craftsperson). Choices over the form, materials and technologies deployed in the creation of material culture are made with reference to other objects (see esp. Gell 1998: 250, 256), to what others are doing, and to expectations about how the object will be used and viewed (Gell 1998: 219–21; Hodder 1990a: 46; Lemonnier 1992: 1–2; 79–80). The material record is thus the result of a series of accretions to, and erosions of, pre-existing material forms. Each replication of, or deviation from, the pre-existing norm is the result of the decision of the individual maker.

An important aspect of this process is the idea in the mind of the craftsperson of how the finished object should look. While, on a theoretical level, the importance of 'artefactual precedent' has been acknowledged in determining actions, and so the choice of subsequent action and behaviour, including that of the maker (Barrett 2000: 61; Wobst 1997; 2000: 41), few archaeological studies have examined the implications of this for material form itself. Exceptions are Ingold, Miller and Shanks (Ingold 1990, 1993a, 1993b; D. Miller 1985, 1987; Shanks 1992, 1999). For Ingold in particular, the desired end point is just as important a consideration in the creation of an object as the choice of raw materials and the techniques available (Ingold 1990; see also J. Dougherty and Keller 1982; Keller and Keller 1996). This is particularly important for the analysis of the following chapters as it implies the existence of an intended viewer for material culture.

Of course, human societies are never as simple as the hypotheses formulated in attempts to understand them. One of the assumptions so far has been that the *habitus* is homogeneous; in fact, quite the opposite is true. The social environments in which individuals live are often diverse and vary between individuals and over time within the same culture. The most frequently cited lines along which society might be structured are age, sex and status. Thus different individuals will be working within, or against, different world-views, and this will affect their behaviour in both the production and perception of objects (Conkey 1991; Meskell 1999). Objects form parts of these conflicting world-views of groups and subgroups within a given society. Though objects are often deployed in order to represent conflicting views, more interestingly they become an arena where the differing views come to be negotiated and explored. This characteristic of material culture is one that will be explored in the discussions of Etruscan material culture in the following chapters, concentrating on the materially based actions of individuals in changing pre-existing attitudes towards certain cultural categories, such as the dead and the living.

The social reception of objects

Much of the discussion so far has centred on the 'socially informed body' and its production of material artefacts, and I have concentrated on the theoretical basis for considering the form of material culture as deliberate and as informed by social and cultural considerations. The active role of the objects themselves in the creation of social reality has been taken for granted somewhat. As Gell has pointed out, approaches derived from the sociological standpoint, though viable on a broad theoretical level, ignore the object itself 'as a concrete product of human ingenuity', concentrating instead on its 'power to mark social distinctions' (Gell 1992: 42–3). For him, it is insufficient to discuss material culture as though it were a 'vehicle for extraneous social and symbolic messages' (Gell 1992: 43); instead we must examine the manner in which objects are active in embodying and creating such social and symbolic messages. In this way, he insists that we acknowledge the power of objects as social agents (Gell 1998: 17–19).

This has been demonstrated in Miller's discussion of the Walbiri hunter-gatherers of Central Australia, in which he shows how cultural and social cosmology is mapped on to the cultural landscape, and how this is in turn mapped on to the features of the geographical landscape. These physical presences then become a means of reflecting and objectifying the social cosmology itself (D. Miller 1985, 1987). Similarly, Pfaffenberger talks of 'social-technical' systems, such as that of the Balinese water supply system, which involves the mobilisation of a host of technical and social factors, such as water temples, priests and irrigation, that 'produce power and meaning as well as goods' (Pfaffenberger 1992: 502).

The concept that objects actively embody meaning is hardly a new one for archaeologists. Since the 1980s there have been calls for a greater emphasis on the active role of material culture (in, for example, contributions to Hodder (ed.) 1982); a little later 'cognitive archaeology' stressed the relationship between cognitive structures and the structures of objects (see for example the contributions in Renfrew and Zubrow (eds.) 1994). Most recently, inquiries into the link between meaning and material have concentrated on the concept of agency (Barrett 1994; Dobres and Robb (eds.) 2000; Hodder 1992; Johnson 1989; Shanks and Tilley 1987a, 1987b; J. Thomas 1996; Tilley 1994).

The work of Gell has taken the agency of objects as its explicit focus. For Gell, humans and inanimate objects act as social agents, prompting and initiating a series of events. Although it is relatively easy to see how a human agent is capable of causing things to happen, the case with an inanimate object may need further elaboration. Gell gives a chillingly powerful example of the land mines deposited by the soldiers of Pol Pot's regime. He argues that the mines, once distributed, are not mere 'tools' made for 'use', but are rather a component of a particular type of social agency (the ideology of Pol Pot). In exploding, killing and maiming, these objects enact and express political ideology (Gell 1998: 17–21; see also D. Miller 1987). This example also serves to highlight the distributed nature of agency (compare Strathern's distributed personhood), whereby agents can exert power in many places simultaneously (so that in this example, the soldier's agency is evident not just where his body is, but also in every mine that he has deposited). Gell's analysis dramatically shows the impact of the agency of objects in the lives and deaths of individuals.

Gell's anthropological treatment of the agency of objects has strong parallels with Bourdieu and Giddens' sociological analyses of the link between the individual and the collective. Just as the social nature of producers has been demonstrated, so has the social nature of objects also come under consideration. According to Gell, objects exist in groups; thus each individual object will be part of a larger family of objects. The characteristic that unifies these groups of objects is commonly referred to as style: each individual object embodies the stylistic principles that form the larger collectivity of a stylistic unit, in the same way that each individual person embodies the cultural principles that form the collectivity of a social unit (Gell 1998: 153–4). For Gell, style is what enables any individual object to be understood in terms of the wholes, or larger units, to which it belongs (Gell 1998: 162–3; see also Hodder's discussion of Boy George, Johnny Rotten, and stiletto heels: Hodder 1990a: 45–7). As a result, objects are seen as necessarily relational – it is through the relationships between them that objects derive and exude meaning.

Style has been an area of debate within archaeology for some thirty years (see Carr and Neitzel (eds.) 1995; Conkey and Hasdorf (eds.) 1990; Gebauer

1987; Hegmon 1992, 1998; Stark (ed.) 1998; for a historical analysis of treatments of style see Conkey 1990; W. Davis 1990; for the debate in classical archaeology see Carstens 2003/4; Whitley 1987). The debate has centred largely on the supposed dichotomy between style and function. Gradually, the view that style and function are separate (see for instance Wobst's distinction between the aspects of an object that were an 'adjunct' and those that were 'functional': Wobst 1977) has been modified by those who see them as complementary to each other (see Sackett's 'isochretism' 1982, 1990), or those who view style as part of a wider cultural discourse (for example Wiessner's emphasis on style defining social boundaries and identities: 1983, 1988, 1990). Despite this concentration on the analysis of style, the results have been largely descriptive; there have been few investigations of how style or groups of material objects behave in the active way that they do (for critique see Dietler and Herbich 1998; Hodder 1990a: 44–5; Lemonnier 1986: 148).

Although, as mentioned above, Gell's work is very open to criticism, in particular over his insistence on primary and secondary agency (for example, Gosden 2001: 164–5), it nonetheless provides one of the few attempts to explore style and material culture on a theoretical and empirical level simultaneously. His attempts to work through the implications of his theoretical position on the data from Polynesia are thus particularly instructive for archaeologists, despite their shortcomings. For him, the relational nature of style is paramount: objects within a style are linked relationally, but more importantly, Gell sees relations not just between objects, but also between such relations themselves (Gell 1998: 163–8). To a certain extent, this is similar to Hodder's treatment of the relationships between stiletto heels and wine glasses, where stylistic references in both refer to one understanding of 'femininity' (Hodder 1990a: 46–7, though this is not the end of Hodder's analysis). In other words, it is possible to see similar principles at work in the creation and manufacture of objects that are traditionally seen as forming discrete categories. There is, then, considerable conceptual slippage between different artefact types, including the human body (through its decoration, clothing and adornment). In addition, there is similar slippage between material culture and other manifestations of culture such as kinship or ritual (Gell 1998: 215), thus allowing us to compare different kinds of objects and different spheres of cultural and social life (Dobres 2000: 199; Hodder 1990a: 46; 1990b; Gell 1998: 168). It is the 'axis of coherence' that gives the similarities across material and cultural categories their homogeneity: in the case of Gell's work on Marquesia this was the concept of 'least difference'; for Hodder, that of 'femininity' and 'domestication'. This book argues that for archaic Etruria the axis of coherence, or structuring principle, was that of surface.

Such an approach need not imply overwhelming homogeneity within a given culture; on the contrary, it is essential to acknowledge the often conflicting desires and motives within a group. Nonetheless, such diverse strategies come together within the collective unity implicit in belonging to a culture. This is similar to Morris's discussion of social structure in the ancient world (itself based on Giddens' theory of structuration), where social structure is seen as informing, rather than dictating social actions (I. Morris 1992).

So far, the discussion has examined the social production of material culture, and the importance of material culture in structuring social practice. The importance of this for the following chapters is that it gives social importance to all aspects of Etruscan material culture. Furthermore, it shows that Etruscan material culture was both the embodiment of and the subsequent framework for the cultural concerns of the Etruscans who used and produced it. The point of departure for the following chapters will therefore be a close examination of Etruscan material culture form, and the changes that took place in it. Such an approach, which emphasises the material form of artefacts, does not argue for a return to empiricist material determinism. On the contrary, the emphasis here is on the interrelationship between objects, their creators and their recipients (Hodder's viewer, or Gell's patient).

Surface and boundaries

For the purposes of the analysis of Etruscan material culture in this book, the physical nature of the object will be taken as the starting point of the inquiry. This is partly due to the archaeological nature of the inquiry, and partly for the theoretical reasons discussed above. Although it is important to remember the relational, non-hierarchical, nature of the links between objects, agency and meaning, the object (be it the human body, portable material objects, or spatial and architectural ones) will be taken as the point at which meaning is generated, interpreted and acted upon.

Given the social production of objects, and the subsequent power of objects to influence culture, the object is the point around which, through the interaction of agents (objects and people), meaning is created. Most importantly, this interaction is dependent on physical and cultural perception; this, in turn, is contingent upon the coming together of the physical entity of the object and the socially cognisant individual. This meeting takes place at the surface of the object. This is the point at which the object creates

meaning, and at which the object is perceived and understood. In his study
of the psychology of perception, Gibson argues that the surface is the point
at which objects are transformed as a result of their agency in the world;
it is where light is reflected (or not), where two substances or objects meet
and touch, and it is the point from which objects transmit themselves to
others, via light, touch or smell (J. J. Gibson 1979: 23). As a result, surfaces
'allow for both persistence and change' (J. J. Gibson 1979: 22). The environment is thus composed of substances that are separated and distinguished
by surfaces, and, importantly, surfaces have characteristics that continue or
alter.

The surface of an object marks the physical boundary between itself and
the wider environment. (As discussed above, this is not to deny that the
agency of the object transcends the extent of its physical being.) Surface is
the means by which agents (individuals and objects) negotiate and articulate
difference. The surface of an object is the point at which the object begins;
it defines and differentiates the object from its surroundings, and marks
the starting point for any engagement with that object. Importantly for
archaeologists, surface encloses and demarcates an object not only in its
physical form, but also as a social, cultural and ideational entity. The surface
acts as a cultural interface between things, people and ideas. It is through
our repeated interaction with and through surface that we develop our
understanding, or, in Deleuze's words, 'sense', of the world (Deleuze 1990).

Of yet greater interest for archaeologists is the mutability of surfaces.
Surfaces are created and used by people in different ways and at different
times. The concept of surface is thus simultaneously culturally specific *and*
transcultural. For example, the manipulation of the surface of the body
by tattooing takes different forms, accrues different meanings and prompts
different responses depending on the time and place in which the tattoos are
seen, and by whom; so that 'LOVE' and 'HATE' inscribed across the knuckles
of a male hand will carry differently charged resonances depending on the
relationship an individual has with the UK justice system, and will clearly
elicit responses different from those prompted by traditional Maori tattoos
(see contributions to Caplan (ed.) 2000).

These different uses and meanings do not undermine the importance
of the surface of the body in transmitting, encoding and shaping cultural
meaning. Though the universal applicability of the concept of surface as an
analytical tool may lead to the criticism that it is too general to be of use,
the malleable nature of surface and its potential for change and manipulation over time make it particularly instructive in a diachronic study. While
anthropologists can assess the significance of surface only in the present or

across cultures, archaeologists are in a uniquely privileged position in being able to discern changes in the treatment and cultural meaning of surface over time. (For an example of the importance of the changing nature of the archaeological marking of cultural notions see Parker Pearson 1993.)

Furthermore, the use of the concept of surface as an 'axis of coherence' allows the conjunction of material that is otherwise difficult to compare. It is both object-specific, in that it can be discerned only in the object itself, and at the same time trans-artefactual, in that it can be applied to many different artefacts, and different kinds of artefact, in a single analysis. For archaeologists, and for historical archaeologists in particular, it allows the combination of artefact categories that are traditionally kept discrete, such as images and buildings. It thus enables us to bridge the unhelpful divide that still exists between art-historical and archaeological material: the iconography of Greek myth on Etruscan mirrors, for example, can be studied alongside the architecture of funerary monuments.

A concept like surface can operate on both a specific and a general level because of the ways in which human beings construct their understanding of the worlds they inhabit. As early as 1942 the anthropologists Bateson and Mead saw 'intangible relationships among different types of culturally standardised behaviour', which meant that 'pieces of behaviour spatially and contextually separated may all be relevant to a single discussion, the same emotional thread running through' (Bateson and Mead 1942: xii). More recently, anthropological and ethnoarchaeological studies have sought to describe and emphasise the interconnectedness of different aspects of cultural life: Bourdieu talks of 'cognitive scheme transfers' (Bourdieu 1977), Gell of 'relations between relations' or 'axes of coherence' (Gell 1998), Carsten of 'cultures of relationships' (Carsten (ed.) 2000), and Tilley of 'metaphor' (Tilley 1999). A recent archaeological contribution by Shore (1995) has emphasised the process of 'analogical schematisation' whereby cultures create and understand meaning through the use of analogy. Individuals process or schematise situations and experiences by means of analogy with other situations and experiences in order to create an understanding of the world. Analogical schematisation means therefore that 'powerful equivalences can be constructed and reconstructed' between different spheres of human experience (Shore 1995).

For these theorists occurrences in any one area of material life are somehow all related to other aspects of material or mental life. Their studies have been fundamental for those whose interest lies in examining ethnicity and cultural identity, so that, in a way parallel to that just discussed, the interrelationships within groups are seen as relating to wider, intra-cultural ones

(J. M. Hall 1997, 2002; Hodder 1982a, 1985; Larick 1986; 1991; S. Jones 1997; Shennan (ed.) 1989). These relationships are ones of mutual definition and redefinition between parallel spheres of human existence (Stewart 1993: 101). However, in order to trace such relationships across spheres, the inquiry has to be sufficiently broad, or distanced. The concept of surface is an analytical device that is both deeply rooted in the particularities of the material under study, and yet versatile enough to be applied in different spheres, to allow the researcher to move within and between different categories of human activity.

The detection of changes in the treatment of surface in a given culture rests on an examination of material form. Though the possibility exists of the non-physical marking of difference (see for example Whitelaw 1994), it is the manipulation of physical surfaces over time that is archaeologically retrievable and will form the basis of the analyses that follow.

As a result, the concept of boundaries will play an important part in this book. Boundaries establish differences between physical or cognitive constructs. For this book, the relationship between surface and boundary is complex and open to change over time: at some points the external, visible surface of an object or space forms the boundary of that object or space; at others, the boundary reaches behind the surface, invisible from the external viewpoint. Thus the articulation of surface and boundary in material culture changes over time: boundaries can be surfaces or have surfaces; they can be physical and/or conceptual.

The concept of boundaries has come under criticism by post-structuralists for the binary oppositions that it implies. The legitimacy of structuralist oppositions such as male/female, living/dead, inside/outside and public/private has been questioned (for example, Pàlsson (ed.) 1993). This book will use such oppositions, not as fixed universals, but rather as ideas around which, and with which, people construct the worlds in which they live. Such oppositions are not 'given', but are constantly open to renegotiation at a cognitive level. This process of renegotiation is embodied in the material changes in Etruscan treatments of boundaries and surfaces. By being both part of the object and the points at which objects begin or end, boundaries allow the definition of both material and ontological difference.

The human body performs a dual role in such an analysis: it is both the cognisant individual that creates, perceives and acts upon the material world, and simultaneously a part of that same material world, with the potential for being perceived itself. A large part of the following discussion rests on an exploration of this latter characteristic, though the former is always implicit. The possibilities presented by considering the body as part of the material world, as a result of adornment, whether permanent (such as scarification or tattooing) or temporary (such as clothing, jewellery and cosmetics), plays a central part in the social incorporation and expression of the individual. However, it is important to emphasise that such discussions of the body are actually concerned with the surface of the body: the skin and its decoration. The importance of the skin as the surface between individual and society has been discussed above (see further Dietler and Herbich 1998: 242; though cf. Meskell 1999, who argues this reduces the body to too passive a role. See below, Chapter 2). The relationship between the inside of the body and its skin has been explored by Stewart, for whom 'the body presents the paradox of the contained and container at once' (Stewart 1993: 104). This contested and shifting yet central relationship means that attention is continually focused on the boundaries or limits of the body. Furthermore, Stewart uses Lacan's 'erotogenic zones'(areas where there are cuts or gaps in the body's surface – eyelids, lips etc.), in order to argue that such zones create a 'sense of "edge", borders or margins' (Stewart 1993: 104). It is no surprise, then, that it is precisely these zones that, anthropologically speaking, are the subject of taboo or elaboration through adornment. By being on the surface, and at the same time punctuating the surface, such apertures serve to define the limits of the body, and ultimately of the self.

For other types of object, including spatial ones (such as architecture and urban form), surfaces are equally important to self-definition and the establishment of boundaries. Spatial structures function as an arena in which social life is enacted, because they are a locus and a medium for the production and reproduction of social roles; at the same time, these social roles produce and reproduce the spatial structures. The articulation of space is carried out by its division, through the creation of architectural boundaries. As Kent has described: 'Architecture creates boundaries out of otherwise unbounded space, while the use of space can be seen as a means to order that unbounded space . . . Architectural partitions usually are conscious manipulations by humans to create boundaries where they do not exist in nature' (Kent 1990b: 2). For some, this concerns social relations and hierarchy (Blanton 1994: 10; Hillier and Hanson 1984: 1); for others, social and cosmological ideas of order are expressed (Richards 1990: 113); while yet others stress the potential of architecture to embody a variety of different orders, from the classification of people to ideas surrounding cleanliness (Parker Pearson and Richards 1994b: 2). In other words, the creation of boundaries goes beyond the physical: 'social boundaries are abstractions and ideological constructs' (Goodby 1998: 161).

Boundaries are thus the point at which social, cultural and ontological categories are created, and changes between these categories take place (Deleuze 1990: 1, 9). Similarly, a 'boundary is not that at which something stops but . . . a boundary is that from which something begins its *presencing*' (Heidegger 1971a: 154, his italics; see also Ardener 1981; 11–12; Deleuze 1990: 186; Kent 1990b: 2; Parker Pearson and Richards 1994b: 24).

Despite such general characteristics, boundaries, like surfaces, are also highly contextualised in their meaning. Anthropological literature attests to the enormous diversity in the boundaries that are represented in different cultures (Conkey 1990; Hodder 1979; Lechtman 1977; Lemonnier 1986; Wiessner 1983). At the same time, if, according to the theory of the *chaîne opératorie*, all aspects of material culture are appropriate for study, such variations in the forms of boundaries must be of central importance to the ideological and social contexts in which they were produced.

Anthropological studies have placed great stress on the precarious and dangerous nature of boundaries. The transition between different marked spaces occurs in special places, set apart and reserved (Lefebvre 1993: 35). These 'weighted spaces' (Parker Pearson and Richards 1994b: 2) mediate between different areas of bounded space. As a result of this, such mediative distances become associated with danger and uncertainty (Douglas 1984; Leach 1972). The same emphasis on boundaries, and points of transition across boundaries, is evident in work on political and territorial borders (Donnan and Wilson 1999: 13), and in a wide range of anthropological discussion of 'art' (Dissanayake 1992).

Doorways are an obvious spatial example of such weighted space, or mediative distances, and the particular significance of doors has been elaborated thus by Lefebvre: 'transitional, symbolic and functional, the object "door" seems to bring a space . . . to an end; and it heralds the reception to be expected in the neighbouring room, or in the house or interior that awaits' (Lefebvre 1991: 209–10). For Bachelard 'the door is an entire cosmos of the half-open' (Bachelard 1994: 222). It is the point at which the state of being inside and outside is undefined and negotiable. Doors and boundaries belong simultaneously to neither and both of the spaces they define. As such they are indefinable in their affinities. In the terminology of structural anthropology they are liminal areas. They allow transition from one space to another, and in so doing allow mediation between physical or ontological states. As a result of their permeability, they are the points of weakness in the boundaries created. They are essential for movement between two states, yet because of this facility they hold potential danger for the maintenance of the distinction between these two states.

The forms that boundaries take are culturally specific (Ardener 1981: 11–12; Douglas 1972: 514; Duncan 1981: 1–2; Lefebvre 1991: 193; Harvey 1990: 216, 222–5; Rapoport 1969: 47), and different cultures draw distinctions between different activities (R. J. Lawrence 1987: 103–10; Harvey 1990: 216, 222–5; Lefebvre 1991: 193). For all these reasons, the spatial treatment of doorways and entrances can reveal much about perceptions of the transitions they mark and facilitate. The way in which a culture marks and deals with these transitional areas casts light on the way that a society thinks about specific boundaries. Any changes in the articulation of these boundaries will signal a corresponding change in such attitudes. It will be argued in the following chapters that the treatment of boundaries changes fundamentally in the late sixth century, and in a way that emphasises the visibility and clarity of those boundaries. Such an approach depends heavily on the concept of a viewer for the newly created surfaces in Etruscan cultural life. In order for any manipulations in surface and material form to have social efficacy, an intended viewer for this behaviour is essential.

Visibility and the viewer

The importance of the visual dimension in social relations has been demonstrated in both anthropological and sociological literature (Fyfe and Law (eds.) 1988; Henny 1986; Marcus and Myers (eds.) 1995; Taylor 1994). Though the ways in which we see may appear obvious, authors have been at pains to point out the historical, social and cultural specificity of seeing. In the face of criticism that there is 'no need to over-intellectualize the moment of looking', Mirzoeff gives a striking illustration of the ways in which seeing is not as obvious as it seems: he takes as an example the legal case brought by the City of Cincinnati against the photographs of Robert Mapplethorpe on the grounds that a jury only had to look at the images to see that they were obscene. However, in the light of the testimonies of curators and art historians, the jury failed to uphold the case (Mirzoeff 1999; 21–2). These witnesses brought different readings (viewings?) to the images before them, which were derived from alternative cultural, social, intellectual and historical perspectives. This social basis for the reception of images is an echo of Bourdieu's work discussed above, and more specifically of his statement that 'any act of perception involved conscious or unconscious deciphering' (Bourdieu 1993: 215), so that 'observation' can no longer be taken as an uncomplicated, or untheorised, given (see also Goldhill and Osborne 1994).

The last twenty years or so have seen attempts to focus on the acts of seeing, largely in art history (both ancient and modern) and anthropology. One of the emphases of these endeavours has been the importance of the social and historical dimensions of seeing (see for example Bryson 1983: xiii–xiv, 87–131; contributions to Foster (ed.) 1988). As Bryson shows, the nineteenth-century concern with vision was a preoccupation with the physiology of the eye and the neurology of the optical apparatus (Bryson 1988). It was, in other words, concerned with the biology of how the eye saw. In the twentieth century, attention moved to perception, and to ensuring that perception was unhindered, so that, for instance, in museums, objects were decontextualised in order to ensure that no superfluous information masked the object from the eye. It is into such a tradition that Gombrich's *Art and Illusion* fits, a tradition that sees all viewers as the same (all eyes are the same).

However, a post-modern position acknowledges that the visual field is one where meanings, not just objects, are perceived, and that these meanings are embedded in verbal and visual networks. These networks are, of course, social constructs. If vision is socially constructed, there must be a relationship between how people learn to see and how the world is seen by them (Heywood and Sandywell (eds.) 1999; Banks and Morphy (eds.) 1997: 22; for classical art history see for example Beard 1991: 14). In this way, images will elicit different reactions and views from different contexts, times and people (Elsner 1995: 1).

Semiotic theory has emphasised the arbitrary nature of signs, so that for instance, individuals familiar with the western artistic conventions, such as the device of perspective, accept two-dimensional pictures as three-dimensional representations. Thus, 'seeing is not believing but interpreting' (Mirzoeff 1999: 13; see also Heywood and Sandywell (eds.) 1999: xi). For Jenks, the social knowledge implicit in such viewing, perception and responses makes the viewer 'artful', that is, knowledgeable both in interpretation and in the behaviour that such knowledge prompts (Jenks (ed.) 1995: 10; see also Beard 1991: 12). For anthropologists, the social dimensions of seeing, like theories of material culture in general, imply an accommodation of the social structuring of the visual world, and, as a result, an exploration of the ways in which phenomena are incorporated within cultural processes, and further, of the ways in which they, in turn, influence the trajectories of socio-cultural systems (Banks and Morphy 1997: 21). Visual systems influence people's behaviour in the world, and their conceptions of it. They are part of the ways in which culture is constituted. Banks's work on Jain representations of the body shows how the relationship between Jain conceptions of the body and soul is replicated in a visual system that includes not only the body of the individual but also other visual forms, such as drawings and sculpture. These images serve to reinforce and uphold conceptions of the nature of the world; thus they are not passive reflections of social constructs, but play an active part in generating those structures in the first place (Banks 1997).

The active or culturally generative role of visual culture has been explored by Davey in terms of what 'viewing directs us to do' (Davey 1999: 13). This is elaborated in detail in Osborne's study of Greek female sculpture, in which he discusses the way in which features such as the position of the head of the sculpture (and therefore its engagement with the viewer) or the variation in composition and textures created by the sculptor affects the viewing of the pieces, so that, 'like it or not, viewers find their attention focused' (Osborne 1994: 86; see also Osborne 1987). Such approaches are open, at first glance, to the criticism that they imply that all viewers will respond in a similar way to variations in light and texture. Yet, as Mirzoeff's treatment of perspective shows, despite the fact that not every viewer (if any) will view an object from the 'intended' (or hypothesised) viewpoint, the internal coherence of such images, or interpretation, makes them credible nonetheless (Mirzoeff 1999: 8). Mirzoeff's analysis is based on perspective in a single image; in a large body of material, Gell's concept of the 'relationships between relations' discussed above gives the same coherence.

Finally, the work of Berger and Bryson has also served to emphasise the active role of viewing, though with an emphasis on the controlling nature of the gaze, or of fixing an object in one's gaze (Berger 1972; Bryson 1983). They emphasise the unequal power relationship between the viewing subject and the viewed object. Thus objects or people that are caught in an objectifying gaze are clearly positioned by the process of being viewed. In this way, viewing defines the object. In the following chapters, the importance of creating visible surfaces in Etruscan material culture will be traced. The creation of viewpoints for objects or spaces is part of their definition and redefinition, and so of their social presence.

Elsner also considers the active role of viewing. Here viewing is taken to be a process which transforms both the viewed and the viewer: the viewer constructs the object by setting it within his pre-existing mental framework, in relation to other similar or dissimilar visual experiences; at the same time, the viewer is redefined according to the new relation to the object in which he or she now stands (Elsner 1992; 1995: 4, 21, 39). In this way, Elsner emphasises the 'reflexivity of viewer and object each constituting each other' (Elsner 1995: 21). Thus, for Etruscans, the viewing of the newly created material world around them would have changed them, and set them in new relationships with each other and the material world. In this way the concept of the viewer dovetails with the concept of the active role of material culture discussed above. The interaction of viewer and the viewed creates a new social reality.

The Etruscan viewer

The identity of the viewer of Etruscan material culture is made up of many possible categories, which may, and doubtless did, overlap. As a result, it is important to acknowledge that individual responses to the same object would have varied, according to characteristics such as, for instance, age, sex, status or wealth. However, as discussed above, the work of Elsner and Osborne in classical art history (Elsner 1995; Osborne 1994), Mirzoeff in visual studies (Mirzoeff 1999), Gell, and the contributors to Banks and Morphy in anthropology (Gell 1998; Banks and Morphy 1997) have shown that the underlying principles of a given visual system operate for all viewers. To concentrate on the individual viewer is, of course, essential to our understanding not only of the object, but also of the social network of which the viewer forms part (as the work on, say, the female or colonial viewer has amply demonstrated: Meskell 1999; Mirzoeff 1999 ch. 4 respectively); however, to concentrate on this to the exclusion of the more general visual system within which all viewers and objects are at work is to underplay the importance of viewing itself. For this reason, in this analysis the term 'viewer' will be taken to refer both to single individuals and to groups of people. The user of a mirror, the pedestrian in an urban environment and the participant in ritual at a sanctuary would have a visual response to the changing environment around them. For such categories it is easy to imagine the quotidian interactions during which, say, the body or the house would be viewed; the process of viewing was one that can be postulated within the day-to-day encounters between individuals and their environments.

The case of burials is more complex, as tombs were sealed after the deposition of the body, raising questions over the applicability of the concept of the viewer for the burial context. However, this lack of a viewer for the tomb is only apparent. First, potential viewers are the participants in the burial ritual. The mourners present at the funeral would experience the tomb at first hand. Second, Etruscan tombs usually contain multiple burials, so unless all the individuals died together, or were ritually killed for coeval burial, individual members of the burying group would re-enter the tomb for subsequent burials. Finally, recent analysis of the skeletal remains from a sarcophagus in the British Museum suggests that excarnation was practised by some Etruscans at least, so that, even in the case of a single deposition, the tomb would have been revisited on several occasions for different stages of the burial process (Swaddling and Prag (eds.) 2002). All these scenarios provide potential viewers for the tomb. Even if these were not the case, it is likely that commemorative ritual activities took place in or near the tombs (a possible explanation for the ramps on the seventh-century burial mounds, and for the steps leading to the roofs of cube tombs: Damgaard Andersen 1993b: esp. 53). The extent to which this involved reopening the tomb cannot be gauged, but a renewed memory of the tomb would have been unavoidable for at least a section of society. Furthermore, the presence of hooks in the ceilings of tombs for lighting illustrates the importance of viewing the inside of the tomb at a certain point it its use. In addition, the earlier burial mounds contain several (up to four) tombs, usually assessed to be a generation later than the previous tomb and containing the 'entourage' of the deceased. The burials within the mounds are thought to be united by familial ties through time, as monuments to the aristocratic families they contained. Again, the recutting of the mound for consecutive burials would heighten awareness of the tomb. Even in an imagined instance when the tomb is not revisited, when all the depositions took place at the same time and the tomb was never opened again, there would still be a collective memory of the inside of the tomb and an awareness of the proximity of the dead on the part of the participants in the original ritual.

This category may or may not have overlapped with a potentially larger group of individuals involved in the construction of the tomb. They too would have carried a memory of the tomb, as would a passer-by during the construction of the tomb, which was certainly no overnight job. The frequency of passers-by would not be insubstantial, as the roads from the city into the territory passed through the cemeteries, so that anyone entering or leaving the city would have walked through the changing architectural landscape of the cemeteries. This would have included visitors from other Etruscan cities and, in the case of coastal Etruria, from other parts of the Mediterranean through the ports such as Pyrgi, Gravisca and Regisvilla. In this way, the viewer of the tomb has become reintegrated with the viewer of Etruscan material culture more generally.

Conclusion

This long chapter has outlined the theoretical framework within which the analysis of the following chapters is set. It has emphasised the deliberate and cognisant creation of Etruscan material culture, and stressed the importance of the close study of changes in material culture form for our understanding of the wider cultural transformations that are at once the product and the cause of those changes. In particular, it has emphasised the visible result of these changes in material culture and, as a result, the role of changing treatments of surface in negotiating cultural differences, and as an analytical tool in an inquiry into material culture change. The rest of this book will examine the changing treatment of surfaces in Etruscan material culture.

2 | Etruscan mirrors: reflections on personal and gender identity

Introduction

In this chapter, the corpus of Etruscan bronze hand mirrors will be used in an investigation of the treatment of the surface of Etruscan bodies. It has two aims: the first is to examine the cultural function of mirrors, or as Serra Ridgway puts it, to look at 'mirrors as *objects* not just "pictures"' (Serra Ridgway 1992: 282). As will be shown, the sudden appearance of mirrors in the archaeological record is closely linked to the function of the mirror in adornment. Adornment, or the manipulation of the surface of the body, is a process that is always bounded by the parameters of social and cultural expectations, and is an essential part of the creation of self-identity. The second aim is to look at the variations in such social and cultural expectations between male and female bodies. This is derived from the images of men and women depicted on the mirrors themselves.

Though the earliest recorded find of an Etruscan hand mirror was in 1507 from a tomb near Castellina in Chianti, it was not until the seventeenth and eighteenth centuries that interest in them became significant. At this time, they were called *paterae*, and were thought to have been used in the pouring of libations. It was not until 1824, when Inghirami published his *Monumenti Etruschi*, that they were identified as mirrors. Inghirami maintained that their use was religious, and this interpretation was not dispelled until later in the century, with the publication by Gerhard of the four-volume *Etruskische Spiegel*, to which a fifth was added by Körte and Klugmann (Gerhard 1834, 1843, 1861, 1862; Körte and Klugmann 1897). This was the first attempt at a systematic survey of Etruscan mirrors. Its focus was on identifying the subject-matter of the engravings on the mirrors, and as a result, the volumes are organised according to the subjects represented on the backs of the mirrors. Despite preliminary work by Ducati, it was not until the 1940s, with the work of Mansuelli, that a chronology was seriously attempted (Ducati 1912; Mansuelli 1942, 1943, 1946, 1947). Modelling his work on that of Beazley on Attic vase painting, Mansuelli tried to establish a relative chronology for the mirrors and to discern different *maestri* by their 'signatures'. Independently, Beazley also made a preliminary attempt at establishing a chronology for these objects (Beazley 1949). Absolute chronologies were obtained through comparison with Attic vase painting, and though the validity of the latter has come under discussion recently (see Cook 1989), the period of contention is largely before the production of Etruscan mirrors, and the Attic chronologies are generally accepted (for chronological accounts, see Del Chiaro 1974; Brendel 1978: 201–2, 285–7, 359–62; de Grummond (ed.) 1982: 140–65. For detailed dating of individual mirrors, see the relevant volumes of the ongoing *Corpus Speculorum Etruscorum*). The dating of later mirrors is more problematic due to the standardised nature of their production (Höckmann 1987a; Salskov Roberts 1983; though, more recently, see Serra Ridgway 2000: 412–6; Szilágyi 1994, 1995). Since the middle of the twentieth century a number of important studies of individual periods (Mayer-Prokop 1967; Pfister-Roesgen 1975), collections (Lambrechts 1978; Rebuffat-Emmanuel 1973) and groups have been carried out (Carpino 2003; Fischer-Graf 1980; Herbig 1955–6; van der Meer 1995), but perhaps the most significant development has been the initiation in 1973 of the *Corpus Speculorum Etruscorum* (hereafter *CSE*), a project that aims, when finished, to provide a complete catalogue of mirrors from museums and private collections (Serra Ridgway 1992, 2000).

The mirrors in question are hand mirrors made of cast and beaten bronze, mostly the latter (Swaddling *et al.* 2000). They comprise a slightly convex reflective disc, which was highly polished on one side. Experiments carried out at the British Museum suggest that if the mirrors were kept tarnish-free by buffing they would have stayed reflective indefinitely (Swaddling pers. comm.). On the other side of this disc there was frequently engraved decoration. In early mirrors this was a simple border decoration, such as a *guilloche* around the edge of the disc, or a simple palmette at the point where the disc met the handle, but in mirrors from the late sixth century onwards, figurative scenes were deployed.

Along with chronologies, the study of these images has formed the bulk of scholarship on Etruscan mirrors. The enormous range of subjects represented on the mirrors has led to their use in illustrating a corresponding range of subjects from Etruscan life. As outlined in Chapter 1, these have included subjects as diverse as clothing (L. Bonfante 1975; 1982: 79–88), domestic furniture (Steingräber 1979: 257–70), religion (Bendinelli 1920; Fiesel 1936: 130–6; Hampe and Simon 1964; Krauskopf 1974; Pfiffig 1975: 117–18; 1980; Salskov Roberts 1993: 287–317), and the role of Greek myth in Etruria (Carpino 1996a, 1996b; Francesco De Angelis 2001; J. J. Schwarz 1997; van der Meer 1995). A more recent focus of attention has been the use of techniques from the physical sciences, for instance in the analysis of the chemical composition of the bronze in order to determine the place and method of manufacture (Caley 1970: 98–9; Craddock 1984: 211–71; Pansieri and Leoni 1956, 1957–8: 49–62; Rowe 1982: 49–60; Wiman 1990). Statistical analysis has also been employed (for instance P. Moscati 1984, 1986; Wiman 1990, 1998), and, most recently, electron microscopy has been used to determine the method of manufacture of the mirrors (Swaddling *et al.* 2000).

The question of who used these mirrors is still unresolved definitively. De Grummond summarises the arguments: representations of mirrors are mostly found on mirrors themselves, where there are few instances of a male user, and those that there are have been explained as attendants holding mirrors for their mistresses. Other evidence used by de Grummond to locate mirrors in the female domain comes from tomb paintings, such as those of the Tomba Bruschi, where female figures are shown using mirrors. Volterran cinerary urns provide twenty-one examples of female figures holding mirrors, and the eight inscriptions of ownership on mirrors indicate female owners. She also uses archaeological contexts to point to the same conclusion: the types of assemblages that contain mirrors are rich and contain consistently female paraphernalia, such as necklaces and spindle-whorls. Osteological evidence is rare in Etruscan archaeology; however, tomb number 10 at Monte Rosello near Sovana contained a female 'cadaver' which had a mirror as part of the grave goods (de Grummond (ed.) 1982: 166–8). More recently, an intact female tomb containing a mirror has been reported (Linington and Ridgway 1997: 45). Although the need for Etruscan men to use mirrors has been argued by Spivey (Spivey 1991b: 62) and shown clearly by van der Meer (van der Meer 1995: 13–27), it is generally accepted that there is a strong link between mirrors and Etruscan women. The work of this chapter goes some way to giving mirrors a male context, and the iconographic evidence would seem to corroborate Spivey's doubts about the exclusively female assignations of mirrors.

The status of the individuals using mirrors is a similarly vexed question, and it would be a naive and partial account of identity that ignored factors such as age or status (see Kampen 1982; Hodder 1991: 11). Like most Etruscan material culture, mirrors have been found in funerary contexts, and recent work on funerary data has shown the dangers of assuming that all members of a society had access to formal, archaeologically visible burial (I. Morris 1987). The funerary record has been shown to be one of representations and idealisations, rather than an accurate reflection of how life was led (Hodder 1982b: 151). It is for this reason that there will be little examination here of the types of men and women represented in the mirrors. My concern is the idealised images of men and women that mirrors indicate. That said, the mirrors are relatively luxurious objects and, though mirrors are not rare in the burial record, the tombs recorded with them are not representative of the total population. We may well be dealing with the self-representation of a small, fairly wealthy sector of Etruscan society.

Mirrors and personal identity: reflection and adornment

Two factors underlie the following discussion of Etruscan mirrors. The first is the archaeological contexts in which they have been found; the second is their function. Both of these factors are important in determining the possible historical and social meanings that these objects have the potential to yield. Etruscan mirrors are found exclusively in funerary contexts (Serra Ridgway 2000: 417). This is not to suggest that mirrors were made only for the tomb, but the chances of a mirror ending up in a grave must have been high, and this must have informed the craftsperson making and decorating the mirror. Burial has been shown to be an important arena for the expression, representation and idealisation of the personal identity of the deceased and of those burying him or her. Similarly, the mirror's function as an object used in adornment and beautification implicates it in the creation of the self-image of its user. In this way mirrors are uniquely placed for the exploration of changing Etruscan attitudes towards the image of the self.

Burial is a type of ritual activity, and the usefulness of funerary data for our understandings of the past is, in large part, due to its ritual nature. Ritual is a particularly effective arena for social expression because we ascribe to it a central ideological position in society, and see it as somehow 'other' in human behaviour. Renfrew uses the work of structuralist anthropologists, such as Leach, to describe ritual as liminal, in other words, simultaneously belonging to 'this world' and 'not this world' (Leach 1976: 77–8; Renfrew 1985: 17). Its otherness from everyday life means that it is particularly laden with cultural and cognitive meanings (Moore and Myerhoff (eds.) 1977: 15). At the same time, ritual's inevitable links with everyday life also mean that it retains 'deep' resonances for the lived experiences of individuals. This is made clear in Geertz's analysis of the Balinese cockfight, where everyday, 'real', relationships between individuals are momentarily challenged, and then reaffirmed in complex, ritualised and metaphorical behaviour (Geertz 1993: 443–5). Building on the work of Durkheim and Turner, where ritual is imagined as an interface between the individual and society, Bell shows that while ritual can be used to bind a social group together, 'ritualisation tends to make ritual activities effective in grounding and displaying a sense of communality *without* overriding the autonomy of individuals of subgroups' (C. Bell 1992: 221–2, her italics; see also C. Bell 1997: 76–83). It is the potential of ritual action for collective and individual expression that makes it such a pertinent tool *and* object for the study of ancient societies.

All aspects of funerary rites, including, most importantly for archaeologists (following Renfrew 1985: 12), the objects chosen for deposition, and the spaces constructed for the ritual, are carefully selected by the predeceased, the buriers and the wider community in the light of these attitudes (Binford 1971; M. Bloch and Parry (eds.) 1982; R. Chapman *et al.* (eds.) 1981; Huntingdon and Metcalf 1979). The selection of funerary rituals (and of the objects used to materialise them) is made as part of the social praxis of individuals, and as such accords with the socially and culturally acceptable range of behaviours for those individuals or that group of individuals. As a result, tombs and the objects they contain hold great potential as sources for understanding a given society's conceptions of life and death.

Funerary behaviour, as a ritual activity, expresses 'the taken for granted norms about the roles and rules which make up society – relationships of power, affection, deference, rights, duties and so on' (I. Morris 1992: 3). Following Bourdieu and Giddens, this learned structure does not determine behaviour, but all actions, especially ritual actions, are informed by it, so that at each funeral the participants choose to challenge, modify or reaffirm these norms and idealisations. While such an approach opens possibilities for our understandings of past societies on a structural level, it also makes impossible the direct reading of burial data as a simplistic representation of 'everyday life'. Instead, we must look for such structural (or, as Geertz might say, 'deep') meanings within the material.

An early attempt to clarify the assumptions behind the 'new' archaeology of death shows that from the outset, identity is inextricably linked to burial, wherein 'the deceased is given a set of representations of his or her social identities while alive, which are given material expression after death' (Parker Pearson 1982: 99). This aspect of mortuary theory is particularly relevant for this discussion of Etruscan mirrors, objects which, it will be argued, are key to the creation of Etruscan personal identity. At its most basic level, mortuary theory assumes that burial and its material remains are somehow related to perceived experiences of individuals while alive. Though this is an extraordinarily complex relationship, it nonetheless underpins all interpretations of objects found in funerary contexts. One aspect of this is the creation of an ideal 'social persona' for the deceased by the buriers, through 'the material expression and objectification of idealised relationships for-mulated about the dead' (Parker Pearson 1982: 110). It must be remembered that 'mortuary practices often distort or invert social reality' (Hodder 1982b: 151), creating an 'idealised' or 'typified' (Pader 1982: 16) representation of the deceased through his or her grave assemblage. Thus, no matter how real-istic or 'quotidian' the images and objects in Etruscan tombs may appear, it is important to acknowledge that they are not representations of life as it was lived, but rather as it was chosen to be represented. The funerary record presents an idealisation of the appearance of the body, not a simple reflection of it. Through the idealisation of the body, burial displays the dynamics of seeing and being seen in a normative way. The expression of these dynam-ics in burial indicates the premium placed on seeing and being seen as an essential, though not unique, component of Etruscan self-representation. Whether the idealised images of the body represented in burial were lit-erally translated on to the bodies of real men and women is of secondary importance, and trying to extrapolate the kinds of individuals who did this is to underestimate the premium placed on self-representation in itself (Engelstad 1991). This aspect of mortuary theory is similar to Stewart's view of 'realistic' forms of writing, which 'do not mirror everyday life; they mirror its hierarchization . . . they are mimetic of values, not the material world' (Stewart 1993: 26). The selection of objects and spaces for Etruscan funerary behaviour must be seen in this socially determined light.

Of course, their deposition in graves is not the only factor which implicates mirrors in the creation of social personae: much more important is their function. The primary function of a mirror is reflection. It is created in order to throw back an image. In doing so, it creates a very specific image: that of the holder of the mirror. As the viewer perceives it, the image is formed immediately, reflecting him or her as he or she 'is'. This gives the holder of the mirror an image of himself or herself as he or she is seen by others. By using the mirror the viewer has the opportunity to change his or her appearance according to how he or she wants to be seen. This manipulation of the surface of the body is always carried out within the confines of social and cultural parameters.

The centrality of bodily experience in the creation and reception of mate-rial culture has been emphasised in recent material culture studies. Following the principles derived ultimately from semiotics, that lay stress on the impor-tance of sign systems (for instance Barthes 1975, 1985, and elaborated by Foucault and others), recent archaeological studies have explored the poten-tial of the body itself as a form of material culture (esp. M. I. Marcus 1993; Sørensen 1991, 2000), and while such approaches have been criticised for making the body passive (Meskell 1999: 34), they provide a useful starting point for an inquiry into the manipulation and social reception of the body. The adornment of the body, whether with clothes, coiffure or cosmetics, involves the socialisation of the body. It turns the skin into a 'social skin': the frontier between society and the self that 'becomes the symbolic stage upon which the drama of socialization is enacted' (T. Turner 1980: 112). Alterations to (or decisions not to alter) the appearance of the body are made in the light of an ideal image of how the individual wants to look. This is, of course, that individual's culturally determined notion of beauty, and is conceptually similar to the desired outcome in the minds of (for instance, Lemonnier's) producers discussed above. The nature of this ideal image is culturally specific and socially informed (for female beauty see Entwhistle 2000; Pacteau 1994: 77–98; W. Perkins (ed.) 2002; for male beauty see Harvey 1995, Robb 1997, Treherne 1997; for the Roman world see Parker 1992, Wyke 1994). For Bourdieu, the principle of beautification 'is nothing other than the [principle of the] *socially informed body* . . . which never escape[s] the structuring action of social determinisms' (Bourdieu 1977: 124, his italics; see also Bourdieu 1989: 192–3); the same phenomenon is called 'social inscription' by Grosz (Grosz 1995: 104). The following analysis of Etruscan mirrors will take as a given the importance of the social moulding of the body elaborated above, while maintaining, of course, that this moulding takes place within the parameters of a set of socially acceptable decisions open to the individuals involved in transforming their bodies.

The analysis will also draw on a related set of results from ethnographic research over the last twenty years which have shown that the appearance of the outside of the body is a crucial factor in the creation and reception of a social identity. Drawing on the work of Hodder (Hodder 1982a) and developments in social psychology (for example J. Turner 1975), Wiessner has stressed the importance of 'social identification via comparison' in an archaeological context (Wiessner 1989: 57). She says that 'when people compare themselves with . . . others and decide whether to simulate, differentiate, emulate etc., they decide how to negotiate their relative identity' (Wiessner 1990: 107). This creation of a self-image via comparison with others is thus culturally and socially informed – it is dependent on the ideals and expectations of the society in which it is created. This social existence is crucial because 'in order to be socially competent, people must know where they stand relative to others' (Wiessner 1989: 57; also Goffmann 1959). The need to identify oneself in relation to those around one seems to be culturally universal, but the forms it takes are culturally specific and varied (Roach and Eicher 1979: 7; Steele 1989a: 15; Wiessner 1989: 57). The degree of variation in the ways and means by which self-images are created can be seen in recent ethnographic literature, which documents, among other processes, tattooing (Caplan (ed.) 2000; Cordwell 1979: 53–8), scarification (Cordwell 1979: 58–60), body painting (Cordwell 1979: 52–3), clothing (Barthes 1985; Comaroff and Comaroff 1992: 69–91; McCracken 1990: 57–70; Sahlins 1976: 179; T. Turner 1980) and jewellery (Pokornowski 1979; Ottenberg 1979). Yet this diversity cannot mask the 'cultural beautification' (Cordwell 1979: 61) of the surface of the body that they all share. Both the anthropological and archaeological literature also shows that, as a form of non-verbal communication (Roach and Eicher 1979: 8–10; Wiessner 1989: 57), the manipulation of the surface of the body can transmit information of many kinds, for example tribal identity (Hodder 1982a; Layton 1989; O'Hanlon 1989) and social hierarchy through age and sex structures (Hodder 1982a: 77–84; Kassam and Megersa 1989; H. M. Cole 1979); it can also carry connotations of ritual, fertility and eroticism (Roach and Eicher 1979: 18–20; O'Hanlon 1989: 134; Pacteau 1994; Coward 1984; Elias 1994: 50).

However, the body is not simply a repository for cultural information (Meskell 1999: 34). The adornment of the body is the mechanism whereby the body shapes and structures the world in which it lives (Grosz 1994: 18). The manipulation of the body through adornment is an essential part in the creation and image of the self, and so of personal identity. Importantly, personal identity is a mutable construct that varies from person to person, but also within individuals according to biological changes or personal experiences. The performance of self-identity through the manipulation of the body is the means of presenting the self to the rest of society. In this performance the body acts as the boundary between the self and others; changes in the nature of that boundary are indicative of changes in the perceived relationship between these categories.

The surface of the body is the individual's only physical contact with the outside world. The manipulation and adornment of the surface of the body form an essential part of the identity of an individual (Sørensen 1991). This surface of the body is a point of negotiation.

One of the most striking features of Etruscan mirrors is their chronological distribution. The Etruscan iron-age, Orientalising and earlier archaic periods have so far provided only four mirrors (Hencken 1968b: 47). In contrast, by the late sixth century, mirrors become increasingly common as grave offerings: it has been estimated that over 3,000 mirrors survive today (L. Bonfante 1994: 245; Serra Ridgway 1992: 282; most recently, Carpino estimates over 4,000 (Carpino: 1996a: 65)). The use of mirrors, then, seems to have exploded in the late Archaic and early Classical periods of Etruscan.

Mirrors could, of course, have been in use before this time and may simply not have survived in the archaeological record. However, the complete
absence of mirrors from settlement or sanctuary contexts would seem to
corroborate the picture gained from the funerary evidence: that of a sudden
and dramatic increase in the deposition (and use) of mirrors towards the
end of the sixth century.

Given the importance of mirrors in personal identity, this sudden increase
in depositions is highly significant. The appearance of mirrors in the archaeological record in the late sixth century indicates the societal premium placed
on idealised images of the body at this time. These images were created on
the bodies and, more importantly, skins of Etruscan individuals, through
decoration and elaboration. Because these adorned bodies, obviously, do
not survive, the presence of mirrors and other toilette objects is a unique
remnant of this process. These artefacts form an important indicator of
the emerging significance of the process of adornment within sixth-century
Etruscan society. The surface of the body is the visible boundary between
individual and society; adornment the process through which that boundary was elaborated and emphasised. The deposition of objects used in this
elaboration shows the cultural importance of this process. The sudden and
dramatic rise in the deposition of these objects in late sixth-century Etruscan
tombs marks the beginning of a new phase of the definition of the self in
Etruscan culture, when the surface of the body became the locus for the
articulation of the construction of the self.

This is not to suggest that self-identity was a new thing in the late sixth
century; in fact, it is difficult to imagine a society, especially one like the
highly structured society of Etruria in the Orientalising period, in which the
expression of self-identity does not, in some form, exist. Snodgrass's work on
the deposition of arms and armour in early Greece has shown that the forum
for the expression and display of wealth or status shifted from funerary to
sanctuary contexts as part of the emergence of the city-state (Snodgrass
1986: 54; see also Osborne 1996a: 101). This is important not because of
the direction of the change (from funerary to sanctuary) but because it
acknowledges the importance of changing contexts for material expression
of social phenomena. Similarly, it is possible that the sudden deposition of
mirrors in Etruria indicates that the expression of self-identities shifted to
the funerary sphere, away from one in which it left little material trace. Yet
it would be going too far to suggest that the archaeological appearance of
mirrors in Etruria indicates a different means of expressing a pre-existing
preoccupation with identity: the evidence for Orientalising-period tombs
is yet to receive a detailed study of such concerns (though contrast Cuozzo

1994 for Pontecagnano), but the material for this period appears to indicate concerns with social hierarchy and the identity of the individual within relationships of social structure (Spivey and Stoddart 1990: 143–51) rather than with the image of the body as a means of articulating self-identity. Though many of the objects of adornment discussed later in this chapter appear in Orientalising-period graves (such as perfume flasks, cosmetics boxes, jewellery, armour, etc.) they form part of a much broader public discourse about elite interaction than the more personal discourse of adornment of the later sixth-century graves. Above all, it is important to remember that the earlier graves do not contain mirrors.

Many Etruscan mirrors show the process of adornment itself. These are scenes where a figure, male or female, appears to be undergoing the process of adornment, either adorning himself or herself, or being adorned by others. Mirrors depicting adornment mostly, though not exclusively, show the female toilette, and as a result, the mirrors discussed here tend to be those relating to female adornment, though the issues that lie behind the images relate equally to male adornment. However, a large number of mirrors had no scene engraved on their backs (de Grummond has calculated that 17.6 per cent of mirrors would have been unengraved, based on the mirrors published in the *CSE* up to 2002 (de Grummond 2002: 309), though van der Meer estimates roughly 50 per cent (van der Meer 1995: 5)). These objects, despite the fact that they do not make explicit reference to the process of adornment through engraving, are equally important in the discourses of adornment and identity. The presence of *any* mirrors indicates a concern with the manipulation of the surface of the body in creating a self-image, and, accompanying this, the deliberate creation of identity. Because of their low art-historical interest, the unengraved examples are a hitherto neglected group of Etruscan mirrors, yet their function implicates them in the same processes of viewing and being viewed as their engraved counterparts.

The self-reflexivity of the adornment scenes is one of their most striking features, as mirrors themselves are often present in such scenes, like the one in Fig. 2.1. That mirrors themselves depict adornment (that is, their own function) on their reverse sides demonstrates the importance attached to this transformative process. The use of a mirror, as itself depicted on a mirror, highlights and underscores its function, drawing attention to the object and to its use in adornment. A similar argument has been put convincingly by Lissarrague for self-reflexive images on Greek vases. In a discussion of sympotic scenes painted on sympotic vessels, he argues that 'the space of the spectator and the space of the picture interfere with each other' (Lissarrague 1994: 16; for a more extended discussion see Lissarrague 1990a). With

2.1 Adornment scene: Malavisch, seated, adorned by lasas, supervised by Turan on the far right (Gerhard CCXIII; scale: 2 cm)

mirrors, however, the relationship between these two spaces is further complicated because the function of the mirror (viewing the body) highlights the active role of the viewer, and the acts of looking and seeing. Whereas in the sympotic scenes dialogue is between the world of the image and the world of the symposium in which it is being used, in the adornment scenes on Etruscan mirrors a further element is added. As well as the world of the image and the toilette scene in which it is used, the action of looking into the mirror implicates the viewer as a third participant. In female toilette scenes on Etruscan mirrors, women are shown looking at their transformed reflections in mirrors that they are holding, or that are being held up for them by others. Even more beguilingly, we know that these scenes were themselves being viewed by the holder of the mirror on which the adornment scene was engraved. When discussing similar images of women looking in mirrors in European painting, Berger concludes that in this way the woman 'joins the spectators of herself' (Berger 1972: 50). That at least one Etruscan mirror-engraver was conscious of this reflexivity is evident in a mirror that shows the toilette of Thethis (Etruscan Thetis), where we see, in the mirror she holds up, the reflected face of Thethis looking back at herself (Gerhard v.96, now *CSE* USA 3.14; discussed further below).

By picking up and using a mirror, an Etruscan woman implicated herself in the rhetoric of adornment that was depicted on the object itself. The mirror would have mirrored her face, just as the image on its back mirrored her behaviour. Many objects are associated with such scenes, both by being depicted in the scenes on the mirrors, or by being found alongside mirrors in burial assemblages. Such objects include perfume dippers (*discerniculae*), jars for perfume (*alabastra, aryballoi*) or cosmetics (*pyxides*), and containers for these objects (*cistae*). The same self-reflexive concern with adornment is echoed in the decoration of these objects, such as perfume dippers whose handles are in the form of female figures holding mirrors (D. K. Hill 1965: figs. 1–4). It might seem easy to dismiss this reflexivity as an irrelevant consequence of the Etruscans' natural creativity: 'What could be more natural for an Etruscan, artistically the child of the Greeks, than to ornament the finest implements with human figures?'(D. K. Hill 1965: 190). However, in the light of the discussion of Chapter 1, it should be conceded that the choice of the kinds of figures and decoration was an active and knowing one. For example, Schneider's analysis of the Ficorini Cista has shown the way in which the selection of the episode of the punishment of Amykos is one that opens up a discourse about physical ideals, including beauty and strength (Schneider 1995). The figures and decoration engraved on these implements were selected because of their relevance. Like the presence of adornment scenes on mirrors, the deliberate representation of the object's function underlines the cultural premium placed on that very function. Although adornment scenes do appear on other objects, such as an early fourth-century Etruscan Red Figure cup (*kylix*) from Chiusi, now in the British Museum, showing three naked female figures in a toilet scene (Walters 1896: number F 478, plate 208; Beazley 1947: 113), the adornment of the body is given repeated and elaborate emphasis in mirrors and other objects involved in the process. Adornment scenes show the primacy given to the process they depict; the process of the transformation of the body according idealised notions of how it should look. This obviously significant issue was played out endlessly on the backs of the mirrors.

So far, the importance of mirrors in the articulation of the self-identity of individuals has been argued from the presence of mirrors in Etruscan graves; further, the sudden rise in the number of these objects at the end of the sixth century has been used to argue for a corresponding rise in concerns with images of the self at this time. The surface of the body, as the interface between the individual and society, was the point at which individual identity was defined, and this was achieved with the help of mirrors in adornment. All mirrors, regardless of whether or not they were engraved, and regardless of the subject engraved on them, were fundamental to the process of defining the identity of their owners. However, personal identity comprises more than the identity of the individual in relation to society; it has many facets, such as age, status, sex and gender. The following section explores one of these facets: gender.

Mirrors and gender identity

The study of Etruscan gender has largely been the study of Etruscan women, and has emphasised the privileged position they held in the ancient world. The comments of ancient sources (notably Athenaeus, *Deipnosphistae* 12.517–8; M. A. Fowler 1994; Shrimpton 1991) set the tone of sexual licence, luxury and beauty that has characterised many later studies (for the sources see Rallo 1989b; Sordi 1981). Archaeological evidence was later incorporated (notably by Pallottino 1955: 151; see also Gasperini 1989; Heurgon 1964; Nielsen 1989; and recently Amann 2000; Rathje 2000). These accounts stress the power, public role, epigraphic prominence and importance of women as mothers (L. Bonfante 1973a, 1973b, 1981, 1986, 1989a, 1989b, 1994; Heurgon 1961, 1964). More recently, accounts have acknowledged the importance of regional and class variation (Baglione 1989: 115; Nielsen 1989 for the former; L. Bonfante 1994; Gasperini 1989: 182; Rallo 1989b: 20; Spivey 1991b for the latter). However, in the most recent studies, Etruscan women are still separated out from their male counterparts in inquiries into Etruscan gender (G. Bartoloni 2000b; Haynes 2000; Rallo 2000; for a notable exception see Amann 2000).

That gender is implicated in the creation of personal identity is apparent in the anthropological (R. A. Schwarz 1979: 28–41; Roach 1979), sociological (Bourdieu 1989: 200–7; Pacteau 1994; Kidwell and Steele (eds.) 1989; Gottdiener 1995: 209–32; Barnes and Eicher (eds.) 1992; Wilson 1985), ethnoarchaeological (Hodder 1982a) and archaeological literature (Gilchrist 1994, 1999; M. I. Marcus 1993; Meskell 1999; Sørensen 2000; Wall 1994). Gendered roles are social constructs and derive from social and cultural attitudes towards the relative behaviours of men and women that are learned in infancy, as is demonstrated by the diversity of gender roles and distinctions between and within cultures. However, despite the variety in the presentation of gender, gender is, nonetheless, a regular axis along which societies choose to define and structure individuals.

Although societies construct models of appropriate gendered behaviour, these structures are not inextricably binding: they are open to refusal and subversion. Men and women choose to what extent, and when, they will conform to the social expectations of them as gendered individuals. Gender identity, like personal identity, is a malleable construct: the experiences of an individual will change over time, and this will alter and be reflected in that individual's evolving gender identity. The active role of the individual in the creation of gendered identity is further explored by Butler (1990: 140; 1993: 12). Echoing Bourdieu's stress on *praxis*, she has emphasised the importance of performance in the construction of gender (see also Strathern 1988: ix). Gender roles are created by the active participation of individuals within society; these roles are selected by individuals from a range of behavioural choices open to them within that society; and this selection is done deliberately and with care. Gilchrist's study of English nunneries provides a pertinent illustration of the ways in which women actively participated in the reproduction and confirmation of wider social norms of female behaviour within (and despite) the confines of these exclusively female environments (Gilchrist 1994).

This last example serves not only to demonstrate the importance of Bourdieu's concept of *habitus* in gender studies, but also to show the relationship between individuals and the wider society of which they are part. This last point is made clearly by Wall's analysis of eighteenth-century New York, where the private gendered roles of individuals were echoed in more public arenas of urban life (Wall 1994).

Finally, it is worth stressing that study of gender relationships is not the same as a study of women (Strathern 1988: ix), and that in discussions of gender, the role of women is not to be overplayed, despite the close ties between feminist and gender archaeologies in the early stages of the subject. In archaeological studies the simple identification of women in the archaeological record – the so-called 'add women and stir' school – was an intellectual position first identified, and rejected, by Wylie (Wylie 1991: 34; see also Moore and Scott 1997: 3). Instead, archaeologists have moved to a more complex exploration of the operation of gender, an initiative which is well under way in other areas of archaeology (for example, Conkey and Spector (eds.) 1984; Wall 1994; Gero and Conkey (eds.) 1991; Gibbs 1987; Gilchrist 1994; Meskell 1999; D. Miller, Rowlands and Tilley (eds.) 1989; Nelson 1997; Sørensen 2000; Walde and Willows (eds.) 1991; Wicker and Arnold (eds.) 1999; Wylie 1991)). However, neither is it a study of men, as some recent attempts to write men into gender studies have suggested. Echoing the way that early feminists 'identified' women in the archaeological record (as noted by Wylie 1991), some studies have tried to redress the undue bias towards women in accounts of gender. Though this has often led to a corresponding series of 'identifications' of men (for example contributions to Foxhall and Salmon (eds.) 1998), such studies have opened the way for more integrated approaches to gender in past societies, approaches that take into account male and female relations and roles as part of a wider social framework (for example Meskell 1999; Wall 1994).

The images engraved on to the backs of the mirrors are a rich source for our understanding of the ways in which gender differences were manifest on the bodies of the Etruscan men and women who used them. As well as scenes of adornment discussed above, the mirrors depict a wide range of subjects, including a large number of recognisable scenes from Greek myth. These images, held in the hand during adornment, reflect the differing norms and expectations of male and female appearance and behaviour in Etruria. In the use of the object in adornment, the engraved image on the back of a mirror is bound together with the image that is created in its reflective field. The two images, one engraved, the other reflected, are thus two sides of the same debate about the appearance of the body. As a result, these images form a vital key to our exploration of the differing manifestations of gender identity in late sixth-century Etruria. This section will explore the manifestations of gender identities as they are represented on the backs of Etruscan mirrors.

The engraved images on the mirrors show both mortal and mythologi-cal characters and many of the latter are recognisably Greek in origin. The question of the reception of Greek myth in early Etruria is fraught with con-troversy (Camporeale 1965; Dohrn 1966/7; Hampe and Simon 1964). The context of the deployment of Greek myth in Etruria has been re-examined in recent years, and it has been argued that Greek myth was a luxurious elite prerogative: specialist knowledge in the hands of a few (Spivey 1991a: 133; 1992: 241; Spivey and Stoddart 1990: 103–6). As such it played an impor-tant part in maintaining that elite's position in relation to those who did not have access to, or understanding of, this knowledge (Izzet 2004). However, by the archaic period, it is assumed that most Etruscans were cognisant with Greek mythology at some level (L. Bonfante 1980: 151; Krauskopf 1974: 35–6; Massa Pairault 1999; Spivey 1997b: 56).

Even when we assume that the holders and beholders of Etruscan mirrors would have understood and recognised the mythological references on them, there are further problems raised by the process of our own identifications of the scenes. Goldhill and Osborne warn that the identification of particular scenes is beset with the hazards of interpretation: simply classifying an image as, say, an adornment scene 'is to engage in more than "mere" identification, not least because such acts of naming construct and imply a relation between an object and a viewer . . . "identification" and "recognition" are inevitably interwoven with a range of ideological presuppositions and interpretive issues' (Goldhill and Osborne 1994: 4). In reading these Etruscan images, we must take care not to transplant a modern idea of what these cultural values were, filtered principally through later textual sources on to them (Spivey 1991b: 56). An understanding of the cultural use of such images is necessary in order to avoid this (Izzet 2005a). Paradoxically, perhaps, this potential pitfall is also one of the great strengths of such images. Although we may be bound to bring to such identifications a raft of presuppositions and former assumptions, this must surely have been the case for the Etruscan viewer too, according to his or her age, sex, status, wealth, experience of Greek culture, and much more. Thus it is possible to infer a range of possible readings for any single image, a range that includes both functional ones as well as highly symbolic and allusive ones (Izzet 2004, 2005b).

Bearing such caution in mind, it is possible to take tentative steps towards the identification of the scenes and figures represented on Etruscan mirrors. Some of the mirrors have captions or labels naming the figures in the scenes. Where there are no inscriptions, iconographic devices can help identify the characters, such as characteristic dress. This includes, for example, the hats, tunics and strapped sandals of the divine twins, Tinas Cliniar (Etruscan Dioskouroi, otherwise known as Castor and Pollux), or the aegis of Menrva (Etruscan Athena). Finally, characteristic positions and poses of the figures can indicate who is represented in the mirrors, such as the framing of the figurative field of the mirror by the Tinas Cliniar.

The images examined in the rest of this chapter are those that explicitly refer to the Etruscan body and its manipulation according to gender norms, though, as discussed above, all mirrors, engraved and unengraved, are implicated in this same process. Although the mirrors will be drawn together into groups according to their subject, such identifications are not intended as the only interpretation of the scene, nor are they to be conceived of as mutually exclusive; for example, the role of Castur and Pultuke in warfare cannot be separated from their other characteristics, such as being athletes, or liminal figures between this world and the next. On the contrary, it is the overlapping associations that such images are able to carry with them from context to context that make their study so rich and complex. It would be implausible to imagine that Etruscan viewers were not capable of such complex and allusive readings. Such potential adds further layering to the reception of these images: 'the production and consumption of images within a culture are highly complex processes in which the full range of a society's perceptual and conceptual apparatus is engaged' (Goldhill and Osborne 1994: 9).

Etruscan mirrors and gender

The rest of this chapter will attempt to go some way towards integrating the implications of recent developments in the archaeology of gender into the Etruscan situation. It will examine the ways in which men and women represented themselves in the period from the late sixth century. It will not simply identify 'women' in the record which has passed down to us, nor merely 'compare and contrast' men and women in Etruria. Instead, gender will be presented as an area where an ideological change in the Etruscans' conceptions of their society is played out. This change is characterised by increased self-awareness and the crystallisation of boundaries, in this case between male and female, through the creation and manipulation of the surfaces of the bodies of men and women.

In the first part of this chapter, it was argued that mirrors, as tools for the creation of self-images, become heavily implicated in the definition of individual identity after the late sixth century. What follows is an icono-graphic analysis of the ways in which the adornment of the surface of the bodies of men and women was used to negotiate changing attitudes towards gender identities. The following analysis is divided into seven sections, each of which deals with a major component of the gendering of Etruscans in, and by, Etruscan mirrors.

Adornment

As mentioned above, most scenes of adornment show female subjects, and, while having relevance for all users of mirrors, they raise issues relating specifically to the female body (Balensiefen 1990: 40–1). For the surface of the skin of Etruscan women it has been suggested that perfumed oils with essences imported from the Orient were involved. Detergents and face packs containing barley, lentils, eggs, narcissus bulbs and honey were used to cleanse the skin. To counter the astringency of these packs, emollient oils were used to hydrate the skin and to restore elasticity. To highlight facial features, natural pigments, such as red and yellow ochre, mulberry essence and a substance to whiten the skin were mixed with an oil base, using worked ivory or bronze sticks and spoons in small silver vessels. It is possible that a henna tincture may have been used to colour the hair (all from Rallo 1989c). In addition, sumptuous jewellery (Carducci 1962: ix–x; Marshall

1911: 108–49, 250–71; Becatti 1955: 67–74, 96–7) and fabrics (L. Bonfante 1975, 1989b) were used to adorn the body. Through such adornment (cosmetics, clothing and jewellery), the surface of the body was manipulated, transformed and hidden. In so doing, it was loaded with deliberately selected cultural significance.

It was argued in the first part of this chapter that the process of adornment should be regarded as the creation of an image of the body, on the surface of the body, according to the conventions of Etruscan society. As a member of that society, through adornment, an Etruscan woman using a mirror imposed on to herself her society's ideals of how her body should appear. This is perhaps most explicit in a group of mirrors that depict the adornment of a figure labelled Malavisch (Fig. 2.1; L. Bonfante 1977; Lambrechts 1992; Mansuelli 1947; van der Meer 1985; 1995: 201–3; Wiman 1992). The label is often translated as 'bride' (G. Bonfante and Bonfante 1983: 148; Sowder 1982: 102). Bonfante notes that, as well as being 'bride', Malavisch may be an Etruscan epithet for Helen, with a certain tentative link to the meaning of 'the adorned one' (L. Bonfante 1990: 34). Interestingly, the name Malavisch may be etymologically related to the Etruscan word for mirror: *malena* (G. Bonfante and L. Bonfante 2002: 201). As Serra Ridgway notes, the mirrors (like other toilette objects: Schneider 1995) 'were generally given as wedding presents' (Serra Ridgway 2000: 416; see also Pandolfini 2000). Such a scene is shown in Fig. 2.1, where we see the surface of the seated body of the woman labelled Malavisch being worked by others, using extremely luxurious materials, to create a superficial image for society and by society. With the connotations of marriage carried both by mirrors in general, and Malavisch in particular, it is thus possible, to take the stance of a structuralist anthropologist, to see adornment as a miniature rite of passage, like the wider rite of passage (marriage) alluded to by Malavisch (Leach 1976: 77–8). Here then we have the socialisation of the female in preparation for her future role.

Adornment in the instance of the Malavisch figures, though carried out by women, is not done for women. Instead the female body is packaged and decorated for the male scrutiny of the groom. This is carried out by unnamed members of her family or more often by divinities, who give an air of 'naturalness' to the whole procedure through the ritualisation of the process (Säflund 1993: 45; J. C. Smith 1991: 86). The divinities form a large and diverse group, but the most popular and appropriate figure is Turan, Etruscan Aphrodite. Although the Malavisch scenes, with their associations of marriage, lend themselves to a reading which draws on rites of passage, all adornment scenes should be seen in a similar way: as the preparation of the body, according to societal norms, for viewing by others.

Adornment scenes are not restricted to the somewhat formulaic Malavisch scenes, which date from the fifth and fourth centuries. Earlier scenes are more diverse and show other aspects of the preparation of the body. For instance, one sixth-century mirror shows a clothed female figure holding a flower towards what has been interpreted as a younger naked male attendant (*CSE* GB 1.18). The attendant holds a mirror in his right hand and what appears to be a pair of pincers or tweezers for depilation in the other. Another mirror shows a scene of bathing (Gerhard v.153). Two naked female figures stand on either side of a large basin, with their hands inside it. Later mirrors continue to show the adornment of Malavisch (Gerhard ccxiii; ccxiv), but also depict the adornment of Turan herself (Gerhard cccxix), of mythological characters (Gerhard v.96) and unidentifiable female figures (Gerhard ccxiv; v.22). Figures are either seated and in the process of being adorned by other women, or represented in bathing scenes (Gerhard cvii).

Adornment scenes show women creating their own images as they wish to be viewed by others. The process is therefore informed by the society's conception of what that image should be. The following three sections examine interrelated aspects of this image.

Turan: seduction and eroticism

One aspect of female gender identity elaborated in images on the mirrors is eroticisation. As already mentioned, a very common figure on Etruscan mirrors was Turan, the Etruscan Aphrodite (for example Gerhard ccxliii.A.i; see also Izzet 1997: catalogue numbers 28–36, 85–91, 340–51, 382–97, 676–721, 1010–22, 1454–73, 1528–32). Such cultural elisions between Greek and Etruscan deities are, of course, dangerous: however, though we cannot assume that all the attributes of Turan correspond with those of Aphrodite, it is accepted that the two goddesses were held in similar regard in their major aspects: the spheres of love and eroticism (R. Bloch 1984; L. Bonfante 1977; Lord 1937; Mansuelli 1946, 1947; Pfiffig 1975: 260–6). In mirrors, Turan is recognised by captions, her clothing, or the perfume dippers and jars that she often carries. In addition to being shown in adornment scenes, and as a single figure on a mirror (which appear in large numbers from the fourth century onwards), Turan also appears in many general mythical scenes, where her association with adornment is less emphasised. Turan is often accompanied by one or more of her circle of attendants (for example Fig. 2.1), or by the lasas (following Serra Ridgway 2000: 417 n. 54). These lasas were a group of winged figures at first identified by scholars as Victories (Martha 1889: 546), though now generally agreed to be local divinities and attendants of Turan (De Agostino 1937; Del Chiaro 1971; Mansuelli 1946: 66–7, 92–5; 1947: 73–4; Rallo 1974). This circle of Turan shares many of her characteristics, the most important of which are seduction and eroticism, and in the specific case of mirrors, adornment. Again, by the fourth century, these attendant lasas became stock figures and were often depicted in a fashion very similar to Turan herself.

As goddess of beauty and seduction, Turan was a particularly appropriate figure for depiction on mirrors, and she reflected these traits on to the user of the mirror. The erotic associations of Turan and her attendants must have been hard to miss, for instance in the seductive naked poses in which they are represented. Turan's particular contribution to adornment therefore carried strong erotic overtones. In Fig. 2.1, the caption tells us that the figure on the far right is Turan. She is carefully supervising the production, watching to ensure that everything is done to her specifications. The concentration of the figures, her attendant lasas, in the central panel, shows the studied care with which the whole process is carried out. The adornment and transformation of the surface of the body are a serious business. Seduction is the key: adornment is a mechanism for seduction, for making the body erotically enticing. The female body, and so the woman herself, is constructed as an erotic object. Women used mirrors as a mechanism for their self-construction, creating a female body that was a malleable erotic object.

In later mirrors Turan is frequently shown alone. In these scenes the single winged figure of Turan fills the field of the mirror and in about half of the single Turan mirrors she holds the tools of her trade: perfume jars and dippers, like that shown in Fig. 2.2. In these images, unlike the 'episodic' scenes in which she is part of the action, she appears to interact more directly with the user of the mirror, who was involved in the process of adornment, using objects similar to those held by Turan. Again, because of Turan's divine status it is possible to see this as a naturalisation of the process of eroticisation and adornment.

However, it is not Turan alone who draws the link with eroticisation on the mirrors. Thirteen mirrors, from the fifth and fourth centuries, show Turan with Atunis, the Etruscan Adonis, the youthful lover of Turan (for example, Gerhard L. 2; see also Izzet 1997: catalogue numbers 81–4 (fifth century), 371–81, and possibly 392 (fourth century); Amorelli 1952; Mansuelli 1946: 69; Rebuffat-Emmanuel 1964). For the Greek world, Detienne has shown the importance of perfume and spice for arousing 'extreme sexual potency

2.2 Turan (Gerhard xxxiv.1; scale: 2 cm)

in the seducer or hyper-sexuality in women' (Detienne 1977: 127–9), and he links this to the cult of Adonis, which was particularly popular in fifth-century Athens, In Etruria, sanctuaries to Atunis have been postulated at Gravisca, and his wider popularity is suggested by the distribution of his image in other parts of Etruria (Torelli 1977, 1997; see also Burn 1987: 42). Depictions of the divine lovers Turan and Atunis contain a distinctly erotic message, and reinforce the link between adornment and eroticism when they are found on mirrors. This link is maintained in four mirrors that depict Atunis alone, through the presence of cosmetic boxes, chests, perfume jars and dippers, all of which were, as discussed above, essential tools in the process of adornment (Gerhard cxiv; *CSE* DDR 1.8; Gerhard cccxxii; v.25).

Another group of mirrors that alludes to the erotic nature of adornment is characterised by Dionysian imagery, with its associations of eroticism, feasting and drinking (Balensiefen 1990: 39; L. Bonfante 1993). This group includes images with Fufluns himself (Etruscan Dionysus), satyrs, maenads, and other figures holding what look like *thyrsi* (the sticks topped with a pine cone and ivy, carried by followers of Dionysus). To this group should be added more general scenes of dancing and dining. An example of the latter

2.3 Female dancers (Gerhard XLIV; scale: 2 cm)

is shown in Fig. 2.3. Cristofani has shown the importance of eroticism at the Etruscan banquet (Cristofani 1987a: 126); the ornate decoration of the two adorned dancing figures in Fig. 2.3, in their coiffure, jewellery and sumptuous dress, shows the attention that was paid by Etruscan women in preparation for attending such banquets.

All the mirrors in this group, from the banqueting scenes to the more explicitly Dionysian, show a wide range of subjects associated with Dionysus and his circle. Cristofani and Martelli believe that the Greek cult of Bacchus was assimilated into the local repertoire of Fufluns during the fifth century (Cristofani and Martelli 1978: 126) and became increasingly popular. Martelli's insight shows that in the fifth and fourth centuries the cult is associated with the 'repertorio "amoroso" degli specchi incisi' (Martelli 1978: 131–2), and it is this erotic aspect of the circle of Dionysus that is echoed in part in the Greek world: 'Wine, music and eros – these are the three focal points of the satyr's activity' (Lissarrague 1990b: 54; 1990c; see also Keuls 1993: 357). By referring to all three of these aspects in depictions of dancing, dining and satyrs, Etruscan mirrors allude to them within the context of adornment. Thus the adornment of the body takes on a specifically erotic aspect.

Elina and the 'male gaze'

Another aspect of female gender identity articulated in the mirrors is the importance of the male viewer for female adornment. The concept of the 'male gaze' was first developed by Berger in his study of European post-Renaissance art, and explored further by Mulvey and others (Berger 1972; Mulvey 1989; Bartky 1990). Its premise is that the act of looking at male and female bodies is imbalanced: women refuse to make eye contact with the viewer, while male figures cast an aggressive and objectifying gaze. Authors such as Berger have shown the ways in which the intended viewer of both the image and the female body within it is assumed to be male. In many scenes on Etruscan mirrors, the so-called 'male gaze' is elaborated. This has been touched upon in the discussion of the scenes of Malavisch above, where the male viewer is the future groom; and it is implied more widely for the use of mirrors in general. However, there are mirrors in which this male gaze is articulated more explicitly. One instance of this is in mirrors depicting stories surrounding Elina, the Etruscan Helen of Troy (Krauskopf 1988). Elina was reputed to have been the most beautiful woman on earth, and the prize given to Alcsentre (Paris) by Turan for having chosen her beauty over that of Uni (Hera) and Menrva (Athena). Various aspects of the story of Elina are depicted in mirrors, and she is often named in captions; however, the most common element of her story in the mirrors is the one in which she herself does not appear: that of the three goddesses and Alcsentre in the scene of judgement for which Elina is the prize (L. Bonfante 1977; Eriksson 1996; Martelli 1976, 1994; Lord 1937; Nagy 1995).

In fifth-century mirrors the most popular theme from the Elina cycle is that of courtship. This includes the courtship of Elina both by Menle (Menelaus, her husband) and by Alcsentre (Paris), the Trojan prince who, as part of his prize for having judged Turan the most beautiful, abducted (or seduced) her. Turan's role in both these aspects of the story is emphasised in the mirrors. In some (for example Gerhard cxcvii), Turan is shown as acting as the intermediary between Elina and Menle; in others (for example Gerhard v.17), Turan holds Elina's face so that it may be viewed by Alcsentre. In these examples, Turan's importance in the courtship is clear, and, as discussed above, she brings with her the associations of eroticism and seduction. The link between the most beautiful goddess and the most beautiful woman on earth is exploited in the mirrors, and brings together

2.4 The judgement of Alcsentre (*CSE* GB 2.4.
Syndics of the Fitzwilliam Museum, Cambridge)

the themes of beauty and adornment. But the importance of the Elina myth
does not end merely in the pertinence of her image on objects used in
beautification; more important is the emphasis on competition and the
judgement of beauty by the male arbiter, Alcsentre (*pace* Osborne 2001:
291). This aspect of the myth is emphasised in the slightly later mirrors that show the episode of the judgement of the three goddesses by
Alcsentre.

The fourth-century mirror illustrated in Fig. 2.4 (*CSE* GB 2.4) shows a
representation of this scene. Alcsentre stands casually, leaning on the edge
of the frame of the mirror. As such, he is in a different position from the

other figures, distanced slightly from the action. He is on the edge of the scene, looking in on the action, just as we are, and just as the Etruscan holder of the mirror would have been. Through this positioning, he includes and implicates us, and the Etruscan viewer, in his own participation in the scene; we are thus encouraged to collude with his judgement. The three goddesses are recognisable by their usual conventions: Menrva by her helmet, Uni by her veil, and Turan by her nudity, as well as by their labels. Here are three female figures under the scrutiny of the male gaze in what is the ultimate beauty contest (Berger 1972: 51–2; see also Keuls 1993: 206). It can be no coincidence for a scene depicted on an Etruscan mirror that the winner is the seductive and erotically charged figure of Turan. Similarly, the gift that Turan gives Alcsentre for selecting her is Elina, the most beautiful of women. Such a scene on a mirror presents a clear message about the importance of female beauty within Etruscan culture, what is at stake in its attainment, and the importance of a male viewer in judging female beauty.

As well as through the numerous depictions of the 'judgement of Alc-sentre', there are several other ways in which the male gaze is made explicit on the backs of Etruscan mirrors. A mirror showing the toilette of Thethis (Etruscan Thetis) has already been mentioned (Gerhard v.96, now *CSE* USA 3.14); it shows Thethis holding a mirror to her face (where her reflection is shown looking back at her), while Pele (Etruscan Peleus) watches her, unseen himself, from behind. As van der Meer notes, Pele is 'struck' by the reflected image in the mirror (van der Meer 1995: 35). To this complex layering of gazes, we can add our own, and that of the (be)holder of the mirror. These gazes, repeatedly reflected back and forth in such a complicated manner, underline the importance of looking at both the process and the product of female adornment.

Another mirror shows a similar male viewer of female adornment. In the mirror in Fig. 2.5 a voyeuristic satyr head pokes over an architectural cornice, watching, unseen, the adornment scene taking place below. This head could be a satyr mask attached to the architecture, such as the satyr-head antefixes found on Etruscan temples (see Chapter 4), or as depicted in a common device of Roman wall-painting (see for example Moormann (ed.) 1993: plate 5), though the lack of symmetry or frontal face makes this unlikely. This head is looking on to the scene from a position similarly removed from the main action of the scene, as is the figure of Alcsentre in the mirror discussed above; yet he is still further removed. As such, he invites parallels between his behaviour as a viewer of adornment and our own. He underlines the importance of the reception of adornment, and in particular its reception by a male viewer. At the same time, given the link

2.5 Adornment scene (Gerhard ccxii; scale: 2 cm)

in Etruscan mirrors between the Dionysiac and the erotic, the imposition of a satyr's gaze on to this mirror adds a further, erotic, dimension to the scene.

The largest group of mirrors that show the importance of the male gaze comprises those with representations of the Tinas Cliniar, the divine twins Castur and Pultuke (Etruscan Castor and Pollux). The popularity of these figures increased to such a degree during the period of mirror manufacture that from the fourth century onwards they form the largest identifiable single group in Etruscan mirrors (Philips 1968; Lambrechts 1968; Bernardy 1927; D. Carandini 1972; De Puma 1973; Del Chiaro 1955; de Grummond (ed.) 1982: 246; Dobrowolski 1994. The same is true of other toilette equipment, notably *cistae*; see for example Schneider 1995). The Tinas Cliniar have a developed and codified iconography which, combined with the large number of inscriptions on mirrors identifying them, makes their identification relatively unproblematic. Identifying characteristics include their dress (tunics and sandals), the stars and moons around their heads, and their pose: standing or sitting at either edge of the decorated area, looking inwards, towards the centre of the mirror.

In the centre of a fourth-century mirror (Gerhard cciii) stands a bejewelled, though otherwise naked, female body flanked by the two male figures of Castur and Pultuke, who gaze at her intently. The female form is caught in the gaze of her onlookers. There are many parallels to this mirror, and in several, the unequal balance between the observed and the observers is exaggerated by the clothing of the two male figures in contrast to the nakedness of the female one (Gerhard cciv). Thus, not only is the female form caught in an unequal gaze, but even when she looks she cannot see as much as she herself reveals. In these instances the naked female body is under the scrutiny of the clothed male onlookers.

Objectification

As an object of scrutiny, the female body is objectified and rendered more passive than the male subject and viewer. This objectification, a further factor at work on the female gender identity, is seen clearly in the Malavisch scenes, discussed earlier (Fig. 2.1). In these scenes, the activity and bustle around the impassive female figure are particularly striking. She sits still, resigned to the consequences of all the alterations her appearance is undergoing. The body of Malavisch, the unnamed, undefined, depersonalised canvas, is preened, groomed, perfumed, and painted to cover any defect, so that it becomes an irresistibly tempting, beautiful object like the mirror itself.

Many of the archaic mirrors demonstrate the ornateness of Etruscan women's adornment. Figure 2.3 shows two female dancers facing each other: they both have carefully coiffured hair showing beneath their mantles, and jewellery, and they wear finely worked fabrics, intricately woven, delicately dyed or meticulously embroidered (L. Bonfante 1975: 12–16); even their shoes are ornately worked. All these elements demonstrate the intricacies and detail of self-representation through female adornment.

However, it is not only the subjects depicted in the mirrors that demonstrate the industry that goes into adornment. Mirrors are themselves the results of skilled craftsmanship. Bronze was a relatively luxurious material, and the mirrors are elaborately worked, as are the many other items of the female toilet: for example, bronze caskets, silver or ivory cosmetics boxes, perfume bottles of alabaster, faience and ceramic, and bone or ivory dippers (Battaglia 1990; D. K. Hill 1965). When the mirror handles were not bronze, they were of carved imported ivory, or of worked bone. Richly painted,

2.6 Adornment scene (Gerhard v.22; scale: 2 cm)

dyed or embroidered fabrics used in clothing the female body have already
been mentioned, though to this should be added Etruscan jewellery, represented on the mirrors as a feature of a woman's adornment, and famous for
its opulence (Cristofani and Martelli 1983; Formigli 1985; Marshall 1911).
In mirrors, women are shown being decorated with necklaces, diadems,
bracelets and earrings (see, for example, Figs. 2.1, 2.5). The serious business of adorning the female body is reflected in the seriousness with which
the paraphernalia of adornment were crafted. The archaeological record
attests to the great technical skill that would have gone into the making
of such objects. The world of adornment is one in which extraordinary
craftsmanship and technical skill are deployed in order to produce beautiful
objects.

   The craftsmanship and creativity of female adornment are represented in
all its stages on the mirror in Fig. 2.6. At the bottom of the border we see a
figure making a necklace. From this spring winged figures, bearing perfume
jars, ribbons, wreaths and more jewellery. In the central scene, the main
figure is being crafted by two technicians who stand behind her, adjusting
her hair and ribbons. The figure to the left holds a perfume dipper in one

2.7 Meeting (Gerhard cdxxi; scale: 2 cm)

hand and a painted alabastron in the other. A small winged figure holds a casket from which he offers more decoration for the 'Christmas tree'. All these objects are known from burial groups and all show exceptional crafts- manship. The winged figures carry the social symbols of adorned women up towards the cultured recipients of all this work at the top of the border: a row of dining men.

Through adornment, the female body becomes a highly crafted decorative object, and this luxuriousness is emphasised through other associations depicted on Etruscan mirrors. Female figures on Etruscan mirrors are often juxtaposed with elaborate and expensive objects or furnishings, and this is often contrasted with the depiction of male figures. In the archaic mirror in Fig. 2.7, the association is emphasised by the vertical division of the surface into a 'natural' male half and a female half full of ornament, decoration and artifice. The vertical division of the mirror is echoed in other mirrors, though the means of that division may vary (see below; also Izzet 2005b). In Fig. 2.7 the shawl, the metal bowl hanging from the bough, and, most importantly, the bed, with its elaborately carved leg and finely woven cover, are all in the female half of the mirror. It is here that the woman herself stands, wearing elaborately embroidered or painted fabrics and jewellery (including a diadem), with intricately coiffed hair, and no doubt cosmetics and perfume. In contrast, the male half is a place of the natural world, represented as a province largely free from such man-made artifice – the man stands amid plants, his head crowned not with metal crafted by human ingenuity but with a simple wreath of leaves. The Etruscan viewer could have imagined a further difference: recent finds have indicated that women's garments may have been dyed in vivid colour, while those of men were left undyed (Eles Masi 1995: 50; Nielsen 1998: 72).

Through her association with such luxury items, and the wealth invested in her appearance, the adorned female became an important addition to a wealthy man's system of status symbols. In the sarcophagus of a married couple from 300 BC, now in Boston Museum (de Grummond (ed.) 1982: fig. 115), this construction is taken to its extreme. The side of the sarcophagus has the same vertical division of space into a male half (on the right) and a female half (on the left) as the mirrors discussed above. The scene is divided symmetrically by the embracing couple in the centre. Each of them is followed by attendants carrying objects associated with them: a stool and military horn for the man; cosmetics boxes and a fan for the woman. This arrangement echoes the divisions outlined above; however, the point made by the sarcophagus does not end there: the female figure is embracing the male, so that the woman's body is itself decorating that of her husband, hanging from his neck like a piece of jewellery. Woman has become an embellishment for the male body. She is a symbol, not of herself, but of her husband's wealth and status. Along with the stool and military horn carried by his servants, she has become part of his insignia. The objects by which she is represented are the tools which give her social identity, not as a person in her own right, but as her husband's wife, and are themselves illustrations of his wealth: two caskets for cosmetics or jewellery (and, no doubt, a mirror) and a highly decorated fan of ostrich feathers, studded with pearls.

A similar transfer of status can be argued for the inscriptions on mirrors, and for the representations of Greek myth. The appearance of writing on mirrors has led many to believe that Etruscan women were literate (L. Bonfante 1973b: 94; 1973a: 245; 1986: 237; 1994: 245; Cantarella 1987: 104; Hodos 1998). Though this may well have been the case, recent studies of literacy in Etruria suggest that other factors may also be at work. Stoddart and Whitley have proposed that lettering and writing were the symbolic tools of a restricted section of the population who were in possession of this rare skill, and who were able to manipulate the magical properties of texts as an ostentatious luxury (Stoddart and Whitley 1988; similarly, see Woolf 1994). As discussed above, a similar argument has been put forward for the understanding of Greek myth in Etruria. Female ownership of both kinds of knowledge, and more importantly, the display of female understanding of it by means of its deployment on mirrors, may well have been an expression not only of the privileged position of Etruscan women, but also of the status that this knowledge would bring to their husbands.

In her analysis of literary representations of women, du Bois singles out the metaphor of the writing tablet for the female body as a 'blank surface, a *tabula rasa* . . . for inscription' and as 'a passive receptive surface' (du Bois 1988: 130–1). The perfume dipper, so common in scenes of Etruscan adornment, is identifiable only through its context. The object itself is barely distinguishable from a writing implement, the stylus. In fact, perfume dippers have often been identified as writing implements in excavation reports (D. K. Hill 1965: 18) – an ambiguity that has rich consequences for the interpretation of gender relations. As well as emphasising the superficiality of adornment, the analogy between perfume dippers and writing implements plays on the passivity of the female body in being inscribed by societal conventions. Du Bois also points out that objects are inscribed with ownership: 'The object of inscription is a possession, a thing, a space defined by the law of property' (du Bois 1988: 165), and she draws an analogy with the tattooing of slaves. Through this association, adornment forms part of the process of the placing of the female body within (male) cultural parameters. Similar readings of the female body (stemming from the work of writers such as Foucault, Giddens and Bourdieu) have recently been criticised as reductivist in conceiving of the body as essentially lacking in agency. In the Etruscan situation, however, the case for such readings is made by the presence of mirrors, and their function within the careful and deliberate elaboration of the surface of the body in adornment (for criticism see Meskell 1999: 25–30, 36; though see above).

Two remaining facets of male agency in female adornment remain to be discussed. The first is illustrated by an inscription found on an exceptional mirror of the fourth century. It bears the inscription *tite cale: atial: turce malstria: cver*, 'Tite Cale gave this mirror to his mother as a gift' (Gerhard cxii; see Izzet 2005b; for an alternative translation see G. Bonfante and Bonfante 2002: 156). On the reverse of the mirror we see Turan and Atunis. Though dedicatory inscriptions are rare (Cristofani 1975; van der Meer 1995: 19), this inscription suggests that men bought or even commissioned expensive mirrors as gifts for women, imposing the male frame of the mirror on to the female form (see also Pandolfini 2000).

The second facet of male agency lies in the makers of the mirrors. Though, due to the lack of inscriptions or makers' signatures, the sex of the makers is not known, they are generally assumed to have been male (by comparison, the maker of the Ficorini Cista was male – Novios Plantios (Schneider 1995). This assumption provides another way in which the male frame of the mirror is imposed on to the bodies of women. At the same time, the repeated use of mirrors by women shows their confirmation of the male frame upon themselves, rather than a refusal of or challenge to it. In constructing an image of herself, the Etruscan woman was acting within the parameters of the culturally informed norms and regulations of Etruscan society.

This discussion has demonstrated the way in which the creation of female identity is inextricably entwined with that of male identity. Gender identities are negotiated through the changing relationships between men and women, and each is constructed in the light of the other. Though the focus so far has been directed towards female gender identity, the analysis has inevitably drawn the male role into this. For the rest of this chapter the emphasis will shift to constructions of male gender identity, with the complementary role of women in this taken as implicit.

Viewing the male body

Representations of Tinas Cliniar, the divine twins Castur and Pultuke, have been introduced above, where they were seen in their characteristic poses either side of the representational space of the mirror, looking at a naked female body between them. Although the Tinas Cliniar appear in earlier mirrors (such as Gerhard v.78), their iconography later becomes standardised, and they are shown in vast numbers, gazing from the edge of the mirror at a (usually) naked figure between them (Del Chiaro 1955; De Puma 1973, 1986; Mansuelli 1941, 1946, 1948; Rebuffat-Emmanuel 1973: 461–74; 483–90; 509–12; for necessary caution in identifications see L. Bonfante 1980: 147–50). The twins make particularly apposite subjects for mirrors, since mirrors are both reflective objects, and objects found almost exclusively in funerary contexts. The twins were born from eggs that were the issue of the union between Zeus and the mortal Leda. This mixed parentage made them part human and part divine, a liminal status that accords with the funerary context of mirrors, in which the deceased makes a journey between the sphere of the living and that of the dead. Furthermore, when Castur was killed fighting, Pultuke asked for his own life to be substituted for that of his brother; instead of granting this request, Zeus allowed them to alternate, each spending a day in the underworld and a day in the world of the living. Thus the two figures exist in a state of flux between this world and the next, reinforcing the liminality bequeathed to them by their parentage (Carpino 1996: 69; Colonna 1996; Nista (ed.) 1994; Rendel Harris 1906: 4). That depictions of the Tinas Cliniar on mirrors are found exclusively in funerary contexts is consistent with their connection with the underworld and the liminality of their position between the sphere of the living and that of the dead. There are many other funerary representations of the pair (Pairault-Massa 1992: 84–6). In one mirror from the fourth century (Gerhard CCLV), Castur and Pultuke are shown winged and carrying a human male figure, which they frame. In other mirrors their liminal role is emphasised by their association with Turms (Etruscan Hermes), the messenger of the gods and the more conventional purveyor of the dead to the underworld (Gerhard v.9; Lambrechts 1968: plate 2; Gerhard CCLXI; *CSE* Denmark 1.15; Gerhard cccxc.1).

As well as their relevance for funerary objects, the Tinas Cliniar are apposite subjects for mirrors: by virtue of being twins, they function as mirror images of each other. In a way similar to the self-referential nature of adornment scenes, their depiction on mirrors underscores the importance of mirror images. At the same time, because of their perpetual state of flux between being alive and being dead, their depiction on mirrors highlights the difficult relationship between image and reality when it comes to adornment.

Finally, we should remember their sibling relationship to Elina, and the resonance of the judgement of bodily beauty that she carries with her. The Tinas Cliniar are frequently shown holding perfume jars. As we have seen, these vases were an integral part of the equipment of adornment, and the association of these objects with the Twins gives them relevance for the context of adornment. In this role, the Tinas Cliniar should not be seen as imposing specific ancient or divine notions of beauty; rather, their association with judgement resonates with the omnipresence of a viewer, and so they confirm the reason behind looking in a mirror. This is equally the case whether they are shown alone, as in Fig. 2.8(a), or in scenes with others. They reiterate one of the messages of the mirror as an object through which one both gazes at oneself and creates an image in order to be gazed at by others.

Images in which the Tinas Cliniar are shown looking at a body are not limited to those in which the body is female. In fact, alongside the objectification of the female body, a number of mirrors indicate the same process at work on the male body, and Castur and Pultuke are frequently implicated in this. Fig. 2.8(b) shows a typical example: Castur and Pultuke are

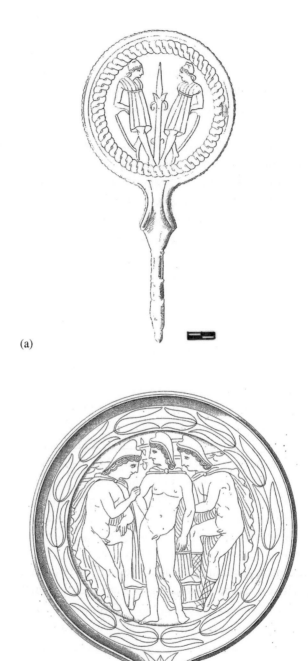

(a)

(b)

2.8 (a) Castur and Pultuke (Gerhard XLVIII.5; scale: 2 cm).
(b) Male figure with Castur and Pultuke (Gerhard CCLVI.1;
scale: 2 cm)

represented in their familiar poses, resting on the inside edges of the frame of the mirror, with a naked male figure in the space between them. The gaze of the divine twins is directed towards this figure. A reading very similar to that given for the naked female figure is possible here: the male body is shown under scrutiny, and in an unequal relationship with those who are viewing it.

As already mentioned, the Tinas Cliniar mirrors have a very distinctive composition, with the Twins standing on the edge of the scene, both framing the figurative space and echoing the shape of the mirror. This composition is resonant of the depiction of the 'judgement of Alcsentre' in Fig. 2.4, discussed above. In the scene of judgement, Alcsentre stands at the left-hand frame of the image, resting against it, in a pose, and garb – he wears sandals and a 'Phrygian' hat – reminiscent of the Tinas Cliniar. In the centre of the scene Turan stands naked, pulling back her veil, with Uni and Menrva on either side of her. Such a composition is echoed in the Tinas Cliniar mirrors, so that the reading of the former – that is, the examination and judgement of the body in terms of beauty – can also be read in the poses of the Tinas Cliniar, as they stand surveying the individuals before them, be they female or male.

Images of the male body under scrutiny are not restricted to the Tinas Cliniar. One mirror (Gerhard CCCLVI) presents an unidentified group of four figures looking at a central naked male body displayed before them in a manner very similar to that of the female figures discussed above. Here, the disembodied head of one of the four viewers, peering from behind the others, is like the voyeur-satyr in the mirror examined earlier (Fig. 2.5). Both see without themselves being seen, placing themselves in a more powerful position than that of the viewed body. The body of the youth under scrutiny is rendered with particular emphasis on the musculature and form of the male anatomy. The male body is shown fully frontal to the viewer of the mirror. The central position of the figure, together with the minimal use of engraving in its execution, creates a large, visually clear area in the middle of the mirror; this forms a stark contrast to the drapery of the other figures in the scene; in this case his naked body is framed by the folds of his own cloak, hanging off his shoulders and down his back. This draws the eye straight towards the displayed male body. We are invited to collude in looking at the body, and as our eye moves out to the rest of the scene we are reassured by the fact that all the figures within the scene are doing the same thing. Interestingly for the female role in the construction of male gender identity, one of the figures is female.

Athleticism

For women, adornment and eroticism were the major components; for men, Etruscan mirrors present a different image. One of the ways in which the male body was transformed was through athletics (Schneider 1995; Thuillier 1985). In contrast to female adornment, male adornment is internalised through athleticism. Running and jumping are depicted on six mirrors from the sixth century (Gerhard ccLxxxix.2; v.138.1; v.138.2; *CSE* USA 2.5; Mayer Prohop 1967: 553, 554; see also Thuillier 1985: 154–6). The corporality of these images is emphasised by the filling of the decorated surface with the single, naked figure. In all cases the figures are male. Emphasis, through the figure's frontality and size, is given to the chest. In Fig. 2.9(a) we see an athlete practising or performing to music with a servant carrying his strigil. The scene is highly reminiscent of those of *palaestrae* or *gymnasia* from Greece or Rome, where a cult of the beautiful body is often cited (for example Osborne 1998: 139; Spivey 1997: 135–45; Starr 1979: 130–5). In all these examples the only viewer is the holder of the mirror. The scene is made up of participants in the action. The absence of a specific viewer in the depiction hints at a more abstract, general viewer. In this example the action takes place on a monumental plinth, setting the scene outside, in public view, as though it were a competition or training for a competition. In Fig. 2.9(b) we see two naked male figures, one of whom is holding up his leg up to apply his strigil to his outer calf. Strigils are frequently associated with perfume jars in burials at this time. Although no evidence survives of *palaestrae* or similar structures in Etruria (Thuillier 1985: 348–9), the elaboration of paraphernalia consistent with such a setting indicates that exercise of this type, together with the material associations of it, was familiar in Etruria (Spivey and Stoddart 1990: 93); Thuillier argues that the Etruscans took part in athletic competition as far back as the late sixth century (Thuillier 1975: 566, 572–4). The presence of strigils in tombs, and in male hands in the iconography of mirrors, is a clear reference to the role of athletics in the male processes of adornment.

One form of exercise for which the Etruscans were famous, especially in southern Etruria, is horse-riding, and this too is represented in mirrors. In these scenes male figures are depicted either riding or strongly associated with horses. In one mirror (Gerhard v.136.2), one such figure is shown leading his mount to the left. Again, his naked, well-muscled torso is shown in the art-historically conventional, and visually striking, full view. Boxing and wrestling are also depicted on mirrors, though they are mythological contests, such as that between Pele and Thethis, or Castur

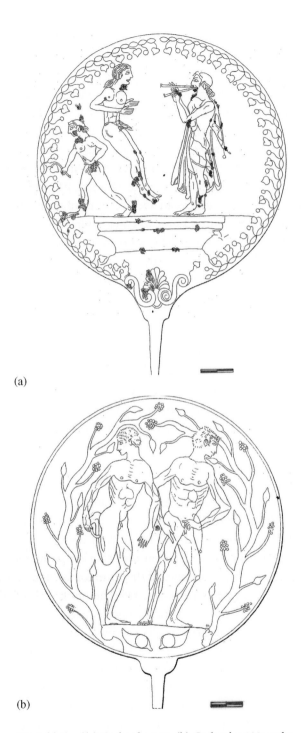

(a)

(b)

2.9 Athletics ((a) Gerhard v.144. (b) Gerhard v.138; scale: 2 cm)

and Pultuke (Gerhard ccxxiv and lvi.1 respectively). In these examples the rendition of the musculature of the naked male body is again emphasised.

As Thuillier has noted, many mirrors exploit the link between the Tinas Cliniar and athleticism (Thuillier 1985: 488–9). The divine twins were great athletes: Castur was a renowned horseman, Pultuke skilled in boxing. Their association as notable sportsmen is highlighted in the mirrors: some scenes show one or both of the Tinas Cliniar holding javelins; in other instances it is horsemanship that is selected for representation. The veneration of this athletic aspect of the Tinas Cliniar in Etruria is apparent in one mirror (Gerhard clxxi) that shows a statue of Pultuke wearing boxing gloves (he is interpreted as a statue because he is on an architectural plinth, unlike the other figures in the scene). To his left a 'real' boxer (identified by his gloves) sits on the plinth. Although inferences concerning the worship of Pultuke have to be tentative, this mirror seems to show that such statues were of particular relevance to boxers, if not to all athletes, and that there was some kind of appreciation of the athletic persona of Pultuke, or of boxers in general. The relation between male adornment and religion is also visible in another mirror (Gerhard ccxxxix), where two naked male figures are shown (possibly Castur and Pultuke, given their shoes and the star behind the head of the left-hand figure) sitting at an altar with a cult statue of Turan. The figure on the left of the cult statue holds a javelin and the other puts his arm around the idol. These images establish a link between athleticism and the Tinas Cliniar, and given the importance of the latter as judges of the body, and the placing of these images on mirrors, they resonate with the importance of athleticism as a form of male adornment. At the same time, they intimate the quasi-religious importance of the process of adornment, and, importantly, the inclusion of Turan carries undertones of eroticism. As a result, the Tinas Cliniar serve not only to impress the importance of athleticism, but also to act as judges of the athletic male body.

The male athletic activity represented on the mirrors is set in a public context; other iconographic evidence corroborates this. The tomb paintings of Tarquinia have been interpreted in this way by Pairault-Massa. She uses the Tombe del Barone, del Triclinio and delle Iscrizioni to place male athleticism in the public sphere, and Thuillier adds riding, boxing, discus-throwing, running and wrestling (Pairault-Massa 1993: 247–79; Thuillier 1993).

One of the key differences in details between male and female adornment and viewing is in the context in which it takes place: whereas female adornment is restricted to the house or interior private space, male adornment takes place in public. This would seem to challenge the traditional views of the greater public visibility of Etruscan women compared to their Greek and Roman counterparts, and suggests greater parallels between the two. In Etruria the process of adornment was carried out in different contexts: the efforts of male adornment, in terms of athletic training, are viewed in public loci, whether funeral games, athletic competitions or training grounds.

Adornment transforms the Etruscan male body, just as the female body was transformed; however, for men the process is internalised. Male adornment is, in a sense, a mirror image of female adornment in that it starts from *within* the body itself, sculpting and shaping it according to culturally desirable forms, rather than *adding* to it in the form of jewellery or pigments. Athletic training is one of the ways in which this is done. Associated with this are the processes of scraping, oiling and, possibly, depilating the body. Through athleticism and physical training the surface of the male body was sculpted into shape. The selective building of musculature from under the skin affected the surface of the body by pushing against the skin, giving it new, desirable contours. In contrast to female adornment, the manipulation of the male body itself, by altering its shape, is almost sculptural: additions to the male body are stripped away, leaving the contoured body, pared down to its minimum, the surface of which was altered through exercise and thus sculpted into the right shape. The addition of sheen through the application of oils to the skin would have added to this sculptural feel.

Warfare

Warfare is the last aspect of Etruscan male gender identity to be discussed here. Images of warfare on Etruscan mirrors depict mythical heroes or seemingly non-specific male warriors (see the sixth-century mirror at Gerhard v.123). The role of warfare in these mirrors should be read in a way similar to the Malavisch scenes discussed above: the images propose the valorisation and codification of the male body in terms of martial adornment, and the creation of the male persona as a warrior, in the same way that adornment and marriage created the female persona as a beautiful wife. This is neatly encapsulated by Pacchioni, who, in an article on the female sarcophagi from Chiusi that contained toilette equipment, calls these objects the 'armamentario della toilette' (Pacchioni 1939: 485). That armour is an equivalent of female adornment has been demonstrated in two earlier European case studies (Robb 1995, 1997; Treherne 1995), and it is shown in two mirrors that represent the arming of Aivas (Ajax) or Achle (Achilles) by Thethis (Thetis) (Fig. 2.10(a); see also Gerhard v.120). In both instances, the pair is flanked by two figures similar to the attendants in female adornment scenes, and

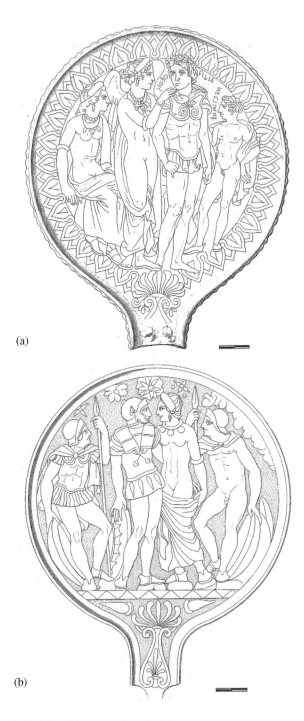

(a)

(b)

2.10 (a) Achle armed by Thethis (Gerhard ccxxxi; scale: 2 cm). (b) Warrior and woman (Gerhard cci; scale: 2 cm)

Thethis, who appears to be placing armour on to the male body in front of her, shows the sort of concentration that typifies such scenes of female adornment. The nature of male arming scenes is thus resonant of female adornment. The equivalence between male arming and female adornment is demonstrated further in the mirror in Fig. 2.10(b). Here, a division of the representational space of the mirror occurs: the male and female are strictly divided down the middle of the mirror; the bejewelled, semi-naked female contrasted with the armed male. In contrast to female adornment, though, this form of male adornment, like athleticism, takes place in the very public arena of warfare.

A related group of mirrors is that showing Menrva, who is identified by her armour and, less frequently, by her aegis (Colonna 1984; Mansuelli 1946: 62–4; 1948; Pfiffig 1975: 255–8; 347–52). As well as her presence in specific mythical scenes, such as the judgement of Alcsentre, early examples from the sixth and fifth centuries show her in less specific contexts: most frequently with a male warrior (for example *CSE* Belgium 1.30), and from the fourth century onwards she is frequently shown as a single figure, like Turan (for example *CSE* Netherlands 3). As goddess of war, her inclusion on mirrors seems a little surprising; however, her divine status, as well as her depiction on an object used in the creation of images of the self, gives such images a normative role: along with athleticism, the heroic warrior ideal was one to aspire to, and one that could be achieved, on a visible level, through appropriate alterations to the body. Menrva would have been an aspirational figure for such a heroic ideal.

Of course, the Tinas Cliniar too have strong links with military heroism: Castur was a famous soldier and taught Heracles swordsmanship and cavalry skills, and the hundreds of examples of Tinas Cliniar mirrors exploit this link. The twins are frequently shown as warriors: often they bear spears and shields (Gerhard XLIX.1), but some representations show helmets and cuirasses as well (Fig. 2.10(b)). The significance of Castur and Pultuke as judges of male athleticism has been noted already. Here, it is suggested that the same normative and judgemental role is expressed in scenes of warfare too. Castur and Pultuke, as exemplary warriors and judges of the manipulation of the surface of the body, were put on mirrors precisely for this reason. Unlike athleticism, though, the creation of the male as warrior does involve the addition of certain features to the body, namely armour.

One particularly elaborate mirror shows the complex interweaving of the different aspects of adornment raised so far (Gerhard V.78). Here, two male figures on the outer edges of the scene, looking in on the central figures, are labelled 'Pultuke' and 'Castur' and they are clearly represented here as warriors: they are armed with spears and wear metal cuirasses. In this mirror, adornment is associated with both male and female beauty: the central figure of Elina, judged to be the most beautiful woman in the world, is flanked on either side by her twin brothers, who are armed and in poses that prefigure their later standardised pose of judgement. Elina's naked, languid pose and jewellery epitomise the aspirations of female adornment, just as her brothers represent heroic warriors. All of this is overseen by their father Tinia (Etruscan Zeus). The complexity of the image allows the association of both the male and female body with arbitration and adornment, while at the same time marking a contrast between female erotic and male warrior ideals.

Conclusion

This discussion has argued that the emergence and proliferation of mirrors in the material record from the late sixth century onwards signal a dramatic change in attitudes towards the representation of the body and the self. This has been traced in two ways: first in attitudes towards individual identity in relation to the rest of society; second in relation to changing gender identities. The first has not been noted until now; the second raises conclusions that differ significantly from many interpretations of the position of women in Etruscan society hitherto. Traditionally, it is the power and status of Etruscan women that are emphasised, and they emerge from the literature, as Spivey has described, as prototype feminists 'who might feel as comfortable in twentieth-century New York as they did in sixth-century BC Tarquinia' (Spivey 1991b: 55). By contrast, the Etruscan women that emerge from the analysis in this chapter are significantly less emancipated (see also Amann 2000). This is due partly to the different theoretical position taken here, and partly to a different chronological focus. Much of the discussion about the high status of Etruscan women has concentrated on the seventh- and sixth-century material, whereas mirrors were deposited only at the end of this period. The two interpretations are not incompatible if the possibility of a change in attitudes towards the relationships between men and women over this period is allowed. Following the argument of this chapter, the emergence of mirrors in the late sixth century marks a significant change in the way that gender roles were imagined and performed in Etruscan society.

Evidence of the representations of Etruscan gender from the earlier period is scarce. However, it is possible that evidence from the eighth- and seventh-century tombs indicates a situation with regard to gender roles that is different from those that follow it (Heurgon 1961, 1964). In fact, the evidence of the iron-age and Orientalising periods would suggest a great degree of ambiguity towards gender relations in early Etruscan society. For the Iron Age, the variety in grave goods, and the so-called 'mixtures' of sexually diagnostic items in graves, have been noted, with graves containing, for instance, both spearheads and male fibulae, or razors and spindle whorls or spools (Cristofani 1969: 17–19; Fedeli 1983: 92; G. V. Gentili 1987; Henken 1968b: 42–7; Toms 1998); and for the Orientalising period, the enormously wealthy female graves containing armour and chariots have been cited (G. Bartoloni and Grottanelli 1989; G. Bartoloni 2000a; Colonna and Colonna 1997; Emiliozzi (ed.) 1997; Martelli 1995; Rathje 2000; Winther 1997). These anomalies have been understood as evidence for particularly powerful Etruscan women (for example warrior princesses) (Bedini 1977; Riva 2000). If this were the case, it would appear to be in contrast to the image presented in the evidence of mirrors and tombs in the later period.

By the late fifth and fourth centuries, the objectifying tendency in the treatment of Etruscan women appears highly developed, culminating in their marginalisation not just in mirrors, but also in other forms of material culture. The mid-fifth-century Tomba 5513 shows the first signs of this process. In what appears to be a standard dining scene, with male and female figures apparently being served by smaller figures, we notice that rather than reclining with the male diners, women are standing behind the couches, attending the men (Steingräber (ed.) 1986: plate 174). In a later tomb-painting in the Tomba degli Scudi (late fourth century), this process of marginalisation has been taken further: while the man reclines on his couch, the woman is not with him but perched on the couch, selecting food for him from the table in front of them. She has been demoted from a position on the couch as equal participant to that of a subordinate servant (Steingräber (ed.) 1986: plate 146). By the fourth century, the presence of Etruscan women at banquets was a privilege that was double-edged at best.

The desire to ascribe to Etruscan women a position of power and influence has underscored most recent work on the subject. No detailed long-term analysis of Etruscan gender has taken place (though for preliminary steps in this direction see Amann 2000; Nielsen 1998; Rathje 2000). With a more careful, diachronic approach to Etruscan gender, it should be possible to trace the elaboration and development of Etruscan gender relations over five centuries. The evidence presented here would suggest that there was a significant change in attitudes towards the role of men and of women during the late sixth and fifth centuries. If this is the case, the marginalisation, objectification and eroticisation of the female from *c.* 530 onwards, as evinced in the mirrors, should be seen as part of that change. By the late sixth century, the norms and expectations of male and female behaviour became more clearly differentiated, with the eroticisation, objectification and domestication of the female body, while the male body became associated with the public activities of athletics and warfare. The definitions and boundaries of gender become heavily implicated in the commission, iconography and funerary deposition of mirrors, and the deposition of mirrors in graves testifies to this.

This chapter has not delineated male or female roles in Etruria. It has looked at one aspect of the ideological change that took place in Etruria: a shift in Etruscan perceptions of the self and the ways in which this shift was materialised on the surfaces of the bodies of individual men and women. The underlying premise of the chapter has been the importance of mirrors as tools in the transformation of the surface of the body, a process that was essential to the negotiation of personal identity. The deposition of mirrors in burial demonstrates the importance of the surface of the body as the boundary on which such negotiation took place. Cultural categories of self and other, and of male and female, were elaborated, through adornment, on the surfaces of the bodies of Etruscan men and women.

Introduction

This chapter takes tomb architecture as the starting point for the examination of changing Etruscan attitudes to surface and boundaries from the seventh century to the fifth. It will argue that the surface of the tomb not only marked the physical distinction between inside and outside the tomb, but also formed the interface between the living and the dead. The period under consideration saw dramatic changes in Etruscan funerary monuments: the massive burial mounds (*tumuli*) of the Orientalising period were characterised by their size and wealth, extending as far as 50 metres in diameter, and containing up to four tombs, each with multiple chambers, all reached by an entrance corridor (*dromos*); by contrast, the sixth century saw a decrease in the size of funerary monuments and a change from circular to rectilinear monuments that were now arranged in orderly rows.

The reasons for such changes have been thought to be increased foreign contacts, technological advances, restrictions of space, or socio-political considerations. An example of the latter is the interpretation of the stylistic unity of the tombs from the late sixth century on, taken together with their increased number and decreased size. With particular reference to the cemeteries of Cerveteri, this has been seen as the result of the rise of a 'ceto medio', or middle class, at the expense of the old elites who had been buried in the large mounds. In other words, the greater uniformity, in terms of the wealth and complexity of tombs in the late sixth century has been understood as the result of a more democratic social structure (Cristofani 1978: 78; Spivey and Stoddart 1990: 143–7). Such a reading has its appeal; however, it should be remembered that the transformation could simply be the result of a change in how social hierarchy was expressed: from the late sixth century onwards, it may have found expression in ways that do not survive, or that we cannot read, or that have not yet been investigated.

More importantly, arguments that focus on the 'new' uniformity in the cube tombs as an indication of the rise of social uniformity ignore the similarity between the earlier mounds. Unfortunately, like most of Etruria, the nature of the excavation of the Banditaccia necropolis at Cerveteri has resulted in a record that pays insufficient attention to the poorer and art-historically less interesting burials at the site, as the complexity of the results of the Lerici Foundation excavations in the Laghetto area of the Banditaccia has shown (Linington 1980; see also Thoden van Velzen 1992). The biases in the evidence from this cemetery and in the Etruscan material record more widely make it difficult to furnish such socio-political interpretations as the sole explanations for change. In addition, such accounts do not explain why the form of late sixth-century tombs was so suited to the expression of 'middle-classness'.

This chapter takes as its starting point the importance of tombs in materialising social and cultural attitudes towards the dead. Changes in tomb form are therefore related to changing perceptions of the place of the dead within the world of the living. If tomb architecture expresses the difference between the living and the dead, changes in architectural form can be seen to express changes in the ontological relationships between the living and the dead. This chapter draws on recent work on architectural space, and on phenomenological understandings of man-made and natural environments.

The importance of social factors over environmental and technological factors in determining the form of the built environment has been emphasised for some time in architectural (Rapoport 1969: 47), anthropological (Douglas 1972: 513–4; King 1980: 2) and archaeological studies (S. Foster 1989: 40; King 1980: 1–2; Sanders 1990: 44–5). Though this is evident in the varying human responses to the need to create dwellings in different cultures, the need to incorporate social explanations into architectural histories has been voiced for many years (Carsten and Hugh-Jones 1995: 36; R. J. Lawrence 1990: 74) As the result of the culturally informed choices and decisions of the builder, architecture bears cultural and social significance (Ardener 1981: 12; Eco 1980: 55).

Architecture is able to embody social meaning because it entails the material manipulation by human beings of otherwise unbounded space. The physical attributes of space necessary for the generation of such meanings are shape, pattern, volume and distance (Harvey 1990: 202). All spaces share such characteristics; however, the meanings of specific spaces, though undeniably linked to these characteristics, are ultimately dependent on usage (Lefebvre 1991: 191; Richards 1990: 113). The attributes of space are variable, and open to an infinite range of possibilities. However, the ways in which these attributes are combined (Heidegger 1971a: 154) and themselves combine with social usage are what relates space to social dynamics. Again, the importance of Bourdieu's *habitus* and *praxis* is evident here in the stress on the social creation and reception of architectural elements as the source of their meanings; in fact, Bourdieu discusses the house, 'the principal locus for the objectification of generative schemes', as the place where social relations are developed, expressed, learned and reiterated (Bourdieu 1977: 89).

The built environment plays a crucial role in providing cues for appropriate (acceptable) social behaviour by encoding the world-view and cultural values of the builders. Studies of past architectures have emphasised the importance of 'a sequence of design decisions, whether made by a professional or lay-builder' in the creation of the built environment (Sanders 1990: 44–5), which is none other than an implicit acknowledgement of the concept of *chaîne opératorie* discussed in Chapter 1. As a result, any inquiry into Etruscan architecture, whether of tombs as is the case here, or of temples and houses, as discussed in the following chapters, must take into account not only the potential for architecture to materialise social meanings, but also the possibility that social meaning resides in all aspects of architectural form.

This theoretical platform allows a detailed analysis of the changing form of Etruscan funerary architecture, most notably the changing importance of surface. To this end, three aspects of funerary space will be examined: the treatment of the entrance of the tomb, the internal structure of chambers, and the location of the architectural decoration of the tomb. In all three areas, changes in the material record mirror changes in attitudes towards the cultural and conceptual placing of the dead.

The tombs that form the basis of this investigation are from the Banditaccia cemetery of Cerveteri, ancient Caere. The tombs of this one cemetery have been chosen as a case study of the chronological development of Etruscan funerary monuments, though other sites are incorporated as much as possible. The site of Cerveteri is one of the best documented in Etruria, originally through the excavation and publication of its monumental cemeteries, which yielded a huge wealth of grave goods, then through the discovery of its port at Pyrgi (Colonna (ed.) 1988–9), and, more recently, through the investigations of the settlement area (Cristofani (ed.) 1992; Cristofani 1997; Cristofani and Nardi (eds.) 1988; Izzet 1999–2000; 2000). The tombs that form the core of the discussion of this chapter date from the seventh to the fifth centuries BC, and come from the Banditaccia cemetery. The chronology of the tombs is established by the dating of grave goods: largely Greek (Corinthian and Attic) pottery; they are therefore precise dates, though they do not account for variations in depositional practices in mortuary contexts. The cemetery was excavated by Mengarelli in the first half of the twentieth century. This was the first systematic excavation of the Banditaccia necropolis, and, despite the limitations of the material, owing to the excavation and recording techniques of the time, it provides one of the largest single multi-period samples available for study from Etruria. In addition, by virtue of the scale of the Mengarelli excavations, the Banditaccia provides a relatively large sample excavated by the same person, using the same techniques, so that differentials in recording technique and method are eliminated. (The excavations were published by Pace *et al.* 1955. This is supplemented here by the careful accounts of Colonna 1986; Pohl 1972; Prayon 1975, 1986.)

As mentioned in Chapter 1, funerary material holds an unusually privileged position in Etruscan studies. Since the beginnings of the discipline, scholarly investigation has centred overwhelmingly on sepulchral monuments. Until relatively recently, all that was known about the Etruscans was derived from funerary remains. This has resulted in a highly biased database for Etruscan culture as a whole (Damgaard Andersen 1997: 334; Thoden van Velzen 1992). In addition, the recording of the funerary material has itself been highly selective. Before the work and influence of Mengarelli (Mengarelli 1915, 1927, 1937, 1938), material from the tombs was not considered of sufficient interest to record unless it was imported and painted. During excavations at Vulci in the mid-nineteenth century, George Dennis witnessed the destruction of coarse, unpainted ware and *bucchero* (Dennis 1883 vol. I: 450). Only in exceptional cases were the architectural elements of the tombs noted: in Bianchi Bandinelli's work on Chiusi, for example, there is very little architectural information, let alone measurements or plans (and when there are plans, they exclude the entrance corridor), because of the overriding emphasis on the material from the graves (Bianchi Bandinelli 1925a). More recent studies of Etruscan funerary monuments have tried to remedy this cursory treatment, and have presented meticulous examinations of the many facets of funerary archaeology (for example Blanck and Proietti 1986; Moretti and Sgubini Moretti (eds.) 1983; Colonna di Paolo and Colonna 1970, 1978; Cristofani 1967). However, this painstaking attention to detail has led to the studies being very localised, taking individual sites or even tombs as their focus. One major exception to this is Prayon's *Frühetruskische Grab- und Hausarchitektur* for the earlier periods of architecture in southern Etruria (Prayon 1975). This influential project attempted to synthesise for the first time the often diverse material from the region, and to set the development of tomb (and house) architecture within broader parameters.

In the light of recent mortuary theory (discussed in greater length in Chapter 2), this chapter sees funerary monuments as being as much a part of the relationships between the living as of the relationships between the living and the dead. Tombs are the physical setting for the ritual act of burial: they enclose the activities associated with the rites of death. This chapter will take as its basis the assumption that the deposition of the body in the tomb is one of the last stages of funerary rituals. Burial is the point of contact between this world and the next, and the ways in which burial takes place are expressive of attitudes towards death. Because tomb form is the result of a series of socio-culturally informed decisions, changes in tomb form must be seen as deliberate and meaningful, reflecting changes in conceptions of social relations and Etruscan attitudes towards death.

This chapter will concentrate on the changing treatment of the ontological difference between the living and the dead, as it is materialised in the physical difference between outside and inside the tomb. In the case of funerary monuments, the entrance to the tomb marks these differences. Entrances and doorways, because they mediate between such differences, are called mediative distance: in Etruscan tombs the mediative distance is the entrance corridor.

Tomb form

The entrance corridor

The treatment of the entrances and doorways of Etruscan tombs changes fundamentally in the second half of the sixth century. However, in order to appreciate the significance of this change, it is necessary to be aware of the preceding 200 years of funerary architecture that led up to this change, and in particular the treatment of doorways and entrances during that period.

The iron-age graves at Cerveteri are simple circular or rectangular pits or trenches cut into the bedrock, known as *pozzi* and *fosse* respectively. The cremated remains or the corpses of the dead, along with a small number of grave goods, were deposited in these modest burials. Towards the end of the eighth century these burials were elaborated by the addition of a small niche (*loculus*), along the inner wall, which probably served to protect the body and grave goods from damage. Later, pseudo-vaulting created by overhanging stone blocks covered by mounds of earth evolved, creating the characteristic cone shape of Caeretan tombs. For stability, the mound was surrounded by a ring of stones. These stones were rough-hewn at first, but were later dressed. At this stage the number of burials in the tombs increases, though single trench graves continued in use at the same time. This continuity in the

3.1 Burial mound, Banditaccia necropolis, Cerveteri

burial record of trench graves, 'probably by poorer people', is used to argue
for cultural continuity from the Iron Age to the Etruscan period (Prayon
1986: 174).

At the end of the eighth and the beginning of the seventh century, funerary
architecture at Cerveteri underwent a decisive change. Containing blocks
were arranged in a circle that enclosed a rectilinear chamber. These eighth-
and early seventh-century mounds have been interpreted as marking a shift
from the relative autonomy of the individual in the Iron Age to a hierarchical
network commanded by the head of the household in the early Orientalising
period (Colonna 1986: 395; Naso 2001).

By the late seventh century, a dramatic increase had taken place in the
scale of some of the funerary monuments at Cerveteri. Giant mounds, up to
50 metres in diameter and 12–15 metres in height, were constructed to house
the burials (Fig. 3.1). The dramatic size of these mounds has been interpreted as 'indubbiamente la massima espressione delle elites aristocratiche'
(Colonna 1986: 398; see also Cristofani 1978: 68), and the frequent appearance of the mounds in pairs or groups is seen as pertaining to the different
branches of the same aristocratic family (Colonna 1986: 398). The mounds
of earth sit on bases carved out of the *tufo*, topped by a cylindrical cornice
of alternating ridges and grooves (Fig. 3.1). The mound is surrounded by
a narrow ditch cut into the bedrock, crossed at one point only by a ramp.

These ramps are thought to have allowed access to the mounds in order to perform commemorative rites (Damgaard Andersen 1993b; Colonna 1986: 389).

The burial chamber in the centre of the mound is reached by a long, narrow entrance corridor. As discussed above, the entrance corridor is a transitional or liminal area between the two ontologically different categories of the living and the dead. The significance of the corridor as a liminal space in the funerary architecture of Cerveteri and elsewhere is highlighted by the presence of sculpture at the beginning of this transitional zone. There is only one example from this date in the sample from the Banditaccia necropolis: this is in the Tomba dei Dolii, where a seated sphinx was found in the entrance corridor (Pace *et al.* 1955: 313–45). It has been argued that this type of sculpture was 'in qualità di "guardiani", in funzione apotropaica' (Cristofani 1978: 72). The apotropaic character of hybrid creatures such as sphinxes, centaurs and griffins, and other wild beasts like lions, has been argued for other sites, principally Vulci (Cristofani 1978: 72–3; Spivey 1988: 15–16). Similar apotropaic finds from other sites include a sculpted lion's head from the south tomb at Castellina in Chianti (Pernier 1916: 271–2, 276–9), and the eponymous sphinx in the Tomba della Sfinge at Blera (Gargana 1932: 500–2). Other apotropaic objects, *cippi* or grave markers, were found in tombs at Vetulonia (Carresi 1985: 128) and possibly in tomb 55 at Marsiliana d'Albegna (Minto 1921a: 107). Given the prevalence of such apotropaic objects in Etruria, it is not inconceivable that similar objects now lost were originally deposited in the entrance corridors of other tombs in the Banditaccia. Rather than simply restricting these sculptures to part of 'lo stimulo verso una scultura di tipo monumentale' (Cristofani 1978: 72), they should be considered as a further element in the emphasis on transition expressed in the entrance corridors.

The Regolini-Galassi tomb at Cerveteri (Fig. 3.2 (a)), from the second quarter of the seventh century, is one of the earliest mound tombs at Cerveteri. Inside the mound, the floor and walls of the tomb have been excavated from the soft *tufo* bedrock, but the ceiling is pseudo-vaulted. The burial chamber is reached by a long corridor, which is partially rock-cut and partially vaulted. The roughly coeval Tomba della Capanna (Fig. 3.2 (b)) is entirely cut out of the rock. This tomb itself consists of two chambers, with convex side walls which join to make a pointed arch in profile, preceded by a 15-metre-long entrance corridor.

In northern Etruria, where the bedrock is at a greater depth, the tombs were often built entirely of stone blocks as, for example, in the cemetery of Populonia or in the Montagnola tomb from Quinto Fiorentino, dating to

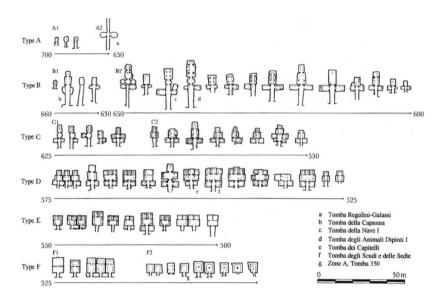

3.2 Chronological scheme of tomb plans from Cerveteri (adapted from Prayon 1975, plate 85)

about 600 BC (Caputo 1962, 1965, 1970; Fedeli 1983; Minto 1921b, 1921c, 1921d, 1925, 1934, 1943; Zifferero (ed.) 1997). In this last example the entrance corridor measures just under 14 metres before the first chamber (Caputo 1962: 115). From the Caeretan examples, the longest entrance corridor is from the Tomba della Capanna (Fig. 3.2(b)), which measures 15 metres (Pace *et al.* 1955: 346–60). Other early corridors from the site measure between 10 and 12 metres (Pace *et al.* 1955: 215–27; 1054–65; 1080–9). A very long entrance corridor is, in fact, a typical feature of early Etruscan mound tombs. For example, at Comeana, the corridor of the Tumulo Montefortini measures 14 metres (Nicosia 1966b: 283); at Cortona, in the Melone di Camucìa, the corridor measures 13 metres (Neppi Modona 1925: 89); at Castellina in Chianti, the corridor of the south tomb measures 6.25 metres (Pernier 1916: 271) and that of the north tomb 7 metres (Pernier 1916: 273); at Populonia the corridor of the Tomba dei Carri is 12.1 metres long (Fedeli 1983: 252; Minto 1914c: 447); that of the Tomba dei Letti Funebri is about 7 metres in length (Fedeli 1983: 261; Milani 1908: 204); and at Vetulonia, the corridor of the Tomba della Pietrera measures 22 metres in length (Carresi 1985: 114; Falchi 1891: 206–13). In addition, long entrance corridors are also noted, though without measurements, at the Tomba Mula, Quinto Fiorentino (Caputo 1962, 1970), and at Vetulonia in the Circolo dei Monili (Falchi 1891: 96–102), the Circolo dei Gemelli (Falchi 1891: 102–4), the Circolo di Bes (Falchi 1891: 104–9), the Tomba del Duce (Falchi 1891: 109–52), the Circolo di Mut (Falchi 1891: 152–6), the Circolo dei due Coni (Falchi 1891: 156–8), and the Circolo del Diavolo (Falchi 1891: 159–60).

These long entrance corridors of the earlier tombs emphasise the difference between inside and outside by stretching the mediative distance between them. At the same time, this creates a discrete space that is a separate entity in its own right. The liminal space of the corridor separates the world of the living from the world of the dead in the burial chamber. In these early tombs, this extended distance must have been felt necessary in keeping these worlds apart (similarly see Parker Pearson 1993: 206). In the corridor the process of entering is prolonged, and impressed on to the consciousness of the entrant by the period of time it takes to travel its extent: going down a corridor of 10–12 metres requires about 16–20 steps. This length is further emphasised by the changing width of the corridor. At Cerveteri, the width of the entrance corridors increases slightly towards the chamber, measuring up to approximately 2 metres at the widest point (Fig. 3.2); the widest is 2 metres (Pace *et al.* 1955: 215–27). This widening gives a sense of inverse funnelling to the structure. The effect of this on entering the tomb is one of propulsion into the widening darkness of the tomb; on leaving, there is almost a sense of urgency, produced by the narrowing walls, towards the hole of light from outside. The widening of the entrance corridor is also evident in non-Caeretan examples, such as the Montagnola and Mulo tombs at Quinto Fiorentino (Caputo 1962: 121; 1970: 369, fig. 1), the Tumulo Montefortini at Comeana (Nicosia 1966b: 283), and the east and north tombs at Castellina in Chianti (Pernier 1916: 266 and 273 respectively).

This argument lays emphasis on the great length of the entrance corridor in these Orientalising tombs. It might be suggested that a long corridor is necessary in order to reach a chamber in a large mound, and is therefore somehow inevitable and thus less culturally significant than a deliberate feature. However, these individual decisions were made in the light of each other, and we cannot assume the order in which they were taken – the choice of a large mound may have been made in order to create a long corridor. Furthermore, if the decision to build a mound led to a culturally undesirably long corridor, the builders could have positioned the chamber at the periphery of the mound. The point is not that either of these scenarios was necessarily the case, but that 'common sense' arguments about material culture form miss the potential for the knowing acceptance of the individual consequences of their actions on the part of the makers.

Towards the end of the sixth century there was a major change in Caeretan funerary architecture. This involved a dramatic diminution in the

3.3 Row of cube tombs, Banditaccia cemetery, Cerveteri

external size of tombs from the preceding monumental mounds to smaller, square monuments, which were constructed out of rectangular *tufo* blocks (Fig. 3.3). These were arranged in a line, with uniform cornices running across the rows of tombs. Colonna has described this as the 'individuazione di una parete esterna' (Colonna 1986: 447). Along with these changes came a change in the length of the entrance corridor. Prayon's chronological scheme of tomb development at Cerveteri (adapted for Fig. 3.2) shows that during the 200 years during which entrance corridors were built, their length in relating to the tomb as a whole was reduced until they reached their shortest point by about 500 BC. This was 0.4 metres in Tomb 113 in Zone A (Pace *et al.* 1955: 543). Tombs from Volterra, Populonia and Tarquinia show a sim-ilarly shortened entrance corridor, where the mid-sixth-century proportion of entrance corridor to chamber length is roughly equal (for Volterra see Minto 1930, for Populonia see Fedeli 1983: 122, fig. 61, and for Tarquinia see Steingräber (ed.) 1986: 386).

By 500 BC in Cerveteri the boundary between outside and inside was now spatially defined in a matter of a few decimetres, a distance covered in less than a single step. This formed a dramatic contrast with the earlier corridors that employed a distance up to twenty times greater to express the same transition. In the later tombs, the mediative distance between the tomb and the outside was condensed to the door lintel itself, which was just marginally thinner than the tomb walls. In this way the exterior surface of the tomb became the boundary, in contrast to the 10 metres or so of excavated rock in earlier tombs.

Important though the diminution of the mediative distance is to the physical experience of entering the tomb, it is equally important to recognise the visual impact of this architectural change. With the shrinking of the entrance corridor, the surface of the tomb became the boundary between the living and the dead. The contestation of the difference between inside and outside now took place on the external, visible surface of the tomb itself. This is a marked change from the earlier mound tombs, where, from the outside, the place of the dead was invisible inside the mound, and the point at which the world of the living ended and the world of the dead began was masked by the long transitional space of the entrance corridor, out of sight, inside the mound (see below, and Fig. 3.5).

The rows of fifth-century tombs from Cerveteri (Fig. 3.3) show the culmination of the dramatic change in the treatment of the entrances to tombs. It is clear that the external appearance of the tomb changed dramatically in this period, from the imposing round burial mounds to smaller rectilinear structures. A very similar development is evident in many other sites, such as the six so-called aedicule tombs at Populonia (De Agostino 1958: 27; Minto 1934b: 388), the 'gabled house' tomb at Blera (Koch, von Mercklin and Weickert 1915: 234–8), the cube tombs at Blera (Koch, von Mercklin and Weickert 1915: 274), the 'house' tomb at Tuscania (Sgubini Moretti 1989), and in the rows of tombs at Orvieto (Bizzari 1962; Bonamici, Stopponi and Tamburini 1994; Klakowicz 1972, 1974). With the reduction in the size of the monuments and in the length of the entrance corridor, the boundary between inside and outside becomes flush with the outer surface of the tomb, and is thus incorporated into the structure of the tomb in a way that was very different from the way the same boundary was expressed in the earlier burial mounds. The locus for the articulation of the difference between the outside and inside of the tomb is now part of the tomb's surface.

That the external, visible surface of the tomb had become the marker of the difference between inside and outside the tomb is also indicated in the materials used to construct the boundary. In the tombs in Fig. 3.3 the entrance is picked out by the use of paler stone, visually highlighting and drawing attention to the location of the entrance. Similarly, the inscriptions on the lintels of Orvietan tombs highlight the importance of the door to the tomb as the beginning of the world of the dead (see below and Fig. 3.9).

A corresponding shift to the externally visible articulation of the difference between inside and outside the tomb is found in the deposition (or lack of it) of the apotropaic objects discussed above. It has been argued that the sculptures of hybrid creatures were a means of protecting the passage between the living and the dead in the early entrance corridors. The example of sculpture from the Banditaccia is early, and the known cases from other sites are all archaic (Martelli 1988). The deployment of such creatures comes to an end, however, with the close of the archaic period. The fifth-century tombs have no such transitional markers within them. Instead, tombs of this period have 'grave markers' in the form of stone *cippi*, cylindrical or casket-shaped carved stones, deposited outside the tomb. They are placed in sockets on stone slabs.

These grave-markers have been found outside tombs from many other sites, for example Marzabotto, Tuscania, where sculpture was also placed on the tomb (Sgubini Moretti 1991: 17, fig. 4), in the Cannicella necropolis (Bonamici, Stopponi and Tamburini 1994: 45, 155) and in the Crocifisso del Tufo necropolis, where five grave-markers have been found *in situ* (for example tomb 3, Bizzari 1962: 117–23; see Fig. 3.9 below, bottom right). For the latter, Bizzari claims that many of the markers found inside the tombs were probably originally placed on the roofs, but fell in when the roofs collapsed (Bizzari 1962: 120). Other grave-markers are noted from on top of tomb 206 at Chiusi (Bianchi Bandinelli 1925a: 281), at the Tomba Ildebranda at Sovana (Bianchi Bandinelli 1929: 71, figs. 24, 80), and at tombs at Vulci (Buranelli 1987: 144).

Most notably, the Tomba dei Demoni from the Ripa S. Angelo necropolis of Cerveteri, dating to the late fourth century, yielded *nenfro* sculptures of pairs of sphinxes and lions, several grave-markers and two exceptional statues of Charun, the god of the underworld. Significantly, these were found not in the tomb but in front of it, in its 'cortile' (Steingräber 1983: 447). Though these objects may have performed an apotropaic function, they often have onomastic inscriptions and so serve a dual purpose of protecting and identifying the dead within the tomb. Again, the communication of these messages takes place in the outer, visible space outside the tomb, a further aspect of the externality characteristic of the changing architecture of the time.

In the fifth- and fourth-century tombs of the rock-cut cemeteries of South Etruria the equation of surface with boundary is taken to its extreme or even inverted. This is particularly true of Castel d'Asso (Colonna di Paolo and Colonna 1970), Norchia (Colonna di Paolo and Colonna 1978; Gargana 1936), San Giuliano (Villa d'Amelio 1963), Sovana (Bianchi Bandinelli 1929), Blera (Koch, von Mercklin and Weickert 1915; Gargana 1932) and Tuscania (Colonna 1967; Sgubini Moretti 1991). In these sites, the rows

3.4 Row of cube tombs from Castel d'Asso

of tombs contain the false doors for which these cemeteries are famous (Fig. 3.4). The exterior surfaces of the tombs are carved with the shape and detail of doors, yet remain solid and impermeable. These doors could be read in many ways. One way is to conclude that the transition between outside and inside has become so problematic that it is no longer viable. However, in the light of the previous analysis of the late sixth-century entrances, these false doors should rather be seen as indicating that the locus for the transition has become so condensed and implicit that simply its representation is sufficient to hint at its existence. It is surface deep, or even externalised, to such an extent that it is actually outside the tomb. This external way of marking the transition between inside and outside is the opposite of that in the mound tombs where the entrance corridors mark the same transition but on the inside of the tomb. The fifth-century doors are, as we have seen, flush with the surface, and in the examples of false doors from Castel d'Asso and Norchia the carved outline of the door actually protrudes from the surface of the tomb (Fig. 3.4). Here the area of transition has been pushed out into the space outside the tomb. This externalisation cannot be mere coincidence; it would surely have been easier to chisel the outline of the door *into* the flat surface of the tomb as it was excavated, rather than leaving a protruding ridge to refine later. Making it stick *out* from the tomb was a deliberate choice and action.

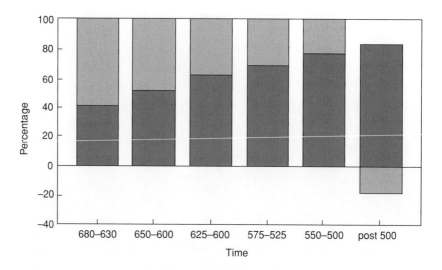

Chart 3.1 Average percentage of the total length of the tomb taken up by the entrance corridor (paler shading) and the chamber (darker shading).

Tombs from the rock-cut cemetery sites show the later extension of the externalisation of the boundary between inside and outside the tomb. These sites contain many examples of portico tombs. These are tombs where the façade was divided into two notional 'storeys' by a protruding tongue of rock supported from below by a row of columns (the eponymous 'vestibule'). Above and below this a false door with raised surround was left in relief on the façade. The appearance of the tomb is that of a completely sealed unit. The 'real' entrance to the tomb is an opening outside the area covered by the visible extent of the tomb. The long, narrow entrance corridor extends from the chamber, out towards the viewer, beneath the façade; in this way it functions as a negative entrance corridor (Fig. 3.5(c)). The visible exterior of the tomb is superficial in the extreme: it is pure representation. The 'business' of the tomb takes place beneath it, and its entrance is not suggested by the architecture of the exterior. Although these examples are not from Cerveteri, the same phenomenon occurs here too, though in a less marked fashion. Chart 3.1 shows the proportion of the tomb length taken up by the entrance corridor and the chamber from the sample of tombs at the site.

It is evident that the importance of the entrance corridor in relation to the chamber decreases over time. In the period 550–500 the average length of the entrance corridor at Cerveteri is at its shortest as a proportion of the average tomb length. As in other sites, after this period the entrance corridor increases in length, for instance in the Tomba dei Rilievi, but instead

outside | inside

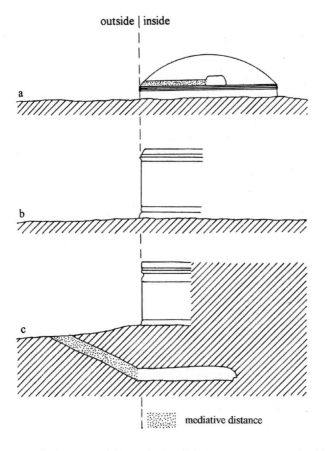

mediative distance

3.5 The location of the mediative distance in Etruscan tombs
(a) before *c.* 530 BC, (b) *c.* 530 BC, (c) after *c.* 530 BC

of retreating back into the monument like the earlier corridors, it runs in
the opposite direction, out in front of the tomb façade, like the negative
corridors of Castel d'Asso (see Fig. 3.5).

Figure 3.5 shows that in the burial mounds the boundary is extended into
the visible body of the tomb. In the late sixth and early fifth centuries this
boundary is condensed so that it is expressed in the walls of the tomb itself.
The surface one sees from the outside is the same as the boundary between
the living and the dead. Later this boundary is extended: the entrance corridor is used again, but now it stretches outwards from chamber and under
the façade of the tomb in a negative way.

The spatial contraction of the boundary between the living and the dead
in the late sixth century does not necessarily imply that this transition is no
longer problematic; instead, it is being expressed in a different way: through

an equation with the external, visible surface of the tomb. This also applies to the negative corridors where, though the transition is being expressed by means of a long tunnel, emphasis is still placed on the visible, flat façade of the cube tombs through the depiction of the false doors on the surface (Fig. 3.4). The contestation of the difference between the living and the dead takes place on the visible surface of the tomb.

The structure of the tomb

Changes in the plan of Etruscan tombs illustrate two further aspects of the importance of visibility and boundedness in the late sixth century. The first, as a result of changing relative size, shape and layout of the chambers, is in the shifting focus of the tomb away from the centre of the mound and towards its edge. The second, by increasing internal divisions, shows an increased concern with differentiating funerary space.

The Tomba della Capanna (Fig. 3.2(b)) illustrates a typical plan of tombs from the earlier period of Etruscan funerary architecture. The overall impression is one of length and narrowness, which is emphasised by its setting in a large mound. It has been noted above that the entrance corridor widened towards the centre of the tomb. At the end of the corridor was a doorway that marked the entrance into a chamber; this, too, widened out, and at its far wall a further doorway led into the final chamber. The dominant feature of this structure was its linearity, or sense of progression towards the final chamber at the centre of the mound. It could even be said that the whole tomb was an elaborated entrance corridor. This is not unique to Cerveteri. The same is true of tombs at Quinto Fiorentino (Caputo 1962: 121; 1970: 369, fig. 1), Comeana (Nicosia 1966b: 283), Cortona (Neppi Modona 1925: 87), Casal Marittimo (Minto 1930: 60), Castellina in Chianti (Pernier 1916: 266–71, 273–4), Populonia and Vetulonia (Carresi 1985: 114, fig. 57; Falchi 1891). Any lateral chambers or niches were incidental to the progress of the entrant to the focus at the end chamber. In the so-called '*tholos* tombs' of northern Etruria, such as those at Quinto Fiorentino (Caputo 1962, 1965, 1970), Comeana (Nicosia 1966a), or Cortona (Neppi Modona 1925: 87), a pillar in the final chamber served as a focal point, emphasising the end point of the sequence. It could be argued, in opposition to such an emphasis on a single element of a tomb, such as the central pillar, that once the decision for corbel vaulting has been made, a central pillar is unavoidable. However, this misses the importance of Gosselain's work in emphasising the importance of every decision in production (Gosselain 1998, 2000); furthermore,

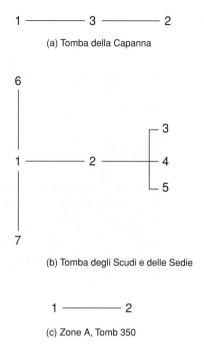

(a) Tomba della Capanna

(b) Tomba degli Scudi e delle Sedie

(c) Zone A, Tomb 350

3.6 Schematic representations of tomb structure, where 1 is the entrance chamber, 2 is the main chamber, and numbers 3 and over are further chambers

it ignores the possibility that such considerations were a part of the initial selection of overall form. The experience of going through the tomb is one of a sequence from the beginning, through the middle, and to the end. The sequential structure of these tombs can be expressed schematically, as shown in Fig. 3.6(a).

This can also be seen in Prayon's sequence of tomb plans at Cerveteri (Fig. 3.2); it is particularly clear in his groups B and C1. In the Tomba degli Animali Dipinti (Fig. 3.2(d)), the sequential nature of the structure is clearly visible in plan, and this is further reinforced by details of the architectural decoration of the interior: strong lines, running parallel with the side walls, carved into the ceiling, draw one further into the tomb. In the tombs with vaulted ceilings in northern Etruria, the rows of overlapping stones, meeting at the central keystone that formed a narrow channel along the length of the entrance corridor, have the same effect. The sequential nature of the tomb is also emphasised by its division into three discrete areas, through which it is necessary to pass in order to reach the main deposition chamber at the end. In the examples from Cerveteri, the transitions between these

3.7 Chamber tomb from the San Cerbone cemetery, Populonia

internal spaces are marked architecturally in the form of doorways; in other parts of Etruria, they are given further emphasis in the selection of materials in the construction of the tomb. For example, in the chamber tombs from Populonia (Minto 1934b: 369, fig. 3; Pernier 1916: 269), these transitions are marked by the use of different coloured stone (Fig. 3.7). In Cerveteri, the elaborated treatment of doorways within the tomb began in the second half of the seventh century, where they received a painted surround, as, for example, in the Tomba degli Animali Dipinti (Naso 1995: 453). The Tomba Campana from Veii had metal sheets nailed around the internal door (Naso 1995: 453). The sequential nature of the tomb is thus impressed upon the entrant by his or her unidirectional path through the aligned spaces; the unidirectionality itself is underlined by the use of different stone or decoration, which visually highlights the transitions.

This sequentiality is still present in the late seventh- and early sixth-century tombs in Prayon's group C2 (Fig. 3.2) where most tombs have at least three stages of progression after the entrance corridor. Between about 670 and 630 the walls of the tomb, which had until then formed a pointed arch, became vertical and there is greater variety in the number of internal spaces. At the same time, the plans of the tombs show the beginnings of a shift in the structural focus of the tomb. For example, in the Tomba della Nave (Fig. 3.2(c)) and the Tomba degli Animali Dipinti (Fig. 3.2(d)), this shift is evident in the central circular chamber. The decreasing size of the chambers as one moves further into the tomb reiterates this change in emphasis in the tomb.

From about 630 BC and into the third quarter of the sixth century, a particularly Caeretan innovation takes place. This is the so-called '*oikos* tomb', or 'vestibule tomb', such as the Tomba dei Capitelli (Fig. 3.2(e)). In these tombs the vestibule, or first chamber, is widened to equal the maximum width of the tomb, and three equal-sized chambers lead from its rear wall. The emphasis on this central chamber marks a dramatic change in the structure of the tomb. After the entrance corridor, instead of continuity in a linear sequence to the final chamber, these central vestibules presented the viewer with an equal choice between three chambers ahead. The sequence is now interrupted at the central chamber of the tomb, and the next stage is not influenced by the architectural layout of the tomb. It is up to the individual which way he or she chooses to progress from that chamber. The same is true of tombs at Chiusi, notably the Tomba del Colle (Bianchi Bandinelli 1925a: 286–9), tomb 166 (Bianchi Bandinelli 1925a: 276), tomb 168 (Bianchi Bandinelli 1925a: 277), and tomb 206 (Bianchi Bandinelli 1925a: 281). This arrangement of rooms is represented schematically in Fig. 3.6(b). By the end of Prayon's group D and group E this process is complete: the central room is the focus of the tomb and the sequential nature of the tomb has disappeared.

The plan of another tomb of this type, the Tomba degli Scudi e delle Sedie (Fig. 3.2(f)), shows aspects of architecture that reiterate the new importance of this central room: it is where most architectural decoration is invested. In the same way, in the Tomba della Scimmia at Chiusi (Bianchi Bandinelli 1925a: 295–8) and the Tomba dei Tori at Tarquinia (Pallottino 1937: 258), it is the location of wall paintings in the central chamber that emphasises the importance of this space within the tomb. By shifting the focus of the tomb in this way, the area of importance was moved away from the centre of the mound and towards its external limit. Traditional interpretations of this architectural configuration have stressed the importance of the ornateness of the furniture in the three rear chambers to suggest the continued cultural importance of these rooms. However, what such interpretations fail to take into account is the equivalent decorative investment in the central chamber of tombs like the Tomba degli Scudi e delle Sedie, or the increased potential of the enlarged central chamber for the communal performance of funerary ritual at the focus of the burial. In the mounds, the physical centre of the mound corresponded to the ritual centre of the tomb; in the vestibule tombs this correspondence was lost and the ritual focus moved closer to the edge of the tomb. When combined with the decreasing length of the tomb entrance, this brings the dead far closer to the living than they had been in earlier tombs. The liminal area between the two was reduced by the shortening of the entrance corridor, and by the articulation of the internal spaces within the tomb.

By the last quarter of the sixth century the process of bringing the ritual focus of the tomb to the edge of the mound reached its culmination. Again, this was achieved by changes to the plan of the tomb. This involved the elimination of most of the chambers. In the plans of the tombs from after *c.* 525 BC the number of tombs with multiple chambers decreases so that eventually, in Prayon's group F2, they become rare. In these tombs there is only the central room of the tomb left (for example Fig. 3.2(g)). Bodies were placed around the perimeters of the chamber. The structure of these tombs is represented schematically in Fig. 3.6(c). On entering, one is immediately at the ritual focus of the tomb; there is no hint of the sequences, much less the linearity, of earlier tombs. In this sense, the effect of the articulation of the tomb's internal spaces echoes that of the shortening of the entrance corridor: both lessen the mediative distance between the living and the dead. Frequently in the later examples from Cerveteri, the focus of the tomb is emphasised by a central column. Elsewhere, the same effect is achieved by the bilateral symmetry of the chamber – for example, the Tomba François at Vulci (Buranelli (ed.) 1987: 59, fig. 1), and the Tomba Ildebranda at Sovana, whose plan is essentially cross-shaped (Bianchi Bandinelli 1929: 85, fig. 32). The two symmetrical lateral niches, and the symmetry of the spaces in front of and behind the entrant, serve to locate the metaphorical centre of the tomb.

By the fourth century, contemporary with the developments in the negative entrance corridor at Castel d'Asso, the immediacy of the burial chamber is taken to its extreme. In the Tomba dell'Alcova, at Cerveteri, the ambulatory nature of the tomb is exaggerated. On the walls, around the four central pillars, are small rectangular recesses like those on either side of the eponymous alcove. Centrality is emphasised by the four pillars in the middle, and by the lowered level of the central area of the tomb. The design of the tomb seems to invite the visitor to step up and look around, but there is no suggestion of the order in which this should take place. In the slightly later Tomba dei Tarquinii or the Tomba dei Rilievi, the same thing occurs, but on a larger scale, and in the latter, the surface is decorated with relief sculpture. Central, focal pillars are surrounded by a regular rectilinear space bounded by the side walls containing niches for the deposition of the dead. The immediacy of entering the ritual focus of the tomb is augmented by the deposition of the 'capostipiti' opposite the entrance, instantly facing the viewer on entry (Blanck and Proietti 1986). In these examples, through architectural form, the tombs have almost become museums for the dead.

Finally in this section, the question of the internal division of the space of the tomb must be considered. In terms of the categorisation of space inside the tombs, an increase in differentiation can be seen in the plans. Between the early seventh and mid-sixth centuries, there was an increased internal segmentation of funerary space, evinced in the increasing number of internal chambers. This indicates the increasing complexity of meanings and symbolism attached to the different spaces within the tombs. The disturbed nature of most Etruscan funerary deposits makes it difficult to assign functions, uses or meanings to the newly created spaces, but this should not detract from the importance of their creation. Whatever the criteria, funerary space became increasingly differentiated, and this was architecturally marked by the increased numbers of chambers.

This is emphasised further by the architectural marking of these different spaces by raised thresholds between the chambers. In contrast to the flat floor running the entire length of the earlier tombs, these thresholds have to be deliberately stepped over. This also happens at other sites; for example, tomb 1 at Volterra (Minto 1930: 30) has a raised threshold between the entrance corridor and chamber. The elaboration of internal doorways, through the use of different coloured stone, paint or metal sheets, seen first in the Orientalising-period tombs, continues in the sixth century; by the time of the sixth-century vestibule tombs, the elaboration was incorporated into the rock from which the tomb was cut, by the presence of carved cordon surrounds. Despite their difference in form from earlier elaborations, these cordons continued to emphasise the transition between the chambers. In other sites the increased number of transitional spaces is marked by wall-paintings. The Tomba dei Tori at Tarquinia (Pallottino 1937: 258), the Tomba della Scimmia (Bianchi Bandinelli 1925a: 295–8) and the Tomba Campana at Veii (Banti 1970) all have painted surrounds to the internal doors. Whatever the form chosen at each site, it is still possible to discern an underlying pattern of elaboration of internal doorways, and so the increased segmentation of the space of the tomb.

The architectural decoration of the tomb

Architectural decoration involves the carving or painting of architectural details, such as ceiling detail or door surrounds on or in the tombs. There are obviously changes in the nature and content of this decoration over time; however, what is important here is the location of the decoration. Any change in the location of decoration is taken to signify a change in the importance of those locations.

The Tomba della Capanna is said to be the first instance of the replication of domestic architecture in a burial context, because of a narrow band running along the centre of the ceiling of the first chamber, often interpreted as the articulation of a ridge pole from a domestic hut (Colonna 1986: 395–6; Cristofani 1978: 68; Prayon 1975: 180, 182). This interest in structural details that appear to parallel those of domestic architecture becomes more striking during the seventh and sixth centuries, with the articulation of ceilings and gables, pillars, doors, windows, and furniture such as beds and chairs. This emphasis on domestic architectural details is seen as an indication of the centrality of the cult of the so-called *gens*: the familial household unit is seen as the core of Etruscan society at this time (Colonna 1986: 420; for the cult of the '*gens*' in the Tomba delle Cinque Sedie, see Prayon 1974).

In the Tomba dei Leoni Dipinti, from the late seventh or early sixth centuries, it is again the roof that receives most attention. The longitudinal axis of the ceiling is picked out along the full length of the chamber by a rectangular ridge. Either side of it, on the sloping roof, small rectangles have been carved out of the rock, perpendicular to the length of the tomb in order to replicate the internal construction of the pitched roof. In the entrance chamber a similar rectangular pattern radiates from a circle against the wall. At the triangular ends of the central chamber the same technique has been employed, this time to depict the support beams at the gables. Both these features can be seen in the ceilings of several tombs at Cerveteri, such as that in Fig. 3.8. The roof receives much attention in tombs from other sites in Etruria, such as the vaulted roofs of the Montagnola tomb (Caputo 1962: 121), and the Tomba della Mulla at Quinto Fiorentino (Caputo 1962: 131–2), the tombs at Casal Marittima (Minto 1930: 58, 60, fig. 38), the pseudo-vaulted roofs of the Tomba del Sodo I at Cortona (Neppi Modona 1925: 84, Pernier 1925: 97) and the Tomba dei Carri at Populonia (Minto 1914c: 447), the relief slabs, which were probably on the ceilings of tombs, at Tarquinia (Pallottino 1937: 202), and the herringbone carvings on the ceiling of tomb 1 at San Giuliano (Villa d'Amelio 1963: 8, fig. 5).

The central chamber of the Tomba dei Leoni Dipinti also contains two pillars, which, though not decorated, add to the architectural complexity of the tomb. Pillars, columns or pilasters are present in other Etruscan tombs from this early period, for example those in the so-called '*tholos* tombs' of Quinto Fiorentino: the Montagnola tomb (Caputo 1962: 128) where the pillar was covered with a clay layer, and the Tomba della Mula (Caputo 1962:

3.8 Carved roof, Banditaccia cemetery, Cerveteri (A. Yoes)

130), those at Casal Marittima (Minto 1930: 68), at Vetulonia in the Tomba delle Pietrera (Carresi 1985: 117), and finally, tomb 1 at San Giuliano, which contains Doric columns (Villa d'Amelio 1963: 7, fig. 4).

It is at roughly this period that one of the most remarked-upon features of Etruscan archaeology develops; tomb-painting (Naso 1996a). The early Orientalising tombs, such as the Tomba dei Leoni Dipinti, are the earliest testimony of this practice at Cerveteri, though slightly earlier examples come from the Tomba dell'Anatre and the Campana Tomb at Veii. In these early tombs, tomb-painting serves a similar function to the architectural detailing: it emphasises structural and architectural elements of the tomb. For example, decoration is concentrated in bands at the join between side wall and ceiling, or on the gables above the internal doors of the tomb. The repertoire of colour at this time is restricted to oranges, blacks and browns.

By the second half of the sixth century, in the Tomba dei Capitelli, the potential for the decoration of pillars and pilasters is realised: the tomb contains two fluted columns with detailed volute capitals, said to be reminiscent of Greek Aeolic capitals (Colonna 1986: 428). The same tomb has an alternating decoration of the ceiling, with the squares between the cross-beams of the roof carved with diagonal striations. As mentioned above, the elaboration of the doorways within the tombs is a feature of Etruscan funerary architecture from the earliest chamber tombs. The Montagnola tomb at Quinto Fiorentino has trilithic stone doorways from the entrance corridor to the chamber and side rooms (Caputo 1962: 121). The Tombe del Sodo I and II at Cortona have monolithic architraves (Neppi Modona 1925: 87); at Casal Marittima, Castellina in Chianti and Populonia, white stone slabs are used to pick out the doorway to the chamber (respectively, Minto 1930: 60; Pernier 1916: 269; Minto 1934b: 369, fig. 3; see above, Fig. 3.7). Later, the internal doors of the chambers are emphasised by decorative architectural cordon surrounds: a convex ridge that surrounds the door and extends out across the top to form a T shape (the so-called "Doric door"), and the raised thresholds mentioned earlier.

Slightly later than the Tomba dei Capitelli, the Tomba delle Colonne Doriche has the door cordons and also two pillars, again fluted but this time with Doric capitals. Windows in the internal walls of the tomb also receive attention, either with *lunette* decoration, or with a raised cordon like those around the doors. Similar cordons to internal doors and windows occur at Tuscania (Colonna 1967: 88, fig. 3) and Blera (Gargana 1932: 500, fig. 18).

A further feature of the internal decoration of tombs dating to before *c.* 525 BC is rock-carved furniture (Steingräber 1979). Prayon argues that the replication of furniture in stone stems from an earlier practice of taking domestic furniture into the tomb at burial (Colonna 1986: 420; Prayon 1986: 182). Early examples come from Populonia and Vetulonia in North Etruria, and from Tarquinia, San Giuliano and Blera in South Etruria (in Populonia: the Tomba dei Carri (Minto 1914c: 447), the Tomba dei Letti Funebri (Milani 1908: 204) and the Tomba dell'Aryballos (Fedeli 1983: 272–3); in Vetulonia: the Tomba delle Pietrera (Falchi 1891: 209, illustrated in Pincelli 1943: plate 7); in Tarquinia: Monterossi tumulus 13 (Pallottino 1937: 195); in San Giuliano: tomb 1 (Villa d'Amelio 1963: 6–12); and in Blera: tomb 13 (Gargana 1932: 496–8), the Tomba della Sfinge (Gargana 1932: 500–2), and the 'gabled house' tomb (Koch, von Mercklin and Weickert 1915: 234–8)). Beds for the dead were carved out of the rock, like the rest of the tomb. In Cerveteri, the gabled ends of the supposedly female beds are interpreted as being representative of the house. Male beds have very carefully carved legs, and semi-circular headrests.

The mid-sixth-century Tomba degli Scudi e delle Sedie (Fig. 3.2(f)) is famous for its intricately carved furniture. It has chairs and beds, and also small footrests by the chairs. Further tombs have a small table in front of the beds, and some contain chairs with moulded cushions and rows of dentil-like decoration under the seat; yet others are incised with decoration (Naso 1996: 345, fig. 251, from Castel Campanile). The contemporary Tomba della Cornice has slightly more elegant chairs with elaborately moulded curved backs and a large architectural cornice running around the walls of the central chamber, about 0.4 metres from the ceiling. A similar cornice in Tomb 236 is decorated with painting (Naso 1996, plate v.1; Pace *et al.* 1955: 712–23). These features are by no means unusual in mid-sixth-century tombs. It is obvious that Etruscans burying their dead at this time invested much in the interior decor of their tombs, in the decoration of the ceilings, windows, doors and furniture.

However, for Colonna, this period is the last in which strong links between the funerary and the domestic spheres are elaborated. The period after the sixth century sees the end of the similarity to domestic buildings at Cerveteri, though the domestic tradition in funerary architecture does still continue, however, in the rock-cut cemeteries of southern Etruria such as Norchia and Castel d'Asso. However, this time it is the outside, rather than the inside, of tombs that is said to reflect domestic architectural forms. The reluctance at Cerveteri to maintain the similarities and ambiguities between the funerary and domestic structures may be one element in the late sixth-century desire to define the funerary sphere more clearly. Through the creation of a distinctly non-domestic architectural language for tombs after the late sixth century, the funerary sphere was clearly distinguished architecturally from the domestic.

Coinciding with the changes in tomb shape discussed above, from the end of the sixth century heavy architectural mouldings began to be made on the outsides of tombs at Cerveteri (Fig. 3.3). These cornices were made up of series of heavy rectangular and convex mouldings, which were carved into the blocks that were used in the construction of the tomb. Other good examples come from Blera (Koch, von Mercklin and Weickert 1915: 247–51) and Orvieto (Fig. 3.6; Klakowicz 1972, 1974).

At Cerveteri, the painted decoration of the inside of tombs ceases around the end of the sixth century (Naso 1996a), with the notable fourth-century exception of the Tomba dei Rilievi (Blanck and Proietti 1986). This decline mirrors the decline in internal architectural elaboration. In some sites, however, this longstanding tradition of tomb-painting continued into the fifth century and beyond, most notably at Tarquinia (though also at Chiusi, Orvieto and Vulci). Although such painting would appear to run counter to the argument that internal elaboration decreased from about the end of the sixth century, in Tarquinia these painted tombs form only an estimated 2 per cent of the total number of tombs (Cristofani 1978: 90; d'Agostino 1983: 2; Weber-Lehmann 1986: 44), and this percentage would be significantly lower at Chiusi, Orvieto and Vulci. Thus, although these paintings are an aspect of Etruscan material culture that is particularly well known, numerically they are rather insignificant. The elite connotations and concerns of

3.9 Inscribed door lintel, Crocifisso del Tufo cemetery, Orvieto

these paintings are generally accepted, though the precise interpretations of these scenes are a matter of some debate, ranging from depictions of life, the afterlife, funerary ritual and elite display (Barker and Rasmussen 1998; Cerchiai 1987; d'Agostino 1989; Spivey 1997; Szilágyi 1981; Walberg 1988). One interpretation that has received corroboration from recent excavations at the cemetery of Pian della Conserva (in the Tolfa mountains) is that the tomb-paintings represent the inside of tents that were erected as part of the burial process. This interpretation, based on the fabric-like, chequered decoration on the ceilings of tombs, and on the explicit pictorial reference to tents in tombs like the Tomba dell Cacciatore (Ross Holloway 1965: 344; Pallottino 1937: 264; 1952: 44; Stopponi 1968), was dismissed by some scholars in favour of the argument that tomb-paintings reflected house structure (Weber-Lehmann 1986: 44). However, the discovery of a set of post holes in front of the entrance of a small sixth-century burial mound from Pian della Conserva suggests that a tent-like temporary structure was erected outside the tombs (Spivey 1997a: 108). If this is the case, the tomb-paintings can be interpreted as depictions of parts of the funerary ritual, such as feasting or athletic competition, and, in some cases, of the 'realia' of funerals (such as wreaths hanging from hooks on the tent poles), behind which we see the landscape in which the funeral was set. According to this interpretation, the false doors painted on to the back walls of the chambers are representations of the entrance to the tomb, as seen from the funerary tent.

In terms of the argument of this chapter, this decoration on the inside of the tomb comes at the very end of the period of emphasis on the inside of tomb scenes, and continues, in this limited number of graves, into the period when elsewhere attention shifts to the outside. This may be a case of particularly conservative retention of established practice by a restricted elite. However, it is ironic that at a time when emphasis is generally focused on the tomb's exterior, the painters and commissioners of these painted tombs chose to represent the outside of the tomb, and the rituals associated with it, in their paintings on the inside of the tomb.

Furthermore, the ways in which painting is deployed in the fifth-century tombs is different from their earlier predecessors: the painting is arranged in large friezes along the side and back walls of the tombs, opening up the imaginary space of the individual wall or room. Often, a certain subject is ascribed to a painted tomb (evident in the names given to the tombs: the Tomba dell Triclinio, etc.), and this is testimony to the potential for narrative content in these tombs, in contrast to the architectural painting or generic animal scenes of the Orientalising tombs. In the same way that the layout of the tomb encourages the division of the interior space of the tomb, the tomb-painting serves a similar function in setting up a 'scene' that the viewer must stop and view, and a narrative that is specific for that individual space. This is particularly true of the late paintings of the François tomb at Vulci, where the narrative of the painting extends around the entire central chamber, establishing the chamber as the focus of the tomb in the same way as the layout of the tomb (Buranelli (ed.) 1987).

A further element of the external elaboration of the tombs in Cerveteri was the use of writing. Though they are rare, some Orientalising tombs contained inscriptions, either painted or inscribed (for instance in the Tomba dei Leoni Dipinti at Cerveteri or the Tomba del Sodo II at Cortona; respectively Naso 1996a; Neppi Modona 1925). By the fifth century in Cerveteri, onomastic inscriptions were often placed above the entrances to these tombs and played a similar part in visually emphasising the exterior of the tomb (Fig. 3.6).

Inscriptions are more popular on non-Caeretan tombs, for instance those at Vulci (Buranelli 1987: 144), Sovana (Rosi 1927: 63), Norchia, San Giuliano, Castel d'Asso, Blera (all in Rosi 1927: 64) and Orvieto (Bizzari 1962: 136–51). The use of writing, a consummately superficial form, reinforces the importance of the external surface as a means of marking the boundary of the tomb.

From the late fifth century onwards, external cornices became ubiquitous. The façades of all the cube tombs at Castel d'Asso have this decorative architectural feature, and it has already been noted that Castel d'Asso is one of the sites where false doors are present (Fig. 3.4). The same occurs at Norchia (Colonna di Paolo and Colonna 1978), Blera (Koch, von Mercklin and Weickert 1915: 238–42) and Tuscania (Sgubini Moretti 1991: 18, figs. 15 and 16). Instead of depictions of doors appearing on the inside of tombs, either painted or as cordons around internal doorways, they are now found exclusively on the exterior. The same cordons from around the 'real' doors inside the earlier chamber tombs, such as in the Tomba dei Capitelli, are deployed here, not to mark a doorway, but to hint at a doorway that is not there. Sometimes these false doors are very detailed, and it is possible to see mouldings that echo the panelling of wooden doors (for example, Fig. 3.4, third tomb from the left).

Perhaps the most impressive of these façades are at Norchia (Rosi 1925: 42–7; Colonna di Paolo and Colonna 1978: plates xii and xiii). The two late so-called 'temple tombs' from the site have the same internal arrangement as contemporary tombs from Castel d'Asso, that is with the chamber below the façade, entered from in front of the tomb through a negative entrance corridor. Outside they are modelled on Greek temple architecture, with a triangular pediment supported by a row of columns. The façades are elaborately carved with a Tuscan-Doric frieze, which contained human heads in relief on the metopes between the triglyphs, a cornice, and winged animal acroteria. The façade of the western tomb had a figured relief representing a number of human figures in mantles (Rosi 1925: 42–4). The exterior form of these tombs is not unique, however, and similarly impressive façades are found at Sovana, such as the colonnaded portico of the Tomba Ildebranda at Sovana. The capitals of the fluted columns here had alternating male and female sculpted heads and floral decoration. Above the colonnade were several cornices and friezes with griffins and vegetal elements in relief (Bianchi Bandinelli 1929: 77–86). The Grotta Pola at the same site had a similarly elaborate façade (Bianchi Bandinelli 1929: 74–6).

While all this elaborate decoration and concentration on the exterior of the tombs were taking place, the reverse process was happening to the interiors. The internal layout of the later tombs is unstructured and roughly hewn from the rock. There is no architectural decoration whatever, and the walls are often irregularly hewn. The absence of internal decoration and complexity is noted by Bianchi Bandinelli with reference to the Tomba Ildebranda: 'la camera sepolchrale, la quale, nella sua mancanza di decorazione e anche rozzezza di esecuzione contrasta singolarmente con la magnificenza dell'edificio superiore' (Bianchi Bandinelli 1929: 82). The same is true of the tomb of Larthia Seianti at Chiusi (Bianchi Bandinelli 1925a: 305–8), the Grotta della Regina at Tuscania (Sgubini Moretti 1991), the Curunas complex at Tuscania (apart from the very rudimentary ridge-pole and rafters; Moretti and Sgubini Moretti (eds.) 1983: 15–18 for tomb 1; 83–6 for tomb 2; 153 for tomb 3), and the tombs from Norchia and Castel d'Asso. In these unelaborated tombs of the rock-cut cemeteries, corpses were placed in narrow channels dug into the rock on either side of a central passage. The creative investment in funerary architecture has now shifted completely to the exterior surface. The same is true of Cerveteri, though not to such an extreme. Here late tombs are simple, roughly hewn chambers, with an unadorned and often poorly executed roof-ridge as the only vestige of the former internal architectural complexity.

The contrast between the inside and outside of these later monuments is the end point of a process that began in the late sixth century. After the internal architectural elaboration of tombs in the preceding 200 years or so, the last quarter of the sixth century saw a shift in this concentration of decoration to the exterior of the tomb. Given the importance of material elaboration and decoration in the preservation and marking of boundaries, discussed in Chapter 1 above, this concentration on the exterior accords with the findings of the analysis of tomb structure and the entrance corridors earlier in this chapter: the physical articulation of the boundary between the living and the dead, or between the inside and outside of the tomb, marked a corresponding shift in the Etruscan conceptions of these areas. From the late sixth century, the difference between the two was expressed in the outer surface of the tomb.

Cemetery organisation

It was not only in the tomb itself that the difference between the living and the dead was clearly articulated; the process extended to the whole cemetery, and to its spatial organisation, both internally and as a discrete unit. Here, the important factor is the relationship between the different tombs in the

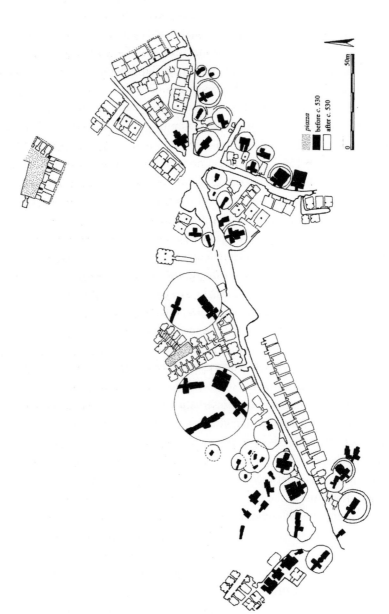

3.10 Phased plan of the Banditaccia cemetery, Cerveteri (adapted from Prayon 1975, fig. 2)

piazza

before c. 530

after c. 530

0   50m

cemetery, and the integration of the tomb within the cemetery itself; in other words, the arrangement of the ritual spaces of the tombs in relation to each other.

To take the example of Cerveteri again, the adapted phased plan (Fig. 3.10) of the Banditaccia cemetery shows the changing attitudes to cemetery organisation over time. Here the shaded tombs are those that date from before 530 BC, while the unshaded ones are from after this date. The diagram shows that over this period a dramatic change took place in the way that the necropolis was organised. The earlier tombs in the monumental mounds are placed with no discernible organisational relationship to each other or to the principal roads running through the cemetery. This is not to say that they were arranged at random: Prayon insists, instead, that they were oriented according to religious doctrine, with their entrances towards the north-west, the part of the sky corresponding to the underworld (Prayon 1975: 85–7; see also Colonna 1986: 367).

After *c.* 530 BC, instead of being aligned according to the relevant part of the sky, the tombs are arranged in rows in direct relation to the roads, with their entrances towards these 'Vie Sepolcrali'. Colonna explains this as the result of the 'inseribilità' of the new modular units as a solution to the problem of lack of space in the cemetery (Colonna 1986: 447; Prayon 1986: 185, 187). Although space may have been a consideration, it is unlikely to have been the only factor at work. As discussed above in this chapter, and in Chapter 1, such a technological explanation needs further elaboration: it would be possible to devise other means of accommodating more depositions (for instance by smaller mounds, taller monuments or the practice of cremation), so the choice of the cube tomb in particular needs further explanation.

In the new organisation of the cemetery, tombs were placed in direct relation to each other, and according to the 'Vie Sepolcrali', rather than according to a part of the sky. In this way, the rows of tombs form a collective façade, with all their entrances on the road. This makes all the entrances to the tombs visible from a single standpoint (Fig. 3.3). The collective nature of the façades is evident in the similarity between the tombs, for example in their doors, which are replicated along the entire row. More dramatically, a thick, moulded cornice runs across the top of the all the tombs in the row, unifying them. Although they have individual entrances, the block of tombs is presented with one, unifying, flat façade. The principal road ran straight through the cemetery site and this was the main way into the settlement. As a result, these rows of tombs would have been seen by visitors and the inhabitants of the town whenever they entered or left the settlement.

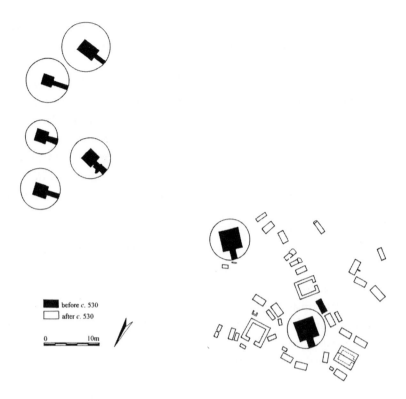

3.11 Phased plan of the San Cerbone cemetery, Populonia (adapted from Fedeli 1983: 122, fig. 61)

Cerveteri is by no means unique with regard to this sudden consciousness of and attention to cemetery layout, though it is one of the few settlements where a long enough sequence exists to show the transition from the seventh century to the fourth. Another example is Populonia, where the San Cerbone necropolis shows a similar realignment of tombs in the late sixth century. In the phased plan in Fig. 3.11 (the dating of the tombs for this diagram is from Fedeli 1983: 222–8; De Agostino 1958: 31), the earlier tombs (shaded) are oriented cardinally, to the north-west. These tombs relate to each other not in their layout, but rather according to the orientation of ritual requirements. The later tombs (unshaded), in contrast, are arranged in rows, approximately parallel or perpendicular to each other, forming a line of monuments. This unidirectionality is emphasised visually by the location of the entrances of the three aedicule tombs in the area, which accord with the rows of tombs.

The Crocifisso del Tufo and Cannicella cemeteries at Orvieto (Fig. 3.12), and, to a certain extent, the East cemetery at Marzabotto (below, Fig. 6.8), show the refinement of this tendency. In the Orvietan cemeteries, the tombs are similar to the contemporary examples from Cerveteri in that their heavy cornices form unified façades, and their doorways are flush with the outer surface of the tomb (Figs. 3.3 and 3.9). In their layout, the tombs are arranged along strictly orthogonal lines, on cemetery streets (Fig. 3.12). These large, imposing blocks of tombs serve to concentrate and thus to emphasise the distinction between inside and outside the tomb, and this is taken yet further by the placement of the blocks along straight streets. Rather than as a response to decreased cemetery space in the form of the greater 'inseribilità' of these tombs (Colonna 1986: 447), this should be seen as part of the changing material expression of the distinction between the living and the dead in the late sixth century.

Open spaces, or 'piazzette', are also incorporated into the cemetery. Such spaces are shown stippled in Figs. 3.10 and 3.12. Not only does this suggest that space was not at such a premium, but it is also indicative of a decision to leave some space in the cemetery 'unbuilt'. At both Cerveteri and Orvieto, some cube tombs are arranged around a space that is not a street: these tombs open out on to a common area, and their orientation is according to this specific space, rather than to any region of the sky. By being built upon or left empty, different types of space are thus created within the cemetery. In Orvieto, the creation of distinct physical spaces within the cemetery is emphasised by the step up from the street to the piazza (Fig. 3.12).

The allocation of space for tombs and space for piazzette is an indication of the need to order and structure cemetery space in two ways. First, it echoes and reinforces the distinctions between the living and the dead that were articulated in the tomb architecture: second, it gives the cemetery a distinct and characteristic form, which the earlier cemeteries lacked. In this latter way, it helps define the cemetery as a distinct and separate space from that around it, especially the city of the living. This has been described elsewhere as a 'sacred halo' around the city (Riva and Stoddart 1996).

Conclusion

This analysis has examined the changes in funerary architecture in order to demonstrate the importance of the surface of the tomb in marking its boundary from about 530 BC onwards. The decreased length of the entrance corridor brings the expression of the difference between inside and outside to the front of the tomb. This is possible because the mediative distance of the entrance corridor is incorporated into the externally visible surface of the tomb. The boundary becomes the façade and the façade becomes the

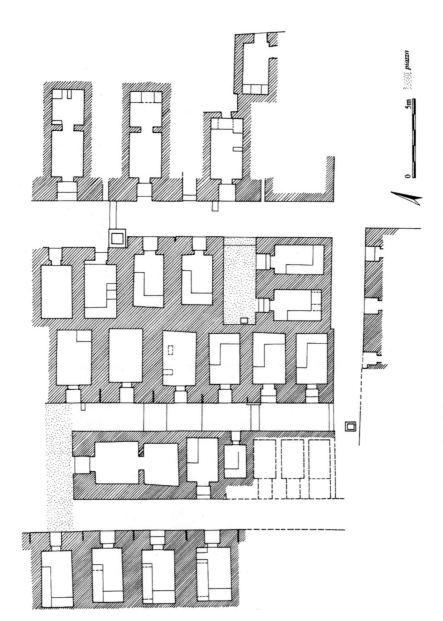

3.12 The Crocifisso del Tufo cemetery, Orvieto (adapted from Bizzari 1962: plate 1)

boundary. In the late, negative chamber tombs, this is taken to an extreme, with the expression of difference being condensed to a dysfunctional, impenetrable façade with a false door. The ontological difference between the inside and the outside of the tombs is expressed through a façade that is impossible to traverse: the façade is pure representation.

Parallel changes take place in the configuration of the internal structure of the tomb. Here, the focus of the tomb shifts to the centre, closer to the outside, shortening the total length of the tomb. In addition, the later tombs have a structure in which the entrant is immediately placed in the ritual centre of the tomb. In the decoration and architectural elaboration of the tomb, the importance of the surface becomes paramount, in this case on the outside of the tomb. Similarly, the arrangement of tombs within the cemetery places emphasis on the front of the tomb as the point at which the world of the dead begins.

Tombs represent and embody cultural meanings, like any material culture. The funerary material culture that survives for our examination is a collection of objects and spaces deliberately selected to indicate the ways in which the Etruscans wanted to be represented in death and, by the implication of mortuary theory, in life. Here too, the process is one of the creation of representations and self-images, but in this instance it is the image not only of the deceased but of the tomb that is created. The living and the dead meet at dangerous boundaries, and it is through an examination of these boundaries that the anxieties surrounding the differences between such areas can be examined.

Funerary architecture formed part of the material expression of changes in Etruscan attitudes and anxieties towards the definition of the living and the dead towards the end of the sixth century: the analysis of the articulation of ritual space over time in this chapter has traced the transformation of these anxieties. As has been argued, the outer surface of tombs and cemeteries became crucial in articulating the desire to express the difference between the living and the dead in an ever more visually striking manner.

4 | Sanctuaries: the sacred and the profane

Introduction

The previous chapter developed an account of Etruscan funerary architecture that demonstrated the importance of creating discrete and readily visible boundaries for the dead. In this chapter, a similar argument will be proposed for the physical and architectural setting of formal ritual practice. In the earlier period of Etruscan history, the locations of religious activity are difficult to perceive archaeologically; however, by the late sixth century it is possible to discern formal sanctuary complexes with architecturally discrete temples. This chapter examines this change in the treatment of ritual space by focusing on two aspects: first, the form and decoration of the temple; and second, the form of sanctuary complex. The stress here is on the planning and construction of temple architecture, with all the choices involved in how this should be accomplished. At every stage, alternatives (both well-established and innovatory) were available and decisions were made on how to move on to the next stage of the construction; every element in temple architecture was made deliberately, and the methods of construction were intentionally selected. As discussed in Chapter 1 this active process of selection applies to all material culture, and all aspects of the Etruscan ritual environment, from the location of the temple in the landscape to the details of the decoration of the gutter tiles. The manner in which objects or buildings are made, decorated or located is never arbitrary; they exist because they have meaning, and they occur in the form that they do because those forms have meanings.

Previous studies have concentrated on temples and sanctuaries as complete phenomena, in order to explain their emergence in the late sixth century. The artefacts from votive deposits, the sculpted terracotta decoration of the temples and the architectural form of the temples have all been a great source of evidence for Etruscologists. The examination of such objects has led to studies that have concentrated on object types (for example Haynes 1985 for bronzes), or have attempted to discern the work of specific hands or workshops. Brendel's 'school of Vulca' for acroterial sculpture has already been noted in Chapter 1 (Brendel 1978: 237–8); Cristofani's description of the distribution of elements of architectural detail in his discussion of the workshops of southern Etruria and Latium has a similar intention (Cristofani 1987b).

Others have concentrated on the more socio-political aspects of sanctuary data. Torelli's work on Gravisca (Torelli 1977, 1997) demonstrates the way in which sanctuaries were points of interaction between Etruscan and other cultures. Although the exclusively Greek nature of this sanctuary has been challenged, it cannot be denied that exchange – cultural, religious and material – was facilitated by sanctuaries (Cristofani 1996b; Serra Ridgway 1990; Spivey and Stoddart 1990: 123–5). Torelli has also examined sanctuaries and their development within the context of changes in Etruscan social structure. He argues that the growth of sanctuaries was stimulated by an attempt on the part of 'tyrants' to wrestle control of ritual from the hands of old aristocracies. The dedicatory plaques at Pyrgi, which tell of the foundation of the sanctuary by one such tyrant, Thefarie Velianas of Cerveteri, are used to document this interpretation (Torelli 1983; 1990: 181; see also Colonna 1985: 134; Cornell 1995a: 147; Pallottino (ed.) 1964). These ideas have been echoed by Pairault-Massa in her work on Etruscan iconography (Pairault-Massa 1992: 60–75).

The development of sanctuaries has also been drawn into debate over the emergence of urbanism in Etruria. Colonna in particular has stressed the importance of urban sanctuaries in the emerging urban entities of the late sixth and fifth centuries (Colonna 1986: 433). More recently, the work of Rendeli and Zifferero has contributed to this debate. For the first, sanctuaries were a point of competition between the emerging Etruscan centres. Drawing on the theory of peer-polity interaction, Rendeli shows, in a diachronic survey of the dimensions of temples from South Etruria and Latium, that temple size was indeed an important element in the competition between, and identity of, the newly formed Etruscan cities (Rendeli 1990; Renfrew and Cherry (eds.) 1986; Snodgrass 1986). Zifferero concentrates not on the size of temples, but on their location, in order to show a similar process. Following de Polignac for Magna Graecia, he demonstrates that the location of sanctuaries on the limits of these new urban units defined and fixed those limits (de Polignac 1995; Zifferero 1995; see also Nardi 1989). The analysis is extended to include sanctuaries as territorial markers (Molinos and Zifferero 1998; Zifferero 1995, 2002; see also Rendeli 1993: 357–60). In a similar way, the new sanctuaries are viewed as points of Etruscan interaction and exchange with Greece and Phoenicia (Cornell 1995a: 108–12; Cristofani 1983: 119–22; Spivey and Stoddart 1990: 123–5).

The interpretative approaches discussed above generally share two characteristics. The first is that they are all, in some way, concerned with marking difference, be it between socio-political systems, between individual cities, or between different territories. The second is a lack of interest in what the temples looked like. Concern with how big a temple was, or where it was located, overrides the specific details of the construction of the temples. Accordingly, the links between these details and the meanings that they carry are not explored; the appearance of a temple is taken so much for granted that it seldom raises comment.

The appearance of the temple is precisely the starting point of the analysis in this chapter. The specifics of the temple's physical form and its decoration will be seen as deeply implicated in the creation and transference of messages about the distinctness of ritual sites. Such elements are usually the domain of the architectural or art historian, but here they will be integrated into a cultural understanding of Etruscan sanctuaries. Though this has been attempted before (Pairault Massa 1992; Spivey 1997), the means by which the physical form of the temple and its decoration embody the cultural boundaries of the divine sphere have not been confronted satisfactorily. Any account that fails to do this denies itself the capacity of explaining fully the appearance of sanctuaries.

Various attempts to explain the emergence of sanctuaries have been discussed above, and their limitations, in terms of ignoring the connection between the choice of form and meaning, have been outlined. The importance of form and the details of sanctuary construction are important because, like all material culture, they are never arbitrary; instead, they are the result of complex series of culturally and socially informed choices about materials, techniques, scale, form, etc. Rather than denying the results of the preceding analyses, this chapter will continue to work with their conclusions that sanctuaries were instrumental in the expression of difference. The emphasis, however, will be on the details of architecture and decoration as a means expressing difference. In other words, it will examine why certain choices were made in the construction of Etruscan ritual architecture, rather than taking the 'sanctuary' or 'temple' as a physical given. A further difference from previous approaches is in the emphasis on other categories of difference that are at stake in the sanctuary, such as inside and outside the sanctuary or temple, or the religious and non-religious. It is precisely because of the elision of these differences that the efficacy of the temple in negotiating them is so great.

There are, of course, several problems inherent in the material that we have in trying to tackle this problem. The first is that not many temples and sanctuaries actually survive. If the numbers from Cerveteri are anything to go by, we have a very small sample of the original whole. For this site, it has been suggested that eight sanctuaries existed in the urban area (Mengarelli 1935, though see Nardi 1989); and of those, only two have been investigated and published. These are the supposed Temple of Hera at the Vigna Parrocchiale and the small Manganello sanctuary (Mengarelli 1935, 1936); a third is currently under excavation at Sant'Antonio (Izzet 1999–2000, 2000; Maggiani and Rizzo 2005). A similar picture emerges at Orvieto, where only two of the nine temples noted have been excavated (Colonna (ed.) 1985: 81). Accordingly, since we have very few examples from which to extrapolate wider trends, questions of the representativeness of our sample must always be borne in mind. The sample size could be increased by the inclusion of sites from Latium (as in, for instance, Cornell 1995: 108–12; Rendeli 1990; Smith 1996; Torelli 1990: 165–70), but this would incorporate sites from a different cultural milieu, thus adding to the difficulties of assessing representativeness. In addition to a small sample size, the few examples that do survive span several centuries, from the sixth-century Piazza d'Armi at Veii to the fourth-century Ara della Regina at Tarquinia (Stefani 1944: 228–90; Romanelli 1948: 238–70). The dating of the sanctuaries is based on the chronologies of the objects found as votives: local and imported ceramics and local bronzes.

The second problem inherent in the material lies in the nature, rather than the quantity of the evidence. Etruscan temples often went through several changes and renovations, so that, for instance, the Belvedere Temple at Orvieto has at least two sets of architectural terracottas associated with it (Andrén 1940: 169; Colonna 1985d: 82; Riis 1941: 100–1), as does Temple B at Pyrgi (Colonna (ed.) 1970: 402–5). This is a particular problem for temples excavated early in the twentieth century, before systematic excavation practices were adopted on Etruscan sites. There are, in fact, few sites that have been excavated recently, giving us very little information derived from modern techniques, such as stratigraphic or palaeo-botanical data. (Notable exceptions to this are Pyrgi (Colonna (ed.) 1988–9: 131–8, 233–4), Punta della Vipera (Torelli 1967) and the ongoing investigations at Sant'Antonio at Cerveteri (Izzet 1999–2000, 2000).) Furthermore, there is a bias in the data in favour of large urban and coastal sites, as opposed to the small rural sanctuaries, the potential for which has been hinted at in Etruria by Zifferero, and demonstrated for Magna Graecia in the *chora* of Metaponto (Zifferero 2002b and Carter 1994 respectively). Finally, though it is easy to talk of an 'Etruscan temple', no two surviving examples are the same, and none fits Vitruvius' description of 'Tuscan' temple exactly. For example, the Belvedere

Temple at Orvieto, though close to the Vitruvian model, is wider at the back than at the front, so that the columns are not aligned with the cella walls as prescribed (Pernier and Stefani 1925: 159).

Such gaps in the available evidence should not prevent us, however, from attempting to understand the surviving material, and in particular from questioning why that material took the form that it did. In this chapter, two main aspects of Etruscan ritual space will be examined. The first is the emergence of a recognisable sanctuary space; the second is the development of specifically temple architecture. In both, the importance of physically marking the cultural difference between sacred and profane, and the importance of surface in marking this distinction, will be shown to have been the most important factor affecting temple or sanctuary form.

The creation of sanctuaries

It is generally accepted that the great period in the foundation of Etruscan sanctuaries was the late sixth century. It is then that sanctuaries were first built, and they quickly developed a standardised architectural form. Before the late sixth century, ritual had taken place in sites dictated by the landscape. These can be categorised according to physical geography such as lakes, caves or mountain-tops, and they are identified by votive deposits (for the best summary of such sites see Edlund 1987b). A famous example of the first type is the Lago degli Idoli at Monte Falterona, about 30 kilometres east of Florence, near the spring of the Arno (Colonna 1960: 589–90; Dennis 1883: 107–11; Edlund 1987a; 1987b: 56–7; Fortuna and Giovannoni 1975). The site is now destroyed, but has yielded one of the richest collections of votive offerings in Etruria. This included several bronze figurines (Brendel 1978: 225–6, fig. 152; Richardson 1983: for example 292–3, plate 204, fig. 692; Riis 1941: 135), as well as anatomical terracottas, coinage, weapons and plentiful *aes rude*. The site could have been the centre of a healing cult, indicated by the presence not only of the anatomical votives, but also of reproductions of suffering and disease – one figure, for instance, has a wounded chest (Dennis 1883: 108). The total number of objects exceeded 600, indicating the considerable popularity of the sanctuary that lasted from the sixth until the fourth century. However, despite this evident popularity, both in terms of the numbers of votives and the time span of the site, there was no architectural structure associated with the cult.

Monte Soracte is possibly the most famous mountain-top ritual site in Etruria, due no doubt in part to Horace's evocation (Edlund 1987b: 46–9;

Horace *Odes* 1, 9). Other literary sources tell us about a cult of the *Hirpi* on the mountain (Pliny the Elder, *NH* 7.19), and poisonous gases and fumes emanating from the site. This is corroborated by archaeological survey, which has noted sulphur fissures on the mountainside (G. D. B. Jones 1963: 126). Pottery finds indicate usage of the site from the Neolithic onwards (Edlund 1987b: 49). Although there seems to be evidence of cultic activity on the site since pre-Etruscan times, there is no evidence of any sort of archaic temple or sanctuary building whatsoever.

Both these examples serve to show the existence of cultic practice in the landscape of central Italy from the Neolithic period onwards. The locations for these activities were dictated by features in the natural landscape: hills, springs, lakes and caves. Religious ceremonies and worship did not need a man-made environment in which to take place. This changed dramatically in the second half of the sixth century, when we see the construction of buildings specifically for cult practice. For the first time in Central Italy, sanctuaries, the specially built locations for ritual practice, emerge and, along with them, codified temple architecture.

This is not to discount completely the possibility that earlier buildings were used for religious purposes. Sanctuaries and temples may have precedents from before the sixth century. It has been argued, for instance, that the seventh-century building #alpha at Roselle served a religious function (Bocci Pacini 1975: 21–33; Colonna (ed.) 1985: 53–6). A similar building has emerged at Tarquinia, where ritual action, including burial, has been demonstrated within a building on the settlement plateau (Bonghi Jovino 1986b, 1986c; Bonghi Jovino and Chiaramonte Treré (eds.) 1986; 1997: 164–94). Perhaps the most convincing suggestion for an early sanctuary is the 'palace' at Murlo. This monumental complex, with its perpetually ambiguous status and function, is often seen as a precursor to the building of sanctuaries in Etruria (Colonna (ed.) 1985: 53; Colonna 1986: 423–4; Prayon 1986: 195; Stopponi (ed.) 1985: 64–154). This suggestion is particularly convincing, given the unequal tripartite division of the building at the end of the 60 metre by 60 metre courtyard, foreshadowing that of the chambers of the Etruscan temple. However, even in this instance the classification of sanctuary does not fit easily. The presence of quotidian paraphernalia, specifically dining equipment (Rathje 1994: 98; Spivey and Stoddart 1990: 73), and the excavator's arguments for a political meeting place of the putative Etruscan League (Phillips 1993: 80–1), as well as those for the domestic residence of a powerful leader (Spivey and Stoddart 1990: 73; Torelli 1983; 1990: 174–81), add to the uncertainty in assigning the complex an exclusively ritual function. Most commentators attempt to pin down the complex's function; in fact, the confusion of modern scholars and the continued debate over the function of the complex may not be accidental, but, rather, may be indicative of ancient ambiguity towards the building's function. Similar ambiguity is evident in discussions of the later so-called '*oikos*' at Piazza d'Armi at Veii, where the identification of the structure as ritual or domestic is difficult to do with certainty (Melis 1985; Stefani 1944–5), and in Damgaard Andersen's discussion of several building types (Damgaard Andersen 1993: 81).

Despite the possible religious or ritualistic function of these buildings, it would be difficult to classify them as temples or sanctuaries in the same sense as the complexes from the late sixth century and beyond. The later complexes share a codified and uniform style of religious architecture in the form of the temple, an outside altar or podium for sacrifices, a boundary wall that surrounds the sanctuary, and the presence of votive deposits (Colonna (ed.) 1985: 23–7). These typical features of Etruscan sanctuaries emerge in the second half of the sixth century from the cultic ambiguity of the preceding centuries. Of course, many of the early 'landscape' shrines and cult locations continue in use after the sixth century (particularly in North Etruria, such as Monte Falterona itself). However, what is significant for this analysis is that they continue alongside the new forms of ritual space: the codified sanctuary. New cult locations are established according to this model rather than the earlier one, and, importantly, the new model incorporates a stronger sense of communal activity in ritual practice.

Thus the appearance alone in the material record of such distinctive features in the late sixth century is significant. After the ambiguity of the earlier buildings, where ritual was one of many activities that took place in a given location, the sudden appearance of a recognisable architectural form in which ritual was housed must be a deliberate attempt to fix ritual spatially. It is important to stress that the mere development of a distinct and archaeologically recognisable architectural language for religious buildings is one of the most significant expressions of the importance of demarcating the ritual sphere; the expression in durable material form is an acknowledgement of the anticipated longevity of the sanctuary. The ways in which the decorative and formal aspects of the temple were bound up in expressing this are discussed below.

Along with the development of specific architecture for the temple, the sacred area of the sanctuary was codified. In many cases this involved the construction of monumental boundary walls, such as those at Veii, Gravisca, Punta della Vipera, Pyrgi and the Belvedere sanctuary at Orvieto (Colonna (ed.) 1970; 1988–9; Colonna 1985d: 80–3; 1985f: 100; Prayon 1986: 197; Spivey and Stoddart 1990: 124; Torelli 1967). In addition, the entrances to the sanctuaries were marked with elaborate gateways. The boundary wall marked the difference between the sacred and profane categorically for the first time. Whatever means were used in order to signal the commencement of ritual activity in the earlier structures – and these may have included cycles of time, the wearing of special clothes, the presence (or absence) of certain individuals or the order in which participants entered and participated – these markers of ritual were ephemeral (Whitelaw 1994). Once complete, and once other kinds of activity were taking place, the only acknowledgement of ritual activity would have been in the memories of the participants. This is not to understate the importance of communal memory in such instances; however, the decision to mark such transitions physically is an important change in how ritual was signalled and conceptualised: that is, as a distinct and enduring spatial category.

The sanctuary space was also defined as different from its surroundings, with regard to what it contained. In addition to the temple, the sanctuary included altars, votive deposits and other sacred buildings. Thus not only temple architecture but also the sanctuary more broadly became codified at this point. The altars were often significant structures, such as those at Marzabotto, Punta della Vipera and the Portonaccio sanctuary at Veii (Brizzolara *et al.* (eds.)) 1980: 105–6; Colonna 1985f: 100; Mansuelli 1972: 130; Stefani 1953; Torelli 1967; see also Steingräber 1982). One of the famous Campana plaques in the Louvre shows such an altar in use (Prayon 1986: 198). Offerings that were not burned on the altars at a sanctuary were left at the site, and, either initially or later, were deposited in votive pits. The catalogues of finds from such deposits, such as the well at Pyrgi or the pit from the Ara della Regina temple at Tarquinia, show the diversity and wealth of objects dedicated to Etruscan divinities. Associated with these cultic features were others, whose function is less clear. From the finds at Pyrgi, with specific reference to the dedications to Astarte at the site, Spivey proposes sacred prostitution; Porticoes G and H (later than the temple itself) at the Portonaccio sanctuary have been identified as treasuries or accommodation for sanctuary staff (Colonna 1985f, 1987; Spivey and Stoddart 1990: 125). The sanctuary at Gravisca had one area, area δ, paved with stone slabs, creating a distinct open space within the sanctuary (Boitani 1985a). Several sanctuaries contained more than one temple, most notably Pyrgi, Marzabotto and the recently excavated sanctuary at Sant'Antonio at Cerveteri (Colonna 1985d: 89; Cristofani 1997; Mansuelli 1972; Spivey and Stoddart 1990: 124). These were built parallel to each other. The collocation, or grouping, of temples is a further element in indicating the growing awareness of ritual as a distinct category of activity: the temples, like the tombs discussed in the last chapter, were laid out in strict relation to each other, giving a spatial unity to the sanctuary. By the late sixth century it was necessary to build for ritual activity a visually, physically and ontologically bounded space. These delineated sacred spaces, both urban and rural, would have stood out in sharp contrast to their surroundings, and this would have been particularly impressive to visitors to the sanctuary from its rural hinterland.

Temple form

So far the emergence of sanctuaries as clearly identifiable, distinctly ritual spaces has been discussed. In what follows, the architectural details of the temple itself will be explored, in order to examine the ways in which the expression of difference is implicated in the building. It will be shown that all elements of Etruscan temple architecture were drawn into the rhetoric of difference. In order to trace this negotiation, it will perhaps be useful, as for funerary architecture, to think in terms of two distinct but interrelated aspects of the temple: decoration and plan.

Architectural decoration

When considering decoration, it is important to distinguish between the subject and content of the decoration, the manner in which it is executed, and its location within the temple's decorative scheme. The Etruscan temple was encrusted with decoration, from the bottom up. As discussed in Chapter 1, when separate categories of any sort are under stress in some way, there is an accompanying cultural emphasis on the points of interaction between those categories. In other words, there seems to be a reinforcing of those threatened categories. In material culture, the reaction to stress takes the form of elaborated boundaries. The physical points of interaction between different types of spaces are given physical emphasis, through monumental-isation or decoration, for example. Differences are emphasised and drawn sharply in order to preserve their integrity.

The base

Etruscan temples were placed on discrete bases (Fig. 4.1). Like the Greek temple, the 'house of the god' was separated clearly from the ground on which it stood. However, unlike the straight steps of the Greek stylobate and stereobate, the Etruscan temple sat on a base that was moulded and carefully

4.1 Belvedere Temple, Orvieto

shaped with convex and concave curves, points and angles. The alternating convex, concave and 'hawk's beak' mouldings were carved in series into the blocks, which fitted together almost seamlessly. Within Etruria itself, the moulded bases of only two temples survive (though it would be possible to cite others from Latium (for instance at the sanctuary of Sant'Omobono; see Cristofani (ed.) 1990: 115–30; Ioppolo 1989; Ross Holloway 1994: 68–80, esp. 75); some continue to see structures B and D at Marzabotto as temples (for example Barker and Rasmussen 1998: 221, caption to fig. 79), though they are generally thought to be altars (Brizzolara *et al.* (eds.)) 1980: 105–6; Colonna 1985d: 89; 1986: 473; Mansuelli 1972: 130). The moulded temple bases from Etruria come from the Belvedere sanctuary at Orvieto, and the fourth-century phase of the Ara della Regina at Tarquinia. In the first, only the moulded blocks, which were not found *in situ*, survive (Minto 1934a: 78); in the second, the base is made up of rectilinear steps, surmounted by one large and one narrow curved stone 'cushion' (Fig. 4.2(c); Romanelli 1948: 242–8). A better idea of the bases may be gained from the surviving altars in Etruria, such as those at Pieve a Socana, Punta della Vipera, Vignanello and Marzabotto, where the alternating bands are particularly elaborate (Fig. 4.2(a) and (b); Brizzolara *et al.* (eds.) 1980: 105–6; Brizio 1891; Colonna (ed.) 1985: 24, 164–7; Mansuelli 1972; Torelli 1967: 332). Both sets of bases are resonant of statue bases, so that the religious appears to be placed on a pedestal, physically raised above, and separated from, the quotidian. The

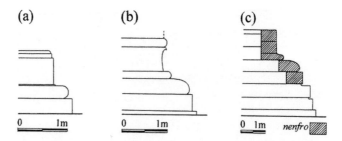

4.2 Altar and temple base profiles: (a) altar from Punta della Vipera (adapted from Torelli 1967: 333); (b) altar at Vignanello (adapted from Colonna (ed.) 1985: 24); and (c) the base of the Ara della Regina temple at Tarquinia (adapted from Colonna 1985d: 73)

interplay of light and shadow caused by the varying undulations in the inter-connecting surfaces of the mouldings would have drawn the eye to this area. At both of the temples with surviving bases, the blocks of the base were faced with a stone different from the rest of the temple; this stone was *nenfro* (Fig. 4.2(c)). The use of a different stone is significant enough in itself in drawing attention to this part of the temple, and alerting us to the fact that something is at stake here. However, *nenfro* is a paler and more fine-grained stone than the surrounding *tufo*, and so would have stood out starkly against the rest of the temple. So, difference is stressed not only by the act of using a different stone *per se*, but also in the specific choice of stone. Such details are integrated more widely into the rhetoric of difference, setting the religious apart, from the foundations upwards.

Terracotta plaques and antefixes

Perhaps the most idiosyncratic element of the decoration of the Etruscan temple was the terracotta plaques (Andrén 1940; see Fig. 4.3 below). These highly decorative slabs of terracotta were moulded and painted, and attached to the temple by bronze nails through holes in the terracotta (for example at Pyrgi; Colonna (ed.) 1970: 710, fig. 550). There were two principal rows of plaques, both running all the way around the temple (Boëthius 1978: 59–63; Colonna (ed.) 1985: 63). The first row was at the point at which the walls of the temples ended and met the overhanging pitched roof. Each plaque consisted of an upper concave cornice ending in a thin beak, decorated with a moulded series of narrow tongues or strigils, and topped by a narrow, vertical fillet. Below the cornice and separated from it by a half round, painted with tri-colour zig-zags was a vertical section or *fascia* that was decorated with a geometric pattern, such as a *guilloche*, lozenges, zig-zags or horizontal lines.

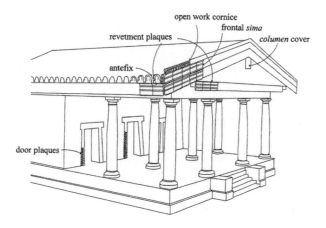

4.3 Reconstruction of an Etruscan temple and its decoration (adapted from Colonna (ed.) 1985: 50, 63)

This in turn was separated by another half round from the bottom section of the plaque, which was decorated with floral patterns such as lotus and palmette (for example at Pyrgi, Temple A: Colonna (ed.) 1970: 346–62; see also Shoe 1965: 215–21).

The second row of plaques ran along the outside edge of the overhanging pitched roof. Here, a row of plaques similar to those described above was surmounted by a row of antefixes along the side walls of the temple, and a row of frontal simas at either end (for example on Temple B at Pyrgi; Colonna (ed.) 1970: 362–71). The frontal sima was made up of three parts, a flat *fascia* and a convex cornice, similar to the revetment plaques, surmounted by an open-work cornice, again usually lotus and palmette.

The details of the decoration serve to emphasise the stress and significance given to temple decoration. These continuous friezes of plaques went all the way round the temple, in repeated motifs and sets of patterns. This results in a frieze where the plaques fit together without seams or joins, producing a constant tonal effect around the monument; there is no change of rhythm or tempo in a frieze decorated in such a way. Through its repetitious nature, the frieze is emphatically non-narrative and as such can have no beginning and no end; it is a continuous, impenetrable whole. Unlike, say, the Parthenon frieze (Osborne 1987: 99–100), it does not invite the viewer in; rather, at the point where roof meets wall, it presents a hard, painted façade all the way round the temple, like an impenetrable halo.

The pitched roof of the Etruscan temple was made up of pantiles covered and sealed by ridged tiles. At the end of each row of ridged tiles was an antefix (Fig. 4.4). These were most commonly faces of gorgons, satyrs, the

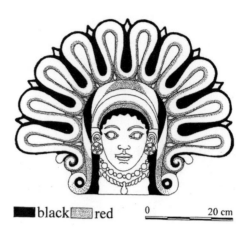

4.4 Female-head antefix from Temple B, Pyrgi
(adapted from Colonna (ed.) 1970: 333)

gods Achlae (Etruscan Achéloos) and Silenus, and maenads, for example
at the Portonaccio sanctuary at Veii (Andrén 1940: 5–8, plates 1–3; Giglioli
1919). All but the last are not particularly surprising subjects, given their
well-attested and widely corroborated apotropaic nature. (This is evident
throughout the range of archaeological material, down to personal orna-
ments, such as necklaces with the face of Achlae (Briguet 1986: 103), which
are the likely precursors of the Roman *bulla*.) These protective deities have
a natural position on a temple. However, one of the factors that contributes
to these characters' apotropaism explains their selection for temples specifically, and also incorporates the maenads. This is, of course, their hybrid
nature. All these creatures are, in some senses, between categories and tran-
scend them, or, in the language of structural anthropology, they are all
liminal (Leach 1976: fig. 7; for a funerary context for such figures in Etruria
see Martelli 1988; Spivey and Stoddart 1990: 116–17; Chapter 3 above). The
gorgon is half woman, half beast; the satyr half man, half beast; Achlae half
man, half bull; the maenad half mad, half sane. By virtue of belonging to
neither category and both simultaneously, these figures are ideal for mediating between one world and another, in this case religious and non-religious,
and temple and non-temple. At the same time, their liminality challenges
the boundaries of categories into which, and between which, they fall. They
therefore act not only as guardians of the boundary between inside and
outside the temple; they are guardians of boundedness itself.

The gorgon and Achlae are particularly apposite in other ways. Achlae, as
a river god, was intrinsically linked with movement and passage, and hence
transition. As well as being a hybrid creature, he was also metamorphic,

with the capacity to transform himself into a bull, serpent or bull-headed man at will. The person of Achlae challenges the categories of his identity through his transformation. This questioning of categories, and thereby the redefinition of them, fits neatly into the broader message of the temple. The gorgons act in a different way. Their images serve, in some ways, normatively. One account tells us that the formerly beautiful Medusa's transformation was a punishment for the crime of sleeping with Poseidon in the Temple of Athena, and thus desecrating the sanctuary. In this sense she is an object lesson in behaviour at sanctuaries. However, more interesting is the danger of her gaze, reputed to petrify and emasculate. It must have been a distinctly disturbing experience to catch the eye of a gorgon in the sanctuary; yet, given her prominent positioning, this would have been almost unavoidable.

As well as their attested mythical attributes, the mode of representing these figures also implicated them in the expression of difference and in the marking off of the temple as different from the space around it. All the characters are disembodied heads, and they are all frontal, staring out from the temple. When looking up at the temple the viewer would have encountered face after face looking down on him or her, angled by the pitch of the roof. The frontal stare of the faces would have confronted and engaged the viewer; they stared straight back, like a mirror. Thus the viewer's gaze is reflected back at him or her, from the very point at which it meets the temple. The antefixes force the viewer to engage directly with their faces; in so doing, they set the limits to, and mark the beginning of, the sacred. In this way the antefixes implicate the viewer in the creation of difference.

Sculpture

The last element of decoration on Etruscan temples is large-scale sculpture. The most complete pedimental group is from Temple A at Pyrgi, dating from about 460–455 BC, which shows a scene from the Theban cycle (Colonna (ed.) 1970: 48–82; Pairault Massa 1992: 72–4). Spivey has argued that this choice of subject-matter is fitting because of the elements of 'hubristic impiety' that attract punishment in the scene (Spivey 1997: 98). So, rather like the lesson of Medusa, the choice of subject is deliberately normative. However, the most famous group of architectural sculptures is probably that from the Portonaccio sanctuary at Veii (Giglioli 1919). Here, larger than life-size terracotta sculptures were placed along the roof-ridge of the temple. At least four figures survive, and again, the liminal nature of two of them is self-evident: Turms and Hercle (Etruscan Hermes and Heracles respectively). The others, Aplu and Letua (Etruscan Apollo and Leto) are more difficult to explain, although Aplu's role as an arbiter may be useful in understanding his presence, if indeed these are correct assignations (the temple is no longer thought to be dedicated to Aplu: Colonna 1986: 468, cf. Andrén 1940: 1–2). Again, beyond their meanings as mythical characters involved with mediation and negotiation, their formal characteristics and visual effects were instrumental in transmitting this message. These moulded and painted figures would have crowned the temple, though their exact order and which way they faced are not clear (compare Spivey 1997: 63, fig. 44, and Boëthius 1978: 62, fig. 51). Whether they faced the front or the back, they would certainly have been seen in profile from the side of the temple. While the antefixes, through their brazen frontality, command and return the viewer's gaze, the roof sculptures, through their studied insouciance, rebuff the viewer. Unlike the pedimental groups with their narrative framework and 'action shots', which we can observe with no difficulty, the sculptures on the roof deliberately avoid our gaze. These figures, with their sublime smiles, looked enigmatically over the heads of the visitor, not giving anything away.

Location of decoration

So far, the ornateness and the subject of the decoration have been the main emphasis. However, it is also important to consider where on the temple the decoration was placed. The sum of all this decoration is a highly ornate building that must have glistened with the moulding, the colour and the pattern that were imprinted upon it. All the decoration discussed so far is from the outside of the temple; making it stand out in the landscape like a jewelled casket. Given the importance of elaboration in marking difference, the extensive decoration of the surface of the Etruscan temple should be seen in terms of marking the importance of the distinction between inside and outside the temple, in other words, between religious and non-religious space. It is not surprising, then, that where these categories meet is precisely where decoration is located on the temple: on the outside. However, the importance of decoration in articulating difference does not end here. The location of the decoration on the outside is also integrated into the dialogue. The choice of which parts of the temple are ornamented gives crucial clues to which differences are particularly at stake in the construction of the temple. It is therefore no surprise that the decoration of Etruscan temples is concentrated on the points of apparent weakness (apparent because they do not coincide with structural weaknesses). All the elements of decoration discussed above are at points where there seems to be a danger of seepage

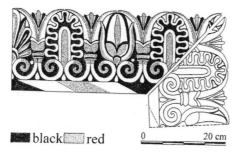

■ black ▨ red   0   20 cm

4.5 Terracotta plaque from the door frame of
Temple B, Pyrgi (adapted from Colonna (ed.)
1970: 380)

between categories: the join between floor and ground, wall and roof, and
roof and sky. At all these points, the integrity of the structure, and the
differences it embodies, are challenged, and protected through ornament.
This is perhaps most explicit in the treatment of doorways, possibly the
weakest point of all. The doors to the chambers were surrounded by more
painted relief plaques (Boëthius 1978: 62), for example on Temple B at Pyrgi,
where the doorjamb terracottas are the most complex and intricate of all
the plaques on the temple (Fig. 4.5; Colonna (ed.) 1970: 380–7).

The care that went into all the temple's plaques underlines the significance
of these pieces. Temple B at Pyrgi provides at least two examples of terracotta
plaques that were made for their specific locations. One is a revetment plaque
from the rear right-hand corner of the temple (Colonna (ed.) 1985: 130); the
other is from the corners of the doorjamb pieces (Fig. 4.5 below; Colonna
(ed.) 1970: 381, 384–5, fig. 302). It was imperative that these areas were
covered with decoration, yet the mass-produced, identical plaques would
not fit into these awkward areas. The solution was the special manufacture
of interlocking pieces, tailor-made for that particular part of the temple.

In addition, two further aspects of the location of the temple's decoration implicate it in negotiating difference. They illustrate most clearly the
manner in which meaning, built form and decoration are not only linked,
but inextricably intertwined within the structure as a whole. The first is
an emphasis on the front of the temple. As well as the decoration running
around the temple, there was an additional concentration of decoration at
the ends of the temple, in the form of pedimental sculpture, for example
those from Temple A at Pyrgi (Colonna (ed.) 1970: 48–82; in fact, the *surviving* Pyrgi example is from the back of Temple A), or the Belvedere Temple
at Orvieto. The form of the temple allows for the placing of this additional

architectural sculpture here, in the triangular gable space under the pitched roof. The placing of extra sculpture here emphasises the longitudinal axis of the temple, setting up a conceptual (and, as it was placed on the ridge-pole, real) central line from which to view the temple. The relationship between front and back is securely established by the location of these sculptural elements. The emphasis on the front cannot, of course, be seen from the sides or back. This does not, however, detract from the ability of the sculpture to emphasise the longitudinal axis and frontality on two counts: first, even if the visitor had never seen an Etruscan temple before, when he or she did get to the front he or she would know it; and second, if the visitor had been to such a site before, he or she would anticipate what was waiting around the corner. For the Portonaccio group of sculptures, Spivey has argued that the placing of sculptures along the roof indicates that the temple 'was clearly to be appreciated by a viewer approaching from the side' (Spivey 1997: 63, caption to fig. 44, though he also admits that the placement is uncertain; see above). However, viewing the sculptures from the side, in profile, would have made it impossible for the viewer to engage with them – their gaze constantly eluding him or her. In order to interact, the viewer would have had to move round to the front, the disdain of the sculptures almost forcing him or her to move and, most importantly, to move to the front. Although the temple could have been appreciated from the side, the visual cues moving the viewer to the front would have ensured that this would not have been for long. Thus the way in which the sculptures were executed (the archaic smile), their composition (the profile view) and their location (axially on the roof) all combine to force an appreciation of the temple from the front.

The second aspect that is emphasised by the location of the decoration is centrality. Etruscan pedimental sculpture, unlike its Greek counterpart, does not extend over the entirety of the triangular space at the front and back of the temple, at least not until the fourth century (for instance at Tarquinia and Talamone; for Tarquinia see Pairault Massa 1992: 101–2; Romanelli 1948: 254–5; for Talamone see Gamburi 1888: 686; Pairault Massa 1992: 240–3). Instead, sculpture is present only in the very centre of the gable triangle (see Fig. 4.3 above). The sumptuous ornamentation, in the form of the extremely deep relief, like that at Pyrgi, is located in line with the central roof-beam (*columen*), and covers it. By being located on the central ridge-pole, the sculpture unites the structural centre of the building with the symbolic centre.

So far, the decoration of the temple and where it was located have been considered. The details of the content and location of the decoration have been shown to be integrated into the broader messaging of the structure

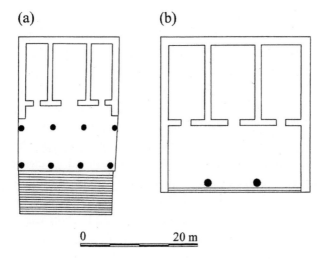

(a)   (b)

0   20 m

4.6 Temple plans: (a) Belvedere Temple, Orvieto; (b) Portonaccio Temple, Veii (adapted from Colonna 1985d: 82 and Colonna
1985f: 100)

in several ways. Subjects and myths explicitly dealing with boundedness
were deliberately selected, the arrangement of the decorative elements was
such that it emphasised difference, and the integration of decoration and
sculpture within its architectural setting was achieved in such a way as to
corroborate this. However, as hinted above, the form of the temple was
equally important in the expression of this meaning.

Columns

The themes of axiality, frontality and centrality play an important part in
the architectural form of the temple (for example Boëthius 1978: 37). The
pedimental sculpture was at both ends of the temple, and the exact placing
of the roof sculptures from Veii is uncertain (Spivey 1997: 63). So, though
it could be argued that the importance of frontality has been overstated in
the discussion of the decoration above; this emphasis seems entirely justi-
fied, however, when examining temple form. The two elements of frontality
and, within that, centrality, are closely knit into the design of the Etruscan
temple, principally in the treatment of columns and steps (Fig. 4.6).

The canonical Etruscan temple had three chambers, with the central one
larger than the others. The columns were aligned with the chamber walls,
and were only at the front of the temple (Castagnoli 1955). Columns should
be considered as part of the architectural elaboration: they are points of
particular concentration in terms of both construction and building, and

also in terms of the viewing of the temple (see Rykwert 1996). Yet again, the concentration of this elaboration is at the front of the building, signalling the most important part of the Etruscan temple. Comparison with Greek temples serves to emphasise the distinctiveness of the Etruscan deployment of columns, and so highlights the specific Etruscan concern with expressing boundedness. Columns themselves are rather ambiguous in their 'allegiance': together they form a line, or colonnade, but this is, necessarily, penetrable. When viewed from the outside of the temple, the columns appear to be an indisputable part of the structure, marking a clear boundary between inside and outside. Yet when viewed from within the colonnade, the status of the columns as a boundary is less clear: they seem to belong to both the external and the internal space of the temple, at the same time both inside and outside the categories that the temple is defining. It is interesting to note that in Greek temples the colonnade acts as a permeable screen around the four sides of the cella; by contrast, in the Etruscan temple, the collonade – the point of transition and mediation between the inside and the outside – is present and possible only at the front.

The number of rows of columns varied from site to site, allowing for even greater emphasis on frontality. At the Portonaccio sanctuary, according to some reconstructions, there were only two columns in total (Fig. 4.6(b)). These were aligned with the central chamber, and the sides of the temple were completely blocked off by the continuation of the chamber walls (Colonna (ed.) 1985: 100; Rendeli 1990: 6; though see Prayon 1986: 198, figs. v-38 and v-39). From the sides and back, the temple would have presented completely blank walls, topped by the decoration mentioned earlier. By the blocking of the sides, and the placing of the columns at the front, the temple signalled the entrance to the sacred most emphatically; it was impossible to enter from anywhere else. Possible movement across the boundary was limited, and restricted to one point only. This was emphasised further by the irregular intercolumnation at the front of the temple. The alignment of the columns with the chamber walls resulted in a wider opening in the centre of the façade, concentrating the location of the boundary at that point. In other temples this is less extreme; some have a row of columns across the entire front (for example Temple A at Pyrgi); in others the number of rows is increased (for example at Orvieto, Fig. 4.6(a)), though this never exceeds two (for an exception from outside Etruria see the temple of Capitoline Jove; see Cristofani (ed.) 1990: 75–6; Gjerstad 1960: 180–4; Prayon 1986: 196). Although in these cases concentration on the centre of the front of the temple is less acute than at the Portonaccio temple, in all of them the location of the columns emphasises frontality and centrality in signalling the beginning of the sacred. Temple form was instrumental in reducing the potential points of entry into or exit from the temple to a single point, and in this way defined and confined the sphere of the sacred.

Steps

The same frontality is evident in another element of temple form: steps. Again, comparison with Greek temples is instructive. Greek temples had a stylobate and stereobate around the entire structure. It would have been possible to step up on to the temple at any given point. In contrast, the Etruscan temple had steps only at the front (Fig. 4.6; for example at Orvieto: Pernier and Stefani 1925: 159; at Tarquinia: Romanelli 1948: 239). In an Etruscan temple it was physically impossible to get up on to the podium by any other way than that which was intended by the builders: by the front. Thus, by being given no other choice, the visitor would have been forced to collude in the definition of the temple. As well as physically dictating the location of the transition between the sacred and the profane, the steps also provided an added visual focus at the front of the temple in a way similar to the moulded base of the temple.

Conclusion

The creation of a distinctly bounded ritual space locates the religious within the urban and rural landscape. Visually and physically, Etruscan temple form within the sanctuary (here the columns and steps in particular) directs and guides the visitor to a certain area, and on the temple, the nature and location of the decoration do the same thing. In doing so, these combined efforts give very clear messages about the location of the front of the temple, and therefore the point from which the temple should be viewed. Creating a viewpoint leads to the objectification of the viewed (Berger 1972; Bryson 1983), and objectification implies control and redefinition. By establishing a viewing point for the temple, the sacred is put in its place within the general order. Simultaneously, by directing the viewer to a certain point, through the visual cues discussed above, temple form exerts control over the viewer. All the elements of the temple are unified in expressing the difference of the sacred from the profane, and thus ordering the relationship between the two. The Etruscan temple that emerges in the late sixth century achieves this on many interlinked levels. First, it is set within its own spatial context, bounded by a wall. Second, difference is expressed in the iconography chosen for the exterior surface of the temple, for instance, the gorgon; in the choice of the form the decoration should take, like the repetitive patterns, frontal faces or aloof stare of the acroterial sculpture; in the location of the decoration, at points of vulnerability or along the longitudinal axis; and in the deployment of architectural features, such as the columns and steps. Obviously, these cannot, in practice, be separated as distinctly as implied here; the elision in the meaning of the location, form and content of the ridge-pole relief sculpture at Pyrgi, or the roof sculpture at Veii, shows this most clearly. Rather, all these factors are in play simultaneously. Inevitably, this results in the separate elements also affecting or influencing one another. The meanings of the individual pieces of ornament or sculpture are constantly reflected in one another, so that the meaning of one is dependent on, and reinforced by, that of another. For instance, the interpretation of the roof sculpture at Veii, above, is related to the importance of frontality, and to the longitudinal axis of the temple. This in turn is mirrored in the far broader Etruscan context of the temple as a mechanism for marking difference (Molinos and Zifferero 1998; Riva and Stoddart 1996; Zifferero 1995, 2002).

Though the rise of sanctuaries and temple architecture in the late sixth century can be explained in terms of urbanism, with temples seen as somehow symptomatic of a city-state, or as a means of competition between cities and territories, it must be remembered that the forms of temple architecture that were chosen were those that were most effective in articulating difference. Once built, the temple becomes instrumental in the creation and structuring of differences as well as in reflecting them. All elements of the temple, from the detail of the terracotta plaques to the topographical location of the site, were implicated in this marking of difference.

5 | Domestic architecture: public and private

Introduction

According to Torelli, the late sixth century was 'un momento cruciale' in the urban development of Etruria (Torelli 1985: 32). This chapter traces the archaeological remains of Etruscan domestic architecture from the Iron Age in order to examine what led to this crucial moment and what form it took. The period from the eighth to the fourth century in Etruria was one that saw great changes in domestic architecture: not only the replacement of curvilinear structures by rectilinear ones, but also an increase in the regularity of these structures, both internally and externally, to such an extent that, by the fifth century, large, regular blocks of houses were constructed. In attempting to understand these wider changes, this chapter will examine the underlying network of smaller changes in the material culture: for example architectural form, the materials used in construction, the internal structure, and the treatment of entrances.

The changes in house form will be considered as a further element of Etruscan culture that will illustrate the importance of boundaries and differentiation in late sixth-century Etruria. As discussed in Chapter 1, the premium placed on the definition of boundaries was materially manifest in the creation and manipulation of surface. In the case of domestic architecture, the most obvious difference articulated is that between the private and the public spheres. Cultural changes in attitudes towards this difference are mirrored in changes in the physical relationship between inside and outside the house.

'The house is an important focus of structures in society' (Yates 1991: 250; see also Donley-Reid 1990: 115; Locock 1994: 9). For this chapter, habitations and domestic architecture will be considered as the materialisations of social ideas about the spheres of public and private. Domestic architecture is an arena for the problematisation and negotiation of social issues in material form. Informing this reading of domestic architecture is the recent theoretical stance that houses 'are the loci for dense webs of signification and affect and serve as basic cognitive models used to structure, think and experience the world' (Carsten and Hugh-Jones 1995: 3).

Recent archaeological analyses of domestic architecture have illustrated the breadth of social information that can be developed from this type of analysis. Social hierarchy (J. Chapman 1990; 1991: 168; Carsten and Hugh-Jones 1995: 21; Duncan 1981: 1; Wallace-Hadrill 1994), individual identity (Duncan 1981: 1; Pratt 1981), gender (Hingley 1990: 139–42; Nevett 1994: 109–10) and social memory (J. Chapman 1991: 164) are all areas that have been elaborated in this way. Such readings are made possible by acknowledging the 'house's role as a complex idiom for social groupings, as a vehicle to naturalise rank, and as a source of symbolic power' (Carsten and Hugh-Jones 1995: 21). As such, Etruscan houses will be examined specifically as problematising concern with the creation and marking of boundaries.

Although domestic buildings had been discovered across Etruria, such as those at Veii and Vetulonia (Colini 1919; Falchi 1898; Stefani 1953), it was not until the mid-twentieth century that systematic excavation took place in Etruscan settlements. The second half of the twentieth century saw a far greater interest in the settlements of the Etruscans, leading to the systematic exploration of sites, following the model established by the Swedish excavations at the sites of San Giovenale and Acquarossa. Since their pioneering work, interest in settlement archaeology has encompassed a range of built environments including small farmsteads and major urban centres (Barker and Rasmussen 1988; Bocci Pacini *et al.* 1975; Donati (ed.) 1994; Cristofani and Nardi 1988; Forsberg and Thomasson (eds.) 1984; Nylander (ed.) 1986; Östenberg 1975; P. Perkins and Attolini 1992; Persson 1986, among many others). In addition to the publication of site-specific studies, the results of these investigations have been usefully incorporated into more general histories of Etruscan architecture and culture (for example Boëthius 1978, Colonna 1986, Prayon 1975, 1986; Torelli 1985).

One obstacle to investigations of Etruscan domestic architecture is the continuity of use of settlement locations. Many former Etruscan centres are now covered by their mediaeval and modern descendants; this necessarily limits the extent and nature of investigations. Another obstacle is the size of the sample available from which to draw broad inferences. The fifty or so years of careful excavation have contributed greatly to our understanding, but cannot compare in volume to the funerary data available.

Furthermore, as Sanders points out, the identification of domestic or public buildings is not unproblematic (Sanders 1990: 53). As a guide he proposes a set of criteria for their identification. These are the presence of a discrete architectural unit, a single entrance, an internal circulation path, a clearly defined outline within the fabric of the settlement, and a distinct set of behavioural markers. To this Melis and Rathje would add examination of the relationships between surrounding buildings, and a study of finds (Melis and

Rathje 1984: 385. See also Nevett 1999). These guidelines have been followed as far as possible.

For much of the discussion of the earlier periods, the sites referred to are limited; evidence comes mainly from San Giovenale and Acquarossa, since these have been excavated in a way that reveals different phases over approximately 200 years of occupation. For this analysis, the different phases are included in their appropriate chronological grouping. The chronology of the houses is based on their finds, and, because of the nature of settlement deposits, these dates are not as precise as they are for the material discussed in previous chapters. In addition, the data also fall within large and often overlapping categories (such as seventh to sixth century, sixth century, late sixth century) depending on the specific diagnostic material that survives at each site. When grouping the evidence chronologically, the principle of *terminus post quem* was applied, putting the groups of houses (dated by the excavators) into order according to the latest possible within the range. For the later periods Marzabotto dominates the material record (23 out of 36 late sixth-century / early fifth-century examples; see Izzet 1997, appendix 3; since the compilation of these data, Marzabotto may now have been superseded by the further publication of the site at Lago dell'Accesa: Camporeale 1997; Camporeale and Giuntoli 2000). Although Marzabotto's representativeness as a site has been questioned (Damgaard Andersen 1997: 343–4; Mansuelli 1979: 354), as Ward-Perkins points out, this was a new settlement, and so not hampered by the presence of previous occupation levels: 'just as it is to the Roman colonies that we look for up-to-date Roman ideas of town-planning, so Marzabotto gives us a measure of Etruscan theory in the fifth century – and a very impressive measure it is' (Ward-Perkins 1958: 114–15). The same problem occurs in studies of early Greek settlements, for example at Lefkandi, where only 2 per cent of the Xeropolis hill has been excavated (Snodgrass 1987: 64–5). The dangers of inferring general trends from so few sites are obvious, as these may not be representative of Etruscan domestic architecture in general, but they are nevertheless the best-excavated and best-published sites that we have.

The evidence for domestic architecture takes the form of ground plans of excavated houses. Rapoport divides the built environment into three different elements, all of which act as clues to behaviour: fixed (architecture), semi-fixed (for example furnishings), and non-fixed (for example people). The fixed elements operate on a high level of redundancy and so embody enough cues to extrapolate meaning (Rapoport 1990: 13). The plans of Etruscan houses should therefore give sufficient information about the settings to understand certain aspects of their form.

Such plans have not always been available. The relative lack of settlement material has meant that scholars have looked elsewhere for clues to the domestic architecture of the Etruscans, specifically to the houses of the dead (Colonna 1986: 371–3; Cristofani 1978: 63; De Albentiis 1990: 72; Torelli 1985: 26, 27). The assumption here has been that 'the interiors of the tombs are often copies of actual houses' (Prayon 1986: 174; see also Boëthius 1960: 4 for iron-age hut-urns). Though the relationship between the houses for the dead and the living in the Etruscan context is a potentially fascinating one, as shown in Bailey's analysis of the Chalcolithic period, or Hodder's study of neolithic Europe (Bailey 1990: 39–43; Hodder 1990b), in exploring Etruscan domestic architecture, this chapter will restrict itself to the evidence from settlement sites alone.

The premise that underlies the work of this chapter is that domestic architecture, like all material culture, is an effective embodiment of social norms, and an effective setting for future social action. Recent work on domestic architecture has shown that house form is never arbitrary or inevitable. As discussed at greater length in Chapters 1 and 2, the choices of materials, techniques and processes that go into determining the forms of dwellings and houses are principally informed by social and cultural factors, rather than being environmentally or technologically determined (Rapoport 1969: 47; more recently Lyons 1996; Parker Pearson and Richards 1994a). As such, domestic buildings are culturally laden with significance, and the forms that dwellings take are never random, but the result of deliberate choices on the part of the builders and/or residents about the built environment in which they live. The creation of Etruscan built environments gives material expression to the desires behind these choices, and the forms chosen are inextricably linked to this. It therefore follows that any changes in these forms are also culturally significant.

House form

The following sections examine the role that domestic architecture plays in the dialectic of boundedness. The cognitive boundaries that are at stake in domestic architecture are, among others, those between public and private, and between different categories of internal domestic space. The evolving relationship between public and private space is played out in the wider dialogue between individual household units and the rest of the settlement. In this chapter, the house will be taken as the private sphere and the rest of the settlement as the public, and it is the dialogue between these areas that

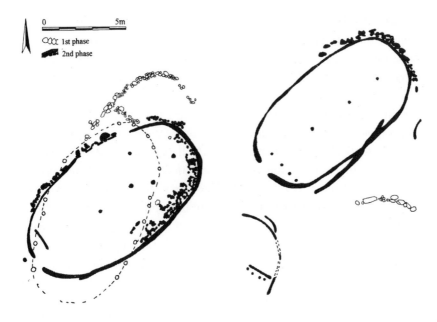

5.1 San Giovenale, Area D (adapted from Boëthius *et al.* 1962: 203)

will be examined here. (This is similar to Dvorsky Rhoner's concept of the 'domestic idea': Dvorsky Rohner 1996: 116.) Of course, such a distinction between public and private is not a cross-cultural universal: for example, Wallace-Hadrill has argued that the Roman house was not as distinctly private as modern houses because of the Roman socio-political institutions of patronage and the accompanying *salutatio* (Wallace-Hadrill 1994).

Unlike previous studies, a strictly chronological approach will not be followed here; instead, different elements of domestic architecture will be examined through time in order to demonstrate changes in attitudes to domestic space, and to emphasise the increasing boundedness of space, and the importance of surface as a means of expressing this from the late sixth century onwards. The first of these elements is house form, which is examined through the plans of domestic units.

Shape

In the Iron Age, habitations generally took the form of curvilinear huts (Fig. 5.1), though several rectilinear huts have been found at Tarquinia (Linington *et al.* 1978; Torelli 1985: 23). For Tarquinia, Colonna argues that the curvilinear huts preceded rectilinear ones (Colonna1986: 390; though see Linington *et al.* 1978: 14). In southern Etruria, where the *tufo* bedrock is close to the surface, excavation has revealed traces of both kinds of huts; some of the best preserved were found at San Giovenale (Boëthius *et al.* 1962; for Acquarossa see Östenberg 1983; Rystedt 2001). The excavators suggest two building phases (Fig. 5.1). In the first, a series of post-holes was cut into the rock, into which the timber frame and hurdles of the hut were inserted. The frame was filled with walling material, and the hut walls were supported all the way around by a row of rubble (Area D, huts A, B and hypothetical C; see Boëthius *et al.* 1962: 289). In the second phase, a continuous channel was dug for the insertion of the walling (Area D, huts D, E, F, G; see Boëthius *et al.* 1962: 289). The walling was made of wattle and daub, which has survived in the form of impressions in the clay used to line the huts (Berggren and Berggren 1980: 10). The huts had thatched roofs, which were supported by the outer walls and by timber uprights inside the hut. These structures appear to show little variation in relation to each other, and Torelli interprets this parity as indicating the lack of differentiation in wealth and power in emerging Etruscan society (Torelli 1985: 23).

During the seventh century a dramatic change took place in habitation construction: buildings became rectilinear, with worked stone foundations, on which sat either stone blocks or mud-brick walls (for example Fig. 5.2). However, as Torelli points out, huts co-existed with masonry buildings for a large part of the century (Torelli 1985: 24). The examples with the new construction technique, plan and decoration of houses are seen as potentially belonging to a 'livello sociale più elevato' (Torelli 1985: 24). Later, in the sixth century, such houses became more numerous. For Colonna this increase in the numbers of domestic residences is the result of competitive emulation; a building form that started as the prerogative of the aristocracy then became more widely adopted (Colonna 1986: 425; De Albentiis 1990: 29–30).

The traditional explanation of the change in shape from curvilinear to rectilinear houses is in terms of construction. The potential roof span of curvilinear structures is restricted (H. W. M. Hodges 1972: 528–9), and so, in order to create larger buildings, rectilinear structures were necessary. However, such an approach privileges technological over cultural factors in determining house form. Instead, such changes need to be examined within a socio-cultural context in the search for fuller explanation (Lyons 1996: 365; Parker Pearson and Richards 1994a: 63–4; Rapoport 1969: 24–5).

The change from curvilinear to rectilinear structures meant that the exteriors of these houses were vertical and flat. From the outside, the earlier, curvilinear huts would have had a three-dimensional quality; in contrast, the later, rectilinear houses would have appeared to have two dimensions only:

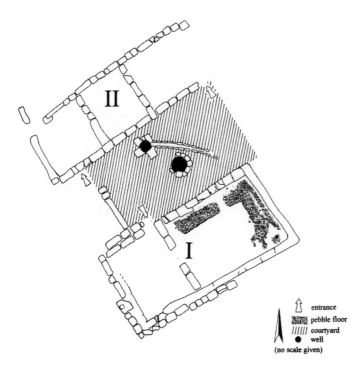

5.2 San Giovenale, Area F, Houses I and II, seventh century (adapted from Nylander (ed.) 1986: 51 and Karlsson 1996: 267). No scale given in original photograph; Karlsson (1996: 267) gives House I measurements as 11 × 5.8 metres

height and width. As was argued for funerary architecture above (Chapter 3), the walls that mark the distinction between inside and outside became more immediate, and, at the same time, more impenetrable. This can be seen, for example, in the well-preserved walls of the Borgo area at San Giovenale (Fig. 5.3). That 'rectilinear compounds provide a sharp definition of inside and outside' is attested in ethnographic examples (Parker Pearson and Richards 1994a: 60). The transition from curvilinear to rectilinear structures cannot be seen simply in terms of constructional motivations. The choice on the part of the builders and inhabitants of these structures is, rather, a deliberate expression of the increased importance of the emphasis between house and non-house, public and private. The form of the domestic unit is manipulated to crystallise this distinction in material form.

Often these houses were conceived of and built, not as single isolated units, but in groups. For example, on the Macchia Grande at Veii, Drews argues that instead of there being one house in different phases, there were three houses and that two of these shared a party wall (Drews 1981:

5.3 The Borgo area, San Giovenale

141; Stefani 1922: 379–85). A more certain example is from the Borgo area of San Giovenale (Fig. 5.4; Blomé 1969: fig. 11; Nylander 1986a: 50), where houses B and C were built together, sharing a party wall. Though unusual at this date (*c.* 600), the building of groups of houses together becomes common so that, by the early fifth century, at Marzabotto the blocks of houses, so-called *insulae*, could contain up to eight houses (below, Fig. 6.1). This increasing homogeneity of domestic architecture is used much like funerary architecture to argue for a 'relativa parità sociale' and a socio-economic equilibrium commensurate with rise of a 'ceto manifatturiero e mercantile' (Colonna 1986: 431; Cristofani 1978: 78; De Albentiis 1990: 68).

In a brief discussion of the urban layout of Turin, Cullum has noted that the 'aligned façades of the buildings . . . exhibit striking uniformity and restraint. The identity of the individual buildings comprising the urban block is subordinated to the continuity of the street façade' (Cullum 1986: 56). In the rows of contiguous Etruscan houses the single, reticent façade, made up of rows of individual houses, thus emphasises the importance of the public space of the street, set against the privacy of the domestic sphere. The façade itself becomes the boundary between the two spheres. In the Etruscan context, then, given the importance of creating just such a boundary in house form, the arrangement of houses in rows must be seen,

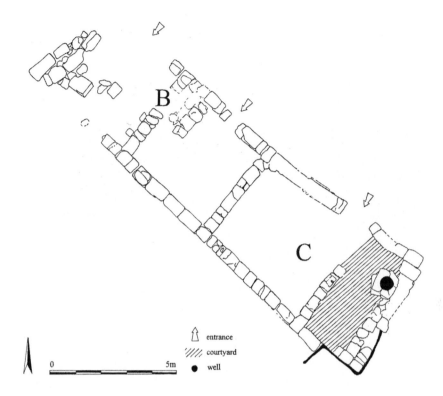

5.4 San Giovenale, Borgo area, Houses B and C (first phase), seventh century (adapted from Blomé 1969: fig. 11)

again, as the expression of the desire to differentiate between domestic and non-domestic spaces.

Blocks of houses are also found at Musarna and Le Murelle, and attested at Tarquinia and Veii (Broise and Jolivet 1985, 1988; Colonna 1977: 213; Pallottino 1937: 380–1; Stefani 1953: 93). In Marzabotto, the blocks of houses measure about 150 metres, and though the houses are individual, without shared walls, they were close enough to have presented a uniform façade, the individual walls joining to form one long, straight wall that runs the length of the street. This is an elaboration of the desire to draw a sharper distinction between house and non-house. The arrangement of houses in blocks makes this distinction clearest. The joining of separate private spheres behind one façade gives the distinction more weight. Whereas, in the seventh and early sixth centuries, individual houses express this to a degree, in the later rows of houses large groups of individual households are joined, giving a far greater impact to the distinction drawn between public and private.

Materials

The second area to be examined concerns the material components and elements of domestic architecture. As well as a change in form, there was also a change in the materials used in domestic architecture; however, the availability of new materials or techniques is not sufficient to explain their deployment: 'just because man can do something, does not mean he will' (Rapoport 1969: 24). Instead, materials and technology enable the creation of spaces, the forms of which are decided on other grounds (Rapoport 1969: 25), primarily socio-cultural factors (Rapoport 1969: 47).

The chronological change in materials used in Etruscan domestic architecture is concurrent with the changes in plan from curvilinear to rectilinear. Wattle and daub walls were replaced by mud-brick walls on stone foundations; thatches were replaced by tiled roofs (though for an earlier funerary context for tiles see Damgaard Andersen and Toms 2001). Torelli asserts that it was the Greeks who taught the Etruscans how to mould terracotta and how to make painted tiles (Torelli 1985: 24–5, who uses Pliny the Elder *HN* 35.152 as a source; see C. Wikander 2001). However, Ridgway and Ridgway have argued for a local tradition of tile manufacture, using the evidenc of Mulro and hut-urns (Ridgway and Ridgway 1994). The walls of the houses were made of rough mud bricks or hurdles reinforced with poles. Clay tiles on a heavy timber framework covered the roofs. By about 600 BC the rectilinear houses of the Borgo area at San Giovenale, on the north side of the terrace, were built on high, carefully constructed sub-structures of ashlar *tufo*. During the course of the sixth century the foundation stones were dressed and became increasingly uniform.

In his analysis of the development of Italian urbanism, Drews sees the introduction of masonry techniques as having Greek origins. While the Greeks were constructing cities, contemporary Etruscans were living in huts: 'it is transparently clear, because they did not know how to build anything better . . . Before 700 the peoples of Central Italy did not know how to build masonry houses' (Drews 1981: 146–7). He goes on to say that at first the masonry city would have seemed an 'incomprehensible phenomenon' to the natives of Central Italy, but, 'once they realised its vast superiority . . . they copied it as carefully as they could' (Drews 1981: 155). Again, the reasons for this putative 'superiority', and why the Etruscans might have perceived it as such, need further investigation.

Drews claims that the most important advantage of the new construction was its durability (Drews 1981: 148). The perishability of the iron-age huts as opposed to the relative permanence of the later houses is an important factor in the choice to change materials. However, this 'improvement' is not reason enough for the change in materials; we need to account for why this would be an improvement in the Etruscan context, and why it was needed at this particular point in time.

The desire to adopt a construction technique that would help guarantee the longevity of the domestic unit should be read as an indication that the unit had become conceived of as a discrete enough entity to require such expression. The choice of durable materials cannot be explained in terms of their durability alone. Instead, durable materials were chosen because their durability gives permanent physical and material expression to specific boundaries and surfaces. The difference between public and private, a distinction that we have already seen expressed in the form of the building, is thus further articulated in a particularly durable and permanent manner by the selection of materials used in construction. The importance of the expression of difference is such that it is no longer adequate to represent it in the relatively perishable materials of the hut. Instead, the distinctions are built into the site in a much more permanent, material way.

In addition to permanence, the change in the materials should also be seen as a result of the advantages of expressing the differences between public and private in a more effective or simply 'better' way. As well as giving permanent expression to the new, more highly defined spatial units, the materials selected are more effective in marking distinction. Walls of brushwood hurdles covered with a layer of clay or wattle and daub would, in addition to being curved, have had irregular surfaces. The weave of the hurdle and the layering of the clay would have resulted in uneven undulations in the surface of the walls, as would the thatched roof. In contrast, squared masonry walls, as well as being straight, would have had a far smoother and crisper surface, as would the terracotta tiles of the roofs. This is less evident in the earlier roof-tiles at Acquarossa, of course; however, finds of tiles at Roselle and Marzabotto suggest an increase in the regularity of tile over time (Donati (ed.) 1994; Brizzolara *et al.* (eds.) 1980; Schifone 1971). This is illustrated in House B of the Borgo at S. Giovenale (Blomé 2001) and its comparison with photographs from huts from the Roman Campagna of the early twentieth century (for example in Brocato and Galluccio 2001). The sharpness resulting from the new materials articulates the difference between inside and outside the house more clearly than the earlier methods.

Thus the change in the choice of the materials used in domestic architecture should be seen in two ways: the first, through durability, as a permanent, physical expression of the house/non-house distinction; the second, through the physical nature of the preferred materials, as a more effective way of expressing this distinction.

Courtyards

A third area where a crystallisation of distinctions is visible is in the relationship between the domestic unit and the non-built space that is often associated with it. Although there is no evidence for any kind of courtyard in the eighth- to seventh-century hut settlements at Luni sul Mignone, Tarquinia, Veii, Acquarossa and San Giovenale, this does not necessarily indicate that such spaces did not exist. It seems highly unlikely that all activities would have taken place inside the hut, and it is possible that the huts had spaces around them that served to complement and extend the space of the hut. (For 'order without architecture' see Parker Pearson and Richards 1994b: 124; Whitelaw 1994.) If they did exist at this date, however, they were not expressed in material form.

By contrast, in the seventh-century settlements at San Giovenale and Acquarossa, low perimeter walls are constructed at the front of some of the houses (Figs. 5.2, 5.4 and 5.5). Given that house form is never arbitrary, then, it would appear that the need to give definition to a previously open space, which had hitherto been only loosely associated with a hut through social convention, was important enough to receive expression in a durable, physical form. In addition, the external space of the courtyard was physically joined to that of the house. Thus, the distinction between public and private was extended outwards to dependent open spaces (see also Dvorsky Rohner 1996: 120–3). The space which had previously been associated with the hut, but was physically part of the public space of the settlement, was now materially incorporated into the private sphere (Parker Pearson and Richards 1994a: 40 cite Redman's work in Morocco as an illustration of how internal courtyards and relative seclusion maintain the public–private distinction). The decision to build a courtyard wall should be read as indicating, first, a need to mark this space physically in a permanent manner and, second, to incorporate this space more definitively within the domestic unit itself. It goes without saying that the use of the courtyard could have been retained on the pre-existing basis, without the construction of the courtyard walls and enclosures, but the social and cultural desires to mark boundaries in material form at this stage clearly overrode this possibility.

Some of the courtyards have wells and it is obvious that the provision of a private water supply would have increased the public–private distinction further by obviating the need to collect water from outside, and by turning the water itself into a private 'ownable' commodity (Figs. 5.2 and 5.4; San Giovenale, Area F, House I: Nylander 1986a: 47; Karlsson 1996: 265; Area F, House II: Nylander 1986a: 48; Area F, House III: Nylander 1986a: 50; Borgo House C, phase I, though this is later appropriated by the public sphere: see below, Chapter 6; Acquarossa, Zone B, House B, phases 1 and 2: Östenberg 1975: 13; Vidén 1986: 50–1; Zone B, House A, phases 1 and 2: Östenberg 1975: 11–13; Vidén 1986: 52; Zone B, House C: Östenberg 1975: 12–13; Vidén 1986: 52–6).

Two sets of houses also articulate another aspect of the definition of the household. These are Houses I and II from Area F at San Giovenale (Fig. 5.2), and Houses B and C from Zone N at Acquarossa. (It should be noted that the most recent work at the site has led to the addition of a phase to House I, and a reinterpretation of its entrance. This would significantly alter the readings below of its relationship to the courtyard space. The final publication of this reinterpretation is awaited; for a preliminary report see Karlsson 2001.) All these houses face a shared courtyard, and the courtyard of the first pair contained two wells (Fig. 5.2). Any relationships between the inhabitants of the two buildings were expressed materially, in the form of the courtyard and wells used in common between them; other houses share partition walls between their associated courtyards (for example Fig. 5.5). Relationships between inhabitants could, for example, be kin- or function-related. What is important is that whatever formed the basis of these relationships, they were being expressed through the material articulation of the courtyard walls and the wells within them – a striking contrast with the physical ambiguity of the earlier period.

As Colonna points out, in houses with external courtyards, it was necessary to pass through the courtyard in order to reach the house, (Colonna 1986: 400; see for example Figs. 5.2 and 5.5 above). By contrast, in the late sixth-century Casa dell'Impluvium at Roselle, and in the early fifth-century houses at Marzabotto (Fig. 5.6), the courtyard is located at the centre of the house, and it is only by going through the house that one arrives at the courtyard. This change can be seen as the next stage in the incorporation of the space of the courtyard into the domestic sphere. Through the new configuration of domestic space, the courtyard space has become embedded within the house. Thus, any activities that would have taken place in such spaces were now firmly located in the private sphere of the domestic unit. In addition, the incorporation of the courtyard within the fabric of the house finally removed any ambiguities of association that such spaces may have

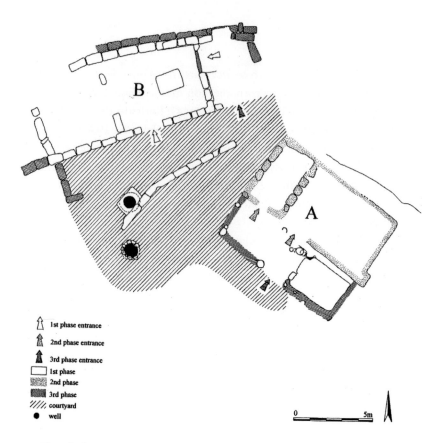

5.5 Phased plan, Acquarossa, Zone B, Houses A and B, seventh–sixth centuries, late seventh to early sixth century, sixth century (adapted from Nylander (ed.) 1986: 54)

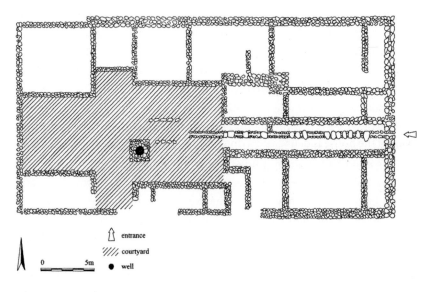

5.6 Marzabotto, Region IV, *Insula* 1, House 2, early fifth century (adapted from Mansuelli 1963: 46)

had. In the earlier courtyards, even though the space was physically defined as an entity associated with the house, uncertainty and ambiguity were still present: the courtyard was both private, in being bounded by a perimeter wall, and yet public, in being outside the house and visible from beyond the perimeter. By the late sixth or early fifth century, with the construction of houses like those at Marzabotto and Roselle, the location of the courtyard behind the façade of the house, and set well within it, removed any ambiguity about its status in the public–private spectrum. Like the parallel treatment of boundaries in funerary architecture, the public–private distinction is condensed to the façade of domestic houses. The exterior surface of the house marks the beginning – and for the viewer the full extent – of the domestic sphere.

Internal structure

It has been argued that the huts of the Iron Age contained internal divisions in the form of brushwood hurdles (Pohl 1977: 94; Prayon 1986: 190). The evidence for this is the presence of post-holes in the area enclosed by the hut (for example Fig. 5.1). This would have resulted in a lengthways division of the hut. At San Giovenale, some of the huts have a channel cut across the hut floor very close to the entrance, which, it has been argued, represented some kind of internal division (for example Area D, Hut D: Boëthius *et al.* 1962: 289). However, the post-holes could have been for roof supports, and the channel associated with the entrance. Either way, the huts of the Iron Age are not internally structured in a *permanent* manner; though the different use of the internal space of a similar structure at Fidene has been argued (Rathje 2001–3: 59), the interior space of the hut is a single complete unit, enclosed by the walls.

From the seventh and sixth centuries onwards, there is a significant change in the articulation of internal space (see for example Fig. 5.2). The internal space of the house is deliberately divided and marked by the construction of internal walls using the same technique as the outer walls. An exception is the first phase of the rectilinear mud-brick building at the north-west gate at Veii, which had internal divisions of brushwood hurdles (Ward-Perkins 1959: 58). An influential contribution to the study of the internal divisions of domestic architecture has been that of Hillier and Hanson, with particular reference to gamma (access) analysis (Hillier and Hanson 1984; for archaeological applications of this work see S. Foster 1989; Donley-Reid 1990: 117; J. Chapman 1990. In Etruscan houses, a similar method has been deployed by Dvorsky Rohner 1996, though she does not use the latest reconstructions of ground plans in Nylander 1986a). Developed as a contribution to contemporary design studies, the conclusions of their study – that structural complexity in architecture is a reflection of social complexity (Hillier and Hanson 1984: 257) – have been applied to archaeological remains to a varying degree, ranging from, for instance, Kent's sympathetic acceptance (Kent 1987: 3; 1990a: 150; see also Rapoport 1990: 17) to a more cautious and qualified view of their relevance (Samson 1990; Fairclough 1992). The caution centres on the cultural specificity of the model – and so on its inapplicability to other cultures (Fairclough 1992: 354) – on the descriptive nature of the results (Samson 1990: 7, 10), and on the fact that the model ignores the symbolic or practical functions of spaces (Fairclough 1992: 351). For these reasons it will not be used in this discussion of the internal division of Etruscan houses.

The internal walls of the seventh- and sixth-century Etruscan buildings were constructed of a wooden framework filled with mud brick, or occasionally stone. These partitions indicate that domestic space was no longer seen as an undifferentiated whole; rather, it appears to have acquired varying meanings and importance. Again, such distinctions may have existed before, but were not expressed materially. If the division of space is never random, the change from not having divisions to having them must be significant. From the seventh and sixth centuries these distinctions are actually marked in the physical form of the house by walls. In addition, it is possible to see a tendency to increase the number of internal divisions in the seventh- and sixth-century houses. The first examples of houses with internal divisions contain only two rooms; the seventh- and sixth-century houses of San Giovenale and Acquarossa usually had two rooms (for example see Fig. 5.2; first and second phases in Fig. 5.5), with a few exceptions that have three rooms (San Giovenale, Borgo House A: Nylander 1986a: 50; Acquarossa, Zone L, House A: Östenberg 1975: 33).

In the sixth century, there is an increase in the number of rooms, with five out of the eight houses at Acquarossa containing three or more spaces (for example the third phase in Fig. 5.5). The largest number of internal spaces is five (see the second phase of Acquarossa, Zone B, House A, including the 'porch': Östenberg 1975: 11–13; Vidén 1986: 52; the second phase of Veii, Macchia Grande, House 1: Stefani 1922: 379–85). The same numbers are evident in structures at Lago dell'Accesa (Fig. 5.7), Acquarossa and Roselle. By the early fifth century, houses at Marzabotto have as many as sixteen discrete spaces articulated in the ground plan (Fig. 5.6).

The increase in the internal division of domestic space expresses physically the cognitive desire to differentiate between internal activities and spaces.

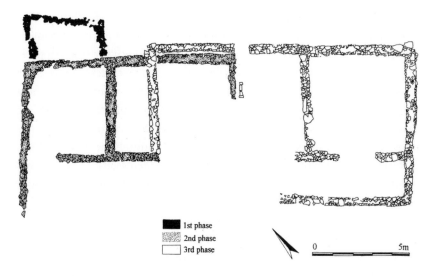

1st phase
2nd phase
3rd phase

0   5m

5.7 Phased plan, Lago dell'Accesa, complesso I (adapted from Camporeale 1985b: 136)

The concern with boundaries that characterises the cultural change that takes place in the late sixth century is made manifest in domestic architecture through the construction of multiple internal divisions to the houses.

The marking and separation of internal domestic space into smaller units have led to conjecture about the use and functions of such rooms; for example, at San Giovenale, the pebble-lined room of House I in Area F (Fig. 5.2) has been associated with sleeping, sitting and dining (Colonna 1986: 400; see also Bergquist 1973; Dvorsky Rohner 1996: 142, n. 10; Karlsson 1996). The desire to assign room function goes beyond San Giovenale (see Colonna 1986: 425, 463; Torelli 1985: 27; Prayon 1986: 190; De Albentiis 1990: 44). However, caution is needed when assigning rooms a specific function. First, the levels of inference in such assignations must move beyond the simplistic equation 'loom weight = cloth production = female space'. Second, assigning rooms a particular function denies the dynamism of the social use of space. As discussed in Chapter 1, spaces are not restricted to one use or meaning (Rapoport 1969: 9; Locock 1994: 5–7); different activities and actions take place in the same space, and the same action can take place in different spaces. In fact, even the use of the word 'room' is so culturally linked with function that, perhaps, its use in this context needs care. Finally, the detail of excavation and publication of Etruscan material is still not yet at a level that would allow the kinds of rich analysis called for by Melis and Rathje (1984: 385; Rathje 2001–3: 59) and demonstrated in some recent Greek studies (for example Cahill 2002; Nevett 1999). This chapter will not assign use or function to the new rooms emerging in Etruscan domestic architecture. That these spaces were used for different functions is not denied; however, the specific uses of the individual rooms are not the concern here. The increased architectural complexity of domestic architecture allows for the physical and spatial differentiation of activity, but whether these new spaces were, for instance, male or female, or used for cooking or sleeping, or to mark social status, is not relevant here. What is important is that distinctions, of whatever nature, were being expressed through the manipulation of the material form of domestic architecture. The increased structural complexity of houses is seen as an indication of the rising importance of spatial patterning and differentiation *per se.*

As well as an increase in the number of internal spaces, the configuration of these spaces also changes over time. Coinciding with the increased articulation of internal domestic space is an increased regularity of plan, (i.e. a 90° angle at the corners) in both the rooms and the complete domestic unit. This regularity of plan appears in the late sixth century and continues to be present, if not to dominate, for the next two centuries, in contrast to a marked absence of regularity before.

The houses at Lago dell'Accesa show this tendency towards a regularisation of space within a single site. 'Complessi' of stone foundations reveal up to four phases of construction; complex I (Fig. 5.7) shows the sequence from irregular to regular layout in the adaptations to and rebuilding of a single building at Lago dell'Accesa. But even the latest sixth-century houses of Lago dell'Accesa do not show the rigidity of the early fifth-century houses at Marzabotto (Fig. 5.6): here each unit, from the individual room to the entire block, is constructed along strictly parallel and perpendicular lines.

The distinctions of Etruscan domestic space are expressed not only physically, but in terms of regularity. A strict order is imposed on to domestic space; they are not simply constructed or appended to existing structures in an arbitrary manner. Instead, they are deliberately planned according to orthogonal principles. The regularisation of these structures, through the use of flat, straight walls of rooms and houses, is particularly effective in slicing previously undifferentiated space into separate units.

Entrances

As discussed in Chapter 1, entrances and doorways form points of potential weakness in the boundaries created by formal architecture. As such they are heavily implicated in the definition of the house, and they are the main point of controlling access to the house. Because only the ground plans of Etruscan houses survive, the possible elaborations of the entrance, either of the threshold or the door and frame, are not generally available for investigation. However, one exception is in the house on the Macchia Grande at Veii. Here, the entrance to the largest room is marked by doorjambs, preserved to a height of 1 metre, of a stone different from the rest of the construction (Stefani 1922: 381). This one example is all we have to suggest that the entrances to Etruscan houses were emphasised in some physical form, and separated from the main fabric of the house through the use of a different stone. In this, domestic architecture appears to employ similar material devices to those used in funerary and temple architecture.

Other aspects of the treatment of entrances are sometimes more archaeologically visible. One of these is the location of the entrance. (These are discussed typologically by Prayon 1975.) In the iron-age huts and the earlier houses the entrance to the unit is generally on the short side of the structure, marked in excavated examples by the absence of the wall gulley in plan. This gives the huts a longitudinal axis (for example Fig. 5.1). In the seventh- and seventh-to-sixth-century houses the entrance shifts to the longer side (for example Figs. 5.2, 5.4 and the first phase in Fig. 5.5), and this tendency is increased in the late seventh to early sixth centuries, and in the sixth and late sixth centuries (for example the second phase in Fig. 5.5, and possibly Fig. 5.7). The principal entrances to such houses were now on their long sides, and as a result the long sides of the houses became the 'front'. This presents the view of the house with an extended façade to the building, emphasising the distinction between house and non-house. The location of the entrance to the unit indicates the conceptual front of the building. The choice of the long side of the building over the short side for the location of the entrance is a further element in confirming the difference between inside and outside: it emphasises the bulk or body of the house beyond the entrance.

In the late sixth century, there is a return to locating the entrance on the shorter side of the building, though this becomes nearly universal only in the fifth century (Fig. 5.6). This would seem to run against the earlier trend of presenting a long, flat façade. However, in this case it must be remembered that though the individual house presents a frontage smaller than it had the potential to do, these houses were constructed in large blocks, with unified fronts, obviating the need for the individual house to express this distinction alone, since it was incorporated into a far longer façade than it could achieve alone (below, Fig. 6.1).

The unified façade of domestic houses from the late sixth century onwards is also evident in the number of external doors. Between the eighth and sixth centuries, houses have a varying number of external entrances (for example House B in Fig. 5.4, the second phase of House B in Fig. 5.5). However, from the late sixth century onwards, houses had only one external entrance (for example the second phase of House A in Fig. 5.5, and Fig. 5.6). Thus, any ambiguity over the location of the boundary between inside and outside the house, or even whether it was a single house, would have been readily clarified by the insistence on only one entrance.

The importance of the definition of the entrance to the house is corroborated by the position of the entrance within the front wall. In the earlier phases of rectilinear houses, those with off-centre entrances dominate (for example Figs. 5.2, 5.4 and the first and second phases of Fig. 5.5); this becomes more acute in sixth- and late sixth-century houses (for example the third phase of Fig. 5.5). However, by the fifth century, all the houses have central entrances (Fig. 5.6). The (single) entrance is placed in the centre of the wall dividing public from private, thus giving it, quite literally, a central role in the negotiation of this difference (Boëthius 1978: 75–6), like that argued for temple architecture in Chapter 3.

Manipulating the treatment of entrances expressed the desire to present a façade in domestic architecture in three ways: by the choice of the long side over the short side for the location of the entrance (until enough houses were strung together to present a longer front than was possible by one individual house); by reducing the number of entrances to one, thus condensing the act of entering to one possible route; and by locating the single entrance in the middle of the façade.

External appearance

Again, because the ground plans are all we have for Etruscan houses, it is difficult to reconstruct their external appearances; iron-age huts and the houses of Marzabotto could have been decorated in ways that have not survived, for instance by painting. Cristofani discusses the possible painted terracotta decoration of houses at Cerveteri, similar to the Boccanera plaques in the British Museum or the Campana plaques in the Louvre dating from the second half of the sixth century (Cristofani 1978: 89; see also Roncalli 1965: 11, 49–50, 63). There is more secure evidence for the external decoration of buildings in the settlement of Acquarossa from the early sixth century, where the extensive use of moulded and painted terracotta friezes and antefixes is attested (Torelli 1989: 26; Nylander 1986a; Rystedt 1983; Rystedt *et al.* (eds.)

1993; C. Wikander 1988). There is no evidence for such decoration after the sixth century. The chronological range of this decoration is surprising given the analysis of this chapter. This could be the result of the particular efficacy of the new forms of domestic architecture in articulating the differences by the early fifth century, so that architectural moulded terracottas were no longer felt necessary. Issues of archaeological survival may also have had a bearing on this chronological pattern: the sites from which these decorations come, San Giovenale and Acquarossa, do not have any houses later than the late sixth century. It is therefore not possible to say whether later houses from these sites would have had plaques. The surviving examples are from a restricted chronological period, so change is not detectable. Finally, the function of the buildings that were so richly decorated is hard to pin down with accuracy; they are largely regarded as having functions beyond the domestic, such as the so-called 'regia' at Acquarossa, which is considered to have been an elite complex used not only to house its owners, but also for ritual feasting and entertaining (Bergquist 1973). These flamboyant early decorations are therefore more likely to be bound up with elite display, and as such are not representative of domestic housing more generally (Flusche 2001).

Conclusion

Behind this analysis of Etruscan domestic architecture is the assumption that house form, like all material culture, is never arbitrary. Traditionally, the development of Etruscan domestic architecture has been seen as an inevitable continuum from huts to houses, where changes in form are seen as somehow obvious, and without the need for explanation. That such a stance is theoretically unsupportable has been shown in Chapter 1. Often, the evolutionist view of Etruscan houses is compounded by the importance placed on the importation of certain features from abroad. Both such emphases give the Etruscans a passive role in the formation of their built environments. In both cases, the 'natural' choice of certain forms denies the Etruscans any real choice in the forms their material culture was to take. Instead, in the light of recent theoretical analyses of domestic space, the premise behind this chapter has been that architectural form is the result of social and cultural factors in Etruria and that 'house form . . . reflects the interaction of cultural norms and the decisions of members of the household' (Blanton 1994: 7).

It has been argued that the choice of rectilinear over curvilinear buildings should be seen in terms of the greater efficacy of the former in physically demarcating differences between the domestic and the non-domestic, the private and the public. This crystallisation of distinctions and of the physical manifestations of social boundaries and differences at the externally visible surface of domestic structures underlies the analyses of other aspects of domestic architecture in this chapter: the choice of durable materials for construction, the incorporation of the courtyard into the domestic unit, the increasing internal division of domestic space, the regularity of the structures and the treatment of the entrance. In all cases, it has been argued, the choice of materials and form is explained, not in terms of an inevitable progression, but rather in terms of the new forms and materials being particularly effective in expressing difference.

As part of a broader examination of the late sixth century, Etruscan domestic architecture reiterates the importance of boundaries and surface at this period. Conceptual differences are emphasised in permanent, physical form, and in a way that concentrates the negotiation of these differences in the surfaces of buildings. The specific means of expression selected by late sixth-century builders should be seen as part of the dialectic of the creation of boundaries through the manipulation of the external surface of the domestic unit.

Introduction

The study of Etruscan cities spans as brief a time as that of domestic architecture. After the somewhat piecemeal excavation of a few sites in the late nineteenth and early twentieth centuries, notably Vetulonia (Falchi 1898) and Marzabotto (Brizio 1891), the first systematic excavation of Etruscan settlements took place in the mid-twentieth century. As a result, traditional studies of Etruscan cities exhibit a heavy reliance on funerary data (see Chapters 1 and 5). As discussed in Chapter 1, the Crocifisso del Tufo cemetery at Orvieto in particular has been used to illustrate the layout of Etruscan cities (Mansuelli 1970b; 1979: 363; 1985: 111; Drews 1981: 148), and the Banditaccia cemetery at Cerveteri has been deployed in a similar way (Gros and Torelli 1988; for doubts about such use of funerary data see Damgaard Andersen 1997). A further similarity with the study of domestic architecture is in the incorporation of urban form into the debate over Etruscan origins. Early in the twentieth century, Haverfield tried to argue that town planning was part of the 'ancestral heritage' of Italy, extending back into the second millennium BC (Haverfield 1913: 72). Such an early date has been dispelled by Ward-Perkins (Ward-Perkins 1958: 109–11). However, in more moderate form, the long-term continuity, at least from the ninth century BC, of the process of urbanisation is a generally accepted principle (Colonna 1970: Castagnoli 1971: 75–81; Gros and Torelli 1988: 6–12; Guidi 1985, 1989; Harris 1989). The importance of local continuity in accounts of Etruscan cities has not, however, excluded the possibility of foreign influence in the accounts of Etruscan urban development (Drews 1981: 146–7; Torelli 1985: 24–5), and, in turn, of the influence of Etruscan cities on the Roman world. The latter is particularly stressed in the areas of water supply and road-building (Gros and Torelli 1988; Owens 1991: 98; Ward-Perkins 1962: 1,637). Owens even goes as far as to suggest that hydraulics was an area where the Etruscans may have influenced the Greeks (Owens 1991: 105). Recently, the debate has been framed in terms of the emergence of complex, state-like polities, and there has been much debate between the camps of Etruscologists and prehistorians over the role played by indigenous, even longer-term influences as opposed to foreign (largely Greek, but also Eastern) stimuli to the Etruscan transformation from village to city (for the debate, see Vanzetti 2002; for 'dal villaggio alla città', see Pacciarelli 2000).

As discussed in Chapter 1, ancient sources stress the importance of religious ritual in the foundation and planning or Etruscan cities (most notably Plutarch, *Rom.* 11.1 and Varro, *Ling.* 5, 143). This involved the taking of auspices, the reading of omens, bird flight, lightning and haruspicy (animal entrails) in the determination of both the location of the city and the day on which it was to be founded. However, again as highlighted in Chapter 1, caution is essential when using such Greek and Roman sources as evidence for Etruscan cultural practices (Dumézil 1970: 261–2; Beard *et al.* 1998).

Material evidence supports the textual evidence in its emphasis on the taking of auspices at the foundation of Etruscan cities. Perhaps the most famous of these is the bronze model of a liver from Piacenza (see Chapter 1; van der Meer 1982: 165; see also Pfiffig 1975: 121–7). This object is discussed extensively in terms of the light it casts on the Etruscan pantheon; however, for the purposes of this chapter it will be taken as an indication that for the Etruscans urban form was cosmologically ordered, and that different aspects of material culture were analogically interrelated (see Chapter 1). As a result, technological or environmental factors appear to have played a far smaller part in determining Etruscan urban form than cultural and social ones.

The construction of formal cities has for a long time been considered a landmark of social development (Childe 1950; Ucko *et al.* (eds.) 1972). In Etruria the phenomena of state formation (e.g. Stoddart 1987) and of urbanism (e.g. Damgaard Andersen 1997) have received particular attention in recent years. While some authors have been at pains to define urbanism (e.g. Damgaard Andersen 1997: 345–53; P. Perkins 2000: 91–2; see also Wells 1984; Whitehouse 1977), others have examined the long-term history of settlement patterns in Etruria (Guidi 1985, 1998; Potter 1979; Peroni and di Gennaro 1986; Stoddart 1987; Rendeli 1991). The latter group has drawn a complex picture of emerging city-state culture from at least the Late Bronze Age. In particular, Stoddart has developed a dynamic and nuanced model which incorporates shifts in power and focus within the settlements of the first half of the first millennium BC (Stoddart 1987, 1989, 1990). This has been elaborated for South Etruria by Rendeli (1991, 1993). Finally, the social and cultural aspects of state formation and urbanism have been explored by Nijboer, in his attempts to link craft specialisation and urbanism (Nijboer 1997, 1998; though see Brandt 2001). These studies have taken a welcome broad approach to the study of urbanism and cities in Etruria (compare Banti

1973) in looking at the underlying processes that prompted and were at the same time part of the wider development of urbanism and state formation in central Italy. One aspect that they neglect, however, is the way in which the material form of urban settlements was part of the same process.

This chapter will examine why the Etruscan city developed in the form that it did. In such an inquiry, the importance of the built environment as a meaningful entity will be foremost (e.g. Bowman 1992; Cormack 1990). As the culturally determined setting for activity, urban form will be examined as articulating the negotiation of cognitive and physical boundaries. Since urban form is not arbitrary, changes in the organisation and layout of the city will be seen as crucial in expressing and materialising the concerns of Etruscan society.

The approach taken to urban form in this chapter follows that proposed by Vance in conceiving of cities as 'the greatest of human physical artefacts' (Vance 1990: 10). There are two obvious ways in which the general discussion above affects the specific analysis of urban form. The first is that cities are the setting for social activity; the second is that, as the setting for such activity, cities reflect social ideology: 'How a city looks and how its spaces are organised form a material base upon which a range of possible sensations and social practices can be thought about, evaluated, and achieved' (Harvey 1990: 66–7). It must be stressed, however, that although the physical nature of the city forms such a base, it does not dictate these sensations or practices. In addition to the obvious debt to Bourdieu in these statements, the stress that Bourdieu himself lays on the dialectical relationship between environment and behaviour allows for a more complex analysis of the city. Social activity is performed in, influenced by, and, in turn, has an influence on the built environment (Bourdieu 1977: 72–8 and 95). Although not specifically developed for analysis of the city, the work of Bourdieu has had a clear influence on recent urban studies. For example, Harvey says that 'spatial practices derive their efficacy through the structure of social relations within which they come to play' (Harvey 1990: 222–3; see also Harvey 1989: 231–41). The 'embeddedness' of practice in space is a recurring feature of his work.

One of the elements of urban experience that Harvey emphasises is that the city provides a backdrop to human action. Paraphrasing Raban's *Soft City*, he describes the city as 'a theatre, a series of stages upon which individuals could work their own distinctive magic while performing a multiplicity of roles' (Harvey 1990: 5; echoed in Gottdiener 1995: 128). The city is conceived as a complex maze of interrelating elements and paths, through which individuals negotiate their quotidian experience. The 'pedestrian rhetoric' implied in this is explored explicitly by de Certeau (de Certeau 1984). He emphasises that it is by walking through such mazes and labyrinths that individuals make sense of the city, react to it and influence its form: the 'swarming mass [of footsteps] is an innumerable collection of singularities. Their intertwined paths give shape to spaces. They weave places together' (de Certeau 1984: 97). Thus, as the setting for social practices and actions, the city, both physically and conceptually, becomes a crucial element in the provision of a *habitus* for social reproduction.

If, as stated above, social actions are located in, locate and inform the urban environment, such an environment must inevitably reflect social ideology (Gottdiener 1995: 73). In the words of Harvey, 'the spaces of the city are created by myriad actions, all of which bear the stamp of human intent' (Harvey 1990: 214; see also Lefebvre 1991: 73). He argues that space, its organisation and its conception are a means of expression. For example, an architect 'tries to communicate certain values through the construction of spatial order' (Harvey 1990: 205–6). At the same time, 'material forms express ideology, just as codified ideology requires material culture as its sign vehicle' (Harvey 1990: 77). As a result of their creation through impounded social actions within them, the spatial forms of cities are symptomatic of the ideologies behind such actions and practices. The forms themselves also feed back into these actions and practices. Socio-semioticians would here emphasise the importance of the material form's relationship to ideology and social change. (Gottdiener 1995: 70–1 uses the work of Foucault to illustrate this; see also Gottdiener and Lagopoulos (eds.) 1986.)

The individual's behaviour in, and understanding of, the city are dependent on socially conditioned judgements about urban space. On entering a specific environment, 'we draw on a repertoire of gestures and interactive competencies in order to negotiate material space as well as communicate with others' (Gottdiener 1995: 73), dependent on the values and meanings that the environment has accrued. These meanings and values are not universal, but are created by social knowledge. There is no universal language of space or the city (Gottdiener and Lagopoulos (eds.) 1986: 10), yet within specific practices the production and use of space can define relations between people, activities, things and concepts (H. Moore 1986).

A frequently neglected aspect of practice is the lapse of time that it inevitably entails. It is through the repeated actions of individuals over time and in space that significance is embodied in the fabric of the city. The passage of time also allows changes in the meanings: 'New meanings can be found in older materialisations of space and time. We appropriate ancient space in very modern ways' (Harvey 1990: 204). Sennett gives ample demonstration of the different prioritisations given to the same space in his

study of ancient and medieval Rome (Sennett 1994: chs. 3 and 4); for example, in the building of the Lateran Basilica, started in AD 313, 'the form of
the ancient court of justice had been recreated', but this time the space was
used not for justice but for ritual (Sennett 1994: 142; see also Vance 1990: 9,
20–1). The appropriation of urban space over time has led many to compare
urban fabric to a palimpsest: 'almost all cities are polysemic agglomerations
of historically variant design practices' (Vance 1990: 9, 20–1) where the
fragmented fabric of the city is repeatedly overlaid with meanings.

   This temporal element of the city allows for an examination of change in
urban form. Many authors stress the importance of 'urbanism as process –
the many ways in which the city's physical frame is adjusted to changing exi-
gencies' (Kostof 1992: 8). These adjustments of the frame are never arbitrary
or random (Kostof 1992: 8; Waterhouse 1993: 10). Changes in the built environments parallel changes in society and culture because the articulation
of the city is a medium for expressing socially, culturally and institutionally
expedient objectives (Ford 1994; Vance 1990: 11).

   The archaeological study of Etruscan urbanism is fraught with difficulties,
many of them shared with domestic architecture. No site has been excavated
in its entirety, so any evidence we have from a particular site may not be representative of the original whole. In addition, many Etruscan centres have
been continuously occupied since Etruscan times, resulting in the destruction of the pre-existing urban fabric, or, in some cases, the remodelling
of the Etruscan remains (such as walls or gates, most notably at Volterra).
This chapter will draw on the evidence from nineteen Etruscan settlement
sites from the eighth to the second centuries, in both South and North
Etruria. The quality and quantity of evidence they yield vary greatly, from
traces of ancient walls in their modern descendants (for instance at Perugia,
Volterra and Cortona) to the results of more systematic and well-reported
excavations (for instance at Acquarossa, San Giovenale and Marzabotto).
The chronological assignation of this material is perhaps the least precise
of all examined in this book. This is due to the difficulties of 'dating' a
city that result from the nature of settlement deposition (and the resulting small quantities of stratified diagnostic material), the shortcomings in
the excavation methodologies of previous archaeological inquiries, and the
variety of data from sites (because of a historical lack of interest and/or continuous occupation of the sites). Most importantly, different parts of any
urban environment are likely to date from different periods. Like domestic
architecture, very wide and overlapping chronologies are put forward by
excavators and for different parts of sites; again like domestic architecture,
these have been put into chronological order according to the last possible

period from which they could come, and the sections of the site that have been individually dated have been treated in the chronologically appropriate part of the discussion that follows. (For more detail see Izzet 1997, appendix 4.)

Picking up several themes of urbanism within such a chronological framework, the main body of this chapter will examine the boundaries between public and private space, between different public spaces, and between urban and non-urban space. It will be argued that the changes in urban form towards the end of the sixth century are motivated by the desire to express, clarify and perpetuate these boundaries.

Public and private

As in domestic architecture, the primary distinction considered here is that between public and private. For domestic architecture, this was manifest in the material form of the buildings: in the flat, straight walls of the houses; in the decrease in the number of entrances and the greater propensity to place entrances centrally; in the unified façades of fifth-century houses; and in the durability of materials chosen for this. The concern of this chapter is the urban matrix of Etruscan towns. Given the concern with public and private argued for the individual unit, this section will first explore the ways in which the domestic unit was integrated into the wider urban make-up by examining the relationship between house and street. This relationship between house and street is one of two ways in which public and private are differentiated in fifth-century urban form; the other, as will be discussed later, is in the differentiation between domestic and non-domestic industrial production.

The street and the house

The outer walls of houses not only marked the beginning of the private sphere; from the perspective of the street they also marked the end of the public sphere. The significance of the imposition of a street grid will be explored in more detail later in this chapter; in this section, the changing form of street layout will be seen as playing a part in the dialogue between public and private through the changing relationship which resulted between street and house. The earlier, irregular arrangement of winding streets, for example in San Giovenale and Acquarossa from the eighth to the sixth century, and in Doganella during the seventh century, was replaced, in early fifth-century sites, such as Marzabotto, by a network of straight roads at right-angles. Houses were arranged according to these streets, laid out along them, and usually parallel or perpendicular to them.

The layout of earlier settlements in Etruria is difficult to assess since no one site has been excavated in its entirety. Nonetheless, some idea of the organisation (or lack of it) of such sites is still possible. The iron-age huts, and early rectilinear structures, were arranged in what appears to be an arbitrary fashion. This can be seen, for example, in the huts in Area D at San Giovenale (Boëthius *et al.* 1962: 289; Berggren and Berggren 1980; 1981; Nylander 1986b), or in the houses from Area B at Acquarossa (Östenberg 1975: 12; Persson 1986: 42). The plans of these areas, Figs. 5.1 and 5.5 respectively, show that houses from this period were placed in no discernible spatial relationship to one another. By contrast, in the sixth century, houses such as those at Lago dell'Accesa showed some rough alignment with one another, as did those in the Piazza d'Armi at Veii (Camporeale 1985b: 132–3, 169; 1997: xxii; Camporeale and Giuntoli 2000: 60; Stefani 1953: 93).

By the late sixth century, however, this irregularity of alignment was lost and the pattern of structures within settlements became strictly regularised; for example in Zones F and N at Acquarossa, where, in the latter case, the regularised area extended for a distance of at least 80 metres (Östenberg 1975: 26, 47; Persson 1994: 300–1). By the fifth century, houses were arranged in a strict orthogonal relationship to the streets, as may be seen, for example, at Doganella (Michelucci 1980: 556; 1981: 102), Roselle (Bocci Pacini *et al.* 1975: 60–73), Le Murelle (Colonna 1977: 213; 1986: 462), and, as shown in Fig. 6.1, at Marzabotto (Brizio 1891: 286; Mansuelli 1963: 46–58; 1979: 358; Staccioli 1967: 114–15; Tripponi 1971: 227). This trend was continued into the fourth century at Musarna (Broise and Jolivet 1985: 365; 1991: 346).

If the houses were oriented according to the street, at the same time the streets inevitably bore a direct relationship to the houses. The street must, therefore, be seen as another area in which the distinction between public and private was played out: from the street, the long rows of late sixth-century houses would have presented one unified façade, arranged in parallel and perpendicular lines. The blocks of houses did not allow passage around the houses as individual units; rather, each unit was one of a block of six or seven houses. In this way, the private sphere was preserved behind the walls of these rows. By the late sixth or early fifth century, the spheres of the private and the public were therefore separated not only from the perspective of domestic architecture, but also in the way that pedestrian routes of the city were configured.

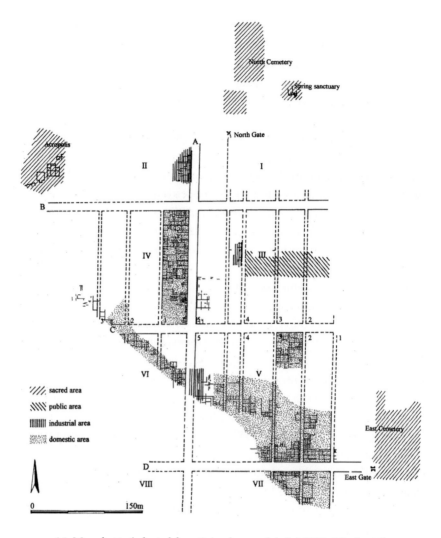

6.1 Marzabotto (adapted from Brizzolara *et al.* (eds.) 1980: 108, fig. 15)

Although the material definition and expression of certain differences, such as public and private, are clear, it is important to remember that once such boundaries were established, there was still potential for ambiguity and uncertainty. For instance, in the distinction between the house and the street, ambiguity would still surround the space that was at the edge of the street. From the late sixth century, pavements were built along the major roads of Etruscan settlements. The earliest examples date from the late sixth century and come from the north-west gate area at Veii (Ward-Perkins 1959: 65). During the late sixth or early fifth centuries, they were built at Le Murelle (Colonna 1977: 213; 1986: 462) and at Roselle (Laviosa 1960:

plate 68) and Marzabotto (Brizzolara *et al.* (eds.) 1980: 108). Later examples survive in the fourth-century levels at Vetulonia (Falchi 1898: 275–6; Carresi 1985: 141–2). In modern western cultures such spaces are considered largely municipal, public spaces; however, in many Mediterranean countries the relationship between the privacy of the house and the public space outside is very blurred in such areas. For instance, pavements are accessible to all users of the street; however, the owners of houses are deemed responsible for the construction, cleaning and often the daily sweeping of such areas. Sometimes it is possible to extend the line of the end of one domestic unit out into the pavement by the difference between a swept section of pavement and an unswept one next to it – as can be seen in modern Italy and Northern Cyprus. Of course, such insight is impossible with Etruscan archaeological material, yet the problematic nature of the evidence should not be forgotten. However, whatever the ambiguities, and however frequently they were negotiated and renegotiated, it is important to remember the significance of the permanent material expression of the overriding boundary between public and private.

Domestic and non-domestic production

A further way in which urban space was differentiated in the late sixth century was according to its function in production. Nijboer has shown the importance of the development of craft specialisation within Etruscan urbanism (Nijboer 1997, 1998). This section explores the spatial organisation of this change. In the seventh- and sixth-century levels of Zone B at Acquarossa, the houses contained traces of small-scale domestic metalworking, giving them what Colonna calls 'un carattere spiccatamente artigianale' (Colonna 1986: 395). In contrast, the sixth-century survey evidence of Doganella shows 'a clear economic and social partition of the settlement' (Spivey and Stoddart 1990: 56). At this time, amphora production was concentrated in the West, and this continued during the fifth century when, in addition, the north-west, unbuilt areas were used for storage and the cultivation of livestock. By the end of the sixth century or in the early fifth century, at Roselle and Marzabotto, and in the San Cerbone and Poggia della Porcareccia areas of Populonia, for example, distinct areas were established within the settlement for industrial production, with concentrations of metalworking at the latter, pottery production at the former, and both at Marzabotto (Fig. 6.2. For Roselle: Bocci Pacini *et al.* 1975: 61; for Populonia: Minto 1954: 305–6; Martelli 1981: 162–3; for Marzabotto: Brizzolara *et al.* (eds.) 1980: 108–15; Mansuelli 1972: 113.). At Cerveteri, a fifth- to fourth-century industrial area has been identified (Mengarelli 1936: 71–3). Even in the later period there are still traces of domestic production in the houses; however, what is important here is that at the same time as this small-scale production was taking place in the domestic sphere, larger, specialised areas and spaces in the city were given over to production of a specific kind. The form of the city was moulded to accommodate this activity, and, at the same time, through the specialisation of space for activity, urban form also expressed the distinctions between domestic and industrial production.

Differentiating public spaces

The street network

'Streets are a primary ingredient of urban existence. They provide the structure on which to weave the complex interactions of the architectural fabric with human organisation' (Çelik *et al.* 1994: 1). The public space of streets is an arena in which quotidian social actions and interactions are enacted; as a result, 'ideology is always present in plans for streets' (Çelik *et al.* 1994: 5). As such, the varying street plans of Etruscan cities over this 500-year period reveal a great deal about changing ideologies towards urban life and its setting.

The relationship between houses and streets has been examined above; now, focus shifts to the street itself, and to the differing treatments of it. As noted above, there is little evidence for early settlement layout in Etruria. However, evidence from San Giovenale, Tarquinia and Veii, for example, suggests that huts were arranged in an arbitrary fashion in relation to one another and to any tracks that linked them. Elsewhere, this pattern has been shown to indicate the organic, unplanned growth of settlements (Çelik *et al.* 1994: 5), and it is plausible to suggest just such a development for early Etruscan sites, with huts being added in a spontaneous manner, where and when they were needed.

This lack of awareness of surrounding structures is true, too, of the earliest rectilinear houses in Etruria. These houses appear to take no account either of the placement of other houses or of the location of streets. For example, the seventh-century Area F at Acquarossa and the Borgo area at San Giovenale give a more regularly laid-out impression than their iron-age predecessors; however, they are by no means orthogonal. In the plan of the Borgo area of San Giovenale shown in Fig. 6.2, rather than being neatly organised, the houses radiated from the north-west (Blomé 1969; Nylander 1986a: 50;

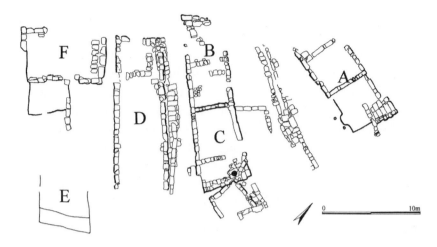

6.2 The Borgo area, San Giovenale (adapted from Blomé 1969: fig. 11)

1986b: 38). Similarly, at Acquarossa, Zones B and L were irregular in plan, with buildings arranged casually (Östenberg 1975: 12; 27; Persson 1986: 41–2).

The late sixth-century area of Zone N at Acquarossa contained the earliest signs of clear orthogonality (Östenberg 1975: 26, 47; Persson 1994: 300–1), and by the late sixth and early fifth century, at sites such as Le Murelle, Roselle and the Piazza d'Armi at Veii, any irregularities in the layout of streets have been almost entirely ironed out (Le Murelle: Colonna 1977: 213; 1986: 462; Roselle: Bocci Pacini *et al.* 1975: 60–73; Laviosa 1960: 313–20; Veii: Stefani 1953: 93).

However, the prime example of this orthogonality, as discussed above, is Marzabotto. Here, the entire site is organised along the axis of a main road that runs north–south, intersected at right-angles by three other roads (Fig. 6.1). The adherence to this north–south alignment is so strict at the site that the buildings of the acropolis, to the north-west, also conform to it. The organisation of the settlement according to this exacting pattern implies an attitude to public space that is very different from that in the earlier, unplanned settlements. Here, public space, in the form of streets and roads, needs to conform to a particular regular pattern. The lack of planned organisation in the earlier settlements indicates that the desire to order urban space and to mark boundaries within it was not perceived or acted upon in the previous centuries. It is only from the late sixth or early fifth century that this desire becomes materialised and expressed in the organisation of urban public space.

The increased evidence for planning in the early Greek colonies of southern Italy, and the scarcity of planning in early Etruscan cities, have been used to argue for the importance of Greek influence on Etruscan urban form (Owens 1991: 96); the layout of Marzabotto 'è chiaramente influenzato dalla dottrina urbanistica greca' (Colonna 1986: 464; see also Torelli 1985: 75, 83), and the '*insulae*' of the same site are seen as being 'of characteristically Greek type' (Owens 1991: 104–5). This may well be the case (though see Chapter 1), but ascribing Greek origins to Etruscan forms fails to explain why such Greek elements were relevant to Etruscan city-builders. These reasons become more apparent with a closer examination of the effects of changing urban form in the late sixth century.

One of the results of the grid layout of the Etruscan town was that, once in place, the grid dictated and restricted movement around the settlement to a much greater extent than in the irregular layout. In the hut and early house settlements, movement was possible around the houses because they were still individual units. In the later settlements, the houses joined together to form large blocks, like those at Marzabotto, where, for instance, block 1 of region IV measures 145 by 35 metres. This would have made movement in certain directions difficult. For instance, to get from the entrance of the house at the centre of this block to the corresponding position on block 2 of region IV (a distance of just over 35 metres) would have required a journey of 180 metres, moving around the whole block (Fig. 6.1). Conversely, other lines of direction were greatly facilitated by the grid: for example, the 400-metre extent of the city could be traversed in a single unbroken journey along two of the minor north–south roads. The pedestrian routes around the city, and thus the pedestrian experience of the city, were therefore influenced by the urban grid in a way very different from those in the earlier settlements.

Similarly, the gridding of the street plan and the conjunction of houses in blocks controlled and restricted lines of sight. In earlier settlements, the relatively small size of the huts and buildings, combined with their arbitrary and single arrangement, would have allowed light and vision to be more diffused, and even to seem multi-directional because of the frequency of spaces between the structures; in contrast, the strict orthogonal plan of later settlements, with long blocks of buildings, would restrict vision to along the straight roads. We do not know the height of the buildings at Marzabotto, but this effect would have been greater with increasing numbers of storeys.

The laying out of an entire settlement according to one grid implies some kind of authority capable of such organisation. It hints at a certain municipality, or centralised planning. This centralised organisation of public space is evident in two discrete though interrelated aspects of the street network: water supply and road paving. Earlier settlements show no signs either of the cobbling of streets or of the provision of water supply on anything but an individual level. For instance, at San Giovenale, House III in Area F and House C:1 on the Borgo had their own wells (Figs. 5.2 and 5.6); in the late sixth-century phase of this last house, the courtyard and well were no longer associated with House C, and the well appears to have become a public one (Colonna 1986: 400; Nylander 1986a: 47; 1986b: 38–40). At Marzabotto, a public well was located on road D (Marzabotto: Brizzolara *et al.* (eds.) 1980: 108), and at Vetulonia a well is attested towards the western end of the 'city excavations' (Falchi 1898: 275).

In addition, drains were incorporated into the urban fabric: at Veii, for instance, subterranean drains and open conduits were constructed in the area of the north-west gate in the late sixth century (Ward-Perkins 1959: 65; 1962: 1, 642; Stefani 1944: 228; see Damgaard Andersen 1997 for the Ponte Sodo; more generally see Bergamini (ed.) 1991). At the same site, Colonna argues that the cistern on the Piazza d'Armi was open, with access from the side by means of steps in the walls (Colonna 1986: 426; Stefani 1953: 105–12; Ward-Perkins 1961: 27; for similar cisterns elsewhere see G. Bartoloni 2001). In the late sixth- and early fifth-century sites of Le Murelle, San Giovenale and Veii, for instance, there were drains along the streets, and, at Marzabotto, the construction of drains, lined with large river pebbles, was integrated into the construction of roads (Le Murelle: Colonna 1977: 213; 1986: 462: San Giovenale: Nylander 1986b: 40; Veii: Stefani 1953: 105–12; Ward-Perkins 1961: 27; Marzabotto: Grillini *et al.* 1970; Brizzolara *et al.* (eds.) 1980: 108). Fig. 6.3 shows the alignment of the drains to the streets at this site, and also illustrates a further element of the municipality of this site. At the point at which the drain runs under the road which is perpendicular to it, the builders have incorporated large stone slabs to form a small bridge or culvert. The drainage of this site was an integral part of the layout of the entire site. Although unusual in its preservation, Marzabotto is not alone in containing such features. The laying of drains along streets continues in the fifth- and fourth-century phases of Doganella, Vetulonia and Roselle (Doganella: Michelucci 1985: 110; Walker 1985a: 448; 1985b: 250. Vetulonia: Falchi 1898: 278; Roselle: Bocci Pacini *et al.* 1975: 90; see also Steingräber 2000: 311).

Towards the end of the sixth century, the construction of the streets themselves also underwent a transformation. Kostof argues for the significance of the paving of streets: 'Paving is important . . . the implication of a delimited surface, an artificially marked off, open space, becomes central to the early development' of what he earlier calls 'the institution of the street' (Kostof

6.3 Drain, Marzabotto

1992: 190; see also Çelik *et al.* 1994). In earlier sites, such as Acquarossa
and San Giovenale, the means of getting around the settlement are defined
only by the absence of buildings. There were no streets as such; passage took
place through the non-built areas. This ends in the late sixth century with
the creation of road surfaces. For example, Acquarossa, Area 80, contains a
small stretch of river pebble road, and in Zones F and N there are stretches
of roads paved with *tufo* pieces; in the former, which is 4 metres wide, the
southern edge of the road is bounded by *tufo* blocks (Östenberg 1975: 25;
Persson 1986: 42; 1994: 301). In early fifth-century Doganella the central

street is cobbled, and those at Marzabotto are bounded by pavements, linked in places by large stones forming 'pedestrian crossings' like those at Pompeii (Doganella: Walker 1985a: 114; P. Perkins and Walker 1990: 15; Marzabotto: Brizzolara *et al.* (eds.) 1980: 108). In contrast to the earlier pathways, the space of the street is therefore physically defined and given expression in the form of paving and edging; it gains a positive form, integrity and, literally, a surface in its own right. This is a completely new feature in Etruscan urbanism.

Public spaces

Along with the laying out of streets and the inherent stress placed on these public spaces, other kinds of public space were also given definition during the sixth century. These include both ritual and non-ritual public areas. For non-ritual public spaces there is no evidence from the earlier period. Again, this is not to say that such spaces did not exist; however, they are not, at this time, embodied in material form. At San Giovenale there is the possibility of a public building of some kind, but its date, and whether it was a ritual or secular building, are not determined. This argument is based on the possible reuse of stone blocks from a previous public building in the fifth-century fortifications (Drews 1981: 150, n. 68). From the late sixth and early fifth centuries there are at least two building complexes of indeterminate function. These are the colonnaded buildings in Zone F of Acquarossa and the large elliptical building at Cerveteri (Acquarossa: Östenberg 1975: 18–25; Bergquist 1973: 21; Cerveteri: Cristofani 1988: 88–92). A parallel though earlier structure, with a similarly undetermined function, is at Murlo (Poggio Civitate: Phillips 1993; Stopponi (ed.) 1985: 41–58, 64–154). These complexes were large and imposing, and would have stood out in relation to the urban fabric that surrounded them. However, their function, whether administrative, ritual or extremely high-status residence, is unclear. Since none of the sites has been fully excavated, the possibility remains that less ambiguous public buildings will emerge from the archaeological record in the future.

At Veii, Colonna argues for open public spaces: 'la prima piazza urbanisticamente definita dell'intera Italia centrale' (Colonna 1986: 426; Stefani 1953: 105–12; Ward-Perkins 1961: 27). This is in the Piazza d'Armi area of the city (Fig. 6.4), an area containing a principal street, 4.65 metres wide, running almost the entire length of the outcrop, crossed by four roads. Towards the mid-point of the site is a block of houses around an open space: Colonna's piazza. It measures 25 by 35–40 metres, with a widening towards the east.

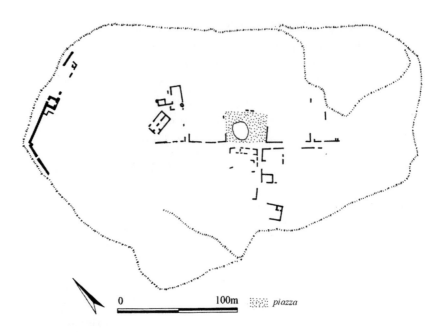

6.4 Piazza d'Armi, Veii (adapted from Colonna 1986: 508, plate 8)

The cistern referred to above is in this piazza. The space, defined by the exterior walls of the surrounding buildings, contains no evidence for ritual activity. This open space within the built-up areas is differentiated from the rest of the site by the very absence of buildings. That this is deliberate and planned is hinted at by the regularity of the surrounding buildings. This is not simply a space in which building has not taken place; it is a space that has been left open.

The differentiation of the entire Piazza d'Armi plateau as a public area of the city is emphasised by a large artificial *fossa*, or ditch, between the outcrop and the rest of the settlement (Colonna 1986: 433; Fontaine 1993: Ward-Perkins 1961: 14), and by the presence of two possible ritual buildings (see Chapter 4 above). Not only is an open space defined, but the whole area of the Piazza d'Armi is itself defined against the rest of the settlement through its monumentalisation (G. Bartoloni *et al.* 2005). This must be seen as a deliberate action to differentiate and emphasise discrete urban spaces within the city. A similar example of the way that non-ritual public space is defined within the form of the city is at Roselle, where public buildings are located in the valley between two residential areas (Colonna 1986: 149). At the beginning of the sixth century, the citadel at Vetulonia was walled with large, irregular blocks (Fig. 6.5; Carresi 1985: 122); at Marzabotto a piazza and a public building of some kind are argued for Regions III and

V (Fig. 6.1); and a fourth-century piazza has been delineated at Musarna (Marzabotto: Campagnano *et al.* 1970: 235; Mansuelli 1972: 130; 1979: 356; Brizzolara *et al.* (eds.) 1980: 115–16; Brizio 1891: 280; Musarna: Broise and Jolivet 1985: 347; 1986: 406; 1987: 505; 1988a: 365).

Ritual spaces

The distinction between ritual and non-ritual was another axis along which urban space was ordered. In fact, the sixth century was a period of 'rivaluazione ed appropriazione del sacro' (Colonna 1986: 433) within the urban fabric. As discussed above in Chapter 4, the late sixth century saw the construction of the monumental sanctuaries in Etruria, many of which were in an urban or suburban context. These sanctuaries comprised not only a temple, but also altars, buildings and other features, such as a ritual pool; all of this was enclosed within a boundary wall. Sacred space was given its own discrete place integrated within the urban environment by its monumentalisation and by its containment within a bounded area of the city, for example at the Belvedere sanctuary at Orvieto (Colonna 1985d: 82). At Marzabotto there is a concentration of ritual buildings in one particular location: the acropolis. This discrete area towards the north-west of the site (Fig. 6.1) contains the foundations and bases of two altars and two temples (there was a fifth structure, now destroyed). These edifices were aligned with the orientation of the settlement (Brizzolara *et al.* (eds.) 1980: 105–6; Colonna 1985d: 89; Mansuelli 1972: 130). Thus, this sacred space is set within the city not just by its location, but also by the alignment of the ritual buildings to the rest of the city, and by its containment within a precinct: the whole area itself was bounded and separated from the non-ritual by 'un robusto muro . . . che delimitava il margine meridionale della terrazza dei templi' (Vitali 1985: 89). The distinctions between sacred and non-sacred were defined through the creation of precincts, through physical boundaries, and through the monumentalisation of these areas with distinctly 'sacred' architecture.

As discussed above, the development of the Etruscan city at the end of the sixth century and beginning of the fifth saw the manipulation and differentiation of public space. Streets became clearly defined as different from the space surrounding them by the imposition of a grid and through paving. Public points of water collection were created and incorporated within the city, and, finally, both ritual and non-ritual public spaces were highly defined within the urban matrix. Thus, within the city itself, a clear definition of the different areas and functions of the city was expressed in material form.

City and non-city

As well as the crystallisation of boundaries within the city, the late sixth century saw increased definition of the difference between the city and the countryside around it. This was achieved through the building of city walls, and accompanying this, monumental entrances, the location of ritual spaces at the edges of the cities, the creation of a self-consciously urban fabric, and a self-consciously rural entity in relation to which the city was defined.

Walls and gateways

Aristotle notes that city walls, as well as serving military purposes, play an equally important role as 'embellishments' of the city (Arist. *Pol.* 7.11). It is on these 'embellishments' that this section will concentrate; though describing the Greek context, Aristotle's proposition raises the possibility of non-military meanings and functions of city walls alongside their defensive ones. This is not to deny the importance of city walls as military defences (see for example A. W. Lawrence 1979; Winter 1971); however, these have been amply elaborated by others, and, for the present, other aspects will be emphasised (Fontaine 1994a: 141–6). One of these is that city walls should be seen as the articulation of the difference between the urban and the non-urban. Walls, gateways and doors, for example between different regions, or between city and countryside, 'contribute to the very definitions of those territorial or urban entities' (Parker Pearson and Richards 1994b: 24). Though the fortification, in the form of a wooden palisade, of the Borgo area of San Giovenale has been suggested for the eighth century BC (Karlsson 1999), and the natural defensibility (cliffs, streams etc.) is a well-noted feature of many Etruscan sites, these perishable or natural features were not permanently marked through the choice of materials. One of the earliest sets of masonry city walls in Etruria comes from the seventh-century phases of Roselle. This rests on a stone pile foundation, 1 metre high and 1.8 metres wide. On top of these foundations, mud bricks, 40–50 centimetres long and 7–8 centimetres high, were laid to form the walls. At roughly the same time, the citadel at Vetulonia was walled (Carresi 1985: 122).

During the sixth century the mud-brick walls of Roselle were replaced by walls consisting of large polygonal stone blocks, which still survive to a height of 5 metres (Fig. 6.5; Bianchi-Bandinelli 1925b: 36; Canocchi 1980: 47–9). These walls were punctuated by seven gates. The sixth century also

6.5 Polygonal walls, Roselle

saw the cutting of a defensive ditch surmounted by quasi-rectangular blocks
at Cerveteri, and the construction of walls around the Piazza d'Armi at
Veii (Cerveteri: Proietti 1986: 217; Veii: Fontaine 1993; Ward-Perkins 1961:
32). In the later sixth century or early fifth century, walls were built around
Cortona, Le Murelle, the upper section of the city at Populonia and the lower
city at Vetulonia (Cortona: Neppi Modona 1925: 51–5; Le Murelle: Colonna
1986: 462; Populonia: Minto 1943: 18–22; Fedeli 1983: 126, 136; Vetulonia:
Falchi 1898: 82–4). During the fifth century, walls were built around the

rest of the city of Veii. In addition, the earlier wall of the Piazza d'Armi was reinforced with short outer walls. In the fourth century, Doganella built a stone circuit wall 6,800 metres in length, Populonia built its second, lower stretch of walls, and Volterra was walled (Doganella: Michelucci 1985: 112–3; Walker 1985a: 114; 1985b: 250; Populonia: Fedeli 1983: 133; Volterra: Fiumi 1976: 14–15). To these, the exceptionally preserved examples at Tarquinia should be added (Fontaine 1994a, 1994b). Whatever the military function of such constructions, their visual impact from both within the city and outside would have been considerable, particularly in the southern cities that were located on higher *tufo* outcrops.

These walls, or 'petrified outlines' of the city (Waterhouse 1993: 6), gave a physically fixed form to the extent of the Etruscan city: 'the settlement is locked in place' by its walls (Kostof 1992: 72). Before the construction of city walls, the point at which the city ended and the countryside began would have been hard to determine. The boundary of the settlement would have been constantly open to change and renegotiation as new buildings were added and occupation patterns changed. The building of walls defined and categorised the extent of the city, and, at the same time, froze the spread of what was perceived as the settlement by imposing a physical restriction. Walls defined what was in the city and what was not; they defined the parameters of the urban and differentiated it from the rural.

Any place is understood by being fixed in relation to another place (Greimas 1986: 27). The city defined itself from within as not being countryside. Walls physically embodied the edges of these differences at a very specific location on the landscape. By doing so, they set up the city as a sealed or semi-sealed unit in the landscape, very different from the surrounding areas. The use of stone to do this would have given permanence to the boundaries they marked: 'the act of hewing stone carries with it a profoundly expressive meaning of impermeable weight' (Waterhouse 1993: 7). Once constructed, they would, in turn, have informed the conceptions of the limits of the city.

Though city walls presented striking visual markers of difference, they were not impermeable. The city was linked to the countryside by monumental gates inserted into its walls, 'funnelling' (Kostof 1992: 36) traffic and people into the city. The earliest city gates are the sixth-century gates of the Piazza d'Armi at Veii, and the east and north gates at Marzabotto of the early fifth century (Veii: Fontaine 1993; Stefani 1922: 390–4; Ward-Perkins 1961: 58. Marzabotto: Mansuelli 1979: 306; Brizzolara *et al.* (eds.) 1980: 117; Brizio 1891: 278). A little later, in the fifth century, the Millstream, Valle La Fata and Capena gates at Veii, and up to seven gates at Perugia, including the Porta Marzia, were built (Veii: Ward-Perkins 1959: 66; 1961: 34–6, 38; Perugia: De Fosse 1980: 741–2). From the late fifth or fourth century, gates survive at Cerveteri, Chiusi, Doganella, Musarna, Orvieto, Populonia and Volterra, including the Porta dell'Arco (Cerveteri: Proietti 1986: 217; Chiusi: Bianchi-Bandinelli 1925a: 236; Doganella: Walker 1985a: 114; 1985b: 250; Musarna: Broise and Jolivet 1993: 446; Orvieto: Bizzari 1970: 153; Populonia: De Agostino 1962: 278; Volterra: Fiumi 1976: 14–15). Such gates were the only points of movement between the inside and outside of the city. As such, the construction of walls and gateways around the city would have restricted and determined points of entry into, and exit from, the city. This would have increased the sense of definition of the city, from both the inside and the outside. The predetermined apertures in the walls were the only ways of getting in or out of the city. They controlled not only how the city was approached, but they also determine how the city would unfold before the visitor, which elements of the city he or she would encounter, and in which order. This control need not necessarily have been imposed from some source of official or individual power, but could have grown up as part of a wider network of informed decisions on the part of the occupants of the city.

One of the Etruscan gateways of Volterra, the Porta all'Arco, survives today (Fig. 6.6). Though it was later modified by the addition of an arch, the lower section is Etruscan. It is made of large yellow *tufo* blocks, into which are set three heads carved from a grey stone. Argument centres around whether these were representations of the founders of the city or of some kind of protective divinities (Fiumi 1976: 14–15). Whatever the specific identification of the figures, it is clear that the boundary of the city was monumentalised and elaborated. A further example may be found in Perugia, where it is argued that the fifth-century Porta Marzia, with its three similar sculpted heads, originally formed one of the Etruscan gateways to the city (Campelli 1935: 25–9; De Fosse 1980: 741–2). The elaboration and monumentalisation of these points of transition from outside to inside emphasise the importance of the transition between these two physically separated states.

Further indications of the importance placed on the crossing of the city limits are provided in cities that were not walled. In Marzabotto, for instance, which does not appear to have been walled (though see Blake 1947: 72), gateways were constructed nonetheless (Fig. 6.7). Perhaps the rigidity of the street plan at this site, with its resulting long blocks of houses, was thought sufficient to define the extent of the city. However, when it came to traversing that difference, the transition was considered important enough to be marked through the building of monumental gateways.

6.6 Porta dell'Arco, Volterra

A concentration of buildings and settlement space would, of course, have been visible without walls, but the construction of walls would have crystallised the presence of the city in the landscape. 'Urban-ness' was defined in relation to the surrounding countryside by detachment from it: by the placing of ritual areas at the points of intersection between these two categories, by the form of the new cities, with their orthogonally arranged buildings and paved streets, by the monumentalisation of transitional areas between the two, and, most importantly, by the slicing through of the landscape with swathes of stonework. The walls – often massive constructions – would have

6.7 East Cemetery and East Gate, Marzabotto

been highly visible from the surrounding countryside. In the same way that domestic houses of the later period formed strict, vertical divisions between the public and the private, the city walls formed a vertical façade to the city. They were a material and visual manifestation of the physical and cognitive entity that was the city. The walls and their gateways indicate the need to express the city as a unit. They were the boundary between city and non-city, and their surface expressed this distinction, from both outside and inside.

'Ritual halos'

In addition to the walls, the separate and highly defined nature of the urban sphere was expressed in other ways. One of these was through the creation of ritualised boundaries. The liminal nature of ritual makes it particularly effective in negotiating and naturalising areas of uncertainty such as city limits. It is interesting to note that the location of many of the sanctuaries of Etruscan towns is on the edge of the settlement. Colonna has noted a tendency for ritual sites to be located near city gates or along the perimeter of the city, and this observation is echoed by Zifferero and, most recently, Nardi (Colonna 1985c: 68 includes Vulci, Tarquinia, Cortona, Cerveteri, Veii, Perugia and Arezzo; Nardi 2005; Zifferero 1995: 333).

These ritual outposts of the city would have acted as markers of the city's jurisdiction in the landscape. A good example of a sanctuary marking the city limits in Etruria is the Belvedere Temple at Orvieto (above, Fig. 4.1). This early fifth-century temple, measuring about 20 by 17 metres, was set within a precinct (Stopponi (ed.) 1985: 81) and was located at the eastern edge of the settlement plateau (Colonna 1985d: 82). At Marzabotto, the ritual space of the acropolis is outside the main area of the city to the west, as is the spring sanctuary to the north (Fig. 6.1; acropolis: Brizzolara *et al.* (eds.) 1980: 105–6; Colonna 1985d: 89; Mansuelli 1972: 130; spring sanctuary: Brizzolara *et al.* (eds.) 1980: 106; Mansuelli 1972: 114; 1979: 356–7). Inhabitants of the city and countryside must always have interacted at certain times and places; such interaction would have been most obviously necessary for exchange or ritual purposes. The sanctuaries, located either just inside or just outside the city, thus play their part in defining the edges of the city.

Cemeteries were also incorporated into the dialectic of city and non-city. (For the importance of the location of cemeteries, see Parker Pearson 1993.) Though the links between individual "villages" and cemeteries are now doubted (Bonghi Jovino and Charamonte Treré (eds.) 1997: 153–60; Guaitoli 1981; Guidi 1989; Mandolesi 1994; Pacciarelli 1991a; 1991b, 1994; *pace*, e.g., Potter 1979: 61), a general spatial association between cemeteries and settlements was established by the Iron Age and continued throughout the Etruscan period. A late sixth- or early fifth-century example is the East cemetery at Marzabotto (Fig. 6.8) where the collocation of the cemetery with the city gate can be seen as merging the transitional areas of the two spheres. Riva and Stoddart stress that funerary architecture is particularly effective in expressing political boundaries because of the liminal aspects of death rituals (Riva and Stoddart 1996: 94). They argue that in the late sixth century, the efficacy of necropoleis in acting as boundaries between the urban and non-urban is increased because of the arrangement of tombs in rows along streets. The location of ritual spaces, through the creation of what the authors call 'ritual halos', was thus brought into the rhetoric of the definition of the city. (See also Zifferero's work on sanctuaries: Zifferero 1995, 2002b.)

Boundary stones

Roughly at the end of the sixth century a new phenomenon appears in the archaeological record, in both urban and non-urban contexts: boundary-markers. These stones are inscribed with the words '*mi tular*', or more unusually '*tular mi*', thought to mean 'I am the boundary' (Cristofani and Torelli 1993: 126; Lambrechts 1970). The inscription on such stones may go on to name the property-owner or to state what boundary the stone marked.

One such stone was found near Tragliatella, on the road between Cerveteri and Veii. It dates from the sixth century (Cristofani and Torelli 1993: 125–7) and contains the inscription '*tular mi*'. Interestingly, an example from near Cortona, on the boundary with Umbria, appears to mark a more public boundary than the usual private-property boundaries expressed in these stones (Stoddart 1990: 48).

The erratic and chance nature of their discovery makes the specific contextual placing of these stones difficult; nonetheless, these are testimony to the increased importance of the boundaries of the city and its territory, or of individual property. Instead of the previously unstated though no doubt communally understood territory or property boundaries, these stones were visible, physical and durable markers of such boundaries. Their deliberate placement in the city or landscape should be seen as part of the wider expression of boundedness and difference from the late sixth century onwards.

City and countryside

A final aspect of the definition of the Etruscan city lies in its relationship to its territory. There is a great need for a synthesis of the results of Etruscan landscape archaeology from the last fifty years or so that not only takes into account the results of major survey work such as that of South Etruria (Potter 1979), the Albegna Valley (A. Carandini *et al.* (eds.) 2002; P. Perkins 1999), Tuscania (Barker and Rasmussen 1988) and the Cecina Valley (Carafa 1994; Terrenato 1998), but also incorporates the results of the few rural excavations (P. Perkins and Attolini 1992; Stefani 1945; Terrenato 1998), as well as more symbolic approaches (Zifferero 1991a, 1995, 2002b). However, this is not the place for such a synthesis. Instead, the following sections will discuss aspects of the rural landscape that have a direct bearing on the subject of this chapter: cities. They will draw on the wealth of recent survey data in order to examine the way in which the exploitation and manipulation of the landscape were part of the definition of the urban entity of the city. This is, of course, to privilege the role of the urban elite within the landscape, a privilege that it already enjoys, to the detriment of the inhabitants of the landscape (Barker 1985; Horden and Purcell 2000: 91). However, I hope that by emphasising the relationship between town and country, the interconnectedness of the daily experience of the average Etruscan in the field and developments in urban form and culture will become apparent. There were two major ways in which the manipulation of the landscape was instrumental in the definition of the city: first, in terms of defining the territorial limits of the city, and second, in the creation of a distinct and organised sense of the landscape as a specific rural entity.

Territorial limits of the city

As well as the importance of sanctuaries in defining city limits, sanctuaries have also been drawn into discussions of the territorial limits of the city. Zifferero, for instance, like de Polignac or Guzzo for Greece, and Carafa for Campania, has emphasised the importance of sanctuary sites as forming a frontier, marking the edge of a city's influence and acting as a locus for the conflicts and resolution of territorial control (Carafa 1998; De Polignac 1995; Guzzo 1987; Zifferero 1995: 333; see also Molinos and Zifferero 1998). In addition, these sites are seen as a 'zona franca' for exchange and interaction, again as argued for Greece by de Polignac (1994: 5–11); see also Rendeli 1993: 357–60; Riva and Stoddart 1996: 91, 99–100.

In a detailed study of the settlement patterns of the territories of Tarquinia and Cerveteri, Zifferero has shown the concentration of small cult sites along the frontier between the two territories, coinciding with the natural frontier posed by the Tolfa mountains. Running inland from the coast, these are Punta della Vipera, foce del Marangone, Poggio Granarolo, Ripa Maiale, Casale dell'Aretta, Bufolareccia, Selvasecca, and Grotta Porcina (Zifferero 1995; 2002b: 251, fig. 4). The chronology for these 'frontier sanctuaries' is complex, but the establishment of the frontier is dated to the sixth century, though some of the settlements that accompany these cult sites may have been established earlier, during the seventh century, as territorial outposts (Zifferero 2002b: 247). Most interestingly, Zifferero argues that, in the case of Cerveteri, through the network of rural sanctuaries it is possible to trace the different phases of the development of the territorial influence of the city, and the different types of control exerted within the territory. In effect, he envisages almost concentric spheres of urban influence from the 'peri-urban' sanctuaries, such as Monte Abbatoncino, which are close to the city, through the rural sanctuaries within the territory, such as Griciano and Procoio di Ceri, which control access to a wider zone, to the 'frontier sanctuaries' of the Tolfa mountains or the coast, including Pyrgi, which allow access to regions beyond the city's territory (Zifferero 2002b: 262). In other words, his analysis shows that the landscape of the urban territory is organised into areas according to their relationship with the city, and that these differences are articulated by the location of rural sanctuaries.

Small fortified hilltop sites form another group of settlements that appears to be strategically located within the landscape. The best-preserved and documented examples of such sites come from the territory of Vulci, (Rendeli 1993: 212–20). The site of Rofalco, for example, is a semi-circular walled settlement occupied from the late sixth century until the third century. The substantial walls extended for 350 metres, were 4 metres wide, and incorporated at least two rectangular towers. Within the walls were the remains of orthogonally placed walls and a cistern. The topographic position of the site is telling: it is placed on the edge of a plateau that dominates the entire plain of Vulci. It is easily defensible, but other advantages are absent, such as good water sources or proximity to communication routes (Rendeli 1985a). An agricultural function for the site therefore seems unlikely, and instead the site has been seen as one of five in the area that are located so as to defend the territorial interests of the city. A similar series of sites has been noted in the Albegna Valley survey, though none is as well preserved (P. Perkins 1999: 21). At Poggio Petricci a pair of hilltops is enclosed by a 1.5-metre-thick wall at the watershed between the Elsa and Tafone Valleys. The site thus controls the route between Vulci and the minor centre of Saturnia. Fortified hilltops have also been identified at Monteti and Capalbio, dominating the coastal strip, and a similar site at Poggio Poggione would have controlled the routes between the Albegna Valley and the coastal strip. Perkins suggests that these sites, along with Rofalco, constituted a chain of strategic late sixth-century locations guarding the routes between the inland settlements of the valley and the coast, protecting the northern and eastern frontiers of the territory of Vulci. The recent excavations at Castellina del Marangone suggest a similar function for this fortified settlement at the territorial boundaries of Tarquinia and Cerveteri (Gran-Aymerich 2005; Prayon 2005). In a more extreme form of a similar argument, Cifani, using the territories of Orvieto and Veii, has argued that the establishment of smaller rural settlements in the landscape were part of a 'colonizing' strategy on the part of major cities, which offered rural land to town-dwellers (Cifani 2002a for Orvieto; Cifani 2005 for Veii).

The establishment of groups of settlements and harbours at the coastal limits of territories should also be seen in this light. In the Albegna Valley, there is a cluster of sites around the mouth of the Chiarone, a river mouth that was probably used as a port in the Etruscan period (P. Perkins 1999: 21). Interestingly, it is equally spaced between two other Etruscan ports or landing points: Orbetello to the north and Regisvilla to the south. The latter was the port of Vulci, founded in about 525 BC, and has been excavated in part. It comprised a rectangular area 600 by 300 metres, with orthogonally arranged streets, and buildings which were each made up of a series of rooms around a covered central courtyard. The principal street was 2.5 metres wide, carefully paved, drained and edged. The ceramic data suggest commercial activity during the fifth century, and the importance of the site in mediating between Vulci and other Mediterranean, principally Greek, cultures (Colonna 1986: 462; Tortorici 1985).

To the north of Orbetello, and at a similar distance from it as the harbour at the mouth of the Chiarone, was another settlement at Bengodi, below the hill of Talamonaccio. The site is probably the location of the sixth-century port site of Doganella, before it moved to Talamonaccio in the fourth century. The site yielded architectural terracottas and loom weights suggesting a ritual dimension and textile manufacture (P. Perkins 1999: 21).

These four coastal sites (Regisvilla, the mouth of the Chiarone, Orbetello and Bengodi) form a regularly spaced series of sites along the maritime limit of the territory, and must have played a part in the territory's definition. Such a role has been argued for the large sanctuary sites of Pyrgi and Gravisca (Spivey and Stoddart 1990; Stoddart 1990: 48). Though further research would be needed to prove it, it is not impossible that these sites were also located within a broader spatial pattern like that of the Albegna Valley sites, which included smaller coastal ritual/commercial sites such as Punta della Vipera at Santa Marinella (Comella 2001; Torelli 1967), and that were part of the wider-scale definition of the territories of Cerveteri and Tarquinia (Stoddart 1990: 48).

The final way in which the territorial control of the city was exerted in the countryside was in the location of minor centres. These were all located in good strategic positions and were evenly distributed throughout the territories of the cities. In the Albegna Valley the intermediate centres were regularly spaced between 10 and 12 kilometres apart. This is corroborated for the Fiora Valley in the territory of Vulci (Rendeli 1993: 173), and is implicit in the Tuscania survey data, where it is suggested that the sites recorded towards the ends of the 10-kilometre transects may belong to other settlement groupings (Barker and Rasmussen 1988: 38). One of the best-preserved examples of such centres is Ghacciaforte, its preservation being largely due to its abandonment after the Etruscan period (Del Chiaro 1976; P. Perkins 1999: 23–4; Rendini 1985). The site is on a hill on the north bank of the Albegna, from where it dominates the valley at the point where the valley narrows between the upper and lower valleys. It was heavily fortified with substantial (4.5 metres thick) walls that included at least three gates, which were recessed and so acted as bastions.

Such defensive and strategic positions typify the minor or intermediate centres of Etruria, such as San Giovenale, Blera or San Giuliano, and must indicate the extension of urban control over the landscape, as does the regular spacing of such sites. These centres were another way in which the territorial interests and limits of the large cities were established and maintained. Of course, the establishment of a road network was a crucial means of achieving this: the spider's-web-like pattern of roads in relation to settlements (see for instance Nardi 1985: 165; Potter 1979: 73, fig. 21, or Ward-Perkins *et al.* 1968: 19, fig. 4) is not only an indication of the focal role that the settlements played in their territories, but were the means by which communication was possible between a centre and its territory. As such, the roads of the territory expressed the extent and control of urban territories; however, it is in their (related) capacity as organisers of territory that roads will be discussed at greater length in the next section.

The creation of a 'rural' landscape

The second way in which the countryside and landscape around cities were implicated in the definition of the city is in the creation of a distinct rural landscape identity – a phenomenon Cifani ascribes to the sixth century (Cifani 2002: 257). This included reorganisation of both the exploitation and the settlement of the landscape. One of the essential factors in this was the opening up of the landscape around cities by the establishment of roads.

In the fifth century a 10.4-metre-wide road was constructed between Cerveteri and its port at Pyrgi, a distance of some 12 kilometres (Colonna 1986: 432; Giuliani and Quilici 1964; Steingräber 2000: 311). It was made of gravel, bounded by *tufo* blocks, and had a central hollow for drainage. Etruscan road-building is attested in other parts of Etruria, though most notably in central southern Etruria, where the *cappellacio* bedrock is very close to the surface. This soft rock was easily worn down and rutted by traffic so that the roads regularly needed to be recut. This has resulted, after centuries of use, in the impressive rock-cut roads of northern Lazio and southern Tuscany, which run like steep-sided ravines from the *tufo* plateaux to valley bottoms, often reaching depths of over 15 metres. The dating of such roads is based on objects from the tombs that lined them or from the material from settlements associated with them. The problems in dating these roads make it difficult to incorporate them into a chronological account with any precision. However, Potter, after Ward-Perkins, has differentiated between the winding, irregular courses of the bronze-age and Villanovan roads and the longer seventh- and sixth-century roads that were more suited to wheeled transport (Potter 1979: 79–84). The road network of Veii provides unusual opportunity for the study of the pre-Roman road network, as the city was largely abandoned at the end of the Etruscan period, and so the roads were not cut, redirected or further manipulated after this point.

In the first phase of road construction, Potter outlines two main types of road around Veii. The first is a series of tracks on valley floors, which followed the natural features of the landscape, and the second is a series of ridgeway tracks, such as the one that preceded the section of the Roman Via Flaminia that passed through the Ager Veientanus (Potter 1979: 81) or that which goes to Nepi and the Monti Sabatini (Ward-Perkins 1961: 3). The route from the La Fata Gate of the city is a frequently cited example of the former, though its traces on the valley bottom are buried under heavy silting. Nonetheless, where the track, which was suitable only for mules and pedestrian traffic, emerges on the other side of the valley, Ward-Perkins noted deeply scored ridges and gulleys winding up the valley side to the opposite plateau, at which point they merged to form a single V-shaped cutting. From this point the road could be traced until the point where it met the later Via Cassia, from where it went to Rome. The antiquity of the route is indicated by the Villanovan cemeteries and habitations that flank it, and the route continued in use until the Roman period. However, in importance it was superseded in the seventh and sixth centuries by more roundabout, though less difficult, roads from the Portonaccio and South-East Gates (Ward-Perkins 1961: 13).

The replacement of early mule and pedestrian routes by what Potter terms 'engineered' roads suitable for wheeled transport was typical of the seventh and sixth century restructuration of the Etruscan landscape. These cross-country routes were not based on natural corridors in the landscape in the same way as the earlier tracks. Instead, they followed longer routes that exploited gentler gradients, and the latter were minimised by cuttings. A good example of such a road is that between Veii and Cerveteri. Here the earlier, irregular, track that wound in and out of valleys was replaced by a longer route suitable for wagons and carts; it avoided the steepest gradients and the remaining slopes were smoothed out by the use of road cuttings (Hemphill 1975: 126).

The cuttings themselves vary in shape and scale. Some could be narrow, tunnel-like passages, others were huge (such as that at the crossing of the Fosso Maggiore gorge by the Nepi–Falerii Veters road, which is 15 metres deep and 200 metres long; Frederiksen and Ward-Perkins 1957: 141–2). Some were straight, such as at the crossing of the Fosso del Sorcelle between Falerii Veteres and Corchiano (Frederiksen and Ward-Perkins 1957: 147), or that leading out of the city at the Formello Gate (Ward-Perkins 1961: 19); others curved and wound their way up and down the plateau sides in order to ease the gradient further (for example, the road leading from the Formello Gate, after crossing the stream, winds its way back up the other side of the valley in a well-marked cutting that swings gently to the right; Ward-Perkins 1961: 20). There were frequently gutters either down the middle of the cuttings or along their sides to mitigate the effects of erosion, as was the case in roads in general (for example Frederiksen and Ward-Perkins 1957: 116–7).

The roads were complemented by complex engineering works, such as bridges and culverts (Boitani 1985b; Hemphill 1975; Potter 1979: 79–84; Ward-Perkins 1962). Streams were most frequently crossed using fords at points where there was an unusually hard shelf of *tufo* on the stream bed – such as those of Veii, where the roads from the North-East (Capena) Gate and the Formello Gate cross streams on leaving the city (Ward-Perkins 1961: 16, 19). Bridges are more unusual, though common. Usually, these must have been simple timber planks, though more impressive structures also survive: one example from the Pietrisco Valley, east of San Giovenale, had abutments of large tufo masonry more than 6 metres high and over 7 metres wide (Colonna and Backe Forsberg 1999; Forsberg 1984). The total span must have been nearly 10 metres, and involved at least two spans of timber supported by piles of stones in mid-stream (Hannell 1962: 304–6). More frequently, the courses of rivers and streams were redirected underground so that the road could pass over them without the need for a ford or bridge. For example, at the point at which the left fork of the road from the North-West Gate of Veii reaches the Fosso di Grotta Gramiccia, the stream runs into a cuniculus (Ward-Perkins 1961: 6); the same thing happened when the Monte Aguzzo road crossed the Fosso di Acqua Viva (Ward-Perkins 1968: 33).

These significant engineering and hydraulic skills involved major manipulations of the Etruscan landscape in order to bring it into line with the demands of the new road systems. The effect of this change in roads was, according to Potter, a complete remodelling of the road network in the seventh and sixth centuries (Potter 1979: 82). However, it was not only the major centres that were linked by roads; the major sites were also connected to minor centres and even to rural sites. For example, one of the routes from the North-East (Capena) Gate of Veii passed out of the city and into the farmland of Monte Aguzzo, where it ended (Ward Perkins 1961: 30–6; 1968: 33, road no. 3). Its purpose was to link rural sites (and produce) with Veii, and, despite its humble function, it was carefully cut and laid out, using cuttings and impressive (500 metres long) cuniculi in the same way that the long-distance routes did (Ward-Perkins 1961: 32). Thus, as a result of the later road network, the entire rural landscape was caught in the ambit of the urban territory. At the same time, the establishment of the road network resulted in the ordering and structuring of the rural landscape.

The ordering and structuring of the landscape through the establishment of a complex road network coincided with the intensification of agricultural practices in the landscape. As Barker and Gamble have shown, what is grown and the systems of husbandry are linked to economic, social and ideological frameworks (Barker and Gamble (eds.) 1985). In Etruria agricultural intensification was achieved through the manipulation of the landscape, and by changes in agricultural practices.

The most dramatic way in which the landscape was physically manipulated was in the construction of extensive networks of land-drainage channels (cuniculi), transforming wet, marginal land, or land that was prone to flooding, into that which was suitable for cultivation (Bergamini (ed.) 1991). Like those used in redirecting streams for the passage of roads, these were series of tunnels and shafts that effectively rerouted water underground for long stretches. Examples are clearly seen in the honeycombed landscape north of Veii (Judson and Kahane 1963; Ward-Perkins 1961: 111, fig. 44). The system of cuniculi was made up of narrow, horizontal tunnels, about 1.6 metres in height, and a series of vertical shafts that linked the tunnels to the surface. The latter were 30–40 metres apart, and provided air for workmen, a means of disposing quarried rock, and help in laying out the system. They usually had footholds for climbing in and out, and were covered with capstones. The network was made up of major cuniculi of impressive length, and tributary cuniculi that fed into them (Ward-Perkins 1968: 32). One of the most famous examples of a cuniculus is the Ponte Sodo between the North East (Capena) and Formello Gates at Veii. This was originally over 100 metres long, and carried the Valchetta stream under a rocky bluff projecting from the plateau, thus eliminating flooding at a sharp bend in the stream. Importantly, the Ponte Sodo antedates the fifth-century fortification of the city, as well as pre-existing cuniculi, thus placing the construction of the cuniculus network around Veii in the sixth century at the latest (T. B. Rasmussen 2005b: 85; Ward-Perkins 1961: 50). More impressive was the 600-metre length of the cuniculus that carried the Formello stream under the ridge on which the city was sited to join the Piordo on the other side of the plateau of Veii, providing a steady water supply all year for the southern and western parts of the town (Ward-Perkins 1961: 49–50).

However, cuniculi were not only for draining and diverting water away; they also provided water, in the same way as an aqueduct. Water could be collected in cisterns that were fed by catchment cuniculi that ran along the water veins in the rock, or it could be carried from streams to cisterns, such as by the cuniculus conveying water from the Piordo stream to the tank in the Portonaccio sanctuary (Ward-Perkins 1961: 48). These complicated arrangements for water management in the Etruscan landscape had the effect of regulating conditions for cultivation, and, like roads, were effective means of ordering the landscape.

Evidence of the intensification of agricultural exploitation of the Etruscan landscape comes from survey data in South Etruria. The three significant surveys in the region (South Etruria, Tuscania and Albegna Valley) all show a dramatic increase in the number of rural sites during the seventh and sixth centuries BC (see below). Though it has been argued that Potter's assertion that almost all the territory of Veii was agriculturally exploited was exaggerated (Potter 1979: 76; Barker and Rasmussen 1998: 195), there was nonetheless a large increase (if on a regionally varying scale) in the number of people living in the landscape, and so both consuming and producing agricultural produce. This was accompanied by an increase in the size of the populations of the larger settlements, again leading to an increased demand for agricultural produce. The increasing numbers of rural sites resulted in larger areas of the landscape being exploited agriculturally. Increasing land clearance and soil erosion similarly point to the incorporation of larger areas into cultivation (Barker and Rasmussen 1998: 41).

However, it was not just the increase in cultivable or cultivated land that suggests increased agricultural intensification. There is a range of evidence to suggest that changes in the ways in which agricultural processes were carried out also intensified production. The increase in 'off-site' material (usually associated with the inadvertent transport of archaeological material into the landscape with manure) in the survey data suggests that the need for increasing soil fertility was addressed, as well as highlighting the increased importance of other activities associated with such material, such as hunting, herding and forest exploitation (Barker and Rasmussen 1988: 33). Similarly, it has been suggested that the (limited) archaeobotanical data evince understanding and practice of crop rotation (of cereals and legumes) as a means of maintaining soil fertility (Barker and Rasmussen 1998: 193–4).

Changes in plant and animal husbandry also indicate the intensification of landscape exploitation. Palaeobotanical data from Etruscan sites are rare; however, what there is suggests an increase in the range of crops cultivated in contrast to the prehistoric and protohistoric periods. Evidence from Narce, Luni sul Mignone and the Fiora Valley suggests that a variety of legumes and vegetables was grown (Barker 1988: 773; Catacchio (ed.) 1983; Helbaek 1967; Jarman 1976). By the Etruscan period, tree cultivation was widespread and systematic. This is shown by the presence of botanical remains, such as grape pips from Cerveteri, Blera, Podere Tartuchino and Pyrgi (respectively, Izzet 2000; Constantini and Giorgi 1987; P. Perkins and Attolini 1992), olive stones from Cerveteri, Podere Tartuchino and Blera (respectively, Barker and Rasmussen 1998: 183; P. Perkins and Attolini 1992; Constantini and Giorgi 1987), as well as a range of fruit stones and pips such as cherry, fig, hazelnut and pear from Cerveteri and Blera (Izzet 2000; Constantini and Giorgi 1987). That this was systematic exploitation is shown by the 'infrastructural' evidence for wine-making and oil-pressing in the region. At Blera, the remains of vine trenches and a wine-press have been excavated, while the sunken storage jar from Podere Tartuchino has been interpreted as part of the secondary fermentation process of wine-making; two stone footings and a post hole close to the jar may be the remains of an associated press (Blera: Ricciardi 1987; Podere Tartuchino: P. Perkins and Attolini 1992). Similar sunken jars, which may have been used for the production of wine or olive oil, or for the storage of agricultural surplus, have been found at a small rural site near Tuscania (A. Grant *et al.* 1992), and at Veii (Stefani 1922). An olive press has recently been excavated in the early fifth-century phase of the Auditorium House, just north of Rome (Terrenato 2001). That this production was an integrated part of a wide network of exchange and redistribution is shown by the wide distribution of Etruscan transport amphorae in the sixth-century Mediterranean on the one hand, and in the large number of transport amphora fragments at the rural site of Podere Tartuchino on the other (P. Perkins and Attolini 1992). The growth of these new tree crops also allowed the increased exploitation of the landscape by allowing the use of valley sides (Barker 1988: 781).

In animal husbandry a similar intensification is evident. The range of animals increased (Clark 1989), as did the importance of secondary products in animal husbandry. The presence of objects used in textile manufacture in rural sites attests the production of cloth, for instance at Podere Tartuchino, and the same site has yielded evidence of cheese production in the form of a hearth and three post holes for a tripod used in cheese-making (Barker and Rasmussen 1998: 192; P. Perkins and Attolini 1992). The presence of older animals in faunal assemblages suggests the use of animals for wool and milk, as well as for meat (Cerveteri: Clark 1989; Populonia: De Grossi Mazzorin 1985, 1987; Acquarossa: Gejvall 1982; Blera: Scali 1987a; San Giovenale: Sorrentino 1981a, 1981b); it also suggests a more intensive use of land. The butchery marks on the faunal remains suggest further systematisation of animal husbandry in their homogeneity: the assemblages from Cerveteri and Populonia suggest standardised carcass processing resulting in standardised parcels of meat for food (or sacrifice) and of bone for tool manufacture (Clark 1989; De Grossi Mazzorin 1985, 1987).

However, it is not only the remains of agricultural practices that indicate the increased exploitation of the Etruscan landscape; the number of settlements, their relative sizes and their interrelationships also suggest such intensification. Despite the pioneering work of the British School at Rome in the middle of the last century, and the renewed calls for a shift in focus to the Etruscan landscape from the mid-1980s onwards (for example Barker 1985), the data available for the countryside of Etruria are largely limited to the results of three survey projects. As a result, the surveys of South Etruria, Tuscania and the Albegna Valley will play the major part in this discussion of the Etruscan landscape, though other projects, such as the survey carried out by Enei in the territory of Cerveteri, will also receive attention (Enei 1992, 1993). The problems of integrating and comparing survey data have been discussed at length (for example contributions to Alcock and Cherry (eds.) 2004), and are particularly relevant in the case of Etruria. In particular, the importance of the region as a pioneer in the area means that the methodology of the early work was underdeveloped, and the long time over which the South Etruria survey took place meant that methodologies changed during the course of the project. When it comes to integrating data from different surveys, projects use different criteria for identifying and characterising sites, and different chronological bands for analysing their results. Nonetheless, these projects provide unique information about this important aspect of Etruscan culture. The discussion will focus on three main aspects of settlement pattern: site numbers, site hierarchy, and the spatial relationships between sites in order to examine both the changing role of the countryside and the changing relationship between city and country in Etruria during the first millennium BC.

The differences in the chronological bands used by the different surveys are evident in the summaries of the data from the projects in Table 6.1, which show site numbers. These differences are a particular problem for examining changing site numbers with a focus on the late sixth century. However, in the broadest of terms their results concur in seeing a major increase in the number of sites at some stage between the seventh and fifth centuries.

For the area around Veii, the South Etruria survey data show a marked increase in sites (from 16 to 137) at a point after the beginning of the seventh century but before the beginning of the fifth century. The same increase emerges, though less extreme (from 79 to 314), from the cumulative data of the whole of the South Etruria survey area. The following period shows a very small increase in both. In Tuscania, a similarly dramatic rise

Table 6.1. Number of sites from survey results in southern Etruria

South Etruria: Veii (Potter 1979: 74, 90)

Date	Number of sites
10th–8th	16
7th–6th	137
5th–4th	127

(Area surveyed: *c.* 250 sq. km)

South Etruria: Totals for all survey area (Potter 1979: 74, 90)

Date	Number of sites
10th–9th	79
7th–6th	314
5th–4th	345

(Area surveyed: nearly 1,000 sq. km)

Tuscania (Barker and Rasmussen 1988: 29–32, 38–9)

Date	Number of sites		
10th–8th	16	+ 5?	= 21
7th–5th	63	+ 29?	= 92
4th–1st	93	+ 31?	= 124

(Area surveyed: *c.* 34 sq. km)

Albegna Valley (P. Perkins 1999: 55–6)

Date	Number of sites
7th	50
6th	81
5th	88
4th	58
3rd	36
2nd	158

(Area surveyed: *c.* 290 sq. km)

Cerveteri (Enei 2001)

Date	Number of sites
8th–7th	21
6th–5th	330
4th–3rd	442

(Area surveyed: *c.* 200 sq. km)

(from 16 to 63) is identified, though this time over a longer period, during the seventh, sixth and fifth centuries. In the Albegna Valley survey the material is divided according to century, and the results show a large increase (from 50 to 81) in the number of sites during the sixth century, and a small further increase in the fifth century. Perhaps the most dramatic increase (from 21 to 330) is in the area of Cerveteri, during the course of the sixth and fifth centuries.

Though these data do not overlap sufficiently to show a very precise picture, it is nonetheless clear that the period around the sixth century was one of considerable increase in the number of sites in the Etruscan landscape. Potter has emphasised the extent of cultivated or grazed land by the fifth century – nearly all the territory of Veii was exploited by this stage, and the same would appear to be the case in the other survey areas (Potter 1979: 76; Ward-Perkins 1968: 69; Barker and Rasmussen 1988: 38; P. Perkins 1999: 169).

The number of sites is not the only factor to change during this period: all the surveys note changes in the nature of the sites in the landscape. This involves the assessment of the level of hierarchy within the settlements, based primarily on the size of the sties, but also related to the spatial relationships between them. The South Etruria survey reveals a landscape of one or two nucleated settlements out of 14 in total in the Bronze Age, and 9 or so for the tenth to eighth century, accompanied by over 70 small rural sites. The Tuscania data do not show any differentiation in the size of settlements in the prehistoric or protohistoric period; the Albegna Valley does not provide data for this period.

In contrast to this picture for the earlier period, the period from the seventh to the fifth centuries sees an increasing differentiation in the size of settlements. In South Etruria, the nucleated settlement of Veii continues to dominate the pattern, but a new order of intermediate sites that are settlements noticeably larger than the rural sites surrounding them emerges. These sites represent either the differential growth of pre-existing sites such as Narce, Nepi and Falerii Veteres, or the emergence of new sites, such as Corchiano, Vignanello and La Ferriera. The Tuscania survey does not provide such evidence because the survey area is not large enough to encompass more that the one intermediate site of Tuscania itself. The Albegna Valley follows a pattern similar to that of South Etruria. Here the seventh century provides some evidence of hierarchy at the lower end of the scale between groups of houses or farms – hamlets or villages – and single farmsteads. At the upper end, the site of the later large city of Doganella was certainly occupied, as was the later intermediate centre of Ghiaccaforte, though the extent of these settlements at this time is uncertain. The greater chronological precision of the Albegna Valley survey data allows us to trace and increase in hierarchy during the sixth century in particular, where the intermediate centres of Talamonaccio, Orbetello, Ghiaccioforte, possibly Saturnia and presumably Doganella appear as such with certainty. Thus the increased population of the Etruscan countryside is accompanied by the increasing hierarchisation of settlements in terms of their relative size.

The Albegna Valley data (and reports) are unique in offering examples of the range of settlements within the territory of an Etruscan city. Below the level of the city and minor centre, there existed two further broad classes of settlement, which are the main component of discussions of the landscape. These are small villages or hamlets and single farmsteads. Although the regions that have been surveyed have not produced a site that is clearly identifiable as a village, Perkins has drawn the settlement at Lago dell'Accesa and the ongoing excavations at La Piana, south of Siena, into his discussion of the group of sites at the mouth of the Chiarone (P. Perkins 1999: 21–2; Colonna (ed.) 1985, 1997; Caccioli and Whitehead 1994 respectively). Such sites are envisaged as groups of individual households with an agricultural base, whose internal organisation is haphazard (though with increasing regularisation of the individual units, see Chapter 5 above).

The individual farmstead or smallholding is better represented in the record. As part of the Albegna Valley survey, excavation was carried out at the site of Podere Tartuchino, a small rural site that has to be taken as representative of this class of site (P. Perkins and Attolini 1992). The structures at the site show two stages of construction. The first, dating to the late sixth or early fifth centuries, is made up of a large single room (12.2 by 5.8 metres), with dry-stone and pebble walls. It had a timber portico running along one of its long sides. The second stage, a modification to the existing structure rather than rebuilding after destruction, is about a generation later. The walls are more carefully constructed, with more evenly sized stones and more accurately laid courses. The site was nearly doubled in size by the addition of three further rooms, and the central room was divided by a change in floor level. This room retained its function as the focus of the unit, and it was where food processing, cooking and eating took place. It was also the place where a large storage jar used in wine-making, referred to above, was found sunk into the beaten-earth floors (probably in use during both phases of the buildings occupation). A large sub-rectangular hearth was also found in the central room, and associated features have led to the suggestion that the inhabitants of the farm made cheese here (Barker and Rasmussen 1998: 192). Other industrial activities took place in the smaller rooms, which were probably also used for sleeping and for penning animals. In front of the building there was a substantial unpaved courtyard. The palaeobotanical data from the site suggest mixed cultivation, with increased soil potential through crop rotation. No faunal remains were recovered, due to the nature of the soils. The excavators have calculated the potential wine-production capacity of the site (from the sunken jar) and suggest a maximum of 1,250 litres, and a minimum 'modest' surplus. This small settlement, even if it produced only a modest surplus, therefore appears to have been involved in networks of exchange and redistribution, a suggestion corroborated by the presence of transport amphora fragments at the site (P. Perkins and Attolini 1992).

Other rural sites have been excavated in Etruria, though the detail available is less. For the present, these confirm that the picture presented by Podere Tartuchino is representative of this level of rural settlement. Excavations at Pietriccioli (5 kilometres east of Marsiliana) show similarities in construction method (dry-stone walls and tiled roof) and layout (rooms around a large yard; P. Perkins 1999, 19), as do the results of a rescue excavation at Montereggi (near Fiesole; Barker and Rasmussen 1998: 169–71) and S. Lucia (near Bagnoregio; Cagiano De Azevedo 1974). Simpler structures have been found in the territory of Tuscania, where a small, simple structure of similar construction, but without a courtyard, has been excavated (A. Grant *et al.* 1993), and at Pianello (east of Castoiglione in Teverina; D'Atri 1986). Of slightly later (fourth-century) date is the small farm building excavated at S. Mario in the territory of Volterra (Terrenato 1998). The structures and finds from such sites confirm the variety of agricultural production, and, in the case of the latter, considerable landscape exploitation, were characteristic of small rural settlements. These sites are considered to have been semi-self-sufficient units that produced (often) significant surpluses. They were thus embedded in wider networks of economic and social exchange, as evinced not only by their productive capacity, but also by the presence of low levels of high-status pottery and other objects (most notably the bronze figurine, gem, coins and finewares from S. Mario, but also decorated terracottas from Montereggi, and the fineware and *aes rude* from Podere Tartuchino) and transport amphora fragments. A complementary case is made in Zifferero's study of the distribution of rouletted or stamped red impasto produced at Cerveteri in the seventh and sixth centuries, which argues for a far more integrated system of communication and exchange between urban centre, secondary sites and an ordered rural landscape (Zifferero 2002a; cf. Pieraccini 2003).

The final aspect of settlement patterns to be examined here is that of the relationships between sites, and thus any hierarchy of power. In the South Etruria survey, the sites of the Bronze Age are located along river valleys, or on the shore of Lake Bracciano, and there appears to be no pattern to their distribution. They are thus sited according to landscape features rather than any other principle (Potter 1979: 60–2). The same haphazard location and lack of relationship to the centre of Tuscania are noted for the same period by Barker and Rasmussen (Barker and Rasmussen 1988: 38); again, the Albegna Valley provides no data for this period.

However, during the seventh and sixth centuries, a change takes place in terms of the spatial relationships between the sites in all the regions. In South Etruria, the intermediate sites appear to act as focal points within the settlement pattern. This is seen most clearly in the area around the major centre of Veii, where there is a concentration of small 'farms' in the first 5 kilometres around the site, but this concentration falls off rapidly beyond that. The same is seen in Tuscania, where the small rural sites are most dense within the first 5 kilometres of the centre, and they fall off in number after that. The concentration of small sites around larger ones suggests that the former are located precisely because of their proximity to the latter. In other words, the settlement centre acts as a focus for the small rural sites; the two are interdependent, and are established in the landscape in relation to each other, rather than in relation to, say, landscape features. The Albegna Valley survey data again provide more chronological precision: the seventh-century sites appear to be widely and thinly scattered through the region, whereas the concentration of settlements around the centres appears in the sixth century. The centrifugal power of the centres therefore emerges at the same time as the growth in settlement numbers and the appearance of size differentiation.

Thus the seventh and sixth centuries saw dramatic changes in the landscape of three regions of southern Etruria at least, changes that resulted in increasing complexity in the landscape record. If we take these data as representative of Etruria as a whole (by no means an unproblematic leap), by the late sixth century the entire landscape of Etruria was densely populated and exploited. For the Albegna Valley, Perkins has proposed an increase in the population from 2,800 in the seventh century to 10,667 in the sixth century. In addition, the relationships between previously undifferentiated sites became increasingly complex, with differences in size and spatial relationships becoming more marked.

This ordered and organised landscape was in contrast to the earlier, less differentiated space of the countryside. This highly organised countryside should be seen as part of the wider restructuring of Etruscan cultural forms in which the landscape was embedded. This inhabited rural landscape would have been defined against the large urban centres of the late sixth century, and would, equally, have played an important part in the definition of those urban centres.

The interrelationship between city and countryside in terms of settlement patterns has been the subject of recent syntheses of these survey data, principally by Rendeli and Stoddart (Rendeli 1993; Stoddart 1987; 1989; Spivey and Stoddart 1990). For Rendeli, concern centres on the appropriation and, in particular, the exploitation of the Etruscan landscape by large settlements for economic motives. Taking three cities (Vulci, Tarquinia and Cerveteri), he describes the changes in the organisation of settlements from the late Bronze Age until the Archaic period. In the territory of Vulci, for example, new centres of settlement, such as Poggio Buco, emerge in the late seventh century (Rendeli 1993: 168), at a distance of about 10–20 kilometres apart – about one day's journey, given the local geography (Rendeli 1993: 173). The affiliation of these sites to Vulci is argued through an analysis of funerary architecture and pottery style (Rendeli 1993: 183–4). In the early sixth century there is an increase in the frequency and decrease in the size of settlements in the territory (Rendeli 1993: 193–4), and, during the same century, there is a marked expansion of the territorial limits of the city (Rendeli 1993: 205). The late sixth century sees a more dramatic change, characterised by a decline in the number of small settlements, with the emergence of a few larger settlements, such as Doganella (Rendeli 1993: 219–20). Rendeli argues that the sixth century was the 'età del cristalizzazione' of the Etruscan landscape, so that by the end of the century the territorial limits of the city were established by a network of dependency within the changing settlement pattern (Rendeli 1993: 356–67; see also Enei 1992, 1993; Guidi 1998; 2000: 194–223; Zifferero 1995). A similarly close relationship between the city and the organisation of territorial frontiers is argued for in the placement of small settlements and sacred areas in the territory of Veii (De Santis 1997).

Stoddart's approach does not emanate from the city alone; rather, it covers the entire landscape, allowing consideration of areas outside the control of any major settlement, the so-called 'buffer zones'. He describes three main changes within the settlement distribution: the emergence of small, politically independent centres in the buffer zones between areas in the seventh and sixth centuries (Stoddart 1987: 213), an increase in small centres dispersed within the territory, and the establishment of sites at the limits of the territory (Spivey and Stoddart 1990: 52). During the sixth century, the extension of the territorial control of the major cities resulted in the destruction of the former independent settlements in the buffer areas, resulting in a 'restructuring of the political balance' of the landscape (Stoddart 1987: 218) and the emergence, instead, of larger sites like Doganella, which he sees as mediating between the large city and the rest of the territory (Spivey and Stoddart 1990: 56). The turn of the century saw a 'renewed phase of centralisation of authority' (Stoddart 1987: 218).

Both these studies serve to reinforce the impression from the individual surveys with regard to two important aspects of Etruscan landscape exploitation. The first is the dramatic changes in settlement patterns, and the second is the stress on the relationship between the city and its surrounding countryside. The city is located within the landscape of its territory, yet the two are clearly defined from each other in material form. Towards the end of the sixth century, the pattern changed from very numerous small settlements that extended over the entirety of the territory to a distribution pattern characterised by far fewer but much larger settlements, such as Doganella. Perkins has suggested that for the area of the Albegna Valley the ratio of urban to rural population was roughly 70:30 in the sixth century (P. Perkins 1999: 167). This concentration of population in urban centres in Etruria is in marked contrast to general estimates of pre-industrial urban populations (Horden and Purcell 2000: 92). This phenomenon should be seen as part of the heightened importance of cities in Etruria at this time, and as another way in which the difference between the city and countryside was emphasised. The city became the place for habitation, while the territory around it became emptier. At the same time, the territories of individual cities expanded, so that there was no neutral space left between them. Thus the entire Etruscan landscape was gradually incorporated into the political geography of the major cities, negating the ambiguity of the formerly neutral 'buffer zones'.

Conclusion

In this discussion of Etruscan urbanisation, a wide range of architectural and landscape evidence has been considered within a chronological framework. In the first part of the chapter, it was argued that changes in urban form served to stress the importance of surface as a means of expressing difference. The walls of houses, the grid street plan and the walls of the city were all manipulated to express difference and categorise space. Cognitive differences are expressed in material form through the creation of physical boundaries. The house, the piazza, the sanctuary and the city itself are highly defined as separate, distinct entities through the articulation of material surfaces and façades. In the second part of the chapter, the city was examined from the perspective of its relationship with its territory, and the role the latter played in its definition. The location of smaller sites within the landscape was shown to be integrated into the definition of the territorial boundaries of the city, and the evidence of roads and other engineering works, agricultural practices and settlement patterns was used to show the ways in which the rural landscape was increasingly differentiated from the urban landscape. This exploitation led, by the late sixth century, to a far clearer, more ordered and idealised 'image' of the Etruscan countryside.

7 | Making Etruscan society: culture contact and (material) culture change

Introduction

The preceding chapters have emphasised the deliberate nature of the creation of all aspects of material culture. In this way, changes in Etruscan material culture are accorded particular importance in the transformation of late sixth-century Etruria. As a result, such changes cannot be explained simply in terms of a natural evolution towards a more 'sensible' form, or in terms of the importation of 'superior' models; instead, the changes in Etruscan material forms are characterised by an increased concern with surface as a means of expressing difference. I have argued that the boundaries of physical entities became, in the sixth century BC, condensed to their visible, exterior surfaces, and further, that such physical distinctions echoed ontological ones. Thus, the outer, visible surface of the body, the tomb, the temple, the house and the city became the point at which these entities conceptually began. Surface thus became crucial for the expression of difference and identity in late sixth-century Etruscan material culture.

The importance of surface is not absolute or universal: the treatment of surfaces and boundaries changes over time and space, and is therefore relational. In the areas of Etruscan material culture examined here, for example, the treatment of surface in the late sixth century is more acute than that in the seventh century. The multiplicity of choices and decisions that were made by artisans in the creation of material culture led to objects and spaces that emphasised, to a greater extent than before, boundaries and distinctions through the explicit manipulation of their visible surfaces. However, while acknowledging that these distinctions are manifest in the archaeological material of the time, and that these distinctions reflected contemporary attitudes towards the bounded entities, it is also important to remember that, once created, these surface boundaries themselves actively helped to shape subsequent reactions and attitudes to those entities.

The emphasis on surface in this period of Etruscan archaeology has not been previously noted. Such an approach allows a local Etruscan motivation for the technological and manufacturing actions that went into the making of Etruscan culture during the second half of the sixth century. However, it is still only a description of the changes that took place, rather than an explanation for them; this last chapter will put forward some hypotheses for why there was such concern with surface in the late sixth century.

Cultural interaction and the creation of identity

My treatment of Etruscan surfaces so far explicitly lays emphasis on the visual aspect of the changes that took place in Etruscan material culture, and this is at the expense of other sensory factors. For example, the difference between inside and outside the tomb would be further impressed on the visitor to the tomb on entering, when changes in the light levels, temperature and acoustic qualities would have emphasised the change in ontological and spatial difference yet further. Although these factors are important, and would have had a significant impact on the visitor to the tomb, the previous analyses have not directed attention to them. The first reason for this is the well-established importance of viewing as a process that transforms the viewer (Elsner 1995); this emphasises the importance of material culture in changing the perceptions of individuals (be they perceptions of femininity, death, the city, etc.). The second (more important) reason for emphasising visuality is that I have wanted to underscore the importance of marking these differences not only to 'insiders' or participants in any given context, but also to non-participants and strangers. This is because it is the relationship with outsiders, and the establishment and clarification of the interactions between insiders and outsiders, that are crucial in explaining change *across* the range of material culture examined so far.

The importance of surface in the creation of identities, be it gender identity, the identity of the living and the dead, or urban and rural identities, has been discussed, explicitly and implicitly, both in theoretical terms and in the workings of the previous chapters. The cultural and historical malleability of physical and social boundaries has already been discussed in Chapter 1, and the importance of surface in defining the entities that they bound has been emphasised. For the purposes of this chapter, the discussion of identity will be extended to include the cultural identities of Etruria.

The relationship between individual and group identities has been explained in terms of the interconnectedness of the two: 'When the identity of a group is threatened, a response on the individual level is mobilised because the identity of the ethnic group has been internalised in the individual, with the consequence that injury to the group is seen as injury to the self' (J. M. Hall 1997: 30). It is thus possible to see the changes in the different levels of Etruscan material culture discussed so far in relation to changes in Etruscan conceptions of their ethnic and cultural identities more widely.

Such an assertion is based on the importance of everyday social and cultural practices in the formation of identity: established modes of differentiation, such as those that exist in gender or status hierarchies, or in those that exist in the organisation of domestic space, have been shown to be incorporated into, and to form essential parts of, the creation of ethnic symbolism (Eriksen 1991; Hodder 1982; S. Jones 1997: 125; Larick 1986; 1991; Olsen and Kobylinski 1991). Most importantly for the argument here *(pace* J. M. Hall 1997: 135), the last decade has seen a growing acknowledgement of the importance of everyday objects within the practices that go to create identity (see for example the work cited in Chapter 1, in particular Dietler and Herbich 1998; Dobres and Hoffman 1994; Gosselain 2000; Lemonnier 1992). In particular, Elsner's assertion that the act of viewing changes the viewer has special importance for underlining the centrality of material culture (and its reception) in the creation of identities (Elsner 1995).

The underlying emphasis that characterises most recent work on ethnicity is the rejection of the instrumentalist views that saw ethnicity as an unchanging category in itself; instead, a 'theory of practice for ethnicity' (S. Jones 1997) emphasises the fluidity and social expediency of ethnic identity (Blinkhorn 1997; J. M. Hall 1997, 2002; S. Jones 1997; Meadows 1997; Pluciennik 1997; Wells 1995, 1998). Just as it has been argued throughout this book that the boundaries of certain categories, including identity, changed over time, so too the saliency of ethnic boundaries and identities varies (J. M. Hall 1997: 30).

Changes in attitudes towards ethnic identity are commonly associated with contact with at least one 'other' group (Eriksen 1992: 34; J. M. Hall 1997: 32; Leach 1982: 58; Pálsson (ed.) 1993: 5, n. 1). Such a position builds on early work on personal identity, where the importance of the differentiation of the self in the light of encounters with others was emphasised (see Chapter 1, and, for example, Wiessner 1983), and has formed the basis of many recent analyses of Greek identity of the fifth century (for example Cartledge 1993; E. Hall 1989; J. M. Hall 1997, 2002) where the threat, and later the effects, of Persian invasion led to a highly defined sense of Greekness. Thus, an increased material expression of identities is a result of a threat to those very identities. If we accept this scenario as a possible explanation for the increased manipulation of surface in late sixth-century Etruria, what forms of stress might have resulted in such an overwhelming and ubiquitous reaffirmation of boundaries and identities?

The most frequently cited 'other' for Etruria is Greece. However, as discussed in Chapter 1, the relationship between the two is usually characterised by Etruscan imitation of culturally 'superior' Greek forms. After dismissing this as an outdated approach to cultural interaction, this chapter will look, with specific reference to Etruria, at how recent changes in our understanding of the workings of the ancient Mediterranean more widely have led to a picture of many cultures coming into contact with one another. The emerging image is one of equal participation and mutual self-definition in the face of this increased and more diverse contact. It will consider briefly the cultures of Greece, Phoenicia and three cultures of early Italy, in order to explore their roles as established or emerging cultural entities in contact with Etruria. Finally, since exogenous explanations are usually insufficient in themselves, the chapter will end with a brief survey of the wider Etruscan context in order to discern any local factors that may have contributed to the increased need to define and express boundaries.

Interactions outside Italy

Greece

The 'Hellenisation' of Etruria

First, this chapter will consider the concept of Hellenisation in relation to the aspects of Etruscan archaeology analysed above. As discussed, it is very common for Hellenic influence, or Hellenisation, to be cited as both a descriptive term and an explanatory device in analyses of material culture change at this time. The following paragraphs will focus more explicitly than in previous chapters on Hellenisation as a motivation for the material culture changes they discussed.

Perhaps the area in which Hellenic influence is easiest to discern is that of urban form. In this case the Greek (Hippodamian) model appears to be replicated within the grid plan of the Etruscan city of Marzabotto. However, Chapter 6 argued that although there may have been elements of Greek planning evident in Etruscan cities, these elements were chosen not merely because they were Greek, but because they were particularly effective in accentuating the external surface for the domestic and urban spheres. In other words, the local relevance of Greek forms, and an Etruscan predilection for them, were active and essential parts of their adoption. A parallel may be drawn with the area of ceramics: Arafat and Morgan have argued that although the volume of Attic vases in Etruscan tombs makes the importance of Greek imports undeniable, the influence on local ceramics was minimal, so that, for instance, the work of the Micali painter retains a strong preference for animal scenes (Arafat and Morgan 1994; for the Micali painter, see Spivey 1987). The vast numbers of Attic vases in Etruria did not have a profound impact on local production; instead, the popularity of Attic pottery derived from its very foreign-ness. These foreign pots, as Arafat and Morgan argue, were valued by Etruscan elites for their ability to set their elite owners apart from those less wealthy individuals, without international contacts, who could not own them. According to such a scenario, a local copy of an Attic pot would be useless (Arafat and Morgan 1994). Similarly, a city built along Greek lines would not perform the functions desired by Etruscan city-builders unless elements of the Greek city form could be used to fulfil specifically Etruscan needs. The same overlap is evident in certain aspects of temple and sanctuary form, where the pedimental front of temples, the use of columns and painted sculptural decoration, and even the use of terracotta tiles, may be seen as signs of Greek influence; however, the different Etruscan deployment of these elements (for example the number and location of columns, and in the use of terracotta for sculptural programmes) suggests that if such features did have an original Greek source, their adoption in an Etruscan context was determined by functions that were different from those in the Greek world.

In other aspects of Etruscan material culture, the case for Greek influence is harder to make. For instance, the deposition of mirrors in Greece takes place primarily in sanctuary contexts and is quite different from the tomb context of Etruscan mirrors. In fact, neither the use nor the form of mirrors in Etruscan culture has direct parallels in mainland Greece. Their function must be seen in relation to local factors rather than external ones. Similarly, though individual elements of domestic architecture have been ascribed to Greek influence, the overall development of Etruscan domestic architecture must be seen as one driven by Etruscan desires, principally the desire to express the difference between inside and outside through the visible surface of the house.

Such an approach, which emphasises the local manipulation of foreign forms, is echoed in the studies of areas of Etruscan material that have not been examined here; in these cases, too, the importance of the Greek contribution has been underplayed in recent years. Four such areas will serve to illustrate this. The first is in the area of mythology, where Spivey has shown that the figures and subjects, notably Ajax, that found their way to Etruria did not constitute a random or arbitrary selection, but were those that were appropriate to local ideas of correct, elite male behaviour (Spivey 1992);

and Small has made a similar case for aesthetic style and structure (Small 1987, 1991–2). At the same time, Scheffer has shown the active selection on a local Etruscan level of Greek motifs used in Etruscan black-figure (Scheffer 1984; see also Osborne 2001; T. B. Rasmussen 2005a). Similarly, Small has shown that the large quantities of sympotic vessels that have been found in Etruscan tombs do not indicate the adoption of the Greek 'symposium' in the Etruscan world, but should be seen as drinking equipment that fitted into a pre-existing Etruscan tradition of elite dining and feasting (Small 1994a). Finally, Snodgrass and d'Agostino have argued that hoplite warfare was inappropriate for the social framework of Etruria, and that, as a result, the finds of Greek hoplite armour found in Etruscan tombs echoed earlier elite use of arms and armour for elite display rather than the adoption of the hoplite phalanx (d'Agostino 1990a; Snodgrass 1965; Spivey and Stoddart 1990: 134–6; see also Stary 1979).

Post-colonial approaches

The preceding paragraphs and chapters have argued that, when examined from the perspective of surface, the relationship between Greek and Etruscan archaeology is more complex than the simplistic model of Greek superiority allows. The Greek elements that are identifiable within the Etruscan material record can be explained not in terms of fundamental Greek influence, still less of Hellenisation, but rather in terms of local needs; in this case, the need to create a surface to express physical boundaries, or to enforce social hierarchies, and thus to maintain social boundaries. Thus the appropriation of Greek material forms should not be seen as a desire on the part of the Etruscans to become, in some way, Greek. First, there are many aspects of Greek culture that the Etruscans reject (such as the hoplite phalanx and the symposium, mentioned above); second, Greek elements appear to be performing different functions in the Etruscan context (such as marking boundaries or social distinctions). As such, the Etruscan contextualisation of the Greek objects made them uniquely Etruscan objects, regardless of their original provenance.

Such readings of Etruscan and Greek interaction accord with recent so-called 'post-colonial' analyses of cross-cultural interaction. It has long been recognised that objects, when they move from one context into another, are transformed in meaning according to the new context in which they find themselves (Appadurai 1986; Gosden and Marshall 1999; Kopytoff 1986; Sahlins 1988; N. Thomas 1991). This is due to the new social and material relationships into which they are placed. This change in function and meaning has been explored in a wide range of ethnographic, anthropological and sociological examples. The importance of pre-existing symbolic structures in determining the reception of objects has been analysed by Gell in his study of the Muria of the Bastar district, Madhya Pradesh, India, and by Lederman in his study of the Mendi of the southern highlands of Papua New Guinea (Gell 1986; Lederman 1986). Similarly, the relevance of local cultural structures in determining, or 'indigenising', the use and meaning of objects has been illustrated by Thomas's study of European trading contacts in the South Pacific. Here the incorporation of European trade goods (such as guns) into local narratives resulted in the reconstitution of such objects according to local cultural schemas (N. Thomas 1991). Appadurai's concept of 'localisation' explores a similar process (Appadurai 1990).

These processes of recontextualisation have been described as hybridisation (Bhabha 1994; García Cancliui 1992), creolisation (Hannerz 1987, 1992; Jourdan 1994), or transculture (Ortiz 1947). The emphasis here is not on the emulation of one culture by another, or even on the selective acquisition of certain elements of one culture by another; instead, these concepts stress the creation of new cultural forms and systems through interaction and conjunction. As a result, indigenous uses of foreign forms can no longer be seen as a failure to copy the original correctly (as early discussions of Greek myth in Etruria – coining the term 'banalizzazione' – would have it). Instead, they are the locally pertinent and appropriate form that is created as a result of interaction. This is illustrated by Comaroff's study of British missionaries in South Africa. As part of their mission to civilise natives, the missionaries wanted to clothe them. However, the result was not a replication of British sartorial customs, but rather an indigenous style that was affected by local ethnic and class divisions, and by local symbolic codes. The most memorable instance of this was the commissioning by one South African chief of a European-style suit in leopard skin, a local sign of chiefly office. Comaroff argues that this was not an instance of a native inexpertly wanting to dress as a white man; instead, by combining the potent local symbol of the leopard skin with the equally powerful style of the European dress, the chief doubled his authority (Comaroff 1996).

Such views differ markedly in two ways from earlier, 'colonialist' perspectives, which have characterised analyses of the ancient and contemporary world. The first difference is in the way that the flow of ideas and goods is conceived: whereas a colonialist perspective characterised this flow as strictly unidirectional, moving from coloniser to colonised, a post-colonialist perspective shows how the inflow of ideas and goods into a receiving culture is itself redirected outwards, through the active reception and domestication – or localisation – of cultural forms. The second, overlapping difference is a shift from the intentionality of the coloniser to that of the colonial consumer, so that, again, the reception of objects is paramount in their meanings (Hannerz 1992; D. Miller 1985; Willis 1990).

In this way, the study of the local context becomes the key to our understanding of objects as they are consumed across and between cultures. The examination of the local context allows us to perceive the particularity of the articulation of goods in any given situation. Douglas and Isherwood have explored the 'assemblages' of objects that people construct through their combination of different objects in different proportions, and they have stressed the importance of these assemblages in assigning new meanings to objects and to the social groups that make them (Douglas and Isherwood 1979).

The 'colonised' is as important as the 'coloniser', therefore, in the construction of the social reality that ensues from contact between the two. As Bhabha has shown in his famous scenario of the patrol officer and the native, both men interacted within a complex web of mutually perceived relationships, including beliefs and ideas about the other, and it was the negotiation and renegotiation of these beliefs through this interaction that shaped their attitudes towards one other: 'native' and 'coloniser' are thus equally enmeshed in the creation of the colonising experience (Bhabha 1994: 95). This example shows the importance of all participants in the colonial or cross-cultural context, as well as highlighting the importance of the small-scale, everyday nature of the creation of that context (see also van Dommelen 1997).

The Mediterranean context

The influence of these ideas has been felt in recent treatments of Greek colonisation and in investigations of the nature of Greek trade and interaction abroad, and, as a result, such ideas have also impacted on the study of the Hellenisation of Etruria, a context that was not 'colonial' (recently, see C. Dougherty and Kurke (eds.) 2003). A combination of new data and new theoretical approaches has led to a reassessment of the role of the Greeks in the Central Mediterranean, and in Etruria in particular. The resulting image of the Greeks is not the traditional one of innate and unchallenged cultural superiority (Blakeway 1932–3; Boardman 1967; 1999; Woodhead 1962: 17); rather, these 'new' Greeks, the product of a recent resurgence of interest in the Greek presence in the central Mediterranean, which has been carried out in the light of the post-colonial theory touched upon above, are ones whose cultural domination has been challenged, from both a Greek and a native perspective, and who are now gradually taking their place in models of ancient Mediterranean trade and exchange as one of many equal partners. Though the model of cultural superiority is inadequate for explaining the changes in Etruscan material culture, there still exists the need to explain the undeniable Greek cultural influence on the world of the Etruscans. The following paragraphs will suggest a model Etrusco-Greek interaction that is less hellenocentric, while proposing a more diverse and heterogeneous network of contacts in the ancient Mediterranean.

What first drove the Euboeans to journey abroad is still not clear. Trade, the search for land and metals, and socio-political cleansing rites have all been proposed (Cawkwell 1992; Boardman 1999; C. Dougherty 1993; Dunbabin 1948; Giardino 1995). For Etruria in particular, the desire to exploit the rich mineral resources (Nijboer 1998: 235–40, 272–7; Zifferero 1991b) has been questioned by d'Agostino in favour of a search for marginal benefits, which he sees as characteristic of Euboean intentions more widely (1996: 309; 1998: 364). What is clear, however, is that around the middle of the eighth century at Pithekoussai the Euboeans established the first Greek settlement outside Greece itself. Burials at the site, which number well over 1,000, have yielded evidence of strong connections with Euboea, in the form of chevron *skyphoi* and burial practices (Buchner and Ridgway 1993). Pithekoussai became the link between Greece and Etruria (Torelli 1996), and chevron *skyphoi* found in burials at Veii are the earliest signs of contact between the two cultures (Close-Brooks and Ridgway 1971; Ridgway 1992). Though early exports to Etruria were from Euboea, local workshops were soon established at Pithekoussai, and, as a result, locally made goods were soon exported to Etruria and neighbouring Campania (d'Agostino 1990b; 1998: 365). However, the contacts between Etruria and Pithekoussai were to be short-lived, as the colony was abandoned towards the end of the eighth century, and with it declined the importance of Euboean material in the Etruscan material record. Yet this was by no means the end of contact between Etruria and Greeks in general. Euboean goods were replaced by those from other emerging Greek settlements in southern Italy, and from Corinth, which was to dominate the Etruscan context until the middle of the sixth century, when Attic pottery came to pre-eminence (Martelli 1979, 1985; Szilágyi 1975).

Along with the important contribution of the results of the Pithekoussai excavations and the contribution they have made to our understanding of early Greek contacts with Etruria, inquiries into the nature of Mediterranean interaction have also changed perceptions of Greek–Etruscan contact. The traditional model of Greek expansion has been challenged on several fronts:

the first questions the terminology of colonisation, and argues that Greek influence was not as unilateral as early accounts suggest; the second challenges the very notion of 'Greeks' as a single, unified group.

As a counterpoint to the view that the Greeks dominated the maritime world of the ancient Mediterranean, the view of a strong Etruscan maritime power has been proposed, drawing on a wide range of archaeological and epigraphic data, including representations of Etruscan ships at sea and engaged in naval battles (Cristofani 1983; Martelli (ed.) 1987: 263–4). At the same time, it has been argued from the presence of Etruscan objects in panhellenic sanctuaries, most notably the Caeretan treasury at Delphi, that Etruscans were travelling throughout the Hellenic world (Colonna 1993; Jacquemin 1999; Kilian 1977; Kilian-Dirlmeier 1985; Martelli 1990; Naso 2000; von Hase 1997). In addition, a votive with an Etruscan dedicatory inscription has been found at the sanctuary of Aphaia on Aegina, attesting not only the presence of an Etruscan trader at a Greek sanctuary, but also his incorporation into local Greek rites (Cristofani 1996b). Finally, the presence of Etruscan traders' marks on Attic pottery found in Etruria indicates that Etruscan traders were in Athens procuring consignments of vases for consumption at home (Johnston 1979: ch. 11).

Such are the arguments that have been put forward in order to refute the idea of Greek maritime hegemony. As well as challenging the hypothesis that Greeks were the dominant power in archaic trade, the one-way nature of Greek–Etruscan trade (which saw only the Greek influence over Etruria) has been questioned, and instead, the influence of Etruscan culture on Attic production has been acknowledged. The output of an Athenian potter called Nikosthenes is the most commonly cited example of Etruscan influence on Greece (for another instance see D. J. Williams 1988). Rasmussen's study of the chronology of four native *bucchero* shapes clearly shows their appearance in Etruscan *bucchero* before they were copied in Greece (T. B. Rasmussen 1985). These Attic copies of Etruscan prototypes were then exported back to the Etruscan market. This example has been used to suggest that at least one Attic potter was making pottery according to what he perceived (it seems correctly) were Etruscan tastes. Most interestingly of all, the provenances of the Nikosthenic copies echo those of their *bucchero* prototypes, so that, for example, both *bucchero* and Nikosthenic amphorae are found almost exclusively at one site, Cerveteri. It has been suggested that this shows not only Etruscan influence over Attic production, and the conformity of Attic production to Etruscan taste, but also that the restriction of Nikosthenic shapes to particular Etruscan sites implies a degree of careful 'market research', or the specific targeting of certain shapes to particular cities in which the prototype had been popular (Scheffer 1988). More generally, Osborne has shown that the pottery from individual Attic workshops is far from randomly distributed throughout the Mediterranean. From this he argues that different parts of the Mediterranean generated different demands, and that these were met by different workshops (R. Osborne 1996b: 38).

An acknowledgement both of the role of Etruscan traders and of the two-way nature of cultural exchange between Greece and Etruria) has emphasised the active role of the Etruscans in Greek–Etruscan interaction. A further part of the challenge to the traditional view of the Greeks overseas has been in the reassessment of the nature of the Greeks themselves. Work on the Euboeans and, more recently, on early Greek colonies in southern Italy and Sicily has led to the discrediting of the notion that the Greeks were a homogenous unit; instead, the differing roles of Euboeans, Corinthians, Lakonians and others in initiating colonisation has been brought to the fore (for example Morris and Papadopoulos 1999). Furthermore, the view of a deliberate colonising or Hellenising agenda in the Greek interactions in the central Mediterranean has been challenged. This has been done on theoretical grounds, by questioning the usefulness of the terminology of 'colonisation' (Franco De Angelis 1998; R. Osborne 1998b: 252; see also Rowlands 1998; van Dommelen 1997), and by examining the archaeological nature of the early Greek foundations abroad. The differences between the foundations suggest different motivations behind the individual settlements. For example, Metapontum has plenty of agricultural land, but few natural resources and a poor harbour, whereas Syracuse has an excellent natural harbour. This diversity of motivation invalidates the notion of a single, unified intent behind the Greek movement towards the west (Graham 1964; R. Osborne 1998b). Finally, the homogeneity of the Greek world has itself been dismissed: the Greek states and colonies were not a united group of cities (C. Dougherty and Kurke (eds.) 2003; J. M. Hall 2004); competition and aggression between colonies were common (Shepherd 1995), and it was possible at the end of the sixth century for an Etruscan city, such as Cerveteri, to have good relations with one Greek state, such as Athens, while being at war with another, Syracuse (Serra Ridgway 1990).

This discussion has placed a heavy emphasis on the diversity of 'Greek' culture in its interaction in the Mediterranean, and with Etruria more specifically. Of course, the same diversity should be remembered when talking about Etruria or Etruscans. There is an extremely well-established tradition within Etruscology of treating individual cities and regions within Etruria in isolation (for instance Banti 1970, Coarelli (ed.) 1975; Dennis 1883; Pallottino 1939). In this sense, the case hardly needs making for Etruria;

and in fact, one of the aims of this book has been to draw together the threads that unify a culture that is otherwise studied disparately. By contrast, the hellenocentrism of studies of the Greek world has traditionally underplayed diversity, with the aim of including everything in the high-status cultural category that the label 'Greek' came to represent. Nonetheless, it is important to remember that when discussing 'Etruscan', this category is equally problematic, and can be readily deconstructed. However, this must be done only at equivalent levels of analysis for both cultures – in other words, one of the significant factors that has affected studies of Greek–Etruscan interaction is the inequity built into a starting point where one culture is seen as a large, unified whole, and the other as a ramshackle collection of differing entities. Given this, it is important to remember the scale of analysis: discussions at the level of the individual must be phrased accordingly, as must discussions at the level of cultural interaction. If identities are created according to the context and scale at which they are operating, then so too must the discussion of groups be appropriately framed. Thus, in a discussion of cultural interaction, it is appropriate to use broad cultural categories, while bearing in mind the problematic nature of such categorisation at a 'micro' level of inquiry.

The reassessment of the role and nature of Greek activities in southern Italy has formed part of a much wider reconsideration of Mediterranean contact (Gras 1985, 1995; Horden and Purcell 2000; Kristiansen 1998: 124–44, 253–73; Sherratt and Sherratt 1993). The picture that is emerging is one in which a single dominant power is replaced by many smaller entities interacting in a more symmetrical manner. Part of this reassessment has resulted in the dismantlement of the concept of long-distance trade, and its replacement with far smaller, regional networks of exchange (Gras 1985). The evidence from the holds of ancient trading vessels, such as those of the Ulu Burun, Giglio or Porticello wrecks, suggests not only mixed cargoes, comprising an assortment of objects from a number of provenances, but also the mixed nature of ancient cargoes in general: in contrast to that at Giglio, the Porticello cargo was largely homogeneous (Bass *et al.* 1989; Bound 1985; Parker 1992). This range in the composition of cargoes suggests that, alongside those vessels that were carrying specific orders, a large number of small-scale, local voyages was taking place. In this way, the model of trade that comprises long-distance voyages in search of large cargoes of raw materials has been replaced by one of small-scale, regional trading networks involving large numbers of small consignments (Kerschner 2004; for a Roman parallel see Laurence 1994: 52; Millett 1993; for the Mediterranean more generally, Horden and Purcell 2000: 149–50, part III). It is into such a framework that Cristofani has placed the Greek trader Sostratos, and his Etruscan counterpart *plavtena*. Cristofani argues that the dedication of the famous anchor by the Aeginetan Sostratos at Gravisca, and the dedication of a cup by the Caeretan *plavtena* in the sanctuary at Aegina, are the material remnants of close, personal, long-term associations between individuals that were typical of archaic trade (Cristofani 1996b). Such personal and small-scale operations are also suggested by the prevalence of the trader's mark 'SO' on the output of the Nikosthenic workshop, indicating close and regular links between one workshop and a particular trader (Arafat and Morgan 1994: 116; Johnston 1979: 80). The system of trade that we should envisage, then, is one that comprises many small traders of different origins, taking part in multiple exchanges on a given voyage, often underpinned by personal, pre-established ties.

Such a system is supported by the evidence found within Etruria itself. The ethnic diversity of the traders in Etruria is attested by the variety of scripts found on traders' marks, thus indicating a mixed community of traders that included Ionians, Aeginetans and Etruscans (Johnston 1979; 1985). Similarly, the heterogeneity of the composition of the deposits at the sanctuaries of the ports of Pyrgi and Gravisca suggests a correspondingly heterogeneous population at these sites: at Pyrgi the gold plaques are testimony to the use of the sanctuary by Etruscans and Phoenicians (Serra Ridgway 1990: 519), and the inscriptions on votives at Gravisca indicate Greeks from a number of states (Cristofani 1996b), as do those on transport amphorae (Colonna 1985a; Slaska 1985). This heterogeneity was not restricted to Etruscan sites: in the Italian sphere a similar mixture of cultures has been postulated for Pithekoussai, where Iberian, Italian, Carthaginian, Levantine and Rhodian objects have been found (Docter and Niemeyer 1994; Ridgway 1994), while, in the Greek sphere, the range of provenances of dedications at the Hellenic sanctuaries discussed above suggests a similarly mixed population of dedicatees (Colonna 1993; Jacquemin 2000; Kilian 1977; Kilian-Dirlmeier 1985; Martelli 1990; Naso 2000; von Hase 1997). Both cases serve to reiterate the independent views of Cristofani and Purcell in emphasising the mobility of individuals in ancient Mediterranean trade (Cristofani 1996a; Giardino 1995; Purcell 1990).

However, this mobility, and the stress on local networks at the expense of trans-Mediterranean networks, should not be considered random and opportunistic, with traders 'tramping' around the Mediterranean, selling and buying as and when they could (for example Hannestad 1989). Instead, such exchanges and interactions were part of 'regular, and in most cases direct, trading links between Athens and individual ports around the Mediterranean' (Osborne 1996: 39).

In addition to this heterogeneous trading population in the Mediterranean, and in Etruscan ports more specifically, there is evidence for a similarly mixed population in Etruscan cities. The earliest evidence for foreigners living and working in Etruria, dating from around the middle of the seventh century, is provided by a mixing bowl found and made in Cerveteri yet signed by a Greek, Aristonothos (Giglioli (ed.) 1962: no. 1; C. Dougherty 2003; Izzet 2004; Martelli (ed.) 1987: 263–4). Slightly later, the so-called 'Rondini and Bearded Sphinx painters', Greeks working in the Etrusco-Corinthian tradition, provide further instances of Greek craftsmen in Etruria (Camporeale 1985a: 80). Ridgway and Williams have also argued that Euboean and Corinthian potters worked in Etruria, Campania and Pithekoussai (Ridgway 1992: 131–3, 136; 2004: 25–6 and n. 32; J. D. Williams 1986). In the sixth century the workshop of the Caeretan *hydriae* was one in which two (Ionian) Greek painters produced vases for a local market (Hemelrijk 1984). It has been assumed that these craftsmen were exiles from their Greek homeland, a migration attributed to the Persian persecution in Ionia (Cristofani 1976, 1978).

Tosto's examination of the construction of Nikosthenic amphorae presents the further possibility of Etruscan craftsmen having visited Athens. He has shown that the similarities between the *bucchero* prototypes and the Attic amphorae are not merely formal, but also structural: the amphorae have a flat 'foot-ceiling', an inconspicuous feature that would not necessarily be copied from looking at the *bucchero* prototype, and is more likely to be the result of first-hand experience in the production of the vases (Tosto 1999: 28; for the unlikelihood of copying such a feature see Gosselain 2000). In other words, either Nikosthenes must have learned this technique from an Etruscan craftsman in Athens, or he must himself have visited Etruria, where he learned how to make the *bucchero* shapes he later manufactured on his return to Athens. Thus we have an instance of either a Greek craftsman in Etruria or an Etruscan craftsman in Greece. One permanent immigrant to whom we can give a name is Demaratus, apparently an exile from Corinth who settled in Tarquinia during the sixth century (Ampolo 1976–7; Musti 1987; Ridgway and Ridgway 1994). In addition to examples of Greeks living in Etruria, there is also evidence of movement away from Etruria: a curse tablet from the Sicilian colony of Selinus contains the name Turana, and it has been argued that this represents an Etruscan woman who had settled in Selinus (Heurgon 1972–3).

So far, this chapter has examined our changing understandings of Etruscan–Greek interaction over the last twenty years. As should now be apparent, the recent reassessment of the nature of Etruscan and Greek interaction has produced a picture of interaction that is more heterogeneous and less hellenocentric in nature. The nature of the Greek 'colonising' movement has been challenged, and the importance of Etruscan traders and cities has been acknowledged. The picture that emerges is one of smaller-scale ventures by both Greeks and Etruscans, based on individual, pre-established links and networks involving a host of individuals in both Greece and Etruria.

The preceding discussion serves two purposes here: the first is to redress the imbalance in earlier studies of Etruscan–Greek contact, restoring Etruscan agency to the process of interaction; the second is to sketch a picture of the workings of archaic Mediterranean trade as it has emerged over recent years. This picture emphasises the extensive networks of multiple interactions on different scales and in different directions within the Mediterranean. Because of the prominence of the Greek 'contribution' to Etruria in discussions so far, this chapter has concentrated on this axis; however, there were other axes of Mediterranean interaction within which Etruscan culture was enmeshed.

Ridgway has emphasised the role of Sardinia in early contacts, as both a valuable source of metals and, from the evidence at the site at Sant'Imbenia, a precedent for eighth-century Pithekoussai (Bafico *et al.* 1997; Ridgway 1995: 79–81; 1998: 316–20; 2000: 182). More generally, the importance of the North Syrians and Phoenicians is being increasingly acknowledged, in terms both of their importance as traders and of their cultural influences on both Greece and Etruria (Aubet and Barthélemy (eds.) 2000; S. Moscati (ed.) 1988; Niemeyer (ed.) 1982). Ridgway has demonstrated the extent of interaction between Greeks and Phoenicians at Pithekoussai, and the importance of the latter in early pan-Mediterranean trade, by arguing for Phoenician residents at the site (Ridgway 1992: 111–18; 1994; also Perserico 1996). He has also used the work of Coldstream and Shepherd in their studies of Greek–native intermarriage to suggest a similar situation for the Phoenicians and Greeks at Pithekoussai (Coldstream 1993; Shepherd 1999). More challengingly, Sherratt and Sherratt have argued that the Phoenician trading network was the model of the later Greek one (Sherratt and Sherratt 1993; also Ridgway 1990: 64). Similarly, Shefton and others have argued that it was Phoenician, not Greek, traders who were responsible for the transportation to the western Mediterranean of much of the archaic Attic pottery that is found there (Morris and Papadopoulos 1999; Shefton

1982). At the same time, Harrison and Aubet have independently demonstrated the importance of the Phoenicians in the western Mediterranean from the early first millennium BC and earlier (Aubet 1993; R. J. Harrison 1988), suggesting that the Greeks were latecomers to this region. While the mechanisms of the Phoenician presence have thus been increasingly elucidated, the cultural influence of the East on Greek forms, both literary and artistic, has been emphasised (Boardman 1999; Burkert 1992; I. Morris 1992; West 1971, 1988). While much of this work centres on the earlier periods of the seventh and sixth centuries, Ridgway extends this Phoenician influence chronologically by stressing the significance of Carthage as a religious and trading centre from the late sixth century onwards (Ridgway 1990; see also Docter 2000). The significance of eastern influence in Etruria is less contested and better established. The work of Strøm and Rathje established the importance of the Phoenicians in Etruria over twenty years ago, as the carriers both of objects from the East and of styles that were incorporated into Etruscan forms (Rathje 1979; Riva 2000; Serra Ridgway 2002; Strøm 1971). More recently Serra Ridgway has shown the importance of eastern traders in later Etruscan ports, such as Pyrgi (Serra Ridgway 1990: 521).

Interactions within Italy

However, it was not only with cultures from outside Italy that Etruscans were coming into contact. The first millennium BC has long been recognised as a formative period in the processes of state formation in the Italian peninsula (Herring and Lomas (eds.) 2000). In addition, the importance of long-distance, intra-regional trade in the peninsula has received attention (Bonomi Ponzi 1996; Malone and Stoddart (eds.) 1994: 136–41). Together, these two factors resulted in far greater interaction between the communities of Italy, and this increased interaction must surely have had an effect on how those communities saw themselves (E. Hall 1989; J. M. Hall 1997, 2004; S. Jones 1997). This section will examine three regions within Italy as examples, in order to understand the cultural contacts that Etruscans were making in the first half of the first millennium BC and in order to explore the Italian world in which the developments outlined in the previous chapters were set. The three regions have been selected on the grounds that they have been the subject of recent primary research and analysis. The later, Roman, terms for the regions are used as shorthand for the often diverse cultural and social categories these regions contained.

Umbria

Two recent publications form the basis for this discussion of the region of Umbria (G. Bradley 2000a; Malone and Stoddart (eds.) 1994). Both agree that urbanisation in Umbria did not take place on any scale until the Roman intervention of the later first millennium BC. However, the studies differ in terms of what this means for our understanding of social complexity before this period. Malone and Stoddart play down political organisation (Malone and Stoddart 1994: 173–4), whereas Bradley argues for considerable complexity that could be termed state formation, though without its usual corollary, urbanisation (Bradley 2000a: 99–100). The divergence between these positions is probably due, to some extent, to the different geographical focus of the two projects: The Gubbio Valley, the subject of Malone and Stoddart's research, is remote and remained so, whereas Bradley focuses more on southern Umbrian sites, such as Plestia, which were on important trade routes through the Apennines, and which were closer to Etruria.

The late bronze-age evidence for Umbria is made up of small, possibly seasonal sites in the upland areas of the region. By the eighth century, sites were located in the foothills, in order to exploit the fertility of valleys and the potential use of the uplands for pasture and woodland. For 400 years these settlements were small and architecturally unimpressive. Far more imposing were the peak sanctuaries that formed highly developed networks around these sites. These sites, one of which, Monte Ansciano, has been excavated (Malone and Stoddart (eds.) 1994), show considerable continuity in use from the bronze-age to the Roman period, and appear to have been linked with specific settlements (such as M. Ansciano with Gubbio). Equally significant were the fortified hilltop settlements that were strategically located along lines of communication and may also have marked territorial limits. Bradley stresses that these phenomena, the establishment of sanctuaries, and the construction of hill forts should not be seen as a pre-urban phase of Umbrian evolution; instead he insists that they are the product of the particular local circumstances of a region in which the volume of trade (particularly between Etruria and Picenum) was high and the local population could exploit this for its own benefit. The seventh century was the period from which this exploitation took place. The increased trading connections between Picenum and Etruria coincided with a considerable increase in social differentiation in the region, with foreign, oriental objects found in wealthy burials. The cemetery of Plestia serves as an example: in the ninth to seventh centuries, burials, including grave goods, were simple and showed little differentiation; the seventh century saw the inclusion of different types of objects – largely weapons and metal ware; but it was from the sixth century that there was a significant increase in the number of burials and in the number and quality of grave goods. The latter included dining equipment, Attic red- and black-figure pottery, and were restricted to a few wealthy burials, indicating complex and hierarchical social organisation that had its origins in the seventh century. Whether this resulting social formation should be called state formation or not, these changes are interpreted as a consequence of increased contact with other cultures, with at least parts of Umbria taking part in a wider Central Italian network, or koine.

Samnium

The region of Samnium must also have been part of such a community. The area has been the subject of extensive recent archaeological inquiry, including the excavation of major settlements sites such as Saepinum and Iuvanum, and field survey, such as the Bifferno Valley and San Vincenzo surveys (Curti *et al.* 1996: 178). Like Umbria, the region shows considerable internal diversity, which is reflected in later urban formation processes. Much of the early revisionist work on Samnium was focused on countering Salmon's view of the region as backward and unsophisticated, and was characterised by emphasis on the sophistication of large cultic centres such as Pietrabbondante, Campochiaro, San Giovanni in Galdo and Vastogiardi in an attempt to compensate for the absence of urban structures (principally in the work of La Regina; see Curti *et al.* 1996: 179; see also Dench 1995). More recently, alternative models of social complexity that do not involve urbanisation have been suggested (Barker 1995).

The Bifferno Valley project is perhaps the most useful guide to the long-term underlying changes that took place in the region in the first millennium BC (Barker 1991, 1995). The settlement data from the Bronze Age consists of small, thinly scattered sites, with little indication of social stratification. This type of settlement and social organisation was transformed at the beginning of the first millennium BC. The number of sites increased by 50 per cent, with a strong bias in their distribution towards the lower valley. Alongside this increase in number, there was an increase in differentiation between the sites: small (50 by 50 metres) domestic sites continued to dominate the sample, but these were accompanied by a few major settlements that were ten times larger than their smaller contemporaries (Arcora, Santa Margherita, Colle Masilli, B287 north of Casacalenda, and Monte Vairano). These major sites were roughly equidistant (10–15 kilometres apart). Excavations at two of these sites (Arcora and Santa Margherita) suggest substantial settlements of 25–35 well-built domestic units. These centres were on well-defended sites, and became the focus for craft production (mainly pottery, metalworking and textile manufacture), and the large numbers of grind-stones, amphorae, and threshing debris suggest that they were also the centre for the processing and storage of the agricultural produce of the small farms around them. At the same time, the construction of hill forts took place in the upland areas (Oakley 1995). The agricultural basis of the rural economy shifted to incorporate the production of wine and possibly olive oil, as well as secondary animal products, especially wool. This increasing complexity was mirrored in the burial data. Excavations at Termoli, Guglionesi, Larino, Campochiaro and Santa Margherita show evidence of warrior graves and social differentiation from the seventh century onwards.

Much of the material expression for this social differentiation was the incorporation of foreign objects, mainly drinking equipment, in the burials. Barker has ascribed a dual role to this imported material: he sees contact with southern Greeks and Campanian Etruscans as both a stimulus to change in Samnium and a means of re-enforcing and reiterating changes in social structure. In both cases, increased contact with external cultures was essential in the transformation of iron-age society.

Latium and Rome

The final region to be examined, Latium, has also been the subject of fervent interest in the last thirty years or so, and the results of numerous studies have transformed our understanding of the region (Cornell 1995a; Purcell 1989; C. J. Smith 1994, 1996). Extensive survey and excavation work has shown that the area of Latium prospered from the beginning of the first millennium BC, during which time the site of Rome was transformed from one of many similarly ranked centres to being the pre-eminent site in Central Italy.

Latial culture is divided into four chronological phases. The Latial I period (1200–900 BC) corresponds to the late Bronze Age, during which period a large number of sites was scattered through the region. The internal organisation of these sites was loose, and evidence from both the Forum in Rome and the sites of the Alban Hills suggests a number of small communities co-existing a few hundred metres apart. Many of these early sites continued to be occupied until the Roman period. There appears to be little social differentiation in either settlement or burial data.

The Latial II period (900–770 BC) saw the decline of many of the hilltop settlements of the Alban Hills, which were abandoned for alternative locations on the coastal plain and valley bottoms, where communication routes, rather than defensibility, appear to have been the determining factor. The growth of these sites, most notably Lavinium, Satricum and Castel di Decima, is evinced in the increase in burials and in settlement size. It has been suggested that their position on the route between Campania and Veii may have accounted for and been a stimulus to their growth.

However, it is not until the Latial III period (770–730 BC) that social stratification becomes significantly emphasised. Although this is a period of limited evidence, new sites such as Antemnae emerge, and pre-existing sites develop at a great rate. For instance, Lavinium provides evidence of habitations and the elaboration of defensive work on the acropolis. In Satricum the burial of children in domestic huts has been interpreted as part of the growth of aristocratic families. In Osteria dell'Osa social structure was significantly emphasised in the use of prestige goods and in the complexity of the tomb construction, and kinship relations appear to be expressed in the spatial patterning of burials. In Rome, the organisation of the settlement becomes much clearer, particularly with the organisation of the Forum Boarium, and differentiation in wealth and status becomes marked in burial evidence. Although imported objects are surprisingly rare in burial, they are more common in other contexts; for example, Greek style pottery (possibly Veientine) was found in the Sant'Omobono area. Domestic huts and possible fortifications have been discovered on the Palatine.

The Latial IV period (730–580) shows the extension of the social differentiation observed in the earlier periods. Local elites appear to be clearly marked in the burial record, in particular at Praeneste, Castel di Decima and Aqua Acetosa Laurentina, where chariot burials and exceptionally rich grave goods testify to inter-elite competition and gift exchange mechanisms. The similarities between these tombs and those of Etruria, as well as the presence of foreign objects (such as Greek ceramics in Tomb 15 at Castel di Decima) suggest that the elite groups in Latium were in contact with one another and with other areas of Central Italy.

During the sixth century a significant shift takes place in the elite expression of wealth – from burial to the construction of temples for communal cult activity, such as sacrifice, most notably the temple complex with four (eventually thirteen) altars at Lavinium. Established settlements continued to flourish, with increasingly dense occupation shown by the agglomeration of previously discrete communities (such as the case of Gabii, which incorporated the population of Osteria dell'Osa among others), and evidence for rudimentary planning and drainage works, as well as more substantial dwellings (such as Lavinium). Whether this agglomeration was synoecism, or the culmination of a process of state formation that stretched back into the Bronze Age, the newly emerging entities had a complex social organisation that was matched by complexity of material culture; they had a distinct sense of their own identities, and were in contact with their neighbouring cultural groups.

It is also at this time that the site of Rome became predominant in the region, and she became 'a unified entity which knew itself as Rome' (C. J. Smith 1996: 100). Communal activities were crucial to this sense, and were not limited to the religious, though there are numerous ritual deposits throughout the city from this date. The area of the Forum, which would have been susceptible to flooding, was filled in with 10,000–20,000 cubic metres of earth (Ammerman 1990), and the *Cloaca Maxima* was constructed to drain the area more effectively. The successive paving of the area included the creation of a ritual focus around the area of the Lapis Niger in the early sixth century (Coarelli 1983: 161–99) and the paving of the Comitium and Curia Hostilia. Furthermore, the building complex known as the regia was repeatedly altered, expanded and monumentalised through its decoration with moulded terracotta relief plaques (Cristofani (ed.) 1990: 97–8), and other impressive aristocratic residences were established in the Forum (A. Carandini 1990). All these factors served to set Rome apart from her Latin neighbours.

It has been argued that this pre-eminence had become formalised by the late sixth century, to such an extent that a treaty drawn up between Carthage and Rome, traditionally dated to 509 BC, was able to refer to the Latin cities as states subject to Rome (Polybius 3.22; Cornell 1995a: 211–14; C. J. Smith 1996: 203). The significance of Rome within the central Mediterranean region can certainly not be overstated: 'The construction of a temple the size of the Capitoline temple is a very clear affirmation of Rome's sense of status. The whole building programme of the sixth century, including the Forum Boarium complex, has the effect of saying something about Rome's place in the world' (C. J. Smith 1994: 291). This place was as one of the leading centres of power and influence (Cornell 1995a: 96).

Rome's pre-eminence in Latium was due to her increasing size and to her greater contacts with foreign cultures, notably that of Etruria (Bietti Sestieri 1992: 70–5; Forsythe 2005: 28–46, 80; though see Pacciarelli 2000; Peroni 1994; A. Carandini 2003, for whom Etruscan contact is insignificant). The Etruscan language is extremely well represented in the inscriptions of this period, suggesting that the earlier contacts between Etruria and Latium continued in Rome. We lack the kinds of inscriptions found at Gravisca that would testify to direct contact between Greeks and Rome, and Rome lacks a coastal harbour; yet the Forum Boarium area acted as the town's harbour, and the inscriptions from this area are Etruscan (C. J. Smith 1996: 226). Furthermore, the similarities between the elite burials of Etruria (Cerveteri) and Latium (Praeneste) suggest links of marriage or elite gift exchange between the two regions. Smith argues that Latium, including Rome, was dependent on Etruria for its trading contacts, rather than being an independent participant in Central Italian trade networks. Though contact with Greek and Phoenician culture was frequent, it was mediated through Etruscan traders (C. J. Smith 1996: 149).

The most significant area in Rome in terms of contact with foreigners was the area of the future Forum Boarium and the sanctuary area of Sant'Omobono. The Forum Boarium was the urban harbour of the city, where cargoes that had been carried up the Tiber (most famously salt, but also oil, wine, livestock and other products) were unloaded and distributed. Though votives and structures from the sixth century have been discovered here (largely Greek ceramics), it was not until the end of the century that a monumental sacred building, decorated with elaborate mythological architectural terracottas, was constructed within a large archaic sanctuary. The deity worshipped has been identified as Mater Matuta (later Fortuna). This identification, and the variety of foreign artefacts from the site, have led Coarelli to compare the site with that of Pyrgi, particularly in terms of the opportunity that the site provided for interchange between Phoenicians, Greeks, Etruscans and Romans from as early as the mid-sixth century (Coarelli 1988: 328–9; see also Cornell 1995a: 112; C. J. Smith 1996: 162). This contact was to leave its mark on the rest of the nascent city of Rome in the form of urban sanctuaries, most notably the temple of Jupiter Optimus Maximus on the Capitoline (Gjerstad 1960: 168–89; C. J. Smith 1996: 162–4).

The influence of Etruria on early Rome has become bitterly debated in the light of this recent research (see Vanzetti 2002 for summary). On the one hand, there are those who see a significant Etruscan contribution, attested by features of Roman topography such as the Capitoline temple of Jupiter Maximus and the *Cloaca Maxima* (see for example Bietti Sestieri 1992; Cristofani (ed.) 1990; C. J. Smith 1996); on the other hand there are those who have disputed the extent of Etruscan power and influence in favour of long-term indigenous development (see for example A. Carandini and Capelli (eds.) 2000; A. Carandini 2003; Cornell 1995a: 151–72; Peroni 1994). It is not important here which of these positions more accurately reflects the ancient reality – this is not a study of the origins of Rome. However, it is important to remember the extraordinary levels of interaction between the Etruscan cities and their neighbours in Latium, including, over time, the newly emerging power of Rome. Such a side-step is possible because, for the 'Etruscologists', foreign contact is important, and for the 'proto-historians' it is irrelevant as it takes place after the crucial period of state formation in the late Bronze Age and very early Iron Age.

Two common features emerge from these studies of pre-Roman cultures in Italy. The first is increasing social complexity in all three areas, expressed in the funerary and settlement data. The second is the importance of foreign contacts, be it Etruscan, Phoenician or Greek, and be it direct or indirect, in the formation of culturally distinct groupings within Central Italy by the middle of the first millennium BC. So far, the focus of study has been the individual region, in terms of its social and cultural development, and the importance of contacts with Etruria to this. When the question is turned round, and examined from the Etruscan perspective, it seems logical therefore that these emerging identities should also have had an important influence on Etruscan culture. If we are to see cultural interaction as a two-way process, the developments in other regions of Italy, for which we have evidence of Etruscan contact, must have played an important role in the creation of Etruscan identity.

The environment for such interaction has been noted for a while, though its importance is becoming increasingly clear. For instance, for the proto-historic period, Peroni suggested wide networks of interaction across the Italian peninsula (Peroni 1969, 1979, 1980; see also Bonomi Ponzi 1996), and for a slightly later period, Ampolo posited an 'open' society for Central Italy (Ampolo 1970/1). Similarly, Bietti-Sestieri, Cristofani and Purcell have all independently stressed the mobility of individuals both within Italy and in the Mediterranean context more widely (Bietti-Sestieri 1997; Cristofani 1996a; Purcell 1990). Most recently, models of interaction and connectivity on a Mediterranean scale have been proposed (Gosden 2004: 69; Horden and Purcell 2000; Kristiansen 1998).

Thus the Etruscans were part of a complex Mediterranean world in which established relationships were reaffirmed and new powers began to emerge. The increase in the volume of traffic and contact between cultures at this time was unprecedented. In the face of such contact, it is not surprising that Etruscans (and, doubtless, Phoenicians, Greeks and Romans) would have undergone a period of reflection and consideration in the light of these encounters, prompting a redefinition of their own place within that world.

In the light of the problematisation of ethnic identity in archaeological thought in the late 1980s and early 1990s (Hall J. M. 1997; S. Jones 1997; Shennan (ed.) 1989), commentators appear to be extremely cautious of discussing ethnic groups and identities in Central Italy for fear of accusations of ethnocentrism or of unjustifiably retrojecting Roman ethnic categories on to earlier social groups (G. Bradley 2000b). In addition, studies have questioned whether ethnic identity was a significant category in ancient conceptions of Italy (Terrenato 1998). While these are obviously pitfalls, more recent (archaeological) treatments of identity have concentrated on the formation of cultural (as opposed to ethnic) identities (for example Díaz-Andreu *et al.* 2005). Rather than concentrating on how and/or whether ethnic identities should be identified, such studies shift emphasis onto the link between identity and a sense of belonging more widely. This builds on two inter-related theoretical strands: the first is the already much discussed relational nature of identity creation, in other words the importance of contact with 'others' in the creation of identities (Cartlege 1993; E. Hall 1989; Hölscher (ed.) 2000; D. Miller 1997); and second the importance of identity creation as an on-going, active process in the light of interaction (Gosden 2004: 69).

The result is that the fluid and mutable nature of all categories of identity must be acknowledged, whether Etruscan, Greek, Umbrian, Samnite or Roman (to remain within the categories discussed here). This means, not that we can no longer talk about 'Etruscans' or 'Greeks', but that such discussions must acknowledge the interrelationships involved in the setting up of these groupings. This not only applies to us as archaeologists, but was true of the everyday experience of negotiating identity in the past. Individuals would have had changing notions of their sex, age, gender, status, ethnic and religious (etc.) identities, and these would have been continually created, recreated, emphasised or diminished according to their setting and their encounters with others.

Because of the relational nature of identity creation, the creation of identities took place at the intersection of cultures. This equates not to spatial areas and boundaries, but to the social contexts in which interaction took place, such as ritualised drinking (Izzet 2004) or ritual activity. Such contexts were the spatial and temporal locations in which individuals came into contact with each other, and at which identities were defined and redefined. As such they are the areas of contestation, or the boundaries, between cultures.

Etruria

However, it is not only externally that we must look in order to gain a sense of why self-definition may have become such an imperative for sixth-century Etruscans. A consideration of state formation in Etruria also provides a clue for the sudden interest in boundedness that derives from within Etruria itself. Stoddart's study of the emergence of Central Italian states in the first half of the first millennium BC centres on a study of settlement hierarchy (Stoddart 1987, 1989; see above, Chapter 6). He argues for local continuity in the process of Etruscan state formation from the late second millennium BC, and in this he is in line with the Roman school of protohistorians, a position in longstanding debate with the Etruscological school, which sees foreign contact as the stimulus for the emergence of complex urban groups in Etruria. According to this model, the late Bronze Age in Central Italy was a period of stable social and economic organisation – the latter based on the local exploitation of ecological zones (for instance of mineral resources). There was no intra-regional exploitation of resources, though intra-regional contacts were extensive, linking lowland and upland areas as well as northern and southern areas in networks of interaction (Peroni 1969, 1979, 1980). The ninth century saw a dramatic change in settlement size and structure in Etruria, caused by an emphasis on nucleation. This move for nucleation is seen, again, not as a response to foreign stimuli, but as the extension of long-established trajectories (Guidi 1998; Stoddart 1989: 96). The nucleation took the form of the concentration of population at pre-existing sites such as Tarquinia (Bonghi Jovino (ed.) 1986), Orvieto (Di Gennaro 1986: 21–2) and Veii (Di Gennaro 1986: 103–4); these sites were often to become the large cities of archaic Etruria. The nucleation of the population in these centres resulted in large tracts of unpopulated landscape, which were later to be repopulated by second-order sites. Recent research has contradicted early interpretations of state formation that saw the gradual synoecism of iron-age villages with corresponding cemeteries (for example Veii: Ward-Perkins 1968). Instead, it appears that these ninth-century centres were integrated settlements from the beginning (for instance Veii (Guaitoli 1981; Guidi 1989); Tarquinia (Bonghi Jovino and Charamonte Treré (eds.) 1997: 153–60; Mandolesi 1994); Vulci (Pacciarelli 1991a, 1991b, 1994)). The resulting effect on settlement rank–size analysis of the nucleation was characterised by a pattern of a few very large, high-ranking centres and many small, low-ranking ones (Guidi 1985).

During the seventh century the settlement organisation changed character again: the population was decentralised, with the population dispersed in small (less than 10 hectares) sites in the landscape (Stoddart 1989: 43). In addition, the formerly empty areas were colonised by second-rank sites, such as Murlo, Acquarossa and Bisenzio, which were of the correct size and distance from the major centres to remain politically autonomous of them. While such sites had existed before, the first half of the sixth century saw an increase in the power and wealth of these sites, evinced for instance in the so-called 'monumental complex' at Acquarossa, or the elaborate courtyard building at Murlo. The growth of these middle-ranking settlements would have posed an obvious threat to the pre-established high-ranking centres, and thus to the urban elites who controlled them. This threat would have taken the form of undermining or diverting control of agricultural surplus, and incoming goods, including luxury goods. Such a change in the political geography of Etruria would have had repercussions that would be felt throughout Etruscan society.

These centres were later perceived as a threat to the urban centres and were destroyed or abandoned by the end of the sixth century, with the extension of control by the primary centres into these previously independent areas. Part of the control that the urban centres exerted was over trade, especially in Greek imported pottery. During the sixth and fifth centuries, the coastal cities of Etruria mediated contact with Greece, a contact that peaked (from the volume of pottery) at this time. This is in contrast to the local distribution of local production; for instance the products of the Micali painter are found within a 42-kilometre radius of their production centre, Vulci (Arafat and Morgan 1994: 119; Spivey 1987).

The work of Stoddart demonstrates the dynamism of geopolitical change, and the resultant insecurity this dynamism brought about in the inhabitants of the Etruscan landscape and cities. This occurred at a time of increasing contact with other cultures, and these taken together must have had a significant effect on challenging and shaping Etruscan cultural identity. Recent work in related fields has demonstrated the links between perceptions of insecurity, monumentalisation and formative periods in cultural development (R. Bradley 1993; J. Thomas 1991: 29–55; Woolf 1996: 30–1). In the preceding chapters, these factors have taken the guise of insecurity in the face of other cultures and internal change, changes in material culture (including monumentalisation) and the creation of a late sixth-century sense of Etruscan identity within the Mediterranean world.

Conclusion: making Etruscan society

As a way of explaining the changes in material culture observed in previous chapters, this chapter has presented several sources of potential insecurity and tension for the emerging identities of Etruria. The increased mobility of individuals during the first millennium BC led to the clarification and establishment of different group identities in the light of one another. Though in the earlier period we may be uncertain about attaching labels to these groups, they were the starting point for the cultural groups that were to take clearer form in the second half of the first millennium BC and the first half of the first millennium AD. Primacy in this process cannot be assigned: growing Greek identity was as much a product of interaction with Etruria (or Persia) as Etruscan identity was formed through contact with Greeks (or Romans); Greek Etruscans, Phoenicians, Umbrians, Sabines and Latins were all involved in mutually constituting their own and one another's identities.

The sense of uncertainty over who one was in relation to – say, the speaker of another language, or to someone from another culture – was paralleled by the uncertainty experienced as a result of the changing geopolitics of the Etruscan region. The sixth-century population shifts and squabbles over territorial control must have indicated a period of great uncertainty, not only for the poorer elements in society, but also for the elites whose lifestyle and pre-eminent position were based on the pre-existing world order. These changes would have led not only to tension, but also to increased contact between the different regions of Etruria. This in turn would have affected an individual's sense of belonging to a specific region or town in Etruria. Increased geographical movement exposed individuals to a wider range of possible ways of living, so that, with the increasing codification of the landscape, the 'urban' experience became more discrete from the 'rural' and vice versa. The increased exploitation of the agricultural landscape, and the control of surpluses, served both to create and to maintain these differences – through the creation of a distinctive rural landscape, and through the display of accumulated and consumed wealth by urban elites in various aspects of their lifestyle, such as public feasting, drinking or horsemanship. This in turn served to maintain the emphasis on intensified agricultural exploitation.

Similarly, categories and differences within the urban sphere would have been questioned: ways of burying, living and worshipping were all renegotiated in terms of where an individual stood in relation to these categories, and in relation to corresponding practices of others or of their own pasts. Clearer boundaries were drawn between different categories of life, such as between the living and the dead, and between current and previous means of expressing this difference. The most acute manifestation of this definition was at the level of the individual persona: the way in which the individual presented him or herself to the rest of society, and to the wider world, was decided daily. Yet other categories were equally important in establishing and re-establishing the emerging order of the world, and the manipulation of the material world was crucial in this.

The discussion of a trans-Mediterranean network of interconnections that started this chapter seems very distant from the domestic image of a woman putting on some make-up, discussed at the beginning of this book. Yet the two are linked by a series of parallel changes that took place in the material culture of Etruria, culminating at the end of the sixth century BC. The analysis of the preceding chapters has brought to prominence the importance of changes in material culture form, and in particular the emphasis on surface, in negotiating, and establishing, difference in sixth-century Etruria. This was in marked contrast to the preceding ambiguity surrounding these aspects of Etruscan material life, and was brought about through a series of personal and cultural interactions. Importantly, the emphasis on visibility and surface in the material forms that were selected for expressing difference shows the centrality of an intended viewer, whether Etruscan, Umbrian or Greek.

The picture that emerges is one in which individual Etruscans were taking innumerable decisions about how they should look, where the dead should be literally and metaphorically placed, and how sacred, domestic and urban space should be organised as a means of expressing new relationships and identities. Etruscan elite commissioners of buildings and artefacts, and the craftspeople they employed, would have been operating within a period of uncertainty and insecurity. The resulting material form of Etruscan material culture should be seen as part of the response to this period of uncertainty, particularly on the part of the urban centres. For them, the assertion of their uniqueness and authority was paramount to their survival, and an attempt to order the rapidly changing world of which they were part. However, the Etruscan use of material was not only a response to threat; the use of material culture was an essential element in the constitution of Etruscan culture. The newly created spaces and categories of Etruscan material culture were not only a strategy of controlling and ordering changing circumstances; they were also crucial in the redefinition of those categories. The material culture of late sixth-century Etruria materialised the contemporary sense of the world, and fixed it in more permanent and visible form. The approach of this book has been to bring together different aspects of Etruscan culture within a single analysis, allowing changes that have otherwise been restricted to a single area to be seen from a unified perspective. This gives a new sense of unity to the social production of Etruscan material, a unity that gives material culture a central role, that restores Etruscan agency to the production of that material culture, and that demonstrates the importance of changes in material culture in transforming the world-view of a culture. The making of Etruscan material culture was thus the making of Etruscan society.

Bibliography

Acquaro, E. (1988) 'Phoenicians and Etruscans', in *The Phoenicians*, ed. S. Moscati, Milan: 532–7.

Agostino, B. d'(1983) 'L'immagine, la pittura e la tomba nell'Etruria arcaica', *Prospettiva* 32: 2–12.

(1985) 'Società dei vivi, communità dei morti: un rapporto difficile', *DArch* 3.1: 47–58.

(1989) 'Image and society in archaic Etruria', *JRS* 79: 1–10.

(1990a) 'Military organisation and social structure in archaic Etruria', in *The Greek City: From Homer to Alexander*, ed. O. Murray and S. Price, Oxford: 59–82.

(1990b) 'Relations between Campania, Southern Etruria and the Aegean in the eighth century BC', in *Greek Colonists and Native Populations: Proceedings of the First Australian Congress of Classical Archaeology. July 1985*, ed. J.-P. Descoeudres. Oxford: 73–85.

(1996) 'Pithekoussai and the first western Greeks', *JRA* 9: 302–9.

(1998) 'Campania in the framework of the earliest Greek colonization in the West', in *Euboica: L'Eubea e la presenza euboica in Calcidia e in Occidente. Atti del convegno internazionale di Napoli 13–16 novembre. AION ArchStAnt* 12, ed. M. Bats and B. d'Agostino. Naples: 355–68.

Alcock, S. E. (1993) *Graecia Capta: The Landscapes of Roman Greece*, Cambridge.

(1994) 'Minding the gap in Hellenistic and Roman Greece', in *Placing the Gods: Sanctuaries and Sacred Space in Ancient Greece*, ed. S. E. Alcock and R. Osborne, Oxford: 247–61.

Alcock, S. E., and Cherry, J. F. (eds.) (2004) *Side-By-Side Survey: Comparative Regional Studies in the Mediterranean World*, Oxford.

Alcock, S. E., and Osborne, R. (eds.) (1994) *Placing the Gods: Sanctuaries and Sacred Space in Ancient Greece*, Oxford.

Allison, P. M. (1997) 'Roman households: an archaeological perspective', in *Roman Urbanism: Beyond the Consumer City*, ed. H. Parkin, London and New York: 112–46.

(1999) 'Labels for ladles: interpreting the material culture of Roman households', in P. M. Allison (ed.), *The Archaeology of Household Activities*, London and New York: 57–77.

(ed.) (1999) *The Archaeology of Household Activities*, London and New York.

Alsayyad, N. (1994) 'Bayn al-Qasrayn: the street between the two palaces', in *Streets: Critical Perspectives on Public Space*, ed. Z. Çelik *et al.*, Berkeley: 71–82.

Amann, P. (2000) *Die Etruskerin: Geschlechterverhältnis und stellung der frau im frühen etrurien (9.–5. Jh. V. Chr.)* (Archäologische Forschungen 5), Vienna.

Ammermann, A. (1990) 'On the origins of the Roman Forum', *AJA* 94: 627–46.

Amorelli, M. T. (1952) 'Nota su uno specchio etrusco inedito', *ArchClass* 4: 91–3.

Ampolo, C. (1970/1) 'Su alcuni mutamenti sociali nel Lazio tra l'VIII sec. e il IV sec.', *DArch* 3–4: 37–99.

(1976/7) 'Demarato: osservazioni sulla mobilità sociale arcaica', *DArch* 9–10: 333–45.

(1980) 'Le origini di Roma e la "cité antique"', *MEFRA* 92: 567–76.

(1996) 'Roma ed i Sabini nel V secolo a.C.', in *Identità e civiltà dei Sabini: Atti del 18 Convegno di studi etruschi ed italici, Rieti – Magliani Sabina, 30 maggio – 3 giugno 1993*, ed. G. Maetzke and L. Perna, Florence: 87–103.

Ampolo, C., *et al.* (1987) *L'Alimentazione nel mondo antico: Gli Etruschi*, Rome.

Anderson, B. (1991) *Imagined Communities: Reflections on the Origin and Spread of Nationalism*, 2nd edn, London.

Andrén, A. (1940) *Architectural Terracottas from Etrusco-Italic Temples*, AIRRS 1.6.

(1974) 'Osservazioni sulle terrecotte architettoniche etrusco-italiche', *AIRRS* 4.31, *ORom* 8: 1–16.

Andrews, A. (1956) *The Greek Tyrants*, London.

Antonaccio, C. M. (1994) 'Placing the past: the Bronze Age in the cultic topography of early Greece', in *Placing the Gods: Sanctuaries and Sacred Space in Ancient Greece*, ed. S. E. Alcock and R. Osborne, Oxford: 79–104.

Appadurai, A. (1986) 'Introduction: commodities and the politics of value', in *The Social Life of Things*, ed. A. Appadurai, Cambridge: 3–63.

(ed.) (1986) *The Social Life of Things*, Cambridge.

(1990) 'Disjuncture and difference in the global cultural economy', *Theory, Culture and Society* 7: 295–311.

Arafat, K., and Morgan, C. (1994) 'Athens, Etruria and the Heuneburg: mutual misconceptions in the study of Greek–Barbarian relations', in *Classical Greece: Ancient Histories and Modern Archaeologies*, ed. I. Morris, Cambridge: 108–34.

Archer, L. J., Fishler, S., and Wyke, M. (eds.) (1994) *Women in Ancient Societies: An Illusion of the Night*, London.

Ardener, S. (1981) 'Introduction', in *Women and Space: Ground Rules and Social Maps*, ed. S. Ardener, London: 11–34.

(ed.) (1981) *Women and Space: Ground Rules and Social Maps*, London.

Aretini, A. (1932) 'Resti dell'antica cerchia urbana di Arezzo', *SE* 6: 533–42.

Arias, P. E. (1953) 'Considerazioni sulla città etrusca a Pian di Misano (Marzabotto)', *Atti e memorie della deputazione di storia patria per le Provincie Romagna* 4: 223–34.

Attema, P., Burgers, G.-J., van Joolen, E., van Leusen, M., and Mater, B. (eds.) (2002) *New Developments in Italian Landscape Archaeology*, BAR International Series 1091, Oxford.

Attema, P., Nijboer, A., and Zifferero, A. (eds.) (2005) *Papers in Italian Archaeology VI: Communities and Settlements from the Neolithic to the Early Medieval Period. Proceedings of the Sixth Conference of Italian Archaeology Held at the University of Groningen, Groningen Institute of Archaeology, The Netherlands, April 15–17 2003*, vol. II, BAR International Series 1452 [II], Oxford.

Aubet, M. E. 1993) *The Phoenicians and the West*, Cambridge.

Aubet, M. E., and Barthélemy, M. (eds.) (2000) *Actas del IV congreso internacional de estudios fenicios y púnicos* (4 vols.), Cadiz.

Azzaroli, A. (1972) 'Il cavallo domestico in Italia dall'età del bronzo agli Etruschi', *SE* 40: 273–306.

Bacchielli, L., and Bonanno Aravantinos, M. (eds.) (1997) *Scritti di antichità in memoria di Sandro Stucchi*, Rome.

Bachelard, G. (1994) *The Poetics of Space*, Boston. (First published in French, 1958.)

Bachofen, J. J. (1861) *Das Mutterrecht*, Basel.
    (1967) *Myth, Religion, and Mother-Right* (selected writings), Princeton.

Bafico, S., Oggiano, I., Ridgway, D., and Garbini, G. (1997) 'Fenici e indegini a Sant'Imbenia (Alghero)', in *Phonikes b shrdn / I Fenici in Sardegna: nuove acquisizioni*, ed. P. Bernardini, R. D'Oriano and P. G. Spanu, Cagliari: 45–53.

Baglione, M. P. (1989) 'Considerazioni sul "ruolo" femminile nell'arcaismo e nel tardo-archaismo', in *Le donne in Etruria*, ed. A. Rallo, Rome: 107–19.

Bagnal, R. (1990) 'The experience and identity of "woman": feminism after structuralism', in *Archaeology after Structuralism*, ed. I. Bapty and T. Yates, London: 103–23.

Bailey, D. W. (1990) 'The living house: signifying continuity', in *The Social Archaeology of Houses*, ed. R. Samson. Edinburgh: 19–48.

Balensiefen, L. (1990) *Die Bedentung des Spiegelbildes als ikonographisches Motiv in der antiken Kunst*, Tübingen.

Bamberger, J. (1974) 'The myth of matriarchy: why men rule in primitive society', in *Woman, Culture and Society*, ed. M. Z. Rosaldo and L. Lamphere, Stanford: 263–80.

Banks, M. (1997) 'Representations of the bodies of the Jains', in *Rethinking Visual Anthropology*, ed. M. Banks and H. Morphy. New Haven: 216–39.

Banks, M., and Morphy, H. (eds.) (1997) *Rethinking Visual Anthropology*, New Haven.

Banti, L. (1970) 'Le pitture della Tomba Campana a Veii', *SE* 38: 27–43.
    (1973) *Etruscan Cities and Their Culture*, London.

Bapty, I., and Yates, T. (eds.) (1990) *Archaeology After Structuralism*, London.

Barber, E. W. (1995) *Women's Work: The First 20,000 Years. Women, Class and Society in Early Times*, New York and London.

Barker, G. (1985) 'The development of landscape archaeology in Italy', in *Papers in Italian Archaeology*, IV: *The Cambridge Conference*, Part I: *The Human Landscape*, BAR International Series 243, ed. C. A. T. Malone and S. K. F. Stoddart. Oxford: 1–19.

(1988) 'Archaeology and the Etruscan countryside', *Antiquity* 62: 772–85.

(1991) 'Two Italys, one valley: an *Annaliste* perspective', in *The Annales School and Archaeology*, ed. J. Bintliff, Leicester: 34–56.

(1995) *A Mediterranean Valley: Landscape Archaeology and Annales History in the Bifferno Valley*, Leicester.

Barker, G., and Gamble, C. (eds.) (1985) *Beyond Domestication in Prehistoric Europe: Investigations in Subsistence Archaeology and Social Complexity*, London.

Barker, G., and Rasmussen, T. (1988) 'The archaeology of an Etrusan *polis*: a preliminary report on the Tuscania project (1986 and 1987 seasons)', *PBSR* 56: 25–42.

(1998) *The Etruscans*, Oxford.

Barnabei, F. (1895) 'Lubriano: tombe etrusche scoperte in Contrada Cantolle', *NSA*: 244–5.

Barnes, R., and Eicher, J. B. (eds.) (1992) *Dress and Gender: Making and Meaning in Cultural Contexts*, New York and Oxford.

Barret, J. C. (1994) *Fragments from Antiquity: An Archaeology of Social Life in Britain, 2900–1200 BC*, Oxford.

(2000) 'A thesis on agency', in *Agency in Archaeology*, ed. M.-A. Dobres and J. Robb, London and New York: 61–8.

Barth, F. (ed.) (1969) *Ethnic Groups and Boundaries: The Social Organisation of Culture Difference*, London.

Barthes, R. (1975) *The Pleasure of the Text*, New York.

(1985) *The Fashion System*, London.

Bartky, S. L. (1990) 'Foucault, femininity, and the modernisation of patriarchal power', in *Femininity and Domination: Studies in the Phenomenology of Oppression*, ed. S. L. Bartky, New York: 63–82.

(ed.) (1990) *Femininity and Domination: Studies in the Phenomenology of Oppression*, New York.

Bartoloni, G. (ed.) (1997) *Le necropoli arcaiche di Veio: Giornata di studio in memoria di Massimo Pallottino*, Rome.

(2000a) 'Il Principe: stile di vita e manifestazioni del potere', in *Principi Etruschi: Tra mediterraneo ed Europa*, eds. G. Bartoloni *et al.*, Venice: 223–70.

(2000b) 'La donna del principe', in *Principi Etruschi: Tra mediterraneo ed Europa*, ed. G. Bartoloni, G., *et al.*, Venice: 308–26.

(2001) 'Evoluzione negli insediamenti capennicoli dell'Italia centrale tirrenica', in *From Huts to Houses: Transformations of Ancient Societies. Proceedings of an International Seminar organised by the Norwegian and Swedish Institutes in Rome, 21–24 September 1997*, ed. J. R. Brandt and L. Karlsson, Stockholm: 361–74.

Bartoloni, G., Acconicia, V., and ten Kortenaar, S. (2005) 'Veio – Piazza d'Armi', in *Dinamiche di sviluppo della città nell'Etruria meridionale: Veio, Tarquinia, Vulci. Atti del XXIII Convegno di Studi Etruschi ed Italici, Roma, Veio, Cerveteri/Pyrgi, Tarquinia, Tuscania, Vulci, Viterbo, 1–6 ottobre 2001*, ed. O. Paoletti and G. Camporeale, Pisa and Rome: 73–85.

Bartoloni, G., Beijer, A. J., and De Santis, A. (1985) 'Huts in the central Tyrrhenian area of Italy during the protohistoric age', in *Papers in Italian Archaeology IV: The Cambridge Conference. Part III: Patterns in Protohistory*, ed. C. A. T. Malone and S. K. F. Stoddart, Oxford: 175–200.

Bartoloni, G., and Cataldi Dini, M. (1980) 'La formazione della città nel Lazio: ll periodo IVA (730/20 – 640/30), *DArch* 13: 125–64.

Bartoloni, G., Delpino, F., Morigi Govi, C., and Sassatelli, G. (eds.) (2000) *Principi Etruschi: Tra mediterraneo ed Europa*, Venice.

Bartoloni, G., and Grottanelli, C. (1989) 'I carri a due ruote nelle tombe femminili del Lazio e dell'Etruria', in *Le donne in Etruria*, ed. A. Rallo, Rome: 55–73.

Bartoloni, P. (ed.) (1983) *Atti del I Congresso internazionale di studi fenici e punici, Roma, 5–10 novembre 1979*, vol. ii, Rome.

Bass, G. F., Pulak, C., Collon, D., and Weinstein, J. (1989) 'The bronze-age shipwreck at Ulu Burun: 1986 campaign', *AJA* 93: 1–29.

Bateson, G., and Mead, M. (1942) *Balinese Character: A Photographic Analysis*, New York.

Bats, M., and d'Agostino, B. (eds.) (1998) *Euboica: L'Eubea e la presenza euboica in Calcidia e in Occidente. Atti del convegno internazionale di Napoli 13–16 novembre, AION ArchStAnt* 12, Naples.

Battaglia, G. B. (1990) *Le ciste prenestine*, Rome.

Bazzichelli, G. (1884, 'Viterbo – intorno a nuove ricerche nel tenimento "Macchia del Conte", riconosciuta sede dell'etrusca "Musarna" nel Viterbese', *NSA*: 215–20.

Beard, M. (1980) 'The sexual status of vestal virgins', *JRS* 70: 12–27.
(1991) 'Adopting an approach II', in *Looking at Greek Vases*, ed. T. Rasmussen and N. Spivey, Cambridge: 12–35.

Beard, M., North, J., and Price, S. (1998) *Religions of Rome*, vol. i: *A History*. Cambridge.

Bearzi, B. (1950–1) 'Considerazioni sulla formazione delle patine e delle corrosioni sui bronzi antichi', *SE* 11: 261–6.

Beazley, J. D. (1942) *Attic Red-Figure Vase-Painters*, Oxford.
(1947) *Etruscan Vase Painting*, Oxford.
(1949) 'The world of the Etruscan mirror', *JHS* 49: 1–17.
(1956) *Attic Black-Figure Vase-Painters*, Oxford.

Becatti, G. (1955) *Oreficerie antiche dalle minoiche alle barbariche*, Rome.

Becatti, G., Bianchi Bandinelli, R., Caputo, G., Devoto, P., and Pugliese Caratelli, G. (eds.) (1965) *Studi in onore di Luisa Banti*, Rome.

Becker, M. J. (1993) 'Seianti Hanunia: an analysis of her skeleton in the sarcophagus at the British Museum', in *La civiltà di Chiusi e del suo territorio. Atti del XVII convegno di studi etruschi ed italici, Chianciano Terme, 28 maggio – 1 giugno 1989*, Florence: 397–405.

Bedini, A. (1975) 'Castel di Decima: la necropoli arcaica', *NSA*: 369.

(1977) 'L'ottavo secolo nel Lazio e l'inizio dell'orientalizzante antico alla luce di recenti scoperte nella necropoli di Castel di Decima', *PP* 32: 274–309.

(1984) 'Struttura ed organizzazione delle tombe 'principesche' nel Lazio. Acqua Acetosa Laurentina: un esempio', *Opus* 3: 377–82.

Beer, C. (1987) 'Comparative votive religion: the evidence of children in Cyprus, Greece and Etruria', in *Gifts to the Gods: Proceedings of the Uppsala Symposium, 1985. Acta Universitatis Upsaliensis. Boreas* 15, ed. T. Linders and G. Nordquist, Uppsala: 21–9.

Bell, C. (1992) *Ritual Theory, Ritual Practice*, New York and Oxford.

(1997) *Ritual: Perspectives and Dimensions*, Oxford and New York.

Bell, E. E. (1995) 'The theme of Perseus and the Gorgon on Etruscan mirrors', abstracts of the papers of the 96th Annual General Meeting of the Archaeological Institute of America, *AJA* 99: 351.

Bendinelli, G. (1914) 'Antichità Tudertine del Museo Nazionale di Villa Guilia', *MonAL* 13: 609–84.

(1920) 'Il tempio etrusco figurato sopra specchi graffitti', *BCAR* 46: 229–45.

Benjamin, A. (1991) *Art, Mimesis and the Avant-Garde: Aspects of a Philosophy of Difference*, London and New York.

Bentz, M. (1992) *Etruskische Votivbronzen des Hellenismus*, Florence.

Bérard, C., *et al.* 1989) *A City of Images: Iconography and Society in Ancient Greece*, Princeton.

Bergamini, M. (ed.) (1991) *Gli Etruschi maestri di idraulica*, Perugia.

Berger, J. (1972) *Ways of Seeing*, Harmondsworth.

Berggren, E., and Berggren, K. (1980) *San Giovenale*, vol. III/3: *The Iron-Age Test Pit in the North-East Part of Area D, AIRRS* 4.26: 3.1.

(1981) *San Giovenale*, vol. II: 2, *Excavations in Area B, 1957–1960, AIRRS* 4.26: 2.2.

Berggren, E., and Moretti, M. (1960) 'San Giovenale', *NSA*: 1–66.

Bergquist, B. (1973) 'Was there a formal dining-room, sacred or civic, on the acropolis of Acquarossa?', *ORom* 9: 21–33.

Bermond Montanari, G. (ed.) (1987) *La formazione della città in Emilia Romagna: prime esperienze urbane attraverso le nuove scoperte archeologiche*, Bologna.

Bernardini, P., D'Oriano, R., and Spanu, P. G. (eds.) (1997) *Phonikes b shrdn / I Fenici in Sardegna: nuove acquisizioni*, Cagliari.

Bernardy, A. A. (1927) 'Collezioni etrusche nei musei di New York e di Boston', *SE* 1: 471–3.

Bhabha, H. (1994) *The Location of Culture*, London.

Bianchi Bandinelli, R. (1925a) 'Clusium: Ricerche archeologiche e topografiche su Chiusi e il suo territorio in età etrusca', *MonAL* 30: 209–552.

(1925b) 'Roselle', *A&R* 6: 35–48.

(1929) *Sovana: Topografia ed arte*, Florence.

(1970) 'L'esplorazione di Roselle', in *Studi sulla città antica: Atti del convegno di studi sulla città etrusca e italica preromana*, ed. G. A. Mansuelli and R. Zangheri, Bologna: 141–4.

Biers, W. R. (1992) *Art, Artefacts, and Chronology in Classical Archaeology*, London and New York.

Bietti-Sestieri, A. M. (1986) 'Italian swords and fibulae of the late Bronze and early Iron Ages', in *Italian Iron-Age Artefacts in the British Museum*, ed. J. Swaddling. London: 3–23.

(1992) *The Iron Age Community of Osteria dell'Osa: A Study of Sociopolitical Development in Central Tyrrhenian Italy*, Cambridge.

(1997) 'Italy in Europe in the Early Iron Age', *Proceedings of the Prehistoric Society* 63: 371–407.

(2000) 'The role of archaeological and historical data in the reconstruction of Italian protohistory', in *Ancient Italy in Its Mediterranean Setting: Studies in Honour of Ellen Macnamara*, ed. D. Ridgway *et al.*, London: 13–31.

Bilde, P. G., Nielsen, I., and Nielsen, M. (eds.) (1993) *Aspects of Hellenism in Italy: Towards a Cultural Unity? Acta Hyperborea* 5, Copenhagen.

Binford, L. R. (1971) 'Mortuary practices: their study and their potential', in *Approaches to the Social Dimensions of Mortuary Practices*, ed. J. A. Brown, *Memoirs of the Society for American Archaeology* 25: 6–29.

Bintliffe, J. (ed.) (1991) *The Annales School and Archaeology*, Leicester.

Bizzari, M. (1962) 'La necropoli di Crocifisso del Tufo in Orvieto', *SE* 30: 1–154.

(1963–4) 'Una importante scoperta per l'antica topografia di Orvieto', *Bollettino dell'Istituto Storico Artistico Orvietano* 9–10, fasc. 1: 118–125.

(1970) 'Trovato in Orvieto il Teichos di Zonara?', in *Studi sulla città antica: Atti del convegno di studi sulla città etrusca e italica Preromana*, ed. G. A. Mansuelli and R. Zangheri, Bologna: 153–6.

Blake, M. E. (1947) *Ancient Roman Construction in Italy from the Prehistoric period to Augustus*, Washington.

Blakeway, A. (1932–3) 'Prologomena to the study of Greek commerce with Italy, Sicily and France in the eighth and seventh centuries BC', *ABSA* 33: 170–208.

Blanck, H., and Proietti, G. (1986) *La Tomba dei Rilievi di Cerveteri*, Rome: De Luca.

Blanck, H., and Steingräber, S. (eds.) (1982) *Miscellanea archaeologica Tobias Dohrn dedicata*, Rome.

Blanton, R. E. (1994) *Houses and Households: A Comparative Study*, New York and London.

Blinkhorn, P. W. (1997) 'Habitus, social identity and Anglo-Saxon pottery', in *Not So Much a Pot, More a Way of Life*, ed. C. C. Cumberpatch and P. W. Blinkhorn, Oxford: 113–124.

Bloch, M. (1981) 'Tombs and states', in *Mortality and Immortality: The Anthropology and Archaeology of Death*, ed. S. C. Humphreys and H. King, London: 137–47.

Bloch, M., and Parry, J. (eds.) (1982) *Death and the Regeneration of Life*, Cambridge.

Bloch, R. (1958) *The Etruscans*, London.

(1983) 'L'alliance étrusco-punique de Pyrgi et la politique religieuse de la republique romaine à l'égard de l'Etrurie et de Carthage', in *Atti del I Congresso internazzionale di studi fenici e punici, Roma, 5–10 novembre 1979*, vol. II, ed. P. Bartoloni, Rome: 397–400.

(1984) 'Turan', *LIMC* 2.1: 169–76.

Blomé, B. (1969) 'Un insediamento arcaico etrusco a San Giovenale (Viterbo): L'applicazione di una moderna metodologia di rilievo', *Palladio* 19: 139–54.

(2001) 'A tentative reconstruction of House B on the Borgo of San Giovenale', in *From Huts to Houses: Transformations of Ancient Societies. Proceedings of an International Seminar Organised by the Norwegian and Swedish Institutes in Rome, 21–24 September 1997*, ed. J. R. Brandt and L. Karlsson, Stockholm: 241–43.

Boardman, J. (1967) *Pre-Classical: From Crete to Archaic Greece*, Harmondsworth.

(1999) *The Greeks Overseas: Their Early Colonies and Trade*, 4th edn, London.

Bocci Pacini, P., *et al.* (1975) *Roselle: Gli scavi e la mostra*, Pisa.

Boëthius, A. (1955–6) 'Vitruvius e il tempio tuscanico', *SE* 24: 137–42.

(1960) *The Golden House of Nero: Some Aspects of Roman Architecture*, Ann Arbor.

(1964) 'Old Etruscan towns: a sketch', in *Classical, Mediaeval and Renaissance Studies in Honour of Berthold Louis Ullman*, Storia e letteratura raccolta di studi e testo 93, ed. C. Henderson Jr, Rome: 3–16.

(1978) *Etruscan and Early Roman Architecture* (revised by R. Ling and T. Rasmussen), Harmondsworth.

Boëthius, A., *et al.* (1962) *Etruscan Culture, Land and People: Archaeological Research and Studies Conducted in San Giovenale and Its Environs by Members of the Swedish Institute in Rome*, New York and Malmö.

Bois, P. du (1982) *Centaurs and Amazons: Women and the Pre-History of the Great Chain of Being*, Ann Arbor.

(1988) *Sowing the Body: Psychoanalysis and Ancient Representations of Women*, Chicago and London.

Boitani, F. (1985a) 'Il santuario di Gravisca', in *Santuari d'Etruria*, ed. G. Colonna, Milan: 141–4.

(1985b) *Strade degli Etruschi: Vie e mezzi di communicazione nell'antica Etruria*, Milan.

Bomati, Y. (1986) 'Phersu et le monde dionysiaque', *Latomus* 45: 21–2.

Bonamici, M., Stopponi, S., and Tamburini, P. (1994) *Orvieto: La necropoli di Cannicella. Scavi della Fondazione per il Museo 'C. Faina' e dell'Università di Perugia (1977)*, Rome.

Bondì, S. F. (1988) 'City planning and architecture', in *The Phoenicians*, ed. S. Moscati, Milan: 284–3.

Bonfante, G., and Bonfante, L. (1983) *The Etruscan Language: An Introduction*, Manchester.

(2002) *The Etruscan Language: An Introduction*, 2nd edn, Manchester.

Bonfante, L. (1973a) 'Etruscan women: a question of interpretation', *Archaeology* 26.4: 242–9.

(1973b) 'The women of Etruria', *Arethusa* 6.1: 91–101.

(1975) *Etruscan Dress*, Baltimore.

(1977) 'The judgement of Paris, the toilette of Malavish and a mirror from the Indiana University Art Museum', *SE* 45: 149–67.

(1980) 'An Etruscan mirror with "Spiky Garland" in the Getty Museum', *The J. Paul Getty Museum Journal* 8: 147–54.

(1981) 'Etruscan couples and their aristocratic society', in *Reflections of Women in Antiquity*, ed. H. P. Foley, New York: 323–42. (Also published in *Women's Studies* 8: 157–87.)

(1982) 'Daily life', in *A Guide to Etruscan Mirrors*, ed. N. T. De Grummond, Tallahassee: 79–88.

(1986) 'Daily life and afterlife', in *Etruscan Life and Afterlife: A Handbook of Etruscan Studies*, ed. L. Bonfante, Warminster: 232–78.

(ed.) (1986) *Etruscan Life and Afterlife: A Handbook of Etruscan Studies*, Warminster.

(1989a) 'Iconografia delle madri: Etruria e Italia antica', in *Le donne in Etruria*, ed. A. Rallo, Rome: 85–106.

(1989b) 'La moda femminile etrusca', in *Le donne in Etruria*, ed. A. Rallo, Rome: 157–71.

(1990) *Etruscan*, London: Trustees of the British Museum.

(1993) 'Fufluns Pacha: the Etruscan Dionysus', in *Masks of Dionysos*, ed. T. Carpenter and C. Faraone, Ithaca and London: 221–35.

(1994) 'Etruscan women', in *Women in the Classical World: Image and Text*, ed. E. Fantham, Oxford and New York: 243–59.

(1999) 'Fama nominis Etruriae', *ARID* 26: 167–71.

Bonfante, L., and von Heintze, H. (eds.) (1976) *In Memoriam Otto J. Brendel: Essays in Archaeology and the Humanities*, Mainz.

Bonghi Jovino, M. (1986a) 'Gli scavi nell'abitato di Tarquinia e la scoperta dei "bronzi" in un preliminare inquadramento', in *Tarquinia – ricerche, scavi e prospettive: Atti del convegno internazionale di studi 'La Lombardia per gli Etruschi'*, ed. M. Bonghi Jovino and C. Chiaramonte Treré. *Milano, 24–25 giugno 1986*, Rome: 59–77.

(1986b) 'La monumentalizzazione dell'area sacra', in *Gli Etruschi di Tarquinia*, ed. M. Bonghi Jovino, Modena: 98–105.

(1986c) 'La prima età del ferro', in *Gli Etruschi di Tarquinia*, ed. M. Bonghi Jovino, Modena: 89–94.

(1986d) 'L'orizzonte protovillanoviano', in *Gli Etruschi di Tarquinia*, ed. M. Bonghi Jovino, Modena: 83–6.

(ed.) (1986) *Gli Etruschi di Tarquinia*, Modena.

(1989) 'Scavi recenti nell'abitato di Tarquinia', in *Atti del secondo congresso internazionale Etrusco. Firenze, 26 maggio – 2 giugno 1985*, vol. I, ed. G. Maetzke, Rome: 315–19.

Bonghi Jovino, M., and Chiaramonte Treré, C. (eds.) (1986) *Tarquinia – ricerche, scavi e prospettive. Atti del convegno internazionale di studi 'La Lombardia per gli Etruschi', Milano, 24–25 giugno 1986*, Rome.

(eds.) (1997) *Tarquinia: Testimonianze archeologiche e riconstruzione storica: scavi sistematici nell'abitato, campagne 1982–1988*, Rome.

Bonnefoy, Y. (ed.) (1991) *Roman and European Mythologies*, London and Chicago.

Bonomi Ponzi, L. (1996) 'La koiné centroitalicha in età preromana', in *Identità e Civiltà dei Sabini: Atti del 18 Convegno di studi etruschi ed italici, Rieti – Magliano Sabina, 30 maggio – 3 giugno 1993*, eds. G. Maetzke and L. Perna, Florence: 393–413.

Bound, M. (1985) 'Una nave mercantile di età arcaica all'isola del Giglio', in *Il commercio etrusco arcaico*, ed. M. Cristofani and P. Pelagatti, Rome: 65–70.

Bourdieu, Pierre (1971) 'The Berber house', in *Rules and Meanings*, ed. M. Douglas, Harmondsworth: 98–110.

(1977) *Outline of a Theory of Practice*, Cambridge.

(1989) *Distinction: A Social Critique of the Judgement of Taste*, London.

(1993) *The Field of Cultural Production*, Cambridge.

Bowman, A. K. (1992) 'Public buildings in Roman Egypt', *JRA* 5: 495–503.

Bowman A. K., and Woolf, G. (eds.) (1994) *Literacy and Power in the Ancient World*, Cambridge

Bradley, G. (2000a) *Ancient Umbria: State Culture and Identity in Central Italy from the Iron Age to the Augustan Era*, Oxford.

(2000b) 'Tribes, states and cities in central Italy', in *The Emergence of State Identities in Italy in the First Millennium* BC, ed. E. Herring and K. Lomas, London.

Bradley, R. (1993) *Altering the Earth*, London.

(1998) *The Significance of Monuments: On the Shaping of Human Experience in Neolithic and Bronze Age Europe*, London.

Braithwaite, M. (1982) 'Decoration as ritual symbol: a theoretical proposal and ethnographic study in southern Sudan', in *Symbolic and Structural Archaeology*, ed. I. Hodder, Cambridge: 80–8.

Brandt, J. R. (2001) 'From craftsmen to specialist: the formation of occupations in late iron age Latium', in *From Huts to Houses: Transformations of Ancient Societies. Proceedings of an International Seminar Organised by the Norwegian and Swedish Institutes in Rome, 21–24 September 1997*, ed. J. R. Brandt and L. Karlsson, Stockholm: 407–13.

Brandt, J. R., and Karlsson, L. (eds.) (2001) *From Huts to Houses: Transformations of Ancient Societies. Proceedings of an International Seminar Organised by the Norwegian and Swedish Institutes in Rome, 21–24 September 1997*, Stockholm.

Brendel, O. J. (1978) *Etruscan Art*, Harmondsworth.

Briffault, R. (1927) *The Mothers: A Study of Sentiments and Institutions* (3 vols.), London.

Briguet, M.-F. (1972) 'La sculpture en pierre fétide de Chiusi au Musée du Louvre', *MEFRA* 84: 847–77.

(1986) 'Art', in *Etruscan Life and Afterlife: A Handbook of Etruscan Studies*, ed. L. Bonfante, Warminster.

Brijder, H. A. G. (ed.) (1984) *Ancient Greek and Related Pottery: Proceedings of the International Vase Symposium in Amsterdam 12–15 April 1984*, Amsterdam.

Briscoe, J. (1981) *A Commentary on Livy Books* xxxiv–xxxvii, Oxford.

Brizio, E. (1891) 'Relazione sugli scavi eseguiti a Marzabotto presso Bologna dal novembre 1888 a tutto maggio 1889', *MonAL* 1: 249–426.

Brizzolara, A. M., Colonna, G., de Maria, S., Gualandi, G., Mansuelli, G. A., Gentili, G. V., and Pairault Massa, F.-H. (eds.) (1980) 'Guida al museo etrusco di Marzabotto', *Emilia Preromana* 8: 97–120.

Broadbent, G., Bunt, R., and Jecks, C. (eds.) (1980) *Signs, Symbols and Architecture*, Chichester.

Brocato, P., and Galluccio, F. (2001) 'Capanne moderne, tradizione antiche', in *From Huts to Houses: Transformations of Ancient Societies. Proceedings of an International Seminar Organised by the Norwegian and Swedish Institutes in Rome, 21–24 September 1997*, ed. J. R. Brandt and L. Karlsson, Stockholm: 283–309.

Broise, H., and Jolivet, V. (1985) 'Musarna (Viterbe)', *MEFRA* 97: 545–7.

(1986) 'Musarna (Viterbe)', *MEFRA* 98: 406–7.

(1987) 'Musarna (Viterbe)', *MEFRA* 99: 505–6.

(1988a) 'Musarna (Com. di Viterbo), *SE* 54: 365–6.

(1988b) 'Musarna (Viterbe)', *MEFRA* 100: 530–2.

(1989) 'Musarna (Viterbe)', *MEFRA* 101: 519–21.

(1990) 'Musarna (Viterbe)', *MEFRA* 102: 477–8.

(1991) 'Musarna (Viterbe)', *MEFRA* 103: 346–7.

(1992) 'Musarna (Viterbe)', *MEFRA* 104: 496–500.

(1993) 'Musarna (Viterbe)', *MEFRA* 105: 444–7.

(1994) 'Musarna (Viterbe)', *MEFRA* 106: 454–62.

Bronson, R. C. (1965) 'Chariot racing in Etruria', in *Studi in onore di Luisa Banti*, ed. G. Becatti *et al.*, Rome: 89–106.

Broude, N., and Garrard, M. D. (eds.) (1982) *Feminism and Art History: Questioning the Litany*, New York.

Brown, A. C. (1974) 'Etrusco-Italic architectural terracottas in the Ashmolean Museum, Oxford', *AR*: 60–5.

Brown, F. E. (1976) 'Of huts and houses', in *In Memoriam Otto J. Brendel: Essays in Archaeology and the Humanities*, ed. L. Bonfante, and H. von Heintze, Mainz: 5–12.

Brown, J. A. (ed.) (1971) *Approaches to the Social Dimensions of Mortuary Practices*, Memoirs of the Society for American Archaeology 25.

(1981) 'The search for ranks in prehistoric burials', in *The Archaeology of Death*, ed. R. Chapman *et al.*, Cambridge: 25–37.

Brown, S. (1993) 'Feminist research in archaeology: what does it mean? Why is it taking so long?', in *Feminist Theory and the Classics*, ed. N. S. Rabinowitz and A. Richlin, New York and London: 237–71.

Brown, W. L. (1960) *The Etruscan Lion*, Oxford.

Bruhl, A. (1953) *Liber Pater: Origine et expansion du culte dionysiaque à Rome et dans le monde Romain*, BEFAR 175, Rome.

Brush, K. A. (1988) 'Gender and mortuary analysis in pagan Anglo-Saxon archaeology', *ARC* 7.1: 76–89.

Bryson, N. (1983) *Vision and Painting: The Logic of the Gaze*, London.

(1984) *Tradition and Desire: From David to Delacroix*, Cambridge.

(1988) 'The gaze in the expanded field', in *Vision and Visuality*, ed. H. Foster, Seattle: 87–108.

Buchli, V. A. (1995) 'Interpreting material culture: the trouble with text', in *Interpreting Archaeology: Finding Meaning in the Past*, ed. I. Hodder, London: 181–93.

Buchner, G., and Ridgway, D. (1993) *Pithekoussai*, vol. i: La Necropoli: tombe 1–723 scavate dal 1952 al 1961, Rome.

Buonamici, G. (1932) *Epigrafica etrusca*, Florence.

(1938) 'Rivista di epigrafia etrusca, 1937–1938', *SE* 12: 303–30.

Buranelli, F. (1987) 'Il corredo: scavo e dispersione', in *La Tomba François di Vulci*, ed. F. Buranelli, Rome: 115–45.

(ed.) (1987) *La Tomba François di Vulci*, Rome.

Burkert, W. (1992) *The Orientalising Revolution: Near Eastern Influence on Greek Culture in the Early Archaic Age*, trans. M. E. Pinder and W. Burkert, Cambridge, Mass.

Burn, L. (1987) *The Meidias Painter*, Oxford.

Burnham, B. J., and Kingsbury, J. (eds.) (1979) *Space, Hierarchy and Society*, Oxford.

Butler, J. (1990) *Gender Trouble: Feminism and the Subversion of Identity*, New York.

(1993) *Bodies that Matter: On the Discursive Limits of 'Sex'*, New York.

Caccioli, D., and Whitehead, J. (1994) 'New researches at La Piana', *AJA* 98: 319–20.

Cagiano De Azevedo, M. (1974) 'Bagnoregio (Viterbo): scavi in località Girella', *NSA*: 21–37.

Cahill, N., 2002) *Household and City Organization at Olynthus*, New Haven and London.

Caley, E. R. (1970) 'Analysis of Etruscan bronze', *AJA* 74: 98–9.

Calzoni, M., and Pierotti, A. M. (1950–1) 'Ricerche su Perugia etrusca: la città e la necropoli urbana', *SE* 21: 275–89.

Cameron, A., and Kuhrt, A. (eds.) (1993) *Images of Women in Antiquity*, London.

Campagnano, L., Grillini, A., and Sassatelli, G. (1970) 'L'esplorazione del settore centro-orientale', *SE* 38: 225–36.

Campelli, V. (1935) 'La cinta murata di Perugia: contributo allo studio dell'architettura etrusca', *RIA* 5: 7–36.

Camporeale, G. (1965) 'Banalizzazioni etruschi di miti greci', in *Studi in onore di Luisa Banti*, ed. G. Becatti *et al.*, Rome: 111–23.

(1967) *Vetulonia: La tomba del Duce*, Florence.

(1985a) 'La cultura dei principi', in *Civiltà degli Etruschi*, ed. M. Cristofani, Milan: 79–84.

(1985b) 'Massa Marittima, Lago dell'Accesa', in *L'Etruria mineraria*, ed. G. Camporeale, Milan: 127–78.

(ed.) (1985) *L'Etruria mineraria*, Milan.

(1986) 'Massa Marittima', *SE* 54: 379.

(1997) *L'Abitato Etrusco dell'Accesa: Il quartiere B*, Rome.

Camporeale, G., and Guintoli, S. (2000) *The Accesa Archaeological Park at Massa Marittima*, Rome.

Cannon, A. (1991) 'Gender, status and the focus of material display', in *The Archaeology of Gender: Proceedings of the 22nd Annual Chacmool Conference, Calgary*, ed. D. Walde and N. D. Willows, Calgary: 144–9.

Canocchi, D. (1980) 'Osservazioni sull'abitato orientalizzante a Roselle', *SE* 48: 31–50.

Cantarella, E. (1987) *Pandora's Daughters: The Role and Status of Women in Greek and Roman Antiquity*, Baltimore and London.

Caplan, J. (ed.) (2000) *Written on the Body: The Tattoo in European and American History*, London.

Caputo, G. (1959) 'Nuova tomba etrusca a Quinto Fiorentino', *SE* 27: 269–76.

(1962) 'La Montagnola di Quinto Fiorentino, L' "Orientalizzante", e le *tholoi* dell'Arno', *BA* 47: 115–52.

(1965) 'L'*obelos* della Montagnola', *SE* 33: 521–2.

(1970) 'La *tholos* della Mula in nuovo rilievo', *SE* 38: 367–72.

Carafa, P. (1994) 'Organizzazione territoriale e sfruttamento delle risorse economiche nell'Agro Volterrano tra l'Orientalizzante e l'età ellenistica', *SE* 59: 109–21.

(1998) 'Le frontiere degli dei: osservazioni sui santuari di confine nella Campagna antica', in *Papers from the EAA Third Annual Meeting at Ravenna, 1997*, vol. I: Pre- and Protohistory, ed. M. Pearce and M. Tosi, Oxford: 211–22.

Carandini, A.(ed.) (1985) *La romanizzazione dell'Eturia: il territorio di Vulci*, Milan.

(1990) 'Il palatino e le aree residenziali', in *La Grande Roma dei Tarquini*, ed. M. Cristofani, Rome: 97–99.

(2003) *La nascita di Roma: dei, lari, eroi, uomini all'alba di una civiltà*, Rome.

Carandini, A., Cambi, F., Celuzza, M., and Fentress, E. (eds.) (2002) *Paesaggi d'Etruria: Valle dell'Albegna, Valle d'Oro, Valle del Chiarone, Valle del Tafone: progetto di ricerca italo-britannico seguito allo scavo di Settefinestre*, Rome.

Carandini, A., and Capelli, R. (eds.) (2000) *Roma: Romolo, Remo e la fondazione della città*, Milan.

Carandini, D. (1972) 'Appunti sul restauro di alcuni specchi in bronzo provenienti dal Museo Nazionale di Tarquinia', *SE* 40: 503–6.

Carducci, C. (1962) *Gold- und Silberschmuck aus dem antiken Italien*, Vienna and Munich.

Carpenter, T., and Faraone, C. (eds.) (1993) *Masks of Dionysos*, Ithaca and London.

Carpino, A. A. (1996a) 'Greek mythology in Etruria: an iconographic analysis of three Etruscan relief mirrors', in *Etruscan Italy: Etruscan Influences on the Civilizations of Italy from Antiquity to the Modern Era*, ed. J. F. Hall, Provo, Utah: 65–91.

  (1996b) 'The delivery of Helen's egg: an examination of an Etruscan relief mirror', *Etruscan Studies* 3: 33–44.

  (2003) *Discs of Splendor: The Relief Mirrors of the Etruscans*, Madison.

Carr, C., and Neitzel, J. E. (eds.) (1995) *Style, Society, and Person: Archaeological and Ethnographic Perspectives*, New York and London.

Carresi, A. (1985) *Vetulonia: Appunti di storia di una città etrusca*, Rome.

Carsten, J. (ed.) (2000) *Cultures of Relatedness: New Approaches to the Study of Kinship*, Cambridge.

Carsten, J., and Hugh-Jones, S. (1995) 'Introduction', in *About the House: Lévi-Strauss and Beyond*, ed. J. Carsten and S. Hugh-Jones, Cambridge: 1–46.

  (eds.) (1995) *About the House: Lévi-Strauss and Beyond*, Cambridge.

Carstens, A. (2003/4) 'Style and context', *Hephaistos* 21/22: 7–28.

Carter, J. C. (1994) 'Sanctuaries in the *chora* of Metaponto', in *Placing the Gods: Sanctuaries and Sacred Space in Ancient Greece*, ed. S. A. Alcock and R. Osborne, Oxford: 161–98.

Cartledge, P. (1977) 'Hoplites and heroes: Sparta's contribution to the techniques of ancient warfare', *JHS* 97: 11–27.

  (1993) *The Greeks: A Portrait of Self and Others*, Oxford.

Castagnoli, F. (1955) 'Peripteros sine postico', *MDAI(R)* 62: 139–43.

  (1956) *Ippodamo di Mileto e l'urbanistica a pianta ortogonale*, Rome.

  (1966–7) 'Sul tempio "italico"', *MDAI(R)* 73–4: 10–14.

  (1971) *Orthogonal Town Planning in Antiquity*, Cambridge, Mass., and London.

Catacchio, N. (ed.) (1983) *Sorgenti della Nova: Una comunità protostorica ed il suo territorio nell'Etruria meridionale*, Rome.

Cateni, G. (1995) *CSE Italia 3 Volterra*, Rome.

Cavagnaro Vanoni, L. (1989) 'Intervento alla civita di Tarquinia della Fondazione Lerici', in *Atti del secondo congresso internazionale etrusco, Firenze, 26 maggio – 2 giugno 1985*, vol. I, ed. G. Maetzke, Rome: 341–5.

Cawkwell, G. (1992) 'Early colonization', *CQ* 42: 289–303.

Çelik, Z. (1994) 'Urban preservations as theme park: the case of Sogukçesme Street', in *Streets: Critical Perspectives on Public Space*, ed. Z. Çelik *et al.*, Berkeley: 83–94.

Çelik, Z., Favro, D., and Ingersoll, R. (1994) 'Streets and the urban process: a tribute to Spiro Kostof', in *Streets: Critical Perspectives on Public Space*, ed. Z. Çelik *et al.*, Berkeley: 1–8.

Çelik, Z., Favro, D., and Ingersoll, R. (eds.) (1994) *Streets: Critical Perspectives on Public Space*, Berkeley.

Cerchiai, L. (1987) 'Sulle tombe del Tuffatore e della Caccia e Pesca: proposta di letteratura iconologica', *DArch* 5: 113–23.

Champion, T. C. (ed.) (1989) *Centre and Periphery: Comparative Studies in Archaeology*, London and New York.

Chapman, J. (1990) 'Social inequality on Bulgarian Tells and the Varna Problem', in *The Social Archaeology of Houses*, ed. R. Samson, Edinburgh: 49–92.

(1991) 'The creations of social arenas in the Neolithic and Copper Age of S. E. Europe: the case of Varna', in *Sacred and Profane: Proceedings of a Conference on Archaeology, Ritual and Religion, Oxford 1989*, ed. P. Garwood, D. Jennings, R. Skeates and J. Toms, Oxford: 152–71.

Chapman, R., Kinnes, I., and Randsborg, K. (eds.) (1981) *The Archaeology of Death*, Cambridge.

Cherfas, J., and Lewin, R. (eds.) (1980) *Not Work Alone: A Cross-Cultural View of Activities Superfluous to Survival*, Beverley Hills.

Cherry, J. F. (1987) 'Power in space: archaeological and geological studies of the state', in *Landscape and Culture: Geological and Archaeological Perspectives*, ed. J. M. Wagstaff, Oxford: 146–72.

Chiaramonte Treré, C. (1986) 'Ristrutturazioni e ricende dell'area sacra: il nuovo assetto del V secolo: l'ultima fase', in *Gli Etruschi di Tarquinia*, ed. M. Bonghi Jovino, Modena: 112–17.

Childe, V. G. (1950) 'The urban revolution', *Town Planning Review* 21: 3–17.

Cifani, G. (2002a) 'Aspects of urbanisation and thenic identity in the Middle Tiber Valley', in *New Developments in Italian Landscape Archaeology*, ed. P. Attema *et al.*, Oxford: 220–28.

(2002b) 'Notes on the rural landscape of central Tyrrhenian Italy in the 6th–5th c. B.C. and its social significance', *JRA* 15: 248–60.

(2005) 'I confini settentrionali del territorio veiente', in *Dinamiche di sviluppo della città nell'Etruria meridionale: Veio, Tarquinia, Vulci. Atti del XXIII Convegno di Studi Etruschi ed Italici, Roma, Veio, Cerveteri/Pyrgi, Tarquinia, Tuscania, Vulci, Viterbo, 1–6 ottobre 2001*, ed. O. Paoletti and G. Camporeale, Pisa and Rome: 151–61.

Claassen, C. (1992) 'Questioning gender: an introduction', in *Exploring Gender through Archaeology: Sixteen Papers from the 1991 Boone Conference*, Monographs in World Archaeology 11, ed. C. Claassen, Madison: 1–9.

(ed.) (1992) *Exploring Gender through Archaeology: Sixteen papers from the 1991 Boone Conference*, Monographs in World Archaeology 11, Madison.

Clark, G. (1989) 'A group of animal bones from Cerveteri', *SE* 55: 253–69.

Clarke, G. W. (1989) *Rediscovering Hellenism: The Hellenic Inheritance and the English Imagination*, Cambridge.

Clarke, J. R. (1991) *The Houses of Roman Italy 100 BC–AD 250: Ritual, Space and Decoration*, Berkeley.

Cleland, C. E. (ed.) (1977) *For the Director: Research Essays in Honour of James B. Griffin*, Museum of Anthropology Paper 61, Ann Arbor.

Clemen, C. (1936) *Die Religion der Etrusker*, Bonn.

Cles-Reden, S. von (1955) *The Buried People*, London.

Close-Brooks, J., and Ridgway, D. (1971) 'Veii in the Iron Age', in *Italy Before the Romans: The Iron Age, Orientalising and Etruscan Periods*, ed. D. Ridgway and F. R. Ridgway. London: 95–127.

Coarelli, F. (1983) *Il foro Romano: Il periodo arcaico*, Rome.

   (1988) *Il foro Boario: Dalle origini alla fine della Repubblica*, Rome.

Coarelli, F. (ed.) (1975) *Etruscan Cities*, London.

Coarelli, F., and Rossi, A. (1980) *Templi dell'Italia antica*, Milan.

Coen, A. (1991) *Complessi tombali di Cerveteri con urne cinerarie tardo-orientalizzanti*, Florence.

   (1999) *Corona etrusca*, Viterbo.

Cohen, M. N., and Bennett, S. (1993) 'Skeletal evidence for sex roles and gender hierarchies in prehistory', in *Sex and Gender Hierarchies*, ed. B. D. Miller, Cambridge: 273–96.

Coldstream, J. N. (1993) 'Mixed marriages at the frontiers of the early Greek world', *OJA* 12: 89–101.

   (1994) 'Prospectors and pioneers: Pithekoussai, Kyme and Central Italy', in *The Archaeology of Greek Colonisation: Essays Dedicated to John Boardman*, ed. G. R. Tsetskladze and Franco De Angelis, Oxford: 47–59.

Cole, H. M. (1979) 'Living art among the Samburu', in *The Fabrics of Culture: The Anthropology of Clothing and Adornment*, ed. J. M. Cordwell and R. A. Schwarz, The Hague: 87–102.

Cole, S. G. (1981) 'Could Greek women read and write?', *Women's Studies* 8: 129–55.

Colini, G. A. (1919) 'Veio – scavi nell'area della città e della necropoli', *NSA*: 3–12.

Colonna, G. (1960) 'Falterona', *EAA* 3: 589–90.

   (1965) 'Il santuario di Pyrgi alla luce delle recenti scoperte', *SE* 33: 193–219.

   (1967) 'Tuscania: monumenti etruschi di epoca arcaica', *Archeologia* 38: 86–93.

   (1970) 'Problemi di topografia storica dell'Etruria meridionale interna', in *Studi sulla città antica: Atti del convegno di studi sulla città etrusca e italica preromana*, ed. G. Mansuelli and R. Zangheri, Bologna: 165–7.

   (ed.) (1970) 'Pyrgi: scavi del santuario etrusco (1959–1967)', *NSA* (second supplement).

   (1973) 'Scavi e scoperte: Cerveteri', *SE* 41: 538–41.

   (1977) 'La presenza di Vulci nelle valli della Fiora e dell'Albegna prima del IV secolo a.C.', in *La civiltà arcaica di Vulci e la sua espansione: Atti del X convegno di studi etruschi ed italici, 29 maggio – 2 giugno 1975*, ed. A. Neppi Modona, Florence: 189–213.

   (1984) 'Menerva', *LIMC* 2.1: 1050–74.

   (1985a) 'Anfore da trasporto a Gravisca', in *Il commercio etrusco arcaico*, ed. M. Cristofani and P. Pelagatti, Rome: 5–18.

(1985b) 'Il culto dei morti', in *Civiltà degli Etruschi*, ed. M. Cristofani, Milan: 290–306.

(1985c) 'I santuari suburbani', in *Santuari d'Etruria*, ed. G. Colonna, Milan: 98–9.

(1985d) 'I santuari urbani', in *Santuari d'Etruria*, ed. G. Colonna, Milan: 67–97.

(1985e) 'Le forme ideologiche della città', in *Civiltà degli Etruschi*, ed. M. Cristofani. Milan: 242–89.

(1985f) 'Santuario in località Portonaccio a Veio', in *Santuari d'Etruria*, ed. G. Colonna, Milan: 99–101.

(ed.) (1985) *Santuari d'Etruria*, Milan.

(1986) 'Urbanistica e architettura', in *Rasenna: Storia e civiltà degli Etruschi*, ed. G. Pugliese Carratelli, Milan: 371–530.

(1987) 'Culti del santuario di Portonaccio', in *Science dell'antichità, Storia Archeologia Antropologia* 1: 419–46.

(1988) 'Il lessico istituzionale etrusco e la formazione della città (especialmente in Emilia Romagna)', in *La formazione della città preromana in Emilia Romagna: Atti del convegno di studi, Bologna-Marzabotto 7–8 dicembre 1985*, ed. G. A. Mansuelli, Bologna: 15–36.

(ed.) (1988–9) 'Pyrgi: scavi del santuario etrusco (1969–1971)', *NSA* (second supplement).

(1993) 'Doni etruschi e di altri barbari occidentali nei santuari panellenici', in *I grandi santuari della Grecia e l'Occidente*, ed. A. Mastrocinque, Trento: 43–67.

(1994) 'A proposito degli dei del Fegato di Piacenza', *SE* 59: 123–39.

(1996) 'Il dokanon, il culto dei Dioscuri e gli aspetti ellenizzati della religione dei morti nell'Etruria tardo arcaico', in *Scritti di antichità in memoria di Sandro Stucchi*, ed. L. Bacchielli and M. Bonanno Aravantinos, Rome: 165–84.

(ed.) (1997) *L'Abitato Etrusco dell'Accesa: Il Quartiere B*, Rome.

Colonna, G., and Backe Forsberg, Y. (1999) 'Le iscrizioni del "sacelle" del Ponte di San Giovenale', *ORom* 24: 63–81.

Colonna, G., and Colonna di Paolo, E. (1997) 'Il letto vuoto, la distribuzione del corredo e la "finestra" della Tomba Regolini Galassi', in *Etrusca et italica*, vol. I: *Scritti in ricordo di M. Pallottino*, eds. G. Nardi *et al.*, Rome and Pisa: 131–72.

Colonna di Paolo, E., and Colonna, G. (1970) *Castel D'Asso, le necropoli rupestri dell'Etruria Meridionale*, vol. I, Rome.

(1978) *Norchia I, le necropoli rupestri dell'Etruria Meridionale*, vol. II, Rome.

Comaroff, J. (1996) 'The empire's old clothes: fashioning the colonial subject', in *Cross-Cultural Consumption: Global Markets, Local Realities*, ed. D. Howes, London and New York: 19–38.

Comaroff, J., and Comaroff, J. (1992) *Ethnography and the Historical Imagination*, Boulder.

Comella, A. (2001) *Il santuario di Punta della Vipera: Santa Marinella, Comune di Civitavecchia*, Rome. Corpus delle stipi votive in Italia, XIII, Regio VII: 6

Conkey, M. W. (1990) 'Experimenting with style in archaeology: some historical and theoretical issues', in *The Uses of Style in Archaeology*, ed. M. W. Conkey and C. A. Hastorf, Cambridge: 5–17.

(1991) 'Contexts of action, contexts for power: material culture and gender in the Magdalenian', in *Engendering Archaeology: Women and Prehistory*, ed. J. M. Gero and M. W. Conkey, Oxford: 57–92.

Conkey, M. W., and Gero, J. M. (1991) 'Tensions, pluralities and engendering archaeology: an introduction to women and prehistory', in *Engendering Archaeology: Women and Prehistory*, ed. J. M. Gero and M. W. Conkey, Oxford: 3–30.

Conkey, M. W., and Hastorf, C. A. (eds.) (1990) *The Uses of Style in Archaeology*, Cambridge.

Conkey, M. W., and Spector, J. D. (1984) 'Archaeology and the study of gender', in *Advances in Archaeological Method and Theory*, vol. VII, ed. M. Schiffer, New York: 1–38.

Connelly, J. B. (1993) 'Narrative and image in Attic vase painting: Ajax and Kassandra at the Trojan Palladion', in *Narrative and Event in Ancient Art*, ed. P. J. Holliday, Cambridge: 88–129.

Constantini, L., and Giorgi, J. A. (1987) 'Blera: I resti vegetali', in *L'Alimentazione nel mondo antico: Gli Etruschi*, ed. C. Ampolo *et al.*, Rome: 83–6.

Cook, R. M. (1972) *Greek Painted Pottery*, London.

(1989) 'The Francis-Vickers chronology', *JHS* 109: 164–70.

Coote, J., and Shelton, A. (eds.) (1992) *Anthropology, Art, and Aesthetics*, Oxford.

Cordwell, J. M. (1979) 'The very human arts of transformation', in *The Fabrics of Culture: The Anthropology of Clothing and Adornment*, ed. J. M. Cordwell and R. A. Schwartz, The Hague: 48–75.

Cordwell, J. M., and Schwartz, R. A. (eds.) (1979) *The Fabrics of Culture: The Anthropology of Clothing and Adornment*, The Hague.

Cormack, R. (1990) 'Byzantine Aphrodisias: changing the symbolic map of a city', *PCPS* 36: 26–41.

Cornell, T. J. (1995a) *The Beginnings of Rome: Italy and Rome from the Bronze Age to the Punic Wars (c. 1000–264 BC)*, London and New York.

(1995b) 'Warfare and urbanization in Roman Italy', in *Urban Society in Roman Italy*, ed. T. J. Cornell and K. Lomas, London: 121–34.

Cornell, T. J., and Lomas, K. (eds.) (1995) *Urban Society in Roman Italy*, London.

(eds.) (1997) *Gender and Ethnicity in Ancient Italy*, London.

Courbin, P. (1968) 'La guerre en Grèce a haute époque d'après les documents archaeologiques', in *Problèmes de la guerre en Grèce ancienne*, ed. J.-P. Vernant, Paris: 119–42.

Coward, R. (1984) *Female Desire: Women's Sexuality Today*, London.

Craddock, P. T. (1984) 'The metallurgy and composition of Etruscan bronze', *SE* 52: 211–71.

Crawford, M. (ed.) (1983) *Sources for Ancient History*, Cambridge.

Cristiansen, J., and Melander, T. (eds.) (1988) *Ancient Greek and Related Pottery*, Copenhagen.

Cristofani, M. (1967) 'Ricerche sulle pitture della tomba "François" di Vulci. I fregi decorativi', *DArch* 1: 186–219.

(1969) *Le tombe di Monte Michele nel museo archeologico di Firenze*, Florence.

(1975) 'Il "dono" nell'Etruria arcaica', *PP* 161: 132–52.

(1976) 'Storia dell'arte e acculturazione: le pitture tombali arcaiche di Tarquinia', *Prospettiva* 7: 2–10.

(1978) *Arte degli Etruschi: Produzione e consumo*, Turin.

(1979) *The Etruscans: A New Investigation*, London.

(ed.) (1981) *Gli Etruschi in Maremma: Popolamento e attività produttive*, Milan.

(1983) *Gli Etruschi del Mare*, 2nd edn, Milan.

(1984) 'Iscrizioni e beni suntuari', *Opus* 3: 319–24.

ed.(1985) *Civiltà degli Etruschi*, Milan.

(1987a) 'Il banchetto in Etruria', in *L'Alimentazione nel mondo antico: Gli Etruschi*, ed. C. Ampolo *et al.*, Rome: 123–31.

(1987b) 'I santuari: tradizione decorative', in *Etruria e Lazio Arcaico*, ed. M. Cristofani, Quaderni di Archeologia Etrusca Rome: 15: 95–120.

ed.(1987) *Etruria e Lazio Arcaico*, Quaderni di Archeologia Etrusca 15, Rome.

(1988) 'L'area urbana', in *Caere 1: Il Parco Archeologico*, ed. M. Cristofani and G. Nardi, Rome: 85–93.

(1989–90) 'Scavi nell'area urbana di Caere: le terrecotte decorative', *SE* 56: 69–84.

(ed.)(1990) *La Grande Roma dei Tarquini*, Rome.

(ed.)(1992) *Caere 3.1: Lo scarico arcaico della Vigna Parrocchiale*, part 1, Rome.

(ed.)(1993) *Gli Etruschi: Una nuova immagine*, Florence.

(1996a) *Etruschi e altre genti nell'Italia preromana: Mobilità in età arcaica*, Rome.

(1996b) 'Sostratos e dintorni', in *Etruschi e altre genti nell'Italia preromana: Mobilità in età arcaica*, M. Cristofani, Rome: 49–57.

(1997) 'Dove vivevano i principi etruschi', *Archeo* 13: 46–54.

Cristofani, M., and Martelli, M. (1978) 'Fufluns Paχies: sugli aspetti del culto di Bacco in Etruria', *SE* 46: 119–33.

(eds.) (1983) *L'Oro degli Etruschi*, Novara.

Cristofani, M., and Michelucci, M. (1981) 'La valle dell'Albegna', in *Gli Etruschi in Maremma: Popolamento e attività produttive*, ed. M. Cristofani, Milan: 97–113.

Cristofani, M., and Nardi, G. (eds.) (1988) *Caere 1: Il Parco Archeologico*, Rome.

Cristofani, M., and Pelagatti, P. (eds.) (1985) *Il commercio etrusco arcaico*, Rome.

Cristofani, M., and Torelli, M. (1993) 'La società e lo stato', in *Gli Etruschi: Una nuova immagine*, ed. M. Cristofani, Florence: 107–138.

Cristofani, M., and Zevi, F. (eds.) (1992) *Atti e memorie della società Magna Grecia*, 3.1.

Crouwel, J. H. (1981) *Chariots and Other Means of Land Transport in Bronze-Age Greece*, Amsterdam.

Cullum, H. (1986) 'The Savoy Hunting Lodge at Venaria Reale', unpublished dissertation, Cambridge.

Cultrera, G. (1932) 'Tarquinia: il primo tumulo della "Doganaccia"', *NSA*: 100–16.

Cumberpatch, C. C., and Blinkhorn, P. W. (eds.) (1997) *Not So Much a Pot, More a Way of Life*, Oxford.

Cuozzo, M. (1994) 'Patterns of organisation and funerary customs in the cemetery of Pontecagnano (SA) during the Orientalizing period', *Journal of European Archaeology* 2.2: 263–98.

Curri, C. B. (1978) 'Nuovi rilievi grafici dei tumuli della Pietrera e del Pozzo dell'Abate', *SE* 46: 255–64.

   (1981) 'Intervento' on the afternoon session of the second day of conference, in *L'Etruria Mineraria: Atti del XII convegno di Studi etruschi ed italici, Firenze 16–20 giugno 1979*, ed. A. Neppi Modona, Florence: 199–202.

Curti, E., Dench, E., and Patterson, J. R. (1996) 'The archaeology of central and southern Italy: recent trends and approaches', *JRS* 86: 170–89.

Damgaard Andersen, H. (1993a) 'Archaic terracottas and their relation to building identification', in *Deliciae fictiles: Proceedings of the First International Conference on Central Italic Architectural Terracottas at the Swedish Institute in Rome, 10–12 December 1990*. AIRRS 4.50, eds. E. Rystedt *et al.*, Stockholm.

   (1993b) 'The Etruscan ancestral cult: its origins, and development, and the importance of anthropomorphization', *ARID* 21: 7–66.

   (1997) 'The archaeological evidence for the origin and development of the Etruscan city in the 7th to 6th centuries BC', in *Urbanization in the Mediterranean in the 9th to 6th centuries BC: ActaHyperborea* 7, ed. H. Damgaard Andersen *et al.*, Copenhagen: 343–82.

Damgaard Andersen, H., Horsnæs, Houby-Nielsen, S., and Rathje, A. (eds.) (1997) *Urbanization in the Mediterranean in the 9th to 6th Centuries BC: Acta Hyperborea* 7, Copenhagen.

Damgaard Andersen, H., and Toms, J. (2001) 'The earliest tiles in Italy?', in *From Huts to Houses: Transformations of Ancient Societies. Proceedings of an International Seminar Organised by the Norwegian and Swedish Institutes in Rome, 21–24 September 1997*, ed. J. R. Brandt and L. Karlsson, Stockholm: 264–8.

Damm, C. (1991) 'From burials to gender roles: problems and potentials in post-processual archaeology', in *The Archaeology of Gender: Proceedings of the 22nd Annual Chacmool Conference, Calgary*, ed. D. Walde and N. D. Willows, Calgary: 130–5.

Danforth, L. M. (1982) *The Death Rituals of Rural Greece*, Princeton.

Davey, N. (1999) 'The hermeneutics of seeing', in *Interpreting Visual Culture: Explorations in the Hermeneutics of the Visual*, ed. I. Heywood and B. Sandywell, London and New York: 3–29.

Davis, N. Z. (1985) *The Return of Martin Guerre*, Harmondsworth.

Davis, W. (1990) 'Style and history in art history', in *The Uses of Style in Archaeology*, ed. M. W. Conkey and C. A. Hastorf. Cambridge: 18–31.

De Agostino, A. (1937) 'Bronzetti e specchi della collezione Bologna di Montepulciano', *SE* 11: 473–6.

(1955–6) 'Nuovi contributi all'archeologia di Populonia', *SE* 24: 255–86.

(1957) 'Populonia: scoperte archeologiche nella necropoli negli anni 1954–1956', *NSA:* 1–52.

(1958) 'La nuova tomba a edicola a Populonia', *SE* 26: 27–35.

(1962) 'La cinta fortificata di Populonia', *SE* 30: 275–82.

(1963) 'La tomba delle antare a Veio', *ArchClass* 15: 219–22.

De Albentiis, E. (1990) *La casa dei Romani*, Milan.

De Angelis, Franco (1998) 'Ancient past, imperial present: the British Empire in T. J. Dunbabin's *The Western Greeks*', *Antiquity* 72: 539–49.

De Angelis, Francesco (2001) 'Specchi e miti: sulla ricezione della mitologia greca in Etruria', *Ostraka* 11.1: 37–73.

De Atley, S. P., and Findlow, F. J. (eds.) (1984) *Exploring the Limits: Frontiers and Boundaries in Prehistory*, Oxford.

D'Atri, V. (1986) 'Castiglione in Teverina (Viterbo)', *SE* 54: 352–4.

De Cazanove, O., and Jolivet, V. (1984) 'Musarna (Viterbe)', *MEFRA* 96: 530–4.

de Certeau, M. (1984) *The Practice of Everyday Life*, Berkeley.

De Fosse, P. (1980) 'Le remparts de Pérouse: contributions à l'histoire de l'urbanism préromain', *MEFRA* 92: 275–820.

De Grossi Mazzorin, J. (1985) 'Reperti faunistici dall'acropoli di Populonia: testimonianza di allevamento e caccia nell III secolo a.C', *Rassegna di Archeologia* 5: 131–71.

(1987) 'Populonia', in *L'Alimentazione nel mondo antico: Gli Etruschi*, ed. C. Ampolo *et al.* Rome: 89–93.

De Puma, R. D. (1973) 'The Dioskuri on four Etruscan mirrors in the Midwestern collections', *SE* 41: 159–70.

(1986) 'Tinas Cliniar', *LIMC* 3.1: 597–608.

(1987) *CSE USA 1*, Ames, Iowa.

(1993) *CSE USA 2*, Ames, Iowa.

(1994) 'Eos and Memnon on Etruscan mirrors', in *Murlo and the Etruscans: Art and Society in Ancient Etruria*, ed. R. D. De Puma and J. P. Small, Madison: 180–9.

De Puma, R. D., and Small, J. P. (eds.) (1994) *Murlo and the Etruscans: Art and Society in Ancient Etruria*, Madison.

De Santis, A. (1997) 'Alcuni considerazioni sul territorio veiente in età orientalizzante e arcaica', in *Le necropoli arcaiche di Veio: Giornata di studio in memoria di Massimo Pallottino*, ed. G. Bartoloni, Rome: 101–41.

Del Chiaro, M. A. (1955) 'Two Etruscan mirrors in San Francisco', *AJA* 59: 277–86.

(1971) 'An Etruscan bronze mirror produced at Caere', *AJA* 75: 85–6.

(1974) 'Etruscan bronze mirrors', *Archaeology* 27: 120–6.

(1976) *Etruscan Ghiaccioforte*, Santa Barbara.

Deleuze, G. (1990) *The Logic of Sense*, trans. M. Lester, London.

Dench, E. (1995) *From Barbarians to New Men: Greek, Roman, and Modern Perceptions of Peoples of the Central Apennines*, Oxford.

Dennis, G. (1883) *The Cities and Cemeteries of Etruria*, 3rd edn, London.

Descoeudres, J.-P. (ed.) (1990) *Greek Colonists and Native Populations: Proceedings of the First Australian Congress of Classical Archaeology. July 1985*, Oxford.

Detienne, M. (1968) 'La phalange: problèmes et controverses', in *Problèmes de la guerre en Grèce ancienne*, ed. J.-P. Vernant, Paris: 119–42.

(1977) *The Gardens of Adonis: Spices in Greek Mythology*, Hassocks.

(1989) *Dionysos at Large*, Cambridge, Mass.

Di Gennaro, F. (1986) *forme di insediamento tra Tevere e fiora dal Bronzo Finale al Principio dell'età del ferro*, Biblioteca di Studi Etruschi 14, Florence.

Díaz-Andreu, M., Lucy, S., Babic, S., and Edwards, D. (eds.) (2005) *The Archaeology of Identity: Approaches to Gender, Age, Status, Ethnicity and Religion*, London and New York.

Dietler, M., and Herbich, I. (1998) 'Habitus, techniques, style: an integrated approach to the social understanding of material culture and boundaries', in *The Archaeology of Social Boundaries*, ed. M. T. Stark, Washington and London: 232–63.

Dissanayake, E. (1992) *Homo Aestheticus: Where Art Comes From and Why*, Seattle.

Dobres, M.-A. (2000) *Technology and Social Agency: Outlining a Practice Framework for Archaeology*, Oxford.

Dobres, M.-A., and Hoffman, C. R. (1994) 'Social agency and the dynamics of prehistoric technology', *Journal of Archaeological Method and Theory* 1.3: 211–58.

Dobres, M.-A., and Robb, J. (eds.) (2000) *Agency in Archaeology*, London and New York.

Dobrowolski, W. (1994, 'I Dioscuri sugli specchi etruschi', in *Thyrrhenoi philotechnoi*, ed. M. Martelli, Rome: 173–81.

Docter, R. F. (2000) 'Carthage and the Tyrrhenian in the eighth and seventh centuries BC: Central Italian transport amphorae and fine wares found under the Decumanus Maximus', in *Actas del IV congreso internacional de estudios fenicios y púnicos* (4 vols.), ed. M. E. Aubet and M. Barthélemy, Cadiz: 329–38.

Docter, R. F., and Niemeyer, H. G. (1994) 'Pithekoussai: the Carthaginian connection: on the archaeological evidence of Eubeo-Phoenician partnership in the eighth and seventh centuries BC', *Apoikia: Annali di Archeologia e Storia Antica* 1: 101–15.

Dohrn, T. (1966–7) 'Die Etrusker und die griechische Sage', *MDAI(R)* 73–4: 15–27.

Dommelen, P. van (1997) 'Colonial constructs: colonialism and archaeology in the Mediterranean', *World Archaeology* 28.3: 305–23.

Donati, L. (ed.) (1994) *La Casa dell'Impluvium. Architettura etrusca a Roselle*, Rome.

(2000), 'Civil, religious and domestic architecture', in *The Etruscans*, ed. M. Torelli, London: 313–33.

Donley-Reid, L. W. (1990) 'A structuring structure', in *Domestic Architecture and the Use of Space: An Interdisciplinary, Cross-Cultural Study*, ed. S. Kent, Cambridge: 114–26.

Donnan, H., and Wilson, T. M. (1999) *Borders: Frontiers of Identity and Nation State*, Oxford and New York.

Doonan, O. (1995) 'The social development of the Italic house, 800–550 BC', abstract of paper from the 96th Annual General Meeting of the Institute of America, *AJA* 99: 351–2.

Dougherty, C. (1993) 'It's murder to found a colony', in *Cultural Poetics in Archaic Greece: Cult, Performance, Politics*, ed. C. Dougherty and L. Kurke, Cambridge: 178–98.

(2003) 'The Aristonothos krater: competing stories of conflict and collaboration', in *Cultures Within Ancient Greek Culture: Contact, Conflict, Collaboration*, ed. C. Dougherty and L. Kurke, Cambridge: 35–56.

Dougherty, C., and Kurke, L. (eds.) (1993) *Cultural Poetics in Archaic Greece: Cult, Performance, Politics*, Cambridge.

(eds.)(2003) *Cultures Within Ancient Greek Culture: Contact, Conflict, Collaboration*, Cambridge.

Dougherty, J., and Keller, C. M. (1982) 'Taksonomy: a practical approach to knowledge structures', *American Ethnologist* 5: 763–74.

Douglas, M. (1972) 'Symbolic orders in the use of domestic space', in *Man, Settlement and Urbanism*, ed. P. J. Ucko *et al.*, London: 513–21.

(1984) *Purity and Danger: An Analysis of the Concepts of Pollution and Taboo*, London.

Douglas, M. (ed.) (1973) *Rules and Meanings*, Harmondsworth.

Douglas, M., and Isherwood, B. (1979) *The World of Goods: Towards an Anthropology of Consumption*, New York.

Dowden, K. (1992) *The Uses of Greek Mythology*, London.

Dragendorff, H. (1928) 'Rappresentazione di un aruspice sopra un vaso aretino', *SE* 2: 177–83.

Drews, R. (1981) 'The coming of the city to central Italy', *AJAH* 6: 133–65.

Ducati, P. (1912) 'Contributo allo studio degli specchi etruschi figurati', *MDAI(R)* 27: 243–85.

(1927) *Storia dell'arte etrusca*, Florence.

Ducrey, P. (1985) *Guerre et guerriers dans la Grèce Antique*, Freibourg.

Dumézil, G. (1970) *Archaic Roman Religion*, London and Chicago.

Dunbabin, T. J. (1948) *The Western Greeks: The History of Sicily and South Italy from the Foundation of the Greek Colonies to 480 BC*, Oxford.

Duncan, J. S. (1981) 'Introduction', in *Housing and Identity Cross-Cultural Perspectives*, ed. J. S. Duncan. London: 1–5.

(ed.) (1981) *Housing and Identity: Cross-Cultural Perspectives*, London.

Dvorsky Rohner, D. (1996) 'Etruscan domestic architecture: an ethnographic model', in *Etruscan Italy: Etruscan Influences on the Civilizations of Italy from Antiquity to the Modern Era*, ed. J. F. Hall, Provo, Utah: 115–45.

Dyer, C., and Haagsma, M. J. (1993) 'A geometric crater from New Halos: results of the 1992 Halos study season', *Pharos* 1: 165–74.

Eco, U. (1976) *A Theory of Semiotics*, Bloomington: Indiana.

(1980) 'Function and sign: the semiotics of architecture', in *Signs, Symbols and Architecture*, ed. G. Broadbent, R. Bunt and C. Jecks, Chichester: 11–69.

Edlund, I. E. M. (1987a) 'Mens sana in corpore sano: healing cults as a political factor in Etruscan religion', in *Gifts to the Gods: Proceedings of the Uppsala Symposium, 1985, Acta Universitatis Upsaliensis, Boreas* 15, ed. T. Linders and G. Nordquist, Uppsala: 51–6.

(1987b) *The Gods and the Place: Location and Function of Sanctuaries in the Countryside of Etruria and Magna Graecia (700–400 BC)*, AIRRS 4.43.

(1991) 'Power and religion: how social change affected the emergence and collapse of power struggles in central Italy', in *Papers of the Fourth Conference of Italian Archaeology*, II, *The Archaeology of Power*, Part 2, eds. E. Herring, R. Whitehouse and J. Wilkins, London: 161–72.

Edmunds, L. (ed.) (1990) *Approaches to Greek Myth*, Baltimore.

Edwards, C. (1996) *Writing Rome: Textual Approaches to the City*, Cambridge.

Eisner, W. R. (1991) 'The consequences of gender bias in mortuary analysis: a case study', in *The Archaeology of Gender: Proceedings of the 22nd Annual Chacmool Conference, Calgary*, ed. D. Walde and N. D. Willows, Calgary: 352–7.

Eldridge, L. G. (1917) 'Six Etruscan mirrors', *AJA* 21: 365–86.

(1918) 'A third century Etruscan tomb', *AJA* 22: 251–94.

Eles Masi, P. V. (1995) *Verucchio, Museo Civico Archeologico*, Rimini.

Elias, N. (1994) *The Civilizing Process*, Oxford.

Elsner, J. (1992) 'Cult and Sculpture: sacrifice in the Ara Pacis Augustae', *JRS* 81: 50–61.

(1995) *Art and the Roman Viewer: The Transformation of Art from the Pagan World to Christianity*, Cambridge.

Emiliozzi, A. (ed.) (1997) *Carri da guerra e principi etruschi*, Rome.

Emmanuel, M. (1927) *The Antique Greek Dance*, trans. H. J. Beauley, New York and London.

Enei, F. (1992) 'Ricognizioni archeologiche nell'Ager Cearetanus: rapporto preliminare', in *Papers of the Fourth Conference of Italian Archaeology*, vol. III, *New Developments*, Part 1, ed. E. Herring, R. Whitehouse and J. Wilkins, London: 71–90.

(1993) *Cerveteri: Ricognizioni archeologiche nel territorio di una città etrusca*, Ladispoli.

(2001) *Progetto Ager Caeretanus: Il literale di Alsium*. Rome.

Engelstad, E. (1991) 'Feminist theory and post-processual archaeology', in *The Archaeology of Gender: Proceedings of the 22nd Annual Chacmool Conference, Calgary*, ed. D. Walde and N. D. Willows, Calgary: 116–20.

Entwhistle, J. (2000) *The Fashioned Body: Fashion, Dress and Modern Social Theory*, Cambridge.

Eriksen, T. H. (1991) 'The cultural contexts of ethnic difference', *Man* 26: 127–44.

(1992) *Us and Them in Modern Societies: Ethnicity and Nationalism in Mauritius, Trinidad and Beyond*, London.

Eriksson, M. C. (1996) 'Two engraved mirrors from the Thordvaldsen Museum, Copenhagen', *ORom* 20: 21–36.

Evans, J. K. (ed.) (1991) *War, Women and Children in Ancient Rome*, London.

Fairclough, G. (1992) 'Meaningful constructions: spatial and functional analysis of medieval buildings', *Antiquity* 66: 348–66.

Falchi, I. (1887) 'Vetulonia: nuovi scavi della necropoli di Vetulonia', *NSA*: 472–530.

(1891) *Vetulonia e la sua necropoli antichissima*, Florence.

(1892) 'Vetulonia: nuovi scavi della necropoli vetuloniese', *NSA*: 381–405.

(1895) 'Vetulonia: scavi dell'anno 1894', *NSA*: 272–317.

(1898) 'Vetulonia: nuove scoperte nell'area della città e della necropoli', *NSA*: 81–112.

(1903) 'Populonia: la necropoli etrusca di Populonia, forse inesplorata', *NSA*: 4–14.

(1908) 'Vetulonia: Nuove scoperte nella necropoli. (Tomba del Tridente)', *NSA*: 419.

Falconi Amorelli, M. T. (1983) *Vulci: Scavi Bendinelli (1919–1923)*, Rome.

(1987) *Vulci: Scavi Mengarelli (1925–1929)*, Rome.

Fantham, E., Foley, H., Kampen, N., Pomeroy, S. B., and Shapiro, H. A. (eds.) (1994) *Women in the Classical World: Image and Text*, New York and Oxford.

Farnell, L. R. (1921) *Greek Hero Cults and Ideas of Immortality*, Oxford.

Fedeli, F. (1983) *Populonia: Storia e territorio*, Florence.

Ferraguti, U. (1937) 'I bronzi di Vulci', *SE* 11: 107–20.

Fiesel, E. (1936) 'The Hercules legend on the Etruscan mirror from Volterra', *AJPh* 57: 130–6.

Finley, M. I. (1968a) 'Etruscheria', in *Aspects of Antiquity: Discoveries and Controversies*, M. I. Finley, London: 102–12.

(1968b) 'The Etruscans and early Rome: new discoveries and controversies', in *Aspects of Antiquity: Discoveries and Controversies*, M. I. Finley, London: 113–28.

(1968c) *Aspects of Antiquity: Discoveries and Controversies*, London.

(1977) 'The ancient city: from Foustel de Coulanges to Max Weber and beyond', *Comparative Studies in Society and History* 19: 305–27.

Fischer, A. (1984) *Africa Adorned*, London.

Fischer-Graf, U. (1980) *Spiegelwerkstätten in Vulci*, Archäologische Forschungen, Bd 8, Berlin.

Fisher, N., and van Wees, H. (eds.) (1998) *Archaic Greece: New Approaches and New Evidence*, London.

Fiumi, E. (1957) 'Contributo alla datazione del materiale volterrano: gli scavi della necropoli del Portone degli anni 1873–74', *SE* 25: 367–415.

(1961) 'La "facies" arcaica del territorio volterrano', *SE* 29: 253–92.

(1976) *Volterra etrusca e romana*, Pisa.

Fletcher, R. (1986) 'Settlement archaeology: world-wide perspectives', *World Archaeology* 18.1: 59–83.

Flusche, L. (2001) 'Aristocratic architectural iconography at Poggio Civitate', in *From Huts to Houses: transformations of Ancient Societies. Proceedings of an International Seminar Organised by the Norwegian and Swedish Institutes in Rome, 21–24 September 1997*, ed. J. R. Brandt and L. Karlsson, Stockholm: 171–7.

Foley, H. P. (1981) 'Introduction', *Women's Studies* 8: 1–2.

   (ed.) (1981) *Reflections of Women in Antiquity*, New York.

Fontaine, P. (1993) 'Véies: les ramparts et la porte de la Piazza d'Armi', *MEFRA* 105: 221–39.

   (1994a) 'Pour une carte archéologique des fortifications étrusques', in *Revue Belge de Philologie et d'Histoire* 75: 121–46.

   (1994b) 'Tarquinia: l'enciente et la porte nord. Contribution à l'architecture militaire étrusque', *Archäologischer Anzeiger*: 73–86.

Foote, S. (1989) 'Challenging gender symbols', in *Men and Women: Dressing the Part*, ed. C. B. Kidwell and V. Steele, Washington: 144–57.

Ford, L. R. (1994) *Cities and Buildings: Skyskrapers, Skid Rows and Suburbs*, Baltimore.

Formigli, E. (1985) *Techniche dell'oreficeria etrusca e romana*, Florence.

Forsberg, S. (1984) 'Il complesso del ponte sul Fosso Pietrisco in San Giovenale', in *San Giovenale: Materiali e problemi. Atti del simposio all'Istituto Svedese di Studi Classici a Roma, 6 aprile 1983, AIRRS* 4.41, ed. S. Forsberg and B. E. Thomasson, Stockholm: 73–5.

Forsberg, S., and Thomasson, B. E. (eds.) (1984) *San Giovenale: Materiali e problemi. Atti del simposio all'Istituto Svedese di Studi Classici a Roma, 6 aprile 1983, AIRRS* 4.41, Stockholm.

Forsythe, G. (2005) *A Critical History of Early Rome: From Prehistory to the First Punic War*, Berkeley and Los Angeles.

Fortuna, A. M., and Giovannoni, F. (1975) *Il lago degli idoli: Testimonianze etrusche in Falterona*, Florence.

Foster, H. (1988) 'Preface', in *Vision and Visuality*, ed. H. Foster, Seattle: ix–xiv.

   (ed.) (1988) *Vision and Visuality*, Seattle.

Foster, S. (1989) 'Analysis of spatial patterns in buildings (access analysis) as an insight into social structure: examples from the Scottish Atlantic Iron Age', *Antiquity* 63: 40–50.

Foucault, M. (1990) *The History of Sexuality*, vol. III: *The Self*, Harmondsworth: Penguin.

Fowler, M., and Wolfe, R. G. (1965) *Materials for the Study of the Etruscan Language*, Madison.

Fowler, M. A. (1994) *Theopompus of Chios: History and Rhetoric in the Fourth Century* BC, Oxford.

Foxhall, L., and Salmon, J. (eds.) (1998, *Thinking Men: Masculinity and Its Self-Representation in the Classical Tradition*, London.

Franchini, E. (1948–9) 'Il Melone di Camucia', *SE* 20: 17–52.

Francis, E. D., and Vickers, M. (1981) '*Leargos Kalos*', *PCPS* 207: 97–136.

(1988) 'The *agora* revisited: Athenian chronology *c.* 500–450 BC', *ABSA* 83: 143–67.

Frascarelli, A. (ed.) (1995) *CSE Italia 2 Perugia I*, Rome.

Frederiksen, M. W., and Ward-Perkins, J. B. (1957) 'The ancient road systems of the central and northern Ager Faliscus', *PBSR* 25: 67–208.

Fridh-Haneson, B. M. (1987) 'Votive terracottas from Italy: types and problems', in *Gifts to the Gods: Proceedings of the Uppsala Symposium, 1985*, Acta Universitatis Upsaliensis, *Boreas*, 15, ed. T. Linders and G. Nordquist, Uppsala: 67–75.

Friedrich, P. (1978) *The Meaning of Aphrodite*, Chicago.

Frontisi-Ducroux, F. (1989) 'In the mirror of the mask', in *A City of Images: Iconography and Society in Ancient Greece*, ed. C. Bérard *et al.*, Princeton: 151–65.

Fyfe, G., and Law, J. (eds.) (1988) *Picturing Power: Visual Depictions and Social Relations*, London.

Galassi Paluzzi, C. (ed.) (1938) *Atti del IV convegno nazionale di studi romani*, Rome.

Gamburi, G. F. (1888) 'Talamone (Comune di Ortebello). Ruderi antiche ed oggetti scoperti sul poggio di Talamonaccio', *NSA*: 682–91.

Gantz, T. N. (1974–5) 'Terracotta figured friezes from the workshop of Vulca', *ORom* 10: 1–22.

García Cancliui, N. (1992) *Culturas híbridas: Estrategias para entrar y salir de la modernidad*, Buenos Aires.

Gargana, A. (1932) 'Bieda – ritrovamenti di tombe etrusche in contrada "Pian del Vescovo"', *NSA*: 485–505.

(1936) 'Norchia (Vetralla) – ritrovamento di tombe etrusche', *NSA*: 268–88.

Garwood, P., Jennings, D., Skeates, R., and Toms, J. (eds.) (1991) *Sacred and Profane: Proceedings of a Conference on Archaeology, Ritual and Religion, Oxford 1989*, Oxford.

Gasperini, L. (1989) 'La dignità della donna nel mondo etrusco e il suo lontano riflesso nell'onomastica personale romana', in *Le donne in Etruria*, ed. A. Rallo, Rome: 181–211.

Gaultier, F., and Briquel, F. (eds.) *Les Etrusques: Les plus religieux des hommes*, Paris.

Gazda, E. K. (ed.) (1991) *Roman Art in the Private Sphere: New Perspectives on the Architecture and Decor of the Domus, Villa and Insula*, Ann Arbor.

Gebauer, A. B. (1987) 'Stylistic analysis: a critical review of concepts, models and applications', *Journal of Danish Archaeology* 6: 223–9.

Geertz, C. (1993) *The Interpretation of Cultures*, London.

Gejval, N. G. 1982. Animal remains from Zone A in Acquarossa, in M. B. Lundgren and L. Wendt (eds.) *Acquarossa III: Zone A*, Stockholm. *AIRRS* 4 38 3: 63–70.

Gell, A. (1986) 'Newcomers to the world of goods: consumption among the Muria Gonds', in *The Social Life of Things*, ed. A. Appadurai, Cambridge: 110–38.

(1992) 'The technology of enchantment and the enchantment of technology', in *Anthropology, Art, and Aesthetics*, ed. J. Coote and A. Shelton, Oxford: 40–67.

(1993) *Wrapping in Images: Tattooing in Polynesia*, Oxford.

(1998) *Art and Agency: An Anthropological Theory*, Oxford.

Gentili, F. (1983) *Populonia*, Florence.

Gentili, G. V. (1987) 'Verucchio', in *La formazione della città in Emilia Romagna: prime esperienze urbane attraverso le nuove scoperte archeologiche*, Studi e documenti di archeologia 3–4, ed. D. Bermond Montanari, Bologna: 207–63.

Gentili, M. D. (1994) *I sarcofagi etruschi in terracotta di età recente*, Rome.

(ed.) (2000) *Aspetti e problemi della produzione degli specchi etruschi figurati*, Rome.

Gerhard, E. D. (1834, 1843, 1861, 1862) *Etruskische Spiegel*, 4 vols., Berlin.

Gernet, L., and Boulanger, A. (1932) *Le génie Grec dans la religion*, Paris: 52–4.

Gero, J. M., and Conkey, M. W. (eds.) (1991) *Engendering Archaeology: Women and Prehistory*, Oxford.

Ghirardini, G. (1898) 'La necropoli primitiva di Volterra', *MonAL* 8: 101–216.

Giannattasio, B. M. (ed.) (1995) *Atti VII Giornata archeologica: Viaggi e commerci nell'Antichità*, Genoa.

Giardino, G. (1995) *Il Mediterraneo Occidentale fra XIV ed VII secolo a.C.: cerchie minerarie e metallurgiche*, Oxford.

Gibbs, L. (1987) 'Identifying gender representations in the archaeological record: a contextual study', in *The Archaeology of Contextual Meanings*, ed. I. Hodder, Cambridge: 79–89.

Gibson, J. J. (1979) *The Ecological Approach to Visual Perception*, Boston and London.

Gibson, K. R., and Ingold, T. (eds.) (1993) *Tools, Language and Cognition in Human Evolution*, Cambridge.

Giddens, A. (1979) *Central Problems in Social Theory: Action, Structure and Contradiction in Social Analysis*, London.

(1984) *The Constitution of Society: Outline of a Theory of Structuration*, Berkeley.

Giglioli, G. Q. (1919) 'Veio: scavi nell'area della città e delle necropoli', *NSA*: 3–37.

(1935) *L'arte etrusca*, Milan.

(1946–7) 'Materiali per un supplemento al "Corpus" degli specchi etruschi figurati: lo specchio etrusco del Victoria and Albert Museum di Londra', *SE* 19: 237–9.

(ed.) (1962) *CVA Italia 36: Musei Capitolini di Roma I*, Rome.

Gilchrist, R. (1991) 'Women's archaeology? Political feminism, gender theory and historical revision', *Antiquity* 65: 495–501.

(1994) *Gender and Material Culture: The Archaeology of Religious Women*, London.

(1999) *Gender and Archaeology: Contesting the Past*, London.

Gill, D. W. J. (1988) 'The temple of Aphaia on Aegina: the date of the reconstruction', *ABSA* 83: 169–77.

Girouard, M. (1978) *Life in the English Country House: A Social and Architectural History*, New Haven and London.

Giuliani, C. F., and Quilici, L. (1964) 'La Via Caere–Pyrgi', *Quaderni dell'Istituto di topografia antica dell'Università di Roma* 1.

Gjerstad, E. (1960) *Early Rome III*, *AIRRS* 4.17.

Glazer, N., and Moynihan, D. P. (eds.) (1975) *Ethnicity, Theory and Experience*, Cambridge, Mass.

Glinister, F. (1997) 'Women and power in archaic Rome', in *Gender and Ethnicity in Ancient Italy*, ed. T. J. Cornell and K. Lomas, London: 115–27.

Goffmann, E. (1959) *The Presentation of the Self in Everyday Life*, Harmondsworth.

Goldhill, S., and Osborne, R. (1994) 'Introduction: programmatics and polemics', in *Art and Text in Ancient Greek Culture*, ed. S. J. Goldhill and R. Osborne, Cambridge: 1–11.

(eds.) (1994) *Art and Text in Ancient Greek Culture*, Cambridge.

Goodby, R. G. (1998) 'Technological patterning and social boundaries: ceramic variability in southern New England', in *The Archaeology of Social Boundaries*, ed. M. T. Stark, Washington and London: 161–82.

Goodman, J. (1993) *Tobacco in History: The Cultures of Dependence*, London and New York.

Gosden, C. (1994) *Social Being and Time*, Oxford.

(1999) *Anthropology and Archaeology: A Changing Relationship*, London and New York.

(2001) 'Making sense: archaeology and aesthetics', *World Archaeology* 33.2: 163–7.

(2004) *Archaeology and Colonialism: Culture Contact from 5000 BC to the Present*, Cambridge.

Gosden, C., and Marshall, Y. (1999) 'The cultural biography of objects', *World Archaeology* 31.2: 169–78.

Gosselain, O. P. (1998) 'Social and technical identity in a clay crystal ball', in *The Archaeology of Social Boundaries*, ed. M. T. Stark. Washington: 78–106.

(2000) 'Materializing identities: an African perspective', *Journal of Archaeological Method and Theory* 7: 187–217.

Gottdiener, M. (1995) *Postmodern Semiotics: Material Culture and the Forms of Postmodern Life*, Oxford.

Gottdiener, M., and Lagopoulos, A. P. (eds.) (1986) *The City and the Sign: An Introduction to Urban Semiotics*, New York.

Gould, R. (1980) *Living Archaeology*, Cambridge.

Grabes, H. (1982) *The Mutable Glass: Mirror-Imagery in Titles and Texts of the Middle Ages and the English Renaissance*, Cambridge.

Graf, F. (1993) *Greek Mythology*, trans. T. Marier, Baltimore.

Graham, J. (1964) *Colony and Mother-City in Ancient Greece*, Manchester.

Gran-Aymerich, J., and Prayon, F. (2005) 'La Castellina près de Civitavecchia. La vocation d'un site aux confines de Caere et de Tarquinia, in *Dinamiche di sviluppo della città nell'Etruria meridionale: Veio, Tarquinia, Vulci. Atti del XXIII Convegno di Studi Etruschi ed Italici, Roma, Veio, Cerveteri/Pyrgi, Tarquinia,*

Tuscania, Vulci, Viterbo, 1–6 ottobre 2001, ed. O. Paoletti and G. Camporeale, Pisa and Rome: 657–64.

Grant, A., Rasmussen, T., and Barker, G. (1993) 'Tuscania: excavations of an Etruscan rural building', *SE* 58: 566–70.

Grant, M. (1980) *The Etruscans*, London.

Gras, M. (1985) *Trafics tyrrhéniens archaïque, BEFAR 258,* Rome.

(1995) *La Méditerranée archaïque*, Paris.

Green, S. W., and Perlman, S. M. (eds.) (1985) *The Archaeology of Frontiers and Boundaries*, Orlando.

Greenhalgh, P. A. L. (1973) *Early Greek Warfare: Horsemen and Chariots in the Homeric and Archaic Ages*, Cambridge.

Greimas, A. J. (1986) 'For a topological semiotics', in *The City and the Sign: An Introduction to Urban Semiotics*, ed. M. Gottdiener and A. P. Lagopoulos, New York: 25–54.

Grenier, A. (1948) *Les religions étrusque et romaine. Mana: Introduction a l'histoires des religions*, vol. II: *Les religions de l'Europe ancienne III*, Paris.

Grillini, A., Sassatelli, G., and Schiassi, A. (1970) 'Verifica delle pendenze delle canalizzazioni', *SE* 38: 327–9.

Grohmann, A. (1981) *Perugia*, Rome and Bari.

Gros, P. (ed.) (1983) *Architecture et société de l'archaïsme grec à la fin de la république romaine*, Rome.

Gros, P., and Torelli, M. (1988) *Storia dell'urbanistica: Il mondo romano*, Rome and Bari.

Grosz, E. (1994) *Volatile Bodies: Toward a Corporeal Feminism*, Bloomington.

(1995) *Space, Time and Perversion*, London and New York.

Grottanelli, C. (1986) 'Yoked horse, twins and the powerful lady: India, Greece, Ireland and elsewhere', *Journal of Indo-European Studies* 14: 125–52.

Grozzadini (1881) 'Bologna: nouve scoperte nella necropoli felsinea nelle terre *Arnoaldi-Veli*', *NSA:* 84–6.

Gruen, E. S. (1990a) *Studies in Greek Culture and Roman Policy*, Leiden.

(1990b) 'The Bacchanalian affair', in *Studies in Greek Culture and Roman Policy*, E. S. Gruen. Leiden: 34–78.

Grummond, N. T. de (ed.) (1982) *A Guide to Etruscan Mirrors*, Tallahassee.

(1988) 'The Dioskuri and other twins on Etruscan mirrors', abstract of paper given at the 89th General Meeting of the Archaeological Institute of America, *AJA* 92: 246.

(2002) 'Etruscan mirrors now', *AJA* 106: 307–11.

Gsell, S. (1891) *Fouilles dans la nécropole de Vulci*, Paris.

Guaitoli, M. (1981) Notizie preliminare su recenti ricognizioni svolte in seminari dell'Istituto, *Quaderni dell'Istituto di Topografia Antica dell'Università di Roma* 9: 79–87.

Guidi, A. (1985) 'An application of the rank-size rule to protohistoric settlements in the middle Tyrhennian area', in *Papers in Italian Archaeology*, vol. IV: *The*

Cambridge Conference, Part 3: *Patterns in Protohistory*, ed. C. A. T. Malone and S. K. F. Stoddart, Oxford: 217–42.

(1989) 'Alcune osservazioni sull'origine delle città etrusche', in *Atti del secondo congresso internazionale etrusco, Firenze 26 maggio – 2 giugno 1985*, vol. I, ed. G. Maetzke, Rome: 285–91.

(1998) 'The emergence of the state in central and northern Italy', *Acta Archaeologica* 69: 139–61.

(2000) *Preistoria della complessità sociale*, Rome and Bari.

Guzzo, P. G. (1987) 'Schema per la categoria interpretativa del "santuario della frontiera"', *Scienze dell'Antichità: Storia, Archeologia, Antropologia* 1: 373–9.

Gwilt, A., and Haselgrove, C. (eds.) (1997) *Reconstructing Iron Age Societies: New Approaches to the British Iron Age*, Oxford.

Haas, J. (1990) *The Anthropology of War*, Cambridge

Hall, E. (1989) *Inventing the Barbarian: Greek Self Definition through Tragedy*, Oxford.

Hall, J. F. (ed.) (1996) *Etruscan Italy: Etruscan Influences on the Civilizations of Italy from Antiquity to the Modern Era*, Provo, Utah.

Hall, J. M. (1997) *Ethnic Identity in Ancient Greece*, Cambridge.

(2002) *Hellenicity: Between Ethnicity and Culture*, Chicago.

(2004) 'How Greek were the early western Greeks?', in *Greek Identity in the Western Mediterranean: Papers in Honour of Brian Shefton*, ed. K. Lomas, Leiden: 35–54.

Hallett, J. (1984) *Fathers and Daughters in Roman Society: Women and the Family*, Princeton.

Halperin, D. M., Zeitlin, F. I., and Winkler, J. J. (eds.) (1990) *Before Sexuality: The Construction of Erotic Experience in the Ancient Greek World*, Princeton.

Hampe, R., and Simon, E. (1964) *Griechische Sagen in der frühen etruskischen Kunst*, Mainz.

Hannay, A. (1990) *Human Consciousness*, London and New York.

Hannell, K. (1962) 'The Acropolis', in *Etruscan Culture, Land and People: Archaeological Research and Studies Conducted in San Giovenale and Its Environs by Members of the Swedish Institute in Rome*, ed. A. Boëthius *et al.*, New York and Malmö: 289–312.

Hannerz, U. (1987) 'The world in creolisation'. *Africa* 57: 546–59.

(1992) *Cultural Complexity: Studies in the Social Organisation of Meaning*, New York.

Hannestad, L. (1989) 'Athenian pottery in Etruria *c.* 550–470 BC', *Acta Archaeologica* 59: 113–30.

Hanson, V. D. (1989) *The Western Way of War: Infantry Battle in Classical Greece*, London.

(ed.) (1991) *Hoplites: The Classical Greek Battle Experience*, London.

Hantman, J. L. (1984) 'Organizational variability on the frontier: history of Mormon settlement in Arizona, 1876–1900', in *Exploring the Limits: Frontiers and*

Boundaries in Prehistory, BAR International series 223, ed. S. P. De Atley and F. J. Findlow, Oxford: 51–65.

Harden, D. (1962) *The Phoenicians*, London.

Harris, W. H. (1989) 'Invisible cities: the beginnings of Etruscan urbanisation', in *Atti del secondo congresso internazionale etrusco, Firenze 26 maggio – 2 giugno 1985*, vol. I, ed. G. Maetzke, Rome: 375–92.

Harrison, J. E. (1903) *Prologomena to the Study of Greek Religion*, Cambridge.

Harrison, R. J. (1988) *Spain at the Dawn of History: Iberians, Phoenicians and Greeks*, London.

Hartog, F. (1988) *The Mirror of Herodotus: The Representations of the Other in the Writing of History*, Berkeley.

Hase, F.-W. von (1997) 'Présence étrusques et italiques dans les sanctuaires grecs (VIII–VII siècle av. J.-C.', in *Les Etrusques: Les plus religieux des hommes*, ed. F. Gaultier and F. Briquel, Paris: 293–323.

Haverfield, F. (1913) *Ancient Town-Planning*, Oxford.

Harvey, D. (1989) *The Urban Experience*, Oxford.

(1990) *The Condition of Postmodernity: An Enquiry into the Origins of Cultural Change*, Oxford.

Harvey, J. (1995) *Men in Black*, London.

Havelock, C. M. (1982) 'Mourners on Greek vases: remarks on the social history of women', in *Feminisim and Art History: Questioning the Litany*, ed. N. Broude and M. D. Garrard, New York: 45–61.

Havelock, E. A., and Hershbell, J. P. (eds.) (1978) *Communication Arts in the Ancient World*, New York.

Haynes, S. (1985) *Etruscan Bronzes*, London.

(2000) *Etruscan Civilization: A Cultural History*, London.

Hegmon, M. (1992) 'Archaeological research on style', *Annual Review of Anthropology* 21: 517–36.

(1998) 'Technology, style and social practices: archaeological approaches, in *The Archaeology of Social Boundaries*, ed. M. T. Stark, Washington and London: 264–79.

Heidegger, M. (1971a) 'Building dwelling thinking', in *Poetry, Language and Thought*, M. Heidegger. London: 143–61.

(1971b) *Poetry, Language and Thought*, London.

Helbaek, H. (1967) 'Agricoltura preistorica a Luni sul Mignone in Etruria, Appendice II', in *Luni sul Mignone e Problemi della Preistoria d'Italia*, AIRRS 4.25, ed. C. E. Östenberg, Lund: 277–9.

Helbig, W. (1888) 'Cornetto-Tarquinnia: nuove esplorazioni della necropoli Tarquiniese', *NSA*: 691–6.

(1889) 'Cornetto-Tarquinia: nuovi scavi della necropoli Tarquiniese', *NSA*: 335–7.

Hemelrijk, J. M. (1984) *Caeretan Hydriae*, Mainz.

Hemphill, P. (1975) 'The Cassia-Clodia survey', *PBSR* 43: 118–72.

Hencken, H. (1968a) *Tarquinia and Etruscan Origins*, London.

(1968b) *Tarquinia, Villanovans and Early Etruscans*, Cambridge, Mass.

Henderson, C., Jr (ed.) (1964) *Classical, Mediaeval and Renaissance Studies in Honour of Berthold Louis Ullman*, Storia e Letteratura raccolta di studi e testo 93, Rome.

Henderson, J. (1994) 'Timeo Danaos: Amazons in early Greek art and pottery', in *Art and Text in Ancient Greek Culture*, ed. S. J. Goldhill and R. Osborne, Cambridge: 85–137.

Henderson, J., and Netherly, P. (eds.) (1993) *Configurations of Power in Complex Societies*, Ithaca.

Henle, J. (1973) *Greek Myths: A Vase Painter's Notebook*, Bloomington and London.

Henny, L. (1986) 'Theory and practice of visual sociology', *Current Sociology* 34.3: 1–76.

Herbig, R. (1955–6) 'Die Kranzspiegelgruppe', *SE* 24: 183–505.

Heres, G. (1986) *CSE Deutsche Demokratische Republik*, vol. i, Rome.

(1987) *CSE Deutsche Demokratische Republik*, vol. ii, Berlin.

Herring, E., Whitehouse, R., and Wilkins, J. (eds.) (1991a) *Papers of the Fourth Conference of Italian Archaeology*, vol. i: *The Archaeology of Power*, Part 1, London.

(eds.) (1991b) *Papers of the Fourth Conference of Italian Archaeology*, vol. ii: *The Archaeology of Power*, Part 2, London.

(eds.) (1992a) *Papers of the Fourth Conference of Italian Archaeology*, vol. iii: *New Developments*, Part 1, London.

(eds.) (1992b) *Papers of the Fourth Conference of Italian Archaeology*, vol. iv: *New Developments*, Part 2, London.

Herring, E., and Lomas, K. (eds.) (2000) *The Emergence of State Identities in the First Millennium BC*, London.

Hershbell, J. P. (1978) 'The ancient telegraph: war and literacy', in *Communication Arts in the Ancient World*, ed. E. A. Havelock and J. P. Hershbell, New York: 81–94.

Heurgon, J. (1957) 'L'état étrusque', *Historia* 6: 63–97.

(1961) 'Valeurs féminines et masculines dans la civilisation étrusque', *MEFRA* 73: 139–60.

(1964) *Daily Life of the Etruscans*, London.

(1972–3) 'Intervento', in *Kokalos* 18–19: 70–4.

Heywood, I., and Sandywell, B. (eds.) (1999) *Interpreting Visual Culture: Explorations in the Hermeneutics of the Visual*, London.

Hill, D. K. (1937) 'Praenestine cist covers of wood', *SE* 11: 121–6.

(1965) 'To perfume the Etruscans and the Latins', *Archaeology* 18: 187–90.

Hill, J. D. (1997) 'The end of one kind of body and the beginning of another kind of body'? Toilet instruments and "Romanisation" in southern England during the first century AD', in *Reconstructing Iron Age Societies: New Approaches to the British Iron Age*, ed. A. Gwilt and C. Haselgrove, Oxford: 96–107.

Hillier, B., and Hanson, J. (1984) *The Social Logic of Space*, Cambridge.

Hingley, R. (1990) 'Domestic organization and gender relations in Iron Age and Romano-British households', in *The Social Archaeology of Houses*, ed. R. Samson, Edinburgh: 125–47.

Höckmann, U. (1987a) 'Die Datierung der hellenistisch-etruskischen Griffspiegel des 2. Jarhunderts v. Chr', *MDAI(R)* 102: 427–89.

(1987b) *CSE Bundesrepublik Deutschland*, vol. i, Munich.

Hodder, I. (ed.) (1978) *The Spatial Organisation of Culture*, London.

(1979) 'Economic and social stress and material culture patterning', *American Antiquity* 44: 446–54.

(1982a) *Symbols in Action: Ethnoarchaeological Studies in Material Culture*, Cambridge.

(1982b) 'The identification and interpretation of ranking in prehistory: a contextual perspective', in *Ranking, Resource and Exchange: Aspects of the Archaeology of Early European Society*, ed. C. Renfrew and S. Shennan, Cambridge: 150–4.

(ed.)(1982) *Symbolic and Structural Archaeology*, Cambridge.

(1984) 'Burials, houses, women and men in the European Neolithic', in *Ideology, Power and Prehistory*, ed. D. Miller and C. Tilley, Cambridge: 51–68.

(1985) 'Boundaries as strategies', in *The Archaeology of Frontiers and Boundaries*, ed. S. W. Green and S. M. Perlman, Orlando.

(1987a) 'Converging traditions: the search for symbolic meanings in archaeology and geography', in *Landscape and Culture: Geological and Archaeological Perspectives*, ed. J. M. Wagstaff, Oxford: 134–45.

(1987b) 'The contextual analysis of symbolic meanings', in *The Archaeology of Contextual Meanings*, ed. I. Hodder, Cambridge: 1–10.

(1987c) 'The meaning of discard: ash and domestic space in Baringo', in *Method and Theory for Activity Area Research: An Ethnoarchaeological Approach*, ed. S. Kent, New York: 424–48.

(ed.)(1987a) *Archaeology as Long-Term History*, Cambridge.

(ed.)(1987b) *The Archaeology of Contextual Meanings*, Cambridge.

(ed.)(1989) *The Meanings of Things: Material Culture and Symbolic Expression*, London.

(1990a) 'Style as historical quality', in *The Uses of Style in Archaeology*, ed. M. W. Conkey and C. A. Hastorf, Cambridge: 44–51.

(1990b) *The Domestication of Europe*, Oxford.

(1991) 'Gender representation and social reality', in *The Archaeology of Gender: Proceedings of the 22nd Annual Chacmool Conference, Calgary*, ed. D. Walde and N. D. Willows, Calgary: 11–16.

(1992) *Theory and Practice in Archaeology*, London.

(1994) 'Architecture and meaning: the example of neolithic houses and tombs', in *Architecture and Order: Approaches to Social Space*, ed. M. Parker Pearson and C. Richards, London and New York: 73–86.

Hodder, I., Shanks, M., Alexandri, A., Buchli, V., Carman, J., Last, J., and Lucas, G. (eds.) (1995) *Interpreting Archaeology: Finding Meaning in the Past*, London.

Hodges, H. W. M. (1972) 'Domestic building materials and ancient settlements', in *Man, Settlement and Urbanism*, ed. P. J. Ucko *et al.*, London: 523–30.

Hodges, R. (1987) 'Spatial models, anthropology and archaeology', in *Landscape and Culture: Geological and Archaeological Perspectives*, ed. J. M. Wagstaff, Oxford: 118–33.

Hodos, T. (1998) 'The asp's poison: women and literacy in Iron Age Italy', *Gender and Italian Archaeology: Challenging the Stereotypes*, ed. R. Whitehouse, London: 197–208.

Hoepfner, W., and Schwandner, E.-L. (1986) *Haus und Stadt in Klassischen Griechenland*, Munich.

Holliday, P. J. (1993) 'Narrative structure in the François Tomb', in *Narrative and Event in Ancient Art*, ed. P. J. Holliday, Cambridge: 175–97.

(ed.) (1993) *Narrative and Event in Ancient Art*, Cambridge.

Hölscher, T. (ed.) (2000) *Gegenwelten zu den Kulturen Griechenlands und Roms in der Antike*, Munich and Leipzig.

(2004) *The Language of Images in Roman Art*, trans. A. Snodgrass and A. M. Künzl Snodgrass, Cambridge.

Horden, P., and Purcell, N. (2000) *The Corrupting Sea: A Study of Mediterranean History*, Oxford.

Howes, D. (ed.) (1996) *Cross-Cultural Consumption: Global Markets, Local Realities*, London and New York.

Humphreys, S. C., and King, H. (eds.) (1981) *Mortality and Immortality: The Anthropology and Archaeology of Death*, London.

Huntington, R., and Metcalf, P. (1979) *Celebrations of Death: The Anthropology of Mortuary Ritual*, Cambridge.

Ingold, T. (1990) 'Society, nature and the concept of technology', *ARC* 9.1: 5–17.

(1993a) 'Tool-use, sociality and intelligence', in *Tools, Language and Cognition in Human Evolution*, ed. K. R. Gibson and T. Ingold, Cambridge: 429–45.

(1993b) 'Technology, language and intelligence: a reconsideration of basic concepts', in *Tools, Language and Cognition in Human Evolution*, ed. K. R. Gibson and T. Ingold, Cambridge: 449–72.

Ioppolo, G. (1989) 'L'architettura del tempio arcaica', in *Il viver quotidiano in Roma arcaica*, ed. G. Pisani Sartorio, Rome: 34–6.

Isaacs, H. R. (1975) 'Basic group identity: the idols of the tribe', in *Ethnicity, Theory and Experience*, ed. N. Glazer and D. P. Moynihan. Cambridge, Mass.: 29–52.

Izzet, V. E. (1996) 'Engraving the boundaries: exploring space and surface in Etruscan funerary architecture', in *Approaches to the Study of Ritual: Italy and the Mediterranean*, ed. J. B. Wilkins, London: 55–72.

(1997) *Declarations of Difference: Boundaries and the Transformation of Archaic Etruscan Society*, unpublished PhD thesis, University of Cambridge.

(1999–2000) 'Etruscan ritual and the recent excavations at Sant'Antonio, Cerveteri', *ARP* 8: 133–48.

(2000) 'The Etruscan Sanctuary at Cerveteri, Sant'Antonio: preliminary report of excavations 1995–1998', *PBSR* 68: 321–35.

(2004) 'Purloined letters: the Aristonothos inscription and krater', in *Greek Identity in the Western Mediterranean: Papers in Honour of Brian Shefton*, ed. K. Lomas, Leiden: 191–210.

(2005a) 'Changing perspectives: Greek myth in Etruria', in *Papers in Italian Archaeology VI: Communities and Settlements from the Neolithic to the Early Medieval Period. Proceedings of the Sixth Conference of Italian Archaeology Held at the University of Groningen, Groningen Institute of Archaeology, The Netherlands, April 15–17 2003*, vol. ii, BAR International Series 1452 (ii), ed. P. Attema *et al.*, Oxford: 822–27.

(2005b) 'The mirror of Theopompus: Etruscan identity and Greek myth', *PBSR* 73: 1–22.

Jackson, A. H. (1991) 'Hoplites and the gods: the dedication of arms and armour', in *Hoplites: The Classical Greek Battle Experience*, ed. V. D. Hanson, London: 228–49.

Jacquemin, A. (1999) *Offrandes monumentales à Delphes*, BEFAR 304, Athens.

Jameson, M. H. (1990) 'Domestic space in the Greek city-state', in *Domestic Architecture and the Use of Space: An Interdisciplinary, Cross-Cultural Study*, ed. S. Kent, Cambridge: 92–113.

(1991) 'Sacrifice before battle', in *Hoplites: The Classical Greek Battle Experience*, ed. V. D. Hanson, London: 197–227.

Jameson, P. (1991) *Centuries of Darkness: A Challenge to the Conventional Chronology of Old World Archaeology*, London.

Jarman, H. N. (1976) 'The plant remains', in *A Faliscan Town in South Etruria: Excavations at Narce 1966–71*, ed. T. W. P. Potter, London: 308–10.

Jenks, C. (ed.) (1995) *Visual Culture*, London and New York.

Johnson, M. (1989) 'Conceptions of agency in archaeological interpretation, *Journal of Anthropological Archaeology* 8.2: 189–211.

Johnston, A. W. (1979) *Trademarks on Greek Vases*, Warminster.

(1985) 'Etruscans in the Greek vase trade', in *Il commercio etrusco arcaico*, ed. M. Cristofani and P. Pelagatti, Rome: 249–55.

Johnstone, M. A. (1937) 'Etruscan collections in the Royal Scottish Museum, Edinburgh and the National Museum of Antiquities of Scotland, Edinburgh', *SE* 11: 388–407.

Jones, G. D. B. (1963) 'Capena and Ager Capenas', *PBSR* 31: 100–58.

Jones, S. (1997) *The Archaeology of Ethnicity*, London and New York.

Jourdan, C. (1994) 'Créolisation, urbanisation et identité aux îles Solomon', *Journal de la Société des Océanistes* 99.2: 177–86.

Judson, S., and Kahane, A. (1963) 'Underground drainageways in Southern Etruria and Northern Latium', *PBSR* 31: 74–99.

Kampen, N. B. (1982) 'Social status and gender in Roman Art: the case of the saleswoman', in *Feminism and Art History: Questioning the Litany*, ed. N. Broude and M. D. Garrard, New York: 63–77.

Kappeler, S. (1986) *The Pornography of Representation*, Cambridge.

Karlin, C., and Julien, M. (1994) 'Prehistoric technology: a cognitive science', in *The Ancient Mind: Elements of Cognitive Archaeology*, ed. C. Renfrew and E. B. Zubrow, Cambridge: 152–64.

Karlsson, L. (1996) 'A dining-room on the acropolis of San Giovenale? Preliminary notes on House 1', *ORom* 20: 265–9.

(1999) 'Excavations at San Giovenale in 1999: fortifications on the Borgo', *ORom* 24: 99–116.

(2001) 'From hut to house: problems of restoring House I on the acropolis of San Giovenale', in *From Huts to Houses: Transformations of Ancient Societies. Proceedings of an International Seminar Organised by the Norwegian and Swedish Institutes in Rome, 21–24 September 1997*, ed. J. R. Brandt and L. Karlsson, Stockholm: 51–3.

Kassam, A., and Megersa, G. (1989) 'Iron and beads: male and female symbols of creation. A study of ornament among Booran Orono (East Africa)', in *The Meanings of Things: Material Culture and Symbolic Expression*, ed. I. Hodder, London: 23–32.

Keller, C. M., and Keller, J. D. (1996) *Cognition and Tool Use: The Blacksmith at Work*, Cambridge.

Kent, S. (1987) 'Understanding the use of space: An ethnoarchaeological approach', in *Method and Theory for Activity Area Research: An Ethnoarchaeological Approach*, ed. S. Kent, New York: 1–60.

(ed.) (1987) *Method and Theory for Activity Area Research: An Ethnoarchaeological Approach*, New York.

(1990a) 'A cross-cultural study of segmentation, architecture and the use of space', in *Domestic Architecture and the Use of Space: An Interdisciplinary, Cross-Cultural Study*, ed. S. Kent, Cambridge: 127–52.

(1990b) 'Activity areas and architecture: an interdisciplinary view of the relationship between use of space and domestic built environments', in *Domestic Architecture and the Use of Space: An Interdisciplinary, Cross-Cultural Study*, ed. S. Kent, Cambridge: 1–8.

(ed.)(1990) *Domestic Architecture and the Use of Space: An Interdisciplinary, Cross-Cultural Study*, Cambridge.

Kerschner, M. (2004) 'Phokäische Thalassokratie oder Phantom-Phokäer? Die frühgriechischen Keramikfunde im Süden Der Iberischen Halbinsel aus der ägäischen Perspektive', in *Greek Identity in the Western Mediterranean: Papers in Honour of Brian Shefton*, ed. K. Lomas, Leiden: 115–48.

Keuls, E. C. (1993) *The Reign of the Phallus: Sexual Politics in Ancient Athens*, Berkeley.

Kidwell, C. B. and Steele, V. (eds.) (1989) *Men and Women: Dressing the Part*, Washington.

Kilian, K. (1977) 'Zwei italische Kannhelme aus Griechenland', in *Etudes Delphiques*, Bulletin de correspondence Hellénique Suppl. 4, Paris: 429–42.

Kilian-Dirlmeier, I. (1985) 'Fremde Weihungen in griechischen Heiligtümern vom 8. bis Beginn des 7. Jhs v. Chr.', *JRGZ* 32: 215–54.

King, A. D. (1980) 'Introduction', in *Buildings and Society: Essays on the Societal Development of the Built Environment*, ed. A. D. King, London: 1–33.

(ed.) (1980) *Buildings and Society: Essays on the Societal Development of the Built Environment*, London.

Klakowicz, B. (1972) *La necropoli annulare di Orvieto*, vol. i: *Crocifisso del Tufo – Le Conce*, Rome.

(1974) *La necropoli annulare di Orvieto*, vol. ii: *Cannicella e terreni limitrofi*, Rome.

Knell, H. (1983) 'Der etruskische Tempel nach Vitruv', *MDAI(R)* 90: 91–101.

Knights, C. (1994) 'The spatiality of the Roman domestic setting: an interpretation of symbolic content', in *Architecture and Order: Approaches to Social Space*, ed. M. Parker Pearson and C. Richards, London and New York: 113–46.

Koch, H., von Mercklin, E., and Weickert, C. (1915) 'Bieda', *MDAI(R)* 30: 161–303.

Koloski-Ostrow, A. O., and Lyons, C. L. (eds.) (1997) *Naked Truths: Women, Sexuality and Gender in Classical Art and Archaeology*, London and New York.

Kopytoff, I. (1986) 'The cultural biography of things: commoditization as process', in *The Social Life of Things*, ed. A. Appadurai, Cambridge: 64–91.

Körte, G., and Klugmann, K. (1897) *Etruskische Spiegel*, vol. v, Berlin.

Kostof, S. (1992) *The City Assembled: The Elements of Urban Form Through History*, London.

(1994) 'His majesty the pick', in *Streets: Critical Perspectives on Public Space*, ed. Z. Çelik *et al.*, Berkeley: 9–22.

Krauskopf, I. (1974) *Der Thebanische Sagenkreis und andere griechische Sagen in der etruskischen Kunst*, Mainz.

(1988) 'Helene-Elina', in *LIMC* 4.1: 563–72.

Kristiansen, K. (1998) *Europe Before History*, Cambridge.

Kristiansen, K., and Rowlands, M. (eds.) (1998) *Social Transformations in Archaeology: Global and Local Perspectives*, London.

Krzyszkowska, O., and Nixon, L. (eds.) (1983) *Minoan Society: Proceedings of the Cambridge Colloquium 1981*, Bristol.

Kus, S., and Raharijaona, V. (1990) 'Domestic space and the tenacity of tradition among some Batsileo of Madagascar', in *Domestic Architecture and the Use of Space: An Interdisciplinary, Cross-Cultural Study*, ed. S. Kent, Cambridge: 21–33.

Lake, A. K. (1935) 'Archaeological evidence for the "Tuscan Temple"', *MAAR* 12: 89–149.

Lambrechts, R. (1968) 'Un miroir étrusque inédit et le mythe de Philoctete', *BIBR* 39: 5–29.

(1970) *Les inscriptions avec le mot 'tular' et le bornage étrusque*, Biblioteca di Studi Etruschi 4, Florence.

(1978) *Les miroirs étrusques et prénestins des Musées royaux d'Art et d'Histoire à Bruxelles.* Brussels.

(1992) 'Malavisch', *LIMC* 6.1: 346–9.

(1995) *CSE Stato della città del Vaticano*, vol. I, Rome.

Lane, E. A. (1937) 'An Etruscan bronze mirror in the Victoria and Albert Museum', *JHS* 57: 219–23.

Larick, R. (1986) 'Age grading and ethnicity in the style of Loikop (Sanbura) spears', *World Archaeology* 18: 269–83.

(1991) 'Warriors and blacksmiths: mediating ethnicity in East African spears', *Journal of Anthropological Archaeology* 10: 299–331.

Larsen, M. T. (ed.) (1979) *Power and Propaganda: A Symposium on Ancient Empires*, Mesopotamia: Copenhagen Studies in Assyriology 7, Copenhagen.

Laurence, R. (1991) 'The urban *vicus*: the spatial organisation of power in the Roman city', in *Papers of the Fourth Conference of Italian Archaeology, Part I*, ed. E. Herring *et al.*, London: 145–51.

(1993) 'Emperors, nature and the city: Rome's ritual landscape', *ARP* 4: 79–87.

(1994) *Roman Pompeii: Space and Society*, London and New York.

Laviosa, C. (1959) 'Rusellae', *SE* 27: 3–40.

(1960) 'Rusellae', *SE* 28: 289–337.

(1961) 'Rusellae', *SE* 29: 31–45.

(1963) 'Rusellae', *SE* 31: 39–65.

(1965) 'Rusellae', *SE* 33: 49–108.

(1969) 'Rusellae', *SE* 37: 577–609.

(1970) 'L'urbanistica delle città archaiche e le strutture in mattoni crudi di Roselle', in *Studi sulla città antica: Atti del convegno di studi sulla città etrusca e italica preromana*, ed. G. A. Mansuelli and R. Zangheri, Bologna: 209–16.

Laviosa, C., *et al.* (1971) 'Rusellae', *SE* 39: 521–66.

Lawrence, A. W. (1979) *Greek Aims in Fortifications*, Oxford.

Lawrence, R. J. (1987) *Housing, Dwellings and Homes: Design Theory, Research and Practice*, Chichester.

(1990) 'Public collective and private space: a study of urban housing in Switzerland', in *Domestic Architecture and the Use of Space: An Interdisciplinary, Cross-Cultural Study*, ed. S. Kent, Cambridge: 73–91.

Layton, R. (1989) 'The political use of Australian body painting and its archaeological impacts', in *The Meanings of Things: Material Culture and Symbolic Expression*, ed. I. Hodder, London: 1–11.

Lazzeri, C. (1927) 'Arezzo etrusca: le origini della città e la stipe votiva alla Fonte Veneziana', *SE* 1: 113–27.

Le Gall, J. (1970) 'Rites de fondation', in *Studi sulla città antica: Atti del convegno di studi sulla città etrusca e italica preromana*, ed. G. A. Mansuelli and R. Zangheri, Bologna: 59–65.

Leach, E. (1972) 'Anthropological aspects of language: animal categories and verbal abuse', in *Reader in Comparative Religion*, 3rd edn, ed. W. Lessa and E. Vogt, New York: 206–20.

(1976) *Culture and Communication: The Logic by which Symbols are Connected*, Cambridge.

(1982) *Social Anthropology*, Glasgow.

Lechtman, H. (1977) 'Style in technology: some early thoughts', in *Material Culture: Styles, Organization, and Dynamics of Technology*, ed. H. Lechtman and R. S. Merrill, St Paul, Minn.: 3–20.

(1984a) 'Andean value systems and the development of prehistoric metallurgy', *Technology and Culture* 25.1: 1–36.

(1984b) 'Pre-Columbian surface metallurgy', *Scientific American* 250: 56–63.

(1993) 'Technologies of power: the Andean case', in *Configurations of Power in Complex Societies*, ed. J. Henderson and P. Netherly, Ithaca: 244–80.

Lechtman, H., and Merrill, R. S. (eds.) (1977) *Material Culture: Styles, Organization, and Dynamics of Technology*, St Paul, Minn.

Lederman, R. (1986) 'Changing times in Mendi: notes towards writing highland New Guinea history', *Ethnohistory* 33.1: 1–30.

Leeuw, S. van de, and McGlade, J. (eds.) (1997) *Time, Process and Structure Transformation in Archaeology*, London.

Leeuw, S. E. van de (1993) 'Giving the potter a choice: conceptual aspects of pottery techniques', in *Technological Choices: Transformation in Material Cultures Since the Neolithic*, ed. P. Lemonnier, London: 238–88.

(1994) 'Cognitive aspects of technique', in *The Ancient Mind: Elements of Cognitive Archaeology*, ed. C. Renfrew and E. B. W. Zubrow, Cambridge: 135–42.

Lefebvre, H. (1991) *The Production of Space*, Oxford.

Leinster, A. C. (1995) 'Herakles and Hera in Etruria: a group of archaic bronze tripods from Vulci', abstract of paper from the 96th Annual General Meeting of the Institute of America, *AJA* 99.2: 351.

Lemonnier, P. (1986) 'The study of material culture today: toward an anthropology of technical systems', *Journal of Anthropological Archaeology* 5: 147–86.

(1989a) 'Bark capes, arrowheads and concorde: on social representations of technology', in *The Meanings of Things: Material Culture and Symbolic Expression*, ed. I. Hodder, London: 156–71.

(1989b) 'Towards an anthropology of technology', *Man* 24: 526–7.

(1990) 'Topsy turvy techniques: remarks on the social representation of techniques', *ARC* 9.1: 27–37.

(1992) *Elements for an Anthropology of Technology*, Anthropological Papers 88, Museum of Anthropology, Ann Arbor.

(ed.) (1993) *Technological Choices: Transformation in Material Cultures Since the Neolithic*, London.

Lerner, S. (1984) 'Defining prehistoric frontiers: a methodological approach', in *Exploring the Limits: Frontiers and Boundaries in Prehistory*, BAR International Series 223, ed. S. P. De Atley and F. J. Findlow, Oxford: 67–80.

Lessa, W., and Vogt, E. (eds.) (1972) *Reader in Comparative Religion*, 3rd edn, New York.

Levi, D. (1933) 'La necropoli etruscha del Lago dell'Accesa e altre scoperte archeologiche nel territorio di Massa Marittima', *MonAL* 35: 5–132.

Linders, T., and Nordquist, G. (1987) (eds.) *Gifts to the Gods: Proceedings of the Uppsala Symposium, 1985*, Acta Universitatis Upsaliensis, *Boreas* 15, Uppsala.

Linington, R. E. (1980) *Lo scavo nella zona Laghetto della necropoli della Banditaccia a Cerveteri, Rassegna di studi del civico museo archeologico e del civico gabinetto numismatico di Milano* 25–6: 1–80.

Linington, R. E., Delpino, F., and Pallottino, M. (1978) 'Alle origine di Tarquinia: scoperta di un abitato villanoviano sui Monterozzi', *SE* 46: 3–23.

Linington, R. E., and Serra Ridgway, F. R. (1997) *Lo scavo del Fondo Scataglini a Tarquinia*, Milan.

Lissarrague, F. (1990a) *The Aesthetics of the Greek Banquet: Images of Wine and Ritual*, Princeton.

(1990b) 'The sexual life of satyrs', in *Before Sexuality: The Construction of Erotic Experience in the Ancient Greek World*, ed. D. M. Halperin *et al.*, Princeton: 53–81.

(1990c) 'Why satyrs are good to represent', in *Nothing to Do with Dionysos? Athenian Drama in Its Social Context*, ed. J. J. Winkler *et al.*, Princeton: 228–36.

(1994) 'Epiktetos egraphsen: the writing on the cup', in *Art and Text in Ancient Greek Culture*, eds. S. J. Goldhill and R. Osborne, Cambridge: 12–27.

Lloyd, G. E. R. (1966) *Polarity and Analogy: Two Types of Argumentation in Early Greek Thought*, Cambridge.

Locock, M. (1994) 'Meaningful architecture', in *Meaningful Architecture: Social Interpretations of Buildings*, ed. M. Locock, Aldershot: 1–13.

(ed.) (1994) *Meaningful Architecture: Social Interpretations of Buildings*, Aldershot.

Lomas, K. (ed.) (2004) *Greek Identity in the Western Mediterranean: Papers in Honour of Brian Shefton*, Leiden.

Lopes Pegna, M. (1964) *L'origine di Arezzo*, Florence.

Loraux, N. (1990) 'La dea: una questione di maternità', in *Storia delle donne in Occidente: L'antichità*, ed. P. Schmitt Pantel. Rome and Bari: 11–44.

Lord, L. E. (1937) 'The judgement of Paris on Etruscan mirrors', *AJA* 41: 602–6.

Lorimer, H. L. (1947) 'The hoplite phalanx with special reference to the poems of Archilochus and Tyrtaeus', *ABSA* 42: 76–138.

(1950) *Homer and the Monuments*, London.

Loudon, M., and Woodford, S. (1980) 'Two Trojan themes: the iconography of Ajax carrying the body of Achilles, and of Aeneas carrying Anchises in black figure vase painting', *AJA* 84: 2–40.

Lovén, L. L., and Strömberg, A. (eds.) (1998) *Aspects of Women in Antiquity: Proceedings of the First Nordic Symposium on Women's Lives in Antiquity, Göteberg 12–15 June 1997*, Jonsered.

Lundgren, M. B. and Wendt, L. (1982) *Acquarossa* 3: *Zone A, AIRRS* 4.38: 3.

Lyons, D. (1996) 'The politics of house shape: round *versus* rectilinear domestic structures in Déla compounds, northern Cameroon', *Antiquity* 70: 351–67.

McCartney, E. S. (1915–16) 'The military indebtedness of early Rome to Etruria', *MAAR* 1: 121–67.

McCloskey, M. A. (1987) *Kant's Aesthetic*, Albany.

McCracken, G. (1990) *Culture and Consumption*, Bloomington.

McDowell, L., and Pringle, R. (eds.) (1992) *Defining Women: Social Institutions and Gender Divisions*, Cambridge.

McEwen, I. K. (1993) *Socrates' Ancestor: An Essay on Architectural Beginnings*, Cambridge, Mass.

McGuire R. H. and Paynter, R. (eds.) (1991) *The Archaeology of Inequality*, Oxford.

McNally, S. (1978) 'The maenad in early Greek art', *Arethusa* 11: 101–35.

Macnamara, E. (1973) *Everyday Life of the Etruscans*, London.

(1990) *The Etruscans*, London.

Maetzke, G. (ed.) (1989) *Atti del secondo congresso internazionale etrusco, Firenze, 26 maggio – 2 giugno 1985*, vol. i, Rome.

Maetzke, G., and Perna, L. (eds.) (1996) *Identità e civiltà dei Sabini. Atti del 18 Convegno di studi etruschi ed italici, Rieti – Magliano Sabina, 30 maggio – 3 giugno 1993*, Florence.

Maggiani, A. (1982) 'Qualche osservazione sul fegato di Piacenza', *SE* 50: 53–88.

Maggiani, A., and Rizzo, M. A. (2005) 'Cerveteri: le campagne di scavo in loc. Vigna Parrocchiale e S. Antonio', in *Dinamiche di sviluppo della città nell'Etruria meridionale: Veio, Tarquinia, Vulci. Atti del XXIII Convegno di Studi Etruschi ed Italici, Roma, Veio, Cerveteri/Pyrgi, Tarquinia, Tuscania, Vulci, Viterbo, 1–6 ottobre 2001*, ed. O. Paoletti and G. Camporeale, Pisa and Rome: 175–84.

Malcus, B. (1984) 'Area D (ovest)', in *San Giovenale: Materiali e problemi. Atti del simposio all'Istituto Svedese di Studi Classici a Roma, 6 aprile 1983, AIRRS* 4.41, ed. S. Forsberg and B. E. Thomasson, Stockholm: 37–60.

Malone, C. A. T. and Stoddart, S. K. F. (eds.) (1985a) *Papers in Italian Archaeology*, vol. iv: The Cambridge Conference, Part 1. *The Human Landscape*, BAR International Series 243, Oxford.

(eds.)(1985b) *Papers in Italian Archaeology*, vol. iv: The Cambridge Conference, Part 3. *Patterns in Prehistory*, BAR International Series 245, Oxford.

(eds.)(1994) *Territory, Time and State: The Archaeological Development of the Gubbio Basin*, Cambridge.

Mancini, R. (1889) 'Orvieto: tombe della necropoli meridionale volsiniese in contrada Cannicella, scoperte nel fondo Onori', *NSA*: 98–9.

Mandolesi, A. (1994) 'Ricerche di superficie relative alla prima età del ferro nell'area di Tarquinia antica e nel territorio immediatamente circostante', in *La presenza etrusca nella Campania meridionale: Atti delle giornate di studia (Salerno-Pontecagnano, 16–18 novembre 1990)*, Biblioteca di Studi Etruschi 28, ed. P. Gastaldi and G. Maetzke, Florence: 329–39.

Manino, L. (1971) 'Kioniskoi di Misano', *SE* 39: 231–48.

Mansuelli, G. A. (1941a) 'Gli specchi etruschi del Museo Civico di Bologna', *SE* 15: 307–16.

(1941b) 'Uno specchio inedito del museo civico di Bologna ed il mito di Erocle alla fronte', *SE* 15: 99–108.

(1942) 'Materiali per un supplemento al "corpus" degli specchi etruschi figurati', *SE* 16: 531–51.

(1943) 'Materiali per un supplemento al "corpus" degli specchi etruschi figurati', *SE* 17: 487–521.

(1946) 'Gli specchi figurati etruschi', *SE* 19: 9–137.

(1947) 'Studi sugli specchi etruschi ıv: la mitologia figurata negli specchi etruschi', *SE* 20: 59–98.

(1963) 'La casa etrusca di Marzabotto: constatazioni nei nuovi scavi', *MDAI(R)* 70: 44–62.

(1970a) *Architettura e città: Problemi del mondo classico*, Bologna.

(1970b) 'La necropoli orvietana di Crocifisso del Tufo: un documento di urbanistica etrusca', *SE* 38: 3–12.

(1972) 'Marzabotto: dix années de fouilles et de recherches', *MEFRA* 84: 111–44.

(1979) 'The Etruscan city', in *Italy Before the Romans: The Iron Age, Orientalising and Etruscan Periods*, ed. D. Ridgway and F. R. Ridgway, London: 353–71.

(1985) 'L'organizzazione del territorio e la città', in *Civiltà degli Etruschi*, ed. M. Cristofani, Milan: 111–20.

(ed.) (1988) *La formazione della città preromana in Emilia Romagna: atti del convegno di studi, Bologna-Marzabotto 7–8 dicembre 1985*, Bologna.

Mansuelli, G. A., and Zangheri, R. (eds.) (1970) *Studi sulla città antica: Atti del convegno di studi sulla città etrusca e italica preromana*, Bologna.

Marcus, G., and Myers, F. (eds.) (1995) *The Traffic in Culture: Refiguring Art and Anthropology*, Berkeley.

Marcus, M. I. (1993) 'Incorporating the body: adornment, gender, and social identity in ancient Iran', *CArchJ* 3.2: 158–78.

Marinatos, N, and Hägg, R. (eds.) (1993) *Greek Sanctuaries: New Approaches*, London.

Marshall, F. H. (1911) *Catalogue of the Jewellery, Greek, Etruscan, and Roman, in the Departments of Antiquities, British Museum, London*, London.

Martelli, M. (1976) 'Regione Toscana, bollettino: musei', *Prospettiva* 5: 70–3.

(1978) '*Fufluns Paχies*: sugli aspetti del culto di Bacco in Etruria', *SE* 46: 130–3.

(1979) 'Prima considerazioni sulla statistica della importazione greche in Etruria nel periodo arcaico', *SE* 47: 37–52.

(1981) 'Scavo di edifici nella zona "industriale" di Populonia', in *L'Etruria Mineraria: Atti del XII convegno di studi etruschi e italici. Firenze, 16–20 giugno 1979*, ed. A. Neppi Modona, Florence: 161–72.

(1985) 'I luoghi e i prodotti dello scambio', in *La civiltà degli Etruschi*, ed. M. Cristofani, Milan: 175–81.

(1987) 'Del pittore di Amsterdam e di un episodo del *nostos* odissaico: ricerche dei ceramografia etrusca orientalizzante', *Prospettiva* 50: 10–17.

(ed.) (1987) *La ceramica degli Etruschi: La pittura vascolare*, Novara.

(1988) 'La cultura artistica di Vulci arcaica', in *Un artista etrusco e il suo mondo: Il pittore di Micali*, ed. M. A. Rizzo, Rome: 22–8.

(1990) 'Scrigni etruschi tardo-arcaici dall'Acropoli de Atene e dall'Illiria', *Prospettiva* 53–6: 17–24.

(1994) 'Sul nome etrusco di Alexandros', *SE* 60: 165–78.

(ed.)(1994) *Thyrrhenoi philotechnoi*, Rome.

(1995) 'Circolazione dei beni suntuarî e stile del potere nell'orientalizzante', in *Atti VII Giornata Archeologica: Viaggi e commerci nell'Antichità*, ed. B. M. Giannattasio, Genoa: 9–26.

Martha, J. (1889) *L'Art etrusque*, Paris.

Massa Pairault, F.-H. (ed.) (1999) *Le myth grec dans l'Italie antique: Fonction et image*, Rome.

Mastrocinque, A. (ed.) (1993) *I grandi santuari della Grecia e dell'Occidente*, Trento.

Mauss, M. (1990) *The Gift: The Form and Reason for Exchange in Archaic Societies*, trans. W. D. Halls, London.

Mayer-Prokop, I. (1967) *Die gravierten etruskischen Griffspiegel archaischen Stils*, MDAI(R) Suppl. 13, Heidelberg.

Meadows, K. I. (1997) 'Much ado about nothing: the social context of eating and drinking in early Roman Britain', in *Not So Much a Pot, More a Way of Life*, ed. C. C. Cumberpatch and P. W. Blinkhorn, Oxford: 21–35.

Meer, L. B. van der (1983) *CSE The Netherlands*, Leiden.

(1985) 'Malavisch: speculum spectans', *BABesch* 60: 94–8.

(1987) *The Bronze Liver of Piacenza: Analysis of a Polytheistic Structure*, Dutch Monographs on Ancient History and Archaeology 2, Amsterdam.

(1995) *Interpretatio Etrusca. Greek Myths on Etruscan Mirrors*, Amsterdam.

Melis, F. (1985) 'L'oikos di Piazza d'Armi', in *Santuari d'Etruria*, ed. G. Colonna, Milan.

Melis, F., and Rathje, A. (1984) 'Considerazioni sullo studio dell'architettura domestica arcaica', *Archeologia Laziale* 8: 382–95.

Mengarelli, R. (1915) 'Cerveteri – nuove esplorazioni nella necropoli di Caere: tombe di età posteriore al V sec. av. Cr., e cippi sepolcrali', *NSA*: 347–86.

(1927) 'Caere e le recenti scoperte', *SE* 1: 145–71.

(1935) 'Il tempio del Manganello a Cerveteri, *SE* 9: 83–94.

(1936) 'Il luogo e i materiali del tempio di *HPA* a Caere', *SE* 10: 67–86.

(1937) 'Caere: iscrizioni su cippi sepolcrali, su vasi fittili, su pareti rocciose, e su oggetti diversi nella città e nella necropoli di Caere', *NSA*: 355–439.

(1938) 'La città di Caere: i pagi, le vie e le ville nel territorio cerite durante il periodo etrusco e il periodo romano', *Atti del IV convegno nazionale di studi romani*, vol. ii, ed. G. Galassi Paluzzi. Rome: 221–9.

Menichetti, M. (1994) *Archeologia del Potere: Re immagini e miti a Roma e in Etruria in età arcaica*, Milan.

Meskell, L. (1999) *Archaeologies of Social Life: Age, Sex, Class et cetera in Ancient Egypt*, Oxford.

Metcalf, P., and Huntingdon, R. (1991) *Celebrations of Death: The Anthropology of Mortuary Ritual*, 2nd edn, Cambridge.

Michelucci, M. (1980) 'Loc. Doganella', *SE* 48: 554–6.

(1981) 'Magliano', in *Gli etruschi in Maremma: Popolamento e attività produttive*, ed. M. Cristofani, Milan: 101–8.

(1983) 'Doganella (comune di Orbetello, Grosseto)', *SE* 51: 448–9.

(1985) 'Doganella – Kalousion: l'identificazione e lo scavo della città', in *La romanizzazione dell'Etruria: il territorio di Vulci*, ed. A. Carandini, Milan: 110–14.

Milani, L. A. (1886) 'Chiusi: sarcofago di terracotta policroma, scoperto a Poggio Canterelli, presso Chiusi', *NSA*: 353–6.

(1894) 'Monteriggioni: di una grande tomba a camera con sarcofaghi, scoperta nella tenuta del Casone', *NSA*: 51–2.

(1908) 'Populonia: relazione preliminare sulla prima campagna degli scavi governativi di Populonia nel comune di Piombino', *NSA*: 199–231.

Miller, B. D. (1993) *Sex and Gender Hierarchies*, Cambridge.

Miller, D. (1985) *Artefacts as Categories: A Study of Ceramic Variability in Central India*, Cambridge.

(1987) *Material Culture and Mass Consumption*, Oxford.

Miller, D., Rowlands, M., and Tilley, C. (eds.) (1989) *Domination and Resistance*, London.

Miller, D., and Tilley, C. (eds.) (1984) *Ideology, Power and Prehistory*, Cambridge.

Miller, M. C. (1997) *Athens and Persia in the Fifth Century BC: A Study in Cultural Receptivity*, Cambridge.

Millett, M. (1993) 'Samian from the sea: Cala Culip shipwreck IV', *JRA* 6: 415–19.

Minto, A. (1914a) 'Perugia: scoperta di un ipogeo etrusco in località denominata San Galigano', *NSA*: 232–44.

(1914b) 'Perugia: tomba a camera, scoperta nella vicinanze di Santa Giuliana', *NSA*: 135–41.

(1914c) 'Populonia: relazione preliminare intorno agli scavi governativi nella necropoli, eseguito nell'anno 1914', *NSA*: 444–63.

(1917) 'Populonia: relazione intorno agli scavi governativi eseguiti nel 1915', *NSA*: 69–93.

(1919) 'S. Quirico D'Orcia: scoperta di un sepolcreto etrusco sul "Poggio dello Lepri"', *NSA*: 89–92.

(1921a) *Marsiliana d'Albegna: le scoperte archeologiche del Principe Don Tommaso Corsini*, Florence.

(1921b) 'Populonia: scavi governativi nell'agro populoniese eseguiti nella primavera del 1920', *NSA*: 197–215.

(1921c) 'Populonia – I: scavi governativi eseguiti nell'autunno del 1920 nella zona di Porto Baratti', *NSA*: 301–16.

(1921d) 'Populonia – II: scavi governativi eseguiti nella primavera del 1921', *NSA*: 317–36.

(1925) 'Populonia: scavi e scoperte fortuite nella località di Porto Baratti durante il 1924–25', *NSA*: 346–73.

(1930) 'Le scoperte archeologiche nell'agro Volterrano dal 1897 al 1899 (da appunti manoscritti di Gherardo Ghirardini)', *SE* 4: 9–68.

(1934a) 'Orvieto: scavi governativi al tempio etrusco di Belvedere', *NSA*: 67–99.

(1934b) 'Populonia: scoperte archeologiche fortuite dal 1931 al 1934', *NSA*: 351–428.

(1937) 'I materiali archeologici', *SE* 11: 335–41.

(1943) *Populonia*, Florence.

(1951) 'La "Tanella Angòri" di Cortona', *Palladio* 1: 60–6.

(1954) 'L'antica industria mineraria in Etruria ed il porto di Populonia', *SE* 23: 291–319.

Mirzoeff, N. (1999) *An Introduction to Visual Culture*, London.

Molinos, M., and Zifferero, A. (1998) 'Political and cultural frontiers', in *Papers from the EAA Third Annual Meeting at Ravenna, 1997*, vol. I: Pre- and Protohistory, BAR International Series 717, ed. M. Pearce and M. Tosi, Oxford: 177–258.

Momigliano, A. (1963) 'An interim report on the origins of Rome', *JRS* 53: 95–121.

(1969a) *Quarto contributo alla storia degli studi classici e del mondo antico*, Rome.

(1969b) 'Tre figure mitiche: Tanaquilla, Gaia Cecilia, Acca Larenzia', in *Quarto contributo alla storia degli studi classici e del mondo antico*, A. Momigliano, Rome: 455–85.

Moore, H. (1986) *Space, Text and Gender*, Cambridge.

(1994) *A Passion for Difference: Essays in Anthropology and Gender*, Cambridge.

Moore, J., and Scott, E. (1997) 'Introduction: on the incompleteness of archaeological narratives', in *Invisible People and Processes: Writing Gender and Childhood into European Archaeology*, ed. J. Moore and E. Scott, London and New York: 1–12.

(eds.) (1997) *Invisible People and Processes: Writing Gender and Childhood into European Archaeology*, London and New York.

Moore, S. F. and Myerhoff, B. G. (eds.) (1977) *Secular Ritual*, Assen and Amsterdam.

Moormann, E. M. (ed.) (1993) *Functional and Spatial Analysis of Wall Painting: Proceedings of the Fifth International Congress on Ancient Wall Painting*, Leiden.

Moretti, M. (1955) 'Necropoli della Banditaccia: Zona B "della Tegola dipinta"', *MonAL* 42: 1049–136.

(1982) *Vulci*, Novara.

(1986) *Cerveteri*, Novara.

Moretti, M., and Sgubini Moretti, A. M. (eds.) (1983) *I Curunas di Tuscania*, Rome.

Morgan, C. (1990) *Athletes and Oracles: The Transformation of Olympia and Delphi in the Eighth Century BC*, Cambridge.

(1993) 'The origins of pan-Hellenism', in *Greek Sanctuaries: New Approaches*, ed. N. Marinatos and R. Hägg, London: 18–44.

(1994) 'The evolution of a sacral "landscape": Istunia, Perachora and the early Corinthian state', in *Placing the Gods: Sanctuaries and Sacred Space in Ancient Greece*, ed. S. E. Alcock and R. Osborne, Oxford: 105–42.

Morgen, S. (ed.) (1989) *Gender and Anthropology: Critical Reviews for Research and Training*, Arlington.

Morley, N. (1996) *Metropolis and Hinterland: The City of Rome and the Italian Economy 200 BC – AD 200*, Cambridge.

Morphy, H., and Banks, M. (1997) 'Introduction: rethinking visual anthropology', in *Rethinking Visual Anthropology*, ed. M. Banks and H. Morphy, New Haven: 1–35.

Morris, I. (1987) *Burial and Ancient Society: The Rise of the Greek City-State*, Cambridge.

(1992) *Death-Ritual and Social Structure in Classical Antiquity*, Cambridge.

(ed.) (1994) *Classical Greece: Ancient Histories and Modern Archaeologies*, Cambridge.

Morris, S. P. (1992) *Daidalos and the Origins of Greek Art*, Princeton.

Morris, S. P., and Papadopoulos, J. (1999) 'Phoenicians and the Corinthian pottery industry', in *Archäologische Studien in Kontaktzonen der antiken Welt*, ed. R. Rolle *et al.*, Göttingen: 251–63.

Moscati, P. (1984) *Ricerche matematico-statistiche sugli specchi etruschi*, Rome.

(1986) *Analisi statistiche multivariate sugli specchi etruschi*, Rome.

Moscati, S. (1968) *The World of the Phoenicians*, London.

(1987) *Italy Before Rome: Greeks, Phoenicians, Italians*, Milan.

(ed.) (1988) *The Phoenicians*, Milan.

Mossé, C. (1968) 'Le role politique des armées dans le monde Grec a l'époque classique', in *Problèmes de la guerre en Grèce ancienne*, ed. J.-P. Vernant, Paris: 221–9.

Mulvey, L. (1989) 'Visual pleasure and narrative cinema', in *Visual and Other Pleasures*, ed. L. Mulvey. London: 14–34.

(ed.) (1989) *Visual and Other Pleasures*, London.

Murray, O. (ed.) (1990) *Sympotica: The Papers of a Symposium on the Symposion, Oxford 1984*, Oxford.

Murray, O., and Price, S. R. F. (eds.) (1990) *The Greek City: from Homer to Alexander*, Oxford.

Musti, D. (1987) 'Etruria e Lazio arcaico nella tradizione (Damarato, Tarquinio, Mezenzio)', in *Etruria e Lazio arcaico*, Quaderni di Archeologia Etrusca 15, ed. M. Cristofani, Rome: 139–53.

Nagy, H. (1995) 'The Judgement of Paris? An Etruscan mirror in Seattle', in *Etruscan Italy: Etruscan Influences on the Civilizations of Italy from Antiquity to the Modern Era*, ed. J. F. Hall, Provo, Utah: 45–63.

Nardi, G. (1985) 'La viabilità di una metropolis: il caso di Caere', in *Strade degli Etruschi: vie e mezzi di communicazzione nell'antica Etruria*, ed. F. Boitani *et al.*, Rome: 155–213.

(1989) *Appunti sui santuari urbani*, Quaderni del centro di studio per l'archeologia etrusco-italica: Miscellenea Ceretana 1, Rome.

(2005) 'L'Area urbana di Cerveteri: nuove acquisitzioni e date riassuntivi', in *Dinamiche di sviluppo della città nell'Etruria meridionale: Veio, Tarquinia, Vulci. Atti del XXIII Convegno di Studi Etruschi ed Italici, Roma, Veio, Cerveteri/Pyrgi, Tarquinia, Tuscania, Vulci, Viterbo, 1–6 ottobre 2001*, ed. O. Paoletti and G. Camporeale, Pisa and Rome: 185–92.

Nardi, G., Pandolfini, M., Drago, L., and Berardinetti, A. (eds.) (1997) *Etrusca et italica*, vol. I: Scritti in ricordo di M. Pallottino, Rome and Pisa.

Naso, A. (1995) 'All'origine della pittura etrusca: decorazione parietale e architettura funeraria in Etruria Meridionale nel VII sec. a. C.', *JRGZ* 37: 439–99.

(1996a) *Architetture dipinte: Decorazioni parietali non figurate nelle tombe a camera dell'Etruria meridionale (VII–V sec. a.C)*, Rome.

(1996b) 'Ossservazioni sull'origine dei tumuli monumentali nell'Italia centrale', *ORom* 20: 69–85.

(2000) 'Etruscan and Italic artefacts from the Aegean', in *Ancient Italy in Its Mediterranean Setting: Studies in Honour of Ellen Macnamara*, ed. D. Ridgway *et al.*, London: 193–207.

(2001) 'Dalla capanna alla casa: riflessi nell'architettura funeraria etrusca', in *From Huts to Houses: Transformations of Ancient Societies. Proceedings of an International Seminar Organised by the Norwegian and Swedish Institutes in Rome, 21–24 September 1997*, ed. J. R. Brandt and L. Karlsson, Stockholm: 29–39.

Naso, A., and Zifferero, A. (1985) 'Etruscan settlement patterns in the Monti della Tolfa area (Lazio)', in *Papers in Italian Archaeology*, vol. IV: The Cambridge Conference, Part I: *The Human Landscape*, BAR International Series 243, ed. C. A. T. Malone and S. K. F. Stoddart, Oxford: 239–59.

Naumann, R., and Hiller, F. (1959) 'Rusellae: Vorläufiger Bericht über die Untersuchungen der Jahre 1957 und 1958', *MDAI(R)* 66: 1–30.

Neils, J. (1994) 'Reflections of immortality: The myth of Jason on Etruscan mirrors', in *Murlo and the Etruscans: Art and Society in Ancient Etruria*, ed. R. D. De Puma and J. P. Small, Madison: 190–5.

Nelson, S. M. (1997) *Gender in Archaeology: Analyzing Power and Prestige*, Walnut Creek and London.

Neppi Modona, A. (1925) *Cortona etrusca e romana nella storia e nell'arte*, Florence.

(ed.) (1977) *La civiltà arcaica di Vulci e la sua espansione: Atti del X convegno di studi etruschi e Italici, 1975*, Florence.

(ed.)(1981) *L'Etruria Mineraria: Atti del XII convegno di studi etruschi e Italici, 16–20 giugno, 1979*, Florence.

Nevett, L. (1994) 'Separation or seclusion? Towards an archaeological approach to investigating women in the Greek household in the fifth to the third centuries BC', in *Architecture and Order: Approaches to Social Space*, ed. M. Parker Pearson and C. Richards, London: 98–112.

(1999) *House and Society in the Ancient Greek World*, Cambridge.

Nicosia, F. (1966a) 'Prov. di Firenze: Comeana (Carmignano)', *SE* 34: 299–300.

(1966b) 'Schedario topografico dell'archeologia dell'Agro Fiorentino', *SE* 34: 277–86.

Nielsen, M. (1989) 'La donna e la famiglia nella tarda società etrusca', in *Le donne in Etruria*, ed. A. Rallo, Rome: 121–45.

(1998) 'Etruscan women: a cross-cultural perspective', in *Aspects of Women in Antiquity: Proceedings of the First Nordic Symposium on Women's Lives in Antiquity, Göteborg 12–15 June 1997*, ed. L. L. in Lovén and A. Strömberg, Jonsered: 69–84.

Niemeyer, H. G. (ed.) (1982) *Phönizer im Westen*, Madrider Beiträge 8, Mainz.

Nijboer, A. J. (1997) 'The role of craftsmen in the urbanization process of Central Italy (8th to 6th centuries BC), in *Urbanization in the Mediterranean in the 9th to 6th Centuries BC*, Acta Hyperborea 7, ed. H. Damgaard Andersen *et al.*, Copenhagen: 383–406.

(1998) *From Household Production to Workshops: Archaeological Evidence for Economic Transformations, Pre-Monetary Exchange and Urbanisation in Central Italy from 800 to 400BC*, Groningen.

Nilsson, M. P. (1929) 'The introduction of hoplite tactics at Rome: its date and its consequences', *JRS* 19: 1–11.

Nista, L. (ed.) (1994) *Castores: L'immagine dei Dioscuri a Roma*, Rome.

Nogara, B. (1916) 'Vignanello – scavi nella città e nella necropoli', *NSA*: 37–86.

North, J. A. (1979) 'Religious toleration in Rome', *PCPS* 25: 85–103.

Nylander, C. (1984) 'Cenni sull'architettura domestica di San Giovenale etrusco', in *San Giovenale: Materiali e problemi. Atti del simposio all'Istituto Svedese di Studi Classici a Roma, 6 aprile 1983*, AIRRS 4.41, ed. S. Forsberg and B. E. Thomasson, Stockholm: 65–9.

(1986a) 'Architettura domestica: San Giovenale', in *Architettura etrusca nel Viterbese: Ricerche svedesi a San Giovenale e Acquarossa, 1956–1986*, ed. C. Nylander, Rome: 47–50.

(1986b) 'Urbanistica: San Giovenale', in *Archittetura etrusca nel Viterbese: Ricerche svedesi a San Giovenale e Acquarossa, 1956–1986*, ed. C. Nylander, Rome: 37–40.

(ed.) (1986) *Archittetura etrusca nel Viterbese: Ricerche svedesi a San Giovenale e Acquarossa, 1956–1986*, Rome.

Oakeshott, R. E. (1960) *The Archaeology of Weapons: Arms and Armour from Prehistory to the Age of Chivalry*, London.

Oakley, S. P. (1995) *The Hillforts of the Samnites*, London.

O'Hanlon, M. (1989) *Reading the Skin: Adornment, Display and Society Among the Wahgi*, London.

Oleson, B., and Kobylinksi, Z. (1991) 'Ethnicity in anthropological research: a Norwegian–Polish perspective', *Archaeologia Polona* 29: 5–27.

Oleson, J. P. (1982) *The Sources of Innovation in Later Etruscan Tomb Design (ca. 350–100 BC)*, Rome.

Olinder, B., and Pohl, I. (1981) *San Giovenale, 2.4. The Semi-Subterranean building in Area B, AIRRS* 4.26: 2.4.

Ortiz, F. (1947) *Cuban Counterpoint: Tobacco and Sugar*, New York.

Osborne, R. (1987) 'The viewing and obscuring of the Parthenon frieze', *JHS* 107: 98–105.

   (1994) 'Looking on – Greek style: does the sculpted girl speak to women too?', in *Classical Greece: Ancient Histories and Modern Archaeologies*, ed. I. Morris, Cambridge: 81–96.

   (1996a) *Greece in the Making (1200–479 BC)*, London and New York.

   (1996b) 'Pots, trade and the archaic Greek economy', *Antiquity* 70: 31–44.

   (1998a) *Archaic and Classical Greek Art*, Oxford.

   (1998b) 'Early Greek colonization? The nature of Greek settlement in the West', in *Archaic Greece: New Approaches and New Evidence*, ed. N. Fisher and H. van Wees, London: 251–69.

   (2001) 'Why did Athenian pots appeal to the Etruscans?', *World Archaeology* 33.2: 277–95.

O'Shea, J. (1981) 'Social configurations and the archaeological study of mortuary practices: a case study', in *The Archaeology of Death*, ed. R. Chapman *et al.*, Cambridge: 39–52.

Östenberg, C. E. (1967) *Luni sul Mignone e Problemi della Preistoria d'Italia*, Lund: *AIRRS* 4.25.

   (1975) *Case Etrusche di Acquarossa*, Rome.

   (1976) 'Acquarossa – Ferentum: campagna di scavo 1975', *ORom* 11: 29–37.

   (1983) 'Acquarossa (Viterbo): rapporto preliminare. Cenni introduttivi, le necropoli e i periodi preistorici e protostorici', *NSA*: 25–96.

Ottenberg, S. (1979) 'Analysis of an African mask parade', in *The Fabrics of Culture: The Anthropology of Clothing and Adornment*, ed J. M. Cordwell and R. A. Schwarz, The Hague: 177–87.

Owens, E. J. (1991) *The City in the Greek and Roman World*, London.

Pacchioni, N. (1939) 'Osservazioni sulle pettinature delle donne etrusche nei sarcofaghi e nelle urne chiusine e perugine', *SE* 13: 485–96.

Pacciarelli, M. (1991a) 'Ricerche topografichea Vulci: dati e problemi relativi all origine della cità medio-tirreniche', *SE* 61: 11–48.

   (1991b) 'Territorio, insediamento, communità in Etruria meridionale agli esordi del processo di urbanizzazione', *Scienza dell'Antichità* 5: 163–208.

   (1994) 'Sviluppi verso l'urbanizzazione nell'Italia tirrenicaprotostorica', in *La presenza etrusca nella Campania meridionale: Atti delle giornate di studia (Salerno-Pontecagnano, 1990)*, Florence: 227–53.

(2000) *Dal villaggio alla città: la svolta protourbana dal 1000 a.C. nell'Italia tirrenica*, Florence.

Pace, B., Vighi, R., Ricci, G., and Moretti, M. (1955) '*Caere*, scavi di Raniero Mengarelli', *MonAL* 42: 1–1136.

Pacteau, F. (1994) *The Symptom of Beauty*, London.

Pader, E. J. (1982) *Symbolism, Social Relations and the Interpretation of Mortuary Rituals*, BAR International Series 130, Oxford.

Page, D. (1955) *Sappho and Alcaeus: An Introduction to the Study of Ancient Lesbian Poetry*, Oxford.

Paglia, C. (1990) *Sexual Personae: Art and Decadence from Nefertiti to Emily Dickinson*, London and New Haven.

Pailler, J.-M. (1988) *Bacchanalia: La répression de 186 av. J.-C. à Rome et en Italie: vestiges, images, tradition*, BEFAR 270, Rome.

Pairault Massa, F.-H. (1981) 'Deux questions religieuses sur Marzabotto', *MEFRA* 93: 127–54.

(1992) *Iconologia e politica nell'Italia antica: Roma, Lazio, Etruria dal VII al I secolo a.C.*, Milan.

(1993) 'Aspects idéologiques de *Ludi*', in *Spectacles sportifs et scéniques dans le monde étrusco-italique*, ed. J.-P. Thuillier, Rome: 247–79.

Pallottino, M. (1937) 'Tarquinia', *MonAL* 36: 5–594.

(1939) 'Sulle facies arcaiche dell'Etruria', *SE* 13: 85–128.

(1952) *Etruscan Painting*, Geneva.

(1955) *The Etruscans*, Harmondsworth.

(ed.) (1964) 'Scavi nel santuario etrusco di Pyrgi', *ArchClass* 16: 49–117.

(1975), *The Etruscans*, London.

(1991a) *A History of Earliest Italy*, London.

(1991b) 'Religion in pre-Roman Italy: the historical framework', in *Roman and European Mythologies*, ed. Y. Bonnefoy, London and Chicago: 25–32.

Pàlsson, G. (1993) 'Introduction: beyond boundaries', in *Beyond Boundaries: Understanding, Translation and Anthropological Discourse*, ed. G. Pàlsson, Oxford: 1–40.

(ed.) (1993) *Beyond Boundaries: Understanding, Translation and Anthropological Discourse*, Oxford.

Pandolfini, M. (2000) 'Iscrizione e didascalie degli specchi etruschi: alcune riflessioni', in *Aspetti e problemi della produzione degli specchi etruschi figurati*, ed. M. D. Gentili, Rome: 209–24.

Pansieri, C., and Leoni, M. (1956) 'Sulla technica di fabbricazione degli specchi di bronzo etruschi', *SE* 25: 305–19.

(1957–8) 'The manufacturing technique of Etruscan mirrors', *Studies in Conservation* 3.2: 49–62.

Paoletti, J. B., and Kregloh, C. L. (1989) 'The children's department', in *Men and Women: Dressing the Part*, ed. C. B. Kidwell and V. Steele, Washington: 22–41.

Papodopoulos, J. K. (1997) 'Phantom Euboeans', *Journal of European Archaeology* 10.2: 191–219.

Pare, C. (1989) 'From Dupljaja to Delphi: the ceremonial use of the wagon in later prehistory', *Antiquity* 63: 80–100.

Pareti, L. (1946) *La tomba Regolini-Galassi del Museo Gregoriana Etrusco e la civiltà dell'Italia centrale nel sec. VII a.C.*, Vatican.

Pardo, V. F. (1986) *Arezzo*, Rome and Bari.

Paribeni, E. (1938) 'I rilievi chiusini archaici: I', *SE* 12: 57–139.

   (1939) 'I rilievi chiusini archaici: II', *SE* 13: 179–202.

Paribeni, R. (1905) 'Civitella S. Paolo: scavi nella necropoli Capenate', *NSA*: 301–62.

Parker, A. (1992) *Ancient Shipwrecks of the Mediterranean and the Roman Provinces*, BAR International Series 580, Oxford.

Parker Pearson, M. (1982) 'Mortuary practices, society and ideology: an ethnoarchaeological study', in *Symbolic and Structural Archaeology*, ed. I. Hodder, Cambridge: 99–113.

   (1993) 'The powerful dead: archaeological relationships between the living and the dead', *CArchJ* 3.2: 203–29.

Parker Pearson, M., and Richards, C. (1994a) 'Architecture and order: spatial representations and archaeology', in *Architecture and Order: Approaches to Social Space*, ed. M. Parker Pearson and C. Richards, London and New York: 38–72.

   (1994b) 'Ordering the world: perceptions of architecture, space and time', in *Architecture and Order: Approaches to Social Space*, ed. M. Parker Pearson and C. Richards, London and New York: 1–37.

   (eds.) (1994) *Architecture and Order: Approaches to Social Space*, London and New York.

Parkin, H. (ed.) (1997) *Roman Urbanism: Beyond the Consumer City*, London and New York.

Pasqui, A. (1885) 'Corneto-Tarquinia: scavi a Villa Tarantola nella necropoli tarquiniese dei Monterozzi', *NSA*: 152–4.

   (1890) 'Sugano: tombe etrusche nella tenuta del Fattoraccio, presso Castelgiorgio', *NSA*: 351–3.

   (1894) 'Degli scavi di antichità nel territorio Falisco: delle tombe di Narce e dei loro corredi', *MonAL* 4: 399–548.

Pearce, M., and Tosi, M. (eds.) (1998) *Papers from the EAA Third Annual Meeting at Ravenna, 1997*, vol. I: *Pre- and Protohistory*, BAR International Series 717, Oxford.

Peebles, C. S., and Kus, S. M. (1977) 'Some archaeological correlates of ranked societies', *American Antiquity* 42.3: 421–48.

Pellegrini, G. (1896) 'Toscanella: tombe antiche scoperte nel territorio del comune', *NSA*: 285–6.

   (1901) 'San Gimignano: tombe etrusche rinvenute nel territorio del comune', *NSA*: 7–10.

Perkins, P. (1991) 'Cities and cemeteries and rural settlements in the Albegna Valley and the Ager Cosanus in the Orientalizing and Archaic period', in *Papers of the Fourth Conference of Italian Archaeology, Part I*, ed. E. Herring *et al.*, London: 135–42.

   (1999) *Etruscan Settlement, Society and Material Culture in Central Coastal Etruria*, BAR International Series 788, Oxford.

   (2000) 'Urbanisation, settlement, burial and people in the Albegna Valley', in *The Emergence of State Identities in the First Millennium BC*, ed. E. Herring and K. Lomas, London: 91–108.

Perkins, P., and Attolini, I. (1992) 'An Etruscan farm at Podere Tartuchino', *PBSR* 60: 71–134.

Perkins, P., and Walker, L. (1990) 'Survey of an Etruscan city at Doganella in the Albegna Valley', *PBSR* 58: 1–143.

Perkins, W. (ed.) (2002) *Fashioning the Body Politic: Dress, Gender, Citizenship*, Oxford and New York.

Pernier, L. (1903) 'Bolsena: tombe etrusco-romane scoperta a Gazzetta, presso Bolsena', *NSA*: 588–600.

   (1907) 'Cornetto Tarquinia: nuove scoperte nel territorio tarquiniese', *NSA*: 43–82.

   (1916) 'Castellina in Chianti: grande tumulo con ipogei paleo-etruschi sul Poggio Montecalvario', *NSA*: 263–81.

   (1920) 'Arezzo: ricerche per la scoperta delle antiche mura urbane laterizie nei terreni di "Fonte Pozzolo" e "Catona"', *NSA*: 167–215.

   (1925) 'Tumulo con tomba monumentale al Sodo presso Cortona', *MonAL* 30: 90–127.

Pernier, L., and Stefani, E. (1925) 'Orvieto: tempio etrusco presso il Pozzo della Rocca', *NSA* 133–61.

Peroni, R. (1969) 'Per uno studio dell'economia di scambio in Italia nel quadro dell'ambiente culturale dei secoli intorno al mille a.C.', *PP* 25: 134–60.

   (1971) *L'età del bronzo nel peninsola italiana*, Florence.

   (1979) 'From Bronze Age to Iron Age: economic, historical and social considerations', in *Italy Before the Romans: The Iron Age, Orientalising and Etruscan Periods*, ed. D. Ridgway and F. R. Ridgway, London: 7–27.

   (1980) 'Per una definizione critica dei facies locali: nuovi strumenti metodologici', in *Il Bronzo Finale*, ed. R. Peroni, Bari: 9–12.

   (ed.) (1980) *Il Bronzo Finale*, Bari.

   (1994) *Introduzione alla protostoria italiana*, Rome.

Peroni, R., and di Gennaro, F. (1986) 'Aspetti regionali dello sviluppo dell'insediamento protostorico nell'italia centro-meridionale alle luce dei dati archeologici e ambientali', *DArch* 2: 193–200.

Perserico, A. (1996) L'interazione culturale Greco-fenicia: dall'Egeo al Tirreno centro-meridionale, in *Alle soglie della classicità: il Mediterraneo tra tradizione e innovazione. Studi in onore di Sabatino Moscati*, ed. E. Acquaro, Rome: 899–916.

Persson, C. B. (1986) 'Urbanistica: Acquarossa', in *Architettura etrusca nel Viterbese: Ricerche svedesi a San Giovenale e Acquarossa, 1956–1986*, ed. C. Nylander, Rome: 40–5.

(1994) 'The field architect's urbanistic notes', in *Acquarossa*, vol. VII: *Trial Trenches, Tombs and Surface Finds, AIRRS* 4.38.7, ed. L. Wendt *et al.*, Stockholm: 289–302.

Pfaffenberger, B. (1992) 'Social anthropology of technology', *Annual Review of Anthropology* 21: 491–516.

Pfiffig, A. J. (1975) *Religio Etrusca*, Graz: Akademische Druck- und Verlagsanstalt.

(1980) *Herakles in der Bilderwelt der Etruskischen Spiegel*, Graz.

Pfister-Roesgen, G. (1973) *Die etruskischen Spiegel des 5. Jhs. V. Chr.* Bern.

Phillips, K. M. (1968) 'Four Etruscan mirrors in the Ella Riegel Memorial Museum at Bryn Mawr College', *SE* 36: 165–8.

(1993) *In the Hills of Tuscany: Recent Excavations at the Etruscan Site of Poggio Civitate (Murlo, Siena)*, Philadelphia.

Pieraccini, L. C. (2003) *Around the Hearth: Caeretan Cylinder-Stamped Braziers*, Rome.

Piggott, S. (1972) 'Conclusion', in *Man, Settlement and Urbanism*, ed. P. J. Ucko *et al.* London: 947–53.

Pincelli, R. (1943) 'Il tumulo Vetuloniese della Pietrera', *SE* 17: 47–113.

Pisani Sartorio, G. (ed.) (1989) *Il viver quotidiano in Roma arcaica*, Rome.

Pluciennik, M. Z. (1997) 'Historical, geographical and anthropological imaginations: early ceramics in Southern Italy', in *Not So Much a Pot, More a Way of Life*, ed. C. C. Cumberpatch and P. W. Blinkhorn, Oxford: 37–56.

Pohl, I. (1972) *The Iron Age Necropolis of Sorbo at Cerveteri, AIRRS* 4.32.

(1977) *San Giovenale*, vol. III/3: *The Iron Age Habitations in Area E, AIRRS* 4.26.3/3.

Pokornowski, I. (1979) 'Beads and personal adornments', in *The Fabrics of Culture: The Anthropology of Clothing and Adornment*, ed. J. M. Cordwell and R. A. Schwarz, The Hague: 103–17.

Polignac, F. de (1994) 'Mediation, competition and sovereignty: the evolution of rural sanctuaries in Geometric Greece', in *Placing the Gods. Sanctuaries and Sacred Space in Ancient Greece*, ed. S. E. Alcock and R. Osborne, Oxford: 3–18.

(1995) *Cults, Territory and the Origins of the Greek City-State*, Chicago.

Pomeroy, S. B. (1975) *Goddesses, Whores, Wives and Slaves: Women in Classical Antiquity*, New York.

Popham, M. R., Sackett, L. H. and Thelmis, P. G. (eds.) (1980) *Lefkandi*, vol. I: *(Text) The Iron Age Settlement and the Cemeteries*, London.

Potter, T. W. (1976) *A Faliscan Town in South Etruria: Excavations at Narce 1966–71*, London.

(1979) *The Changing Landscape of South Etruria*, London.

(1991a) 'Power politics and territory in South Etruria', in *Papers of the Fourth Conference of Italian Archaeology*, vol. II, *The Archaeology of Power*, Part 2, ed. E. Herring, R. Whitehouse and J. Wilkins, London: 173–84.

(1991b) 'Towns and territories in Southern Etruria', in *City and Country in the Ancient World*, ed. J. Rich and A. Wallace-Hadrill, London: 191–209.

Poursat, J.-C. (1968) 'Les représentations de danse armée dans la céramique attique', *BCH* 92: 550–615.

Pratt, G. (1981) 'The house as an expression of social worlds', in *Housing and Identity: Cross-Cultural Perspectives*, ed. J. S. Duncan, London: 135–80.

Prayon, F. (1974) 'Zum ursprünglichen Aussehen und zur Deutung des Kult-raums in der Tomba delle Cinque Sedie bei Cerveteri', *Marburger Winckelmann-Programm*: 1–15.

(1975) *Frühetruskische Grab- und Hausarchitektur*, MDAI(R) Suppl. 22, Heidelberg.

(1986) 'Architecture', in *Etruscan Life and Afterlife: A Handbook of Etruscan Studies*, ed. L. Bonfante, Warminster: 174–201.

(2005) 'Lo sviluppo urbanistico del sito etrusco di Castellina del Marangone (comune di Santa Marinella, prov. di Roma)', in *Dinamiche di sviluppo della città nell'Etruria meridionale: Veio, Tarquinia, Vulci. Atti del XXIII Convegno di Studi Etruschi ed Italici, Roma, Veio, Cerveteri/Pyrgi, Tarquinia, Tuscania, Vulci, Viterbo, 1–6 ottobre 2001*, ed. O. Paoletti and G. Camporeale, Pisa and Rome: 665–75.

Price, S. R. F. (1994) *Rituals and Power: The Roman Imperial Cult in Asia Minor*, Cambridge.

Proietti, G. (1977) 'Scavi e scoperte: Cerveteri', *SE* 45: 442–4.

(1980) 'Scavi e scoperte: Cerveteri', *SE* 48: 522–3.

(1986) *Cerveteri*, Rome.

Pryce, F. N. (1931) *Catalogue of Sculpture in the Department of Greek and Roman Antiquities of the British Museum*, London.

Pugliese Carratelli, G. (ed.) (1986) *Rasenna: Storia e civiltà degli Etruschi*, Milan.

(ed.)(1996) *The Western Greeks: Classical Civilization in the Western Mediterranean*, London.

Purcell, N. (1989), 'Rediscovering the Roman Forum', *JRA* 2: 156–66.

(1990) 'Mobility and the polis', in *The Greek City from Homer to Alexander*, ed. O. Murray and S. R. F. Price, Oxford: 29–50.

Quilici, L. (1990) 'Forma e urbanistica di Roma arcaica', in *La Grande Roma dei Tarquini*, ed. M. Cristofani, Rome: 29–44.

Rabinowitz, N. S. (1993) 'Introduction', in *Feminist Theory and the Classics*, ed. N. S. Rabinowitz and A. Richlin, London and New York: 1–20.

Rabinowitz, N. S., and Richlin, A. (eds.) (1993) *Feminist Theory and the Classics*, London and New York.

Rallo, A. (1974) *Lasa: Iconografia e Esegesi*, Studi e Materiali di Etruscologia e Antichità italiche 12, Rome.

(1989a) 'Classi sociali e mano d'opera femminile', in *Le donne in Etruria*, ed. A. Rallo, Rome: 147–56.

(1989b) 'I fonti', in *Le donne in Etruria*, ed. A. Rallo, Rome: 15–33.

(1989c) 'La cosmesi', in *Le donne in Etruria*, ed. A. Rallo, Rome: 173–9.

(ed.) (1989) *Le donne in Etruria*, Rome.

(2000) 'The woman's role', in *The Etruscans*, ed. M. Torelli, London: 131–40.

Randall-MacIver, D. (1924) *Villanovans and Early Etruscans*, Oxford.

(1927) *The Etruscans*, Oxford.

Ransborg, K. (1981) 'Burial, succession and early state formation in Denmark', in *The Archaeology of Death*, ed. R. Chapman *et al.*, Cambridge: 105–21.

Raper, R. (1979) 'Pompeii: planning and social implications', in *Space, Hierarchy and Society*, BAR International Series 59, ed. B. C. Burnham and J. Kingsbury, Oxford: 137–48.

Rapoport, A. (1969) *House Form and Culture*, London.

(1990) 'Systems of activities and systems of settings', in *Domestic Architecture and the Use of Space: An Interdisciplinary, Cross-Cultural Study*, ed. S. Kent, Cambridge: 9–20.

Rasmussen, T. B. (1979) *Bucchero Pottery from Southern Etruria*, Cambridge.

(1985) 'Etruscan shapes in Attic pottery', *Antike Kunst* 28: 33–9.

(2005a), 'Herakles' apotheosis in Etruria and Greece', *Antike Kunst* 48: 30–9.

(2005b) 'Urbanisation in Etruria', *Proceedings of the British Academy* 126: 70–91.

Rasmussen, T., and Spivey, N. (eds.) (1991) *Looking at Greek Vases*, Cambridge.

Rathje, A. (1979) 'Oriental imports in Etruria in the eighth and seventh centuries BC: their origins and implications', in *Italy Before the Romans: The Iron Age, Orientalising and Etruscan Periods*, ed. D. Ridgway and F. R. Ridgway, London: 145–83.

(1983) 'A banquet scene from the Latin city of Ficana', *ARID* 12: 7–26.

(1990) 'The adoption of the Homeric banquet in central Italy in the Orientalizing period', in *Sympotica: The Papers of a Symposium on the Symposion, Oxford 1984*, ed. O. Murray, Oxford: 279–88.

(1994) 'Banquet and ideology: some new considerations about banqueting at Poggio Civitate', in *Murlo and the Etruscans: Art and Society in Ancient Etruria*, ed. R. D. de Puma and J. P. Small. Madison: 95–9.

(2000) '"Princesses" in Etruria and Latium Vetus?', in *Ancient Italy in Its Mediterranean Setting: Studies in Honour of Ellen Macnamara*, ed. D. Ridgway *et al.*, London: 295–300.

(2001–3) 'Huts, houses and palaces: life in central Italy in the Archaic period', *ARP* 9: 57–67.

Rebuffat-Emmanuel, D. (1964) 'Turan et Adonis sur un miroir d'Arezzo', *SE* 32: 173–83.

(1973) *Le miroir étrusque, d'après la collection du Cabinet des Medailles*, BEFAR 20, Rome.

Renard, M. (ed.) (1962) *Hommages à Albert Grenier*, Collection Latomus 58, Brussells.

Rendel Harris, J. (1906) *The Cult of the Heavenly Twins*, Cambridge.

Rendeli, M. (1985a) 'L'*oppidum* di Rofalco nella Selva del Lamone', in *La romaniz-zazione dell'Etruria: Il territorio di Vulci*, ed. A. Carandini, Milan: 60–1.

(1985b) 'Settlement patterns in the Castro area (Viterbo)', in *Papers in Italian Archaeology*, vol. IV: The Cambridge Conference, Part 1: *The Human Landscape*, BAR International Series 243, ed. C. A. T. Malone and S. K. F. Stoddart, Oxford: 261–73.

(1990) '"Muratori, ho fretta di erigere questa casa" (*Ant. Pal.* 14. 136): concorranza tra formazioni urbane dell'Italia centrale tirrenica e la costruzione di edifici di culto arcaici', *RIA* 12: 1–20.

(1991) 'Sulla nascità della communità urbane in Etruria Meridionale, *AION* 13: 9–45.

(1993) *Città aperte: Ambiente e paesaggio rurale organizzato nell'Etruria merid-ionale costiera durante l'età orientalizzante e arcaica*, Rome.

Rendini, P. (1985) 'Ghiaccaforte', in *La romanizzazione dell'Etruria: Il territorio di Vulci*, ed. A. Carandini, Milan: 131–2.

Renfrew, C. (1985) *The Archaeology of Cult: The Sanctuary at Phylakopi*, The British School at Athens, Suppl. 18, London.

(1994) 'The archaeology of religion', in *The Ancient Mind: Elements of Cognitive Archaeology*, ed. C. Renfrew and E. B. W. Zubrow, Cambridge: 47–54.

Renfrew, C., and Cherry, J. F. (eds.) (1986) *Peer Polity Interaction and Socio-Political Change*, Cambridge.

Renfrew, C., and Shennan, S. (eds.) (1982) *Ranking, Resource and Exchange: Aspects of the Archaeology of Early European Society*, Cambridge.

Renfrew, C., and Zubrow, E. B. W. (eds.) (1994) *The Ancient Mind: Elements of Cognitive Archaeology*, Cambridge.

Rhodes, R. F. (1995) *Architecture and Meaning on the Athenian Acropolis*, Cambridge.

Ricci, G. (1955) 'Necropoli della Banditaccia: Zona A "del recinto"', *MonAL* 42: 201–1036.

Ricciardi, L. (1987) 'Blera: l'insediamento agricolo di Le Pozze', in *L'Alimentazione nel mondo antico: Gli Etruschi*, C. Ampolo *et al.*, Rome: 83.

Rich, J., and Wallace-Hadrill, A. (eds.) (1991) *City and Country in the Ancient World*, London.

Richards, C. (1990) 'The late neolithic house in Orkney', in *The Social Archaeology of Houses*, ed. S. Samson, Edinburgh: 111–24.

Richardson, E. (1964) *The Etruscans: Their Art and Civilisation*, Chicago and London.

(1983) *Etruscan Votive Bronzes*. Mainz.

Richlin, A. (ed.) (1992) *Pornography and Representation in Greece and Rome*, New York and Oxford.

Ridgway, D. (1981) *The Etruscans*, Edinburgh.

(1982) 'Buried evidence', *Times Literary Supplement*, 27 August: 926.

(1983) 'The bones of the past', *Times Literary Supplement*, 7 January: 21.

(1990) 'The first western Greeks and their neighbours, 1935–1985', in *Greek Colonists and Native Populations: Proceedings of the First Australian Congress of Classical Archaeology, July 1985*, ed. J.-P. Descoeudres, Oxford: 61–72.

(1992) *The First Western Greeks*, Cambridge.

(1994) 'Phoenicians and Greeks in the West: a view from Pithekoussai', in *The Archaeology of Greek Colonisation: Essays Dedicated to John Boardman*, ed. G. R. Tsetskladze and Franco De Angelis, Oxford: 35–46.

(1995) 'Archaeology in Sardinia and South Italy, 1989–94', *AR* 1994–5: 75–96.

(1998) 'L'Eubea e l'Occidente: nuovi spunti sulle rotte dei materiali', in *Euboica: L'Eubea e la presenza euboica in Calcidia e in Occidente. Atti del convegno internazionale di Napoli 13–16 novembre, AION ArchStAnt* 12, ed. M. Bats and B. d'Agostino, Naples: 311–22.

(2000) 'The first western Greeks revisited', in *Ancient Italy in Its Mediterranean Setting: Studies in Honour of Ellen Macnamara*, ed. D. Ridgway *et al.*, London: 179–91.

(2004) 'Euboeans and others along the Tyrrhenian Seaboard in the 8th century BC', in *Greek Identity in the Western Mediterranean: Papers in Honour of Brian Shefton*, ed. K. Lomas, Leiden: 15–33.

Ridgway, D., and Ridgway, F. R. (eds.) (1979) *Italy Before the Romans: The Iron Age, Orientalising and Etruscan Periods*, London.

(1994) 'Demaratus and the archaeologists', in *Murlo and the Etruscans: Art and Society in Ancient Etruria*, ed. R. D. de Puma and J. P. Small, Madison: 6–15.

Ridgway, D., Serra Ridgway, F. R., Pearce, M., Herring, E., Whitehouse, R. D., and Wilkins, J. B. (eds.) (2000) *Ancient Italy in Its Mediterranean Setting: Studies in Honour of Ellen Macnamara*, London.

Riis, P. J. (1941) *Tyrrhenika: An Archaeological Study of Etruscan Sculpture in the Archaic and Classical Periods*, Copenhagen.

Riva, C. (2000) 'The Genesis of the Etruscan State', unpublished PhD thesis, University of Cambridge.

Riva, C., and Stoddart, S. K. F. (1996) 'Ritual landscapes in archaic Etruria', in *Approaches to the Study of Ritual: Italy and the Ancient Mediterranean*, ed. J. B. Wilkins, London: 91–109.

Rix, H. (1991) *Etruskische Texte*, Tübingen.

Rizzo, M. A. (ed.) (1988) *Un artista etrusco e il suo mondo: Il pittore di Micali*, Rome.

(1989) 'Cerveteri – il tumulo di Montetosto', in *Atti del secondo congresso internazionale etrusco, Firenze, 26 maggio – 2 giugno 1985*, vol. I, ed. G. Maetzke, Rome: 153–61.

Roach, M. E. (1979) 'The social symbolism of women's dress', in *The Fabrics of Culture: The Anthropology of Clothing and Adornment*, ed. J. M. Cordwell and R. A. Schwarz, The Hague: 415–22.

Roach, M. E., and Eicher, J. B. (1979) 'The language of personal adornment', in *The Fabrics of Culture: The Anthropology of Clothing and Adornment*, ed. J. M. Cordwell and R. A. Schwarz, The Hague: 7–21.

Robb, J. (1995) 'Female beauty and male violence in early Italian society', abstract of paper from the 96th Annual General Meeting of the Institute of America, *AJA* 99: 303.

(1997) 'Female beauty and male violence in early Italian society', in *Naked Truths: Women, Sexuality and Gender in Classical Art and Archaeology*, ed. A. O. Koloski-Ostrow and C. L. Lyons, London and New York: 43–65.

Roberts, B. K. (1987) 'Landscape archaeology', in *Landscape and Culture: Geological and Archaeological Perspectives*, ed. J. M. Wagstaff, Oxford: 77–95.

Rolle, R., Schmidt, K., and Docter, R. (eds.) (1999) *Archäologische Studien in Kontaktzonen der antiken Welt*, Göttingen.

Romanelli, P. (1934) 'Tarquinia: saggi di scavo nell'area dell'antica città', *NSA*: 438–43.

(1948) 'Tarquinia: scavi e ricerche nell'area della città', *NSA*: 193–270.

Romualdi, A. (1985) 'Il popolamento in età ellenistica a Populonia: le necropoli', in *L'Etruria mineraria*, ed. G. Comporeale, Milan: 185–6.

Roncalli, F. (1965) *Le lastre dipinte da Cerveteri*, Rome.

Rosaldo, M. Z., and Lamphere, L. (eds.) (1974) *Woman, Culture and Society*, Stanford.

Rosaldo, R. (1986) 'Ilongot hunting as story and experience', in *The Anthropology of Experience*, ed. V. Turner and E. Bruner, Urbana, Ill.: 137–65.

(1989) *Culture and Truth: The Remaking of Social Analysis*, Boston.

Rose, H. J. (1911) 'On the alleged evidence for mother-right in early Greece', *Folk-lore* 22: 277–91.

(1920) 'Mother-right in ancient Italy', *Folk-lore* 31: 93–108.

Rosi, G. (1925) 'Sepulchral architecture as illustrated by the rock façades of central Etruria', *JRS* 15: 1–59.

(1927) 'Sepulchral architecture as illustrated by the rock façades of central Etruria: ii', *JRS* 17: 59–96.

Ross Holloway, R. (1965) 'Conventions of Etruscan painting in the Tomb of Hunting and Fishing at Tarquinia', *AJA* 69: 341–7.

(1994) *The Archaeology of Early Rome and Latium*, London.

Roth, R. E. (2001–3) 'Ritual abbreviations in the Etruscan funeral', *ARP* 9: 93–103.

Rowe, P. (1982) 'The manufacturing process', in *A Guide to Etruscan Mirrors*, ed. N. T. de Grummond. Tallahassee.: 49–60.

Rowlands, M. (1998) 'The archaeology of colonialism', in *Social Transformations in Archaeology: Global and Local Perspectives*, ed. K. Kristiansen and M. Rowlands, London: 327–32.

Ruiz, A. (1998) *The Archaeology of the Iberians*, Cambridge.

Ruyt, F. de (1973) 'Une cité étrusque d'époque archaïque à Acquarossa (Viterbe)', *AC* 42: 584–6.

Rykwert, J. (1976) *The Idea of a Town: The Anthropology of Urban Form in Rome, Italy and the Ancient World*, London.

(1996) *The Dancing Column*, Cambridge, Mass.

Rystedt, E. (1983) *Acquarossa*, vol. iv: *Early Etruscan Akroteria from Acquarossa and Poggio Civitate (Murlo)*, Stockholm, *AIRRS* 4.38.4.

(2001) 'Huts *vis-à-vis* houses: a note on Aquarossa', in *From Huts to Houses: Transformations of Ancient Societies. Proceedings of an International Seminar Organised by the Norwegian and Swedish Institutes in Rome, 21–24 September 1997*, ed. J. R. Brandt and L. Karlsson. Stockholm: 24–7.

Rystedt, E., Wikander, C., and Wikander, Ö. (eds.) (1993) *Deliciae fictiles: Proceedings of the First International Conference on Central Italic Architectural Terracottas at the Swedish Institute in Rome, 10–12 December 1990*, Stockholm, *AIRRS* 4.50.

Sackett, J. R. (1982) 'Approaches to style in lithic archaeology', *Journal of Anthropological Archaeology* 1: 59–112.

(1985) 'Style and ethnicity in the Kalahari: a reply to Wiessner', *American Antiquity* 50.1: 154–9.

(1990) 'Style and ethnicity in archaeology: the case for isochretism', in *The Uses of Style in Archaeology*, ed. W. M. Conkey and C. A. Hastorff, Cambridge: 32–43.

Säflund, G. (1993) *Etruscan Imagery: Symbol and Meaning*, Jonsered.

Sahlins, M. (1976) *Culture and Practical Reason*, Chicago.

(1988) 'Cosmologies of capitalism: the trans-Pacific sector of "the world system"', *PBA* 74: 1–51.

Said, E. W. (1978) *Orientalism*, London.

Salmon, J. (1977) 'Political hoplites?', *JHS* 97: 84–101.

Salskov Roberts, H. (1981) *CSE Denmark*, vol. i, Rome.

(1983) 'Later Etruscan mirrors: evidence for dating from recent excavations', *ARID* 12: 31–54.

(1993) 'The creation of a religious iconography in Etruria in the Hellenistic period', in *Aspects of Hellenism in Italy: Towards a Cultural Unity?* Acta Hyperborea 5, ed. P. G. Bilde *et al.*, Copenhagen: 287–317.

Samson, R. (1990) 'Introduction', in *The Social Archaeology of Houses*, ed. R. Samson, Edinburgh: 1–18.

(ed.) (1990) *The Social Archaeology of Houses*, Edinburgh.

Sanders, D. (1990) 'Behavioral conventions and archaeology: methods for the analysis of ancient architecture', in *Domestic Architecture and the Use of Space: An Interdisciplinary, Cross-Cultural study*, ed. S. Kent, Cambridge: 43–72.

Sassatelli, G. (ed.) (1981) *CSE Italia*, vol. i: *Bologna*, ii, Rome.

Saunders, T. (1990) 'The feudal construction of space: power and domination in the nucleated village', in *The Social Archaeology of Houses*, ed. R. Samson, Edinburgh: 181–96.

Savignoni, L. (1900) 'Perugia: Tomba etrusca contenente ricca suppellettile funeraria, scoperta presso la città', *NSA*: 553–61.

Saxe, A. A. (1970) 'Social Dimensions of Mortuary Practices', unpublished PhD thesis, University of Michigan.

Scali, S. (1987) Bolsena-Gran Carro: I resti faunisitici, in *L'Alimentazione nel mondo antico: gli Etruschi*, ed. G. Barbieri, Rome: 67–70.

Scheffer, C. (1981) *Acquarossa*, vol. ii/1: *Cooking and Cooking Stands in Italy, 1400–400 BC*, *AIRRS* 4.38.2/1, Stockholm.

(1984) 'The selective use of Greek motifs in Etruscan black-figured vase painting', in *Ancient Greek and Related Pottery: Proceedings of the International Vase Symposium in Amsterdam 12–15 April 1984*, ed. H. A. G. Brijder, Amsterdam: 229–33.

(1988) 'Workshop and trade patterns in Athenian Black figure', in *Ancient Greek and Related Pottery*, ed. J. Cristiansen and T. Melander, Copenhagen: 536–46.

Schefold, K. (1966) *Myth and Legend in Early Greek Art*, trans. A. Hicks, London.

(1992) *Gods and Heroes in Late Archaic Greek Art*, trans. A. Griffiths, Cambridge.

Schiffer, M. (ed.) (1984) *Advances in Archaeological Method and Theory*, vol. VII, New York.

Schifone, C. (1971) 'Antefisse fittili', *SE* 39: 249–65.

Schlanger, N. (1994) 'Mindful technology: unleashing the *Chaîne Opératoire* for an archaeology of mind', in *The Ancient Mind: Elements of Cognitive Archaeology*, ed. C. Renfrew and E. B. W. Zubrow, Cambridge: 143–51.

Schneider, R. M. (1995) 'Gegenbilder und verhaltensideale auf der Ficorinischen Ciste', *SE* 60: 105–23.

Schreier, B.A. (1989) 'Introduction', in *Men and Women: Dressing the Part*, ed. C. B. Kidwell and V. Steele, Washington: 1–5.

Schwarz, J. J. (1997) 'Greek Myths on Etruscan Mirrors', *JRA* 10: 326–9.

Schwarz, R. A. (1979) 'Uncovering the secret vice: towards an anthropology of clothing and adornment', in *The Fabrics of Culture: The Anthropology of Clothing and Adornment*, ed. J. M. Cordwell and R. A. Schwarz. The Hague: 23–45.

Sciama, L. (1981) 'The problem of privacy in Mediterranean anthropology', in *Women and Space: Ground Rules and Social Maps*, ed. S. Ardener, London: 89–111.

Scullard, H. H. (1967) *The Etruscan Cities and Rome*, London.

Seamuzzi, E. (1940) 'Contributi per la Carta Archeologica dell'Etruria: di alcuni recenti trovamenti archeologici interessanti la topografia dell'Etruria', *SE* 14: 353–7.

Sennett, R. (1994) *Flesh and Stone: The Body and the City in Western Civilization*, Boston, Mass., and London.

Serra Ridgway, F. R. (1990) 'Etruscan, Greeks, Carthaginians: the sanctuary at Pyrgi', in *Greek Colonists and Native Populations: Proceedings of the First Australian Congress of Classical Archaeology, July 1985*, ed. J.-P. Descoeudres, Oxford: 511–30.

(1992) 'Etruscan mirrors in the Louvre and the Corpus', *JRA* 5: 278–83.

(2000) 'Etruscan mirrors and archaeological context', *JRA* 13: 407–18.

(2002) 'Oriental(ising) motifs in Etruscan art', *ORom* 27: 109–22.

Sgubini Moretti, A. M. (1980) 'Tuscania', *SE* 48: 545–6.

(1989) 'Tomba a casa con portico nella necropoli di Pian di Mola a Tuscania', in *Atti del secondo congresso internazionale etrusco, Firenze, 26 maggio – 2 giugno 1985*, vol. I, ed. G. Maetzke, Rome: 321–35.

(1991) *Tuscania: Il Museo Archeologico*, Rome.

Shanks, M. (1993) 'Style and the design of a perfume jar from an archaic city state', *Journal of European Archaeology* 1: 77–102.

(1999) *Art and the Early Greek State: An Interpretive Archaeology*, Cambridge.

Shanks, M., and Tilley, C. (1982) 'Ideology, symbolic power and ritual communication: a reinterpretation of neolithic mortuary practices', in *Symbolic and Structural Archaeology*, ed. I. Hodder, Cambridge: 129–54.

(1987a) *Social Theory and Archaeology*, Cambridge.

(1987b) *Re-Constructing Archaeology*, Cambridge.

Sharrock, A. R. (1991) 'Womanufacture', *JRS* 81: 36–49.

Shefton, B. B. (1982). 'Greeks and Greek imports in the south of the Iberian peninsula: the archaeological evidence', in *Phönizer im Westen*, Madrider Beiträge 8, ed. H. G. Niemeyer, Mainz: 337–406.

Shennan, S. (1989) 'Introduction: archaeological approaches to cultural identity', in *Archaeological Approaches to Cultural Identity*, ed. S. Shennan, London: 1–32.

(ed.) (1989) *Archaeological Approaches to Cultural Identity*, London.

Shepherd, G. (1995) 'The pride of most colonials: burial and religion in the Sicilian colonies', in *Ancient Sicily*, Acta Hyperborea 6, ed. T. Fischer-Hansen, Copenhagen: 51–82.

(1999) 'Fibulae and females: intermarriage in the Western Greek colonies and the evidence from the cemeteries', in *Ancient Greeks East and West*, ed. G. Tsetskhladze, Leiden: 267–300.

Sherratt, A., and Sherratt, S. (1991) 'From luxuries to commodities: the nature of Mediterranean bronze age trading systems', in *Bronze Age Trade in the Mediterranean: Papers Presented at the Conference Held at Rewley House, Oxford, in December 1989*, Studies in Mediterranean Archaeology 90, ed. N. H. Gale, Jonsered: 351–86.

(1993) 'The growth of the Mediterranean economy in the early first millennium BC', *World Archaeology* 24.3: 361–78.

Shoe, L. (1965) 'Etruscan and Republican Roman mouldings', *MAAR* 28: 1–232.

Shore, B. (1995) *Cultures in Mind: Cognition, Culture and the Problem of Meaning*, New York and Oxford.

Shrimpton, G. S. (1991) *Theopompus the Historian*, Montreal and Kingston.

Silverblatt, I. (1988) 'Women in States', *Annual Review of Anthropology* 17: 427–60.

Slaska, M. (1985) 'Le anfore da trasporto a Gravisca', in *Il commercio etrusco arcaico*, ed. M. Cristofani and P. Pelagatti. Rome: 19–21.

Small, J. P. (1987) 'Left, right, and center: direction in Etruscan art', *ORom* 16: 125–35.

(1991–2) 'The Etruscan view of Greek art', *Boreas* 14/15: 51–65.

(1994a) 'Eat, drink and be merry: Etruscan banquets', in *Murlo and the Etruscans: Art and Society in Ancient Etruria*, ed. R. D. De Puma and J. P. Small, Madison: 85–94.

(1994b) 'Scholars, Etruscans, and Attic painted vases', *JRA* 7: 34–58.

Smith, C. J. (1994) 'A review of the archaeological studies in Iron-Age and Archaic Latium', *JRA* 7: 285–302.

(1996) *Early Rome and Latium: Economy and Society*, Oxford.

Smith, J. C. (1991) 'Gender and the construction of reality', in *The Archaeology of Gender: Proceedings of the 22nd Annual Chacmool Conference, Calgary*, ed. D. Walde and N. Willows, Calgary: 84–95.

Snodgrass, A. M. (1965) 'The hoplite reform and history', *JHS* 85: 110–22.

(1980) *Archaic Greece: The Age of Experiment*, London and Toronto.

(1983) 'Archaeology', in *Sources for Ancient History*, ed. M. Crawford, Cambridge: 137–84.

(1986) 'Interaction by design: the Greek city-state', in *Peer Polity Interaction and Socio-Political Change*, ed. C. Renfrew and J. F. Cherry, Cambridge: 47–58.

(1987) *An Archaeology of Greece: The Present State and Future Scope of a Discipline*, Berkeley and London.

Sogliano, A. (1885) 'Cuma', *NSA*: 322–3.

(1889) 'Di un dipinto murale rinvenuto in una tomba Cumana', *MonAL* 1: 953–6.

Sordi, M. (1981) 'La donna etrusca', in *Misoginia e maschilismo in Grecia e in Roma*, Genoa: Istituto di Filologia Classica e Medievale: 49–67, reprinted in Sordi (1995), 159–73.

(1995) *Prospettive di Storia Etrusca*, Como.

Sordini, G. (1893) 'Bolsena: nuove scoperte nella necropoli Barano, presso la città', *NSA*: 64–8.

Sørensen, M. L. S. (1991) 'The construction of gender through appearance', in *The Archaeology of Gender: Proceedings of the 22nd Annual Chacmool Conference, Calgary*, ed. D. Walde and N. D. Willows, Calgary: 121–9.

(2000) *Gender Archaeology*, Cambridge.

Sorrentino, C. (1981a) 'La fauna', in *San Giovenale II. 2: Excavations in Area B*, 157–1960, ed. E. Berggren and K. Berggren, Rome, *AIRRS* 4.26.2.2: 58–64.

(1981b) Appendix, in *San Giovenale II. 4. The Subterranean Building in Area B*, ed. E. Berggren and K. Berggren, Rome; *AIRRS* 4.26.2.4: 85–9.

Sourvinou-Inwood, C. (1993) 'Early sanctuaries, the eighth century and ritual space: fragments of a discourse', in *Greek Sanctuaries: New Approaches*, ed. N. Marinatos and R. Hägg, London: 1–17.

Sowder, C. L. (1982) 'Etruscan mythological figures', in *A Guide to Etruscan Mirrors*, ed. N. T. De Grummond, Tallahassee: 100–28.

Spector, J. D. and Whelan, M. K. (1989) 'Incorporating gender into archaeology courses', in *Gender and Anthropology: Critical Reviews for Research and Training*, ed. S. Morgen, Arlington.

Spivey, N. J. (1987) *The Micali Painter and His Followers*, Oxford.

(1988) 'Il pittore Micali', in *Un artista etrusco e il suo mondo: Il pittore di Micali*, ed. M. A. Rizzo, Rome: 11–21.

(1991a) 'Greek vases in Etruria', in *Looking at Greek Vases*, ed. N. J. Spivey and T. Rasmussen, Cambridge: 131–50.

(1991b) 'The power of women in Etruscan society', *ARP* 2: 55–67.

(1992) 'Ajax in Etruria', *Atti e memorie della società Magna Grecia* 3.1, ed. M. Cristofani and F. Zevi, Taranto: 233–42.

(1997a) *Greek Art*, London.

(1997b) *Etruscan Art*, London.

Spivey, N. J., and Stoddart, S. K. F. (1990) *Etruscan Italy*, London.

Staccioli, R. A. (1967) 'Sulla struttura dei muri delle case della città etrusca di Misano a Marzabotto', *SE* 35: 113–26.

(1970) 'A proposito della casa etrusca a sviluppo verticale', in *Studi sulla città antica: Atti del convegno sulla città etrusca e italica preromana*, ed. G. A. Mansuelli and R. Zangheri, Bologna: 129–33.

Stark, M. T. (ed.) (1998) *The Archaeology of Social Boundaries*, Washington.

Starr, C. G. (1977) *The Economic and Social Growth of Early Greece, 800–500 B.C.*, New York.

Stary, P. F. (1979) 'Foreign elements in Etruscan arms and armour: eighth to third centuries BC', *Proceedings of the Prehistoric Society* 45: 179–206.

Steele, V. (1989) 'Appearance and identity', in *Men and Women: Dressing the Part*, ed. C. B. Kidwell and V. Steele, Washington: 6–21.

(1989) 'Clothing and sexuality', in *Men and Women: Dressing the Part*, ed. C. B. Kidwell and V. Steele. Washington: 42–63.

Stefani, E. (1922) 'Veio: esplorazioni dentro l'area dell'antica città', *NSA*: 379–404.

(1929) 'Veio: saggi e scoperte fortuite nella necropoli', *NSA*: 325–51.

(1944–5) 'Scavi archeologici a Veio in Contrada Piazza d'Armi', *MonAL* 40: 177–290.

(1945) 'Grottarossa: ruderi di una villa republicana', *NSA*: 52–72.

(1953) 'Veio: tempio detto dell'Apollo – esplorazione e sistemazione del santuario', *NSA*: 29–112.

(1954) 'Ardea (Contrada Casalinaccio): resti di un antico tempio scoperto nell'area della città', *NSA*: 6–30.

Steingräber, S. (1979) *Etruskische Möbel*, Rome.

(1982) 'Überlegungen zu etruskischen Altären', in *Miscellanea archaeologica Tobias Dohrn dedicata*, ed. H. Blanck and S. Steingräber, Rome: 103–16.

(1983) *Città e necropoli dell'Etruria*, Rome.

(ed.) (1986) *Etruscan Painting*, New York.

(2000) 'Etruscan urban planning', in *The Etruscans*, ed. M. Torelli, London: 291–311.

Stewart, S. (1993) *On Longing: Narratives of the Miniature, the Gigantic, the Souvenir, the Collection*, Durham, N.C., and London.

Stoddart, S. K. F. (1987) 'Complex Polity Formation in North Etruria and Umbria, 1200–500 BC', unpublished PhD thesis, University of Cambridge.

(1989) 'Divergent trajectories in central Italy, 1200–500 BC', in *Centre and Periphery: Comparative Studies in Archaeology*, ed. T. C. Champion, London and New York: 88–101.

(1990) 'The political landscape of Etruria', *ARP* 1: 39–51.

Stoddart, S. K. F., and Whitley, J. (1988) 'The social context of literacy in archaic Greece and Etruria', *Antiquity* 62: 761–72.

Stone, E. C. (1993) 'Chariots of the gods in old Babylonian Mesopotamia (*c.* 2000–1600 BC)', *CArchJ* 3/1: 83–107.

Stopponi, S. (1968) 'PARAPETASMATA Etruschi', *BA* 53: 60–2.

(1985) 'Il santuario del Belvedere a Orvieto', in *Santuari d'Etruria*, ed. G. Colonna, Milan: 80–3.

(ed.) (1985) *Case e palazzi d'Etruria*, Milan.

Strandberg Olofson, M. (1989) 'On the reconstruction of the monumental area at Acquarossa', *ORom* 17: 163–83.

Strathern, M. (1988) *The Gender of the Gift: Problems with Women and Problems with Society in Melanesia*, Berkeley.

Strazzulla, M. J. (1994) 'Attestazioni figurative dei Dioscuri nel mondo etrusco', in *Castores: L'immagine dei Dioscuri a Roma*, ed. L. Nista, Rome: 39–52.

Strøm, I. (1971) *Problems Concerning the Origin and Early Development of the Etruscan Orientalising Style*, Odense.

Strømberg, A. (1993) *Male or Female? A Methodological Study of Grave Gifts as Sex-Indicators in Iron Age Burials from Athens*, Studies in Mediterranean Archaeology and Literature 123, Jonsered.

Swaddling, J. (ed.) (1986) *Italian Iron Age Artefacts in the British Museum*, London.

Swaddling, J., Craddock, P. T., La Niece, S., and M. Hockey (2000) 'Breaking the mould: the overwrought mirrors of Etruria', in *Ancient Italy in Its Mediterranean Setting: Studies in Honour of Ellen Macnamara*, ed. D. Ridgway *et al.*, London: 117–40.

Swaddling, J., and Prag, J. (eds.) (2002) *Seienti Hanunia Tlesnasa: The Story of an Etruscan Noblewoman*, London.

Szilágyi, J. G. (1975) *Etruszko-Korinthosi vásafestézct*, Budapest.

(1981) 'Impletae modis saturae', *Prospettiva* 24: 2–23.

(1994) 'Discorso sul metodo: contributo al problema della classificazzione degli specchi tardo-etruschi', in *Tyrrhenoi philotechnoi*, ed. M. Martelli, Rome: 161–72.

(1995) 'Discourse on method: a contribution to the problem so classifying late Etruscan mirrors', *Etruscan Studies* 2: 35–52.

Szilágyi, J. G., and Bouzek, J. (1992) *CSE Hongrie-Tchécoslovaquie*, Rome.

Tajfel, H. (ed.) (1982) *Social and Intergroup Relations*, Cambridge.

Talocchini, A. (1963) 'La città e la necropoli di Vetulonia secondo i nuovi scavi (1959–1962)', *SE* 31: 435–51.

(1981) 'Ultimi dati offerti dagli scavi vetuloniesi (Poggio Pelliccia e Costa Murata)', in *L'Etruria Mineraria: Atti del XII convegno di studi etruschi e italici, Firenze, 16–20 giugno 1979*, ed. A. Neppi Modona, Florence: 99–138.

Taylor, L. (ed.) (1994) *Visualizing Theory: Selected Essays from V.A.R. 1990–1994*, New York.

Terrenato, N. (1998) 'Tam Firmum Municipium: the Romanization of Volterrae and its cultural implications', *JRS* 88: 94–114.

(2001) 'The Auditorium site in Rome and the origins of the villa', *JRA* 14: 5–32.

Thoden van Velzen, D. (1992) 'A game of tombs: the use of funerary practices in the conflict between Etruscans and Romans in the 2nd and 1st centuries BC in Chiusi, Tuscany', *ARC* 11.1: 65–76.

Thomas, J. (1991) *Rethinking the Neolithic*, Cambridge.

(1996) *Time, Culture and Identity: An Interpretive Archaeology*, London and New York.

Thomas, J., and Whittle, A. (1986) 'Anatomy of a tomb: West Kennet revisited', *OJA* 5.2: 129–56.

Thomas, N. (1991) *Entangled Objects: Exchange, Material Culture and Colonialism in the South Pacific*, Cambridge, Mass.

Thuillier, J.-P. (1975) 'Denis d'Halicarnasse et les jeux romains (*Antiquités Romaines* VII, 72–73)', *MEFRA* 87: 563–81.

(1985) *Les jeux athlétiques dans la civilisation étrusque*, Rome.

(1993) 'Les représentations sportives dans l'oeuvre du Peintre di Micali', in *Spectacles sportifs et scéniques dans le monde étrusco-italique*, ed. J.-P. Thuillier, Rome: 21–44.

(ed.) (1993) *Spectacles sportifs et scéniques dans le monde étrusco-italique*, Rome.

Tilley, C. (1994) *A Phenomenology of Landscape: Places, Paths, and Monuments*, Oxford.

(1999) *Metaphor and Material Culture*, Oxford.

Tomlinson, R. (1992) *From Mycenae to Constantinople: The Evolution of the Ancient City*, London.

Toms, J. (1998) 'The construction of gender in iron age Etruria', in *Gender and Italian Archaeology: Challenging the Stereotypes*, ed. R. Whitehouse, London: 157–79.

Torelli, M. (1967) 'Terza campagna di scavi a Punta della Vipera (S. Marinella)', *SE* 35: 331–52.

(1974–5) 'Tre studi di storia etrusca', *DArch* 8.1: 3–78.

(1977) 'Il santuario Greco di Gravisca', in *PP* 32: 398–458.

(1983) '*Polis* e "palazzo": architettura, ideologia e artigianato greco in Etruria tra VII e VI sec. a.C.', in *Architecture et société de l'archaïsme grec à la fin de la république romaine*, ed. P. Gros, Rome: 471–99.

(1985) 'Introduzione', in *Case e palazzi d'Etruria*, ed. S. Stopponi, Milan: 21–40.

(1990) *Storia degli Etruschi*, Rome and Bari.

(1992a) 'Iconologia selvaggia ed altro', *Ostraka* 1: 259–301.

(1992b) *L'arte degli Etruschi*, Rome and Bari.

(1996) 'The encounter with the Etruscans', in *The Western Greeks: Classical Civilization in the Western Mediterranean*, ed. G. Pugliese Carratelli, London: 567–76.

(1997) 'Les Adonies de Gravisca: archéologies d'une fête', in *Les Etrusques: Les plus religieux des hommes*, ed. F. Gaultier and F. Briquel, Paris: 233–92.

(1999) *Tota Italia: Essays in the Cultural Formation of Roman Italy*, Oxford.

(ed.) (2000) *The Etruscans*, London.

Tortorici, E. (1985) 'Regisvilla', in *La romanizzazione dell'Eturia: Il territorio di Vulci*, ed. A. Carandini, Milan: 53.

Tosto, V. (1999) *The Black-Figure Pottery Signed ΝΙΚΟΣΘΕΝΕΣΕΠΟΙΕΣΕΝ*, Amsterdam.

Treherne, P. (1995) 'The warrior's beauty: the masculine body and self-identity in Bronze Age Europe', *Journal of European Archaeology* 3.1: 105–44.

Tripponi, A. (1971) 'Esplorazione di un edificio nella zona sud-orientale (Reg. V. Ins. I)', *SE* 39: 219–30.

Tsetskhladze, G. R (ed.) (1999) *Ancient Greeks East and West*, Leiden.

Tsetskhladze, G. R., and De Angelis, Franco (eds.) (1994) *The Archaeology of Greek Colonisation: Essays Dedicated to John Boardman*, Oxford.

Turchi, N. (1922) *Manuale di storia delle religioni*, 2nd edn, Turin.

Turner, F. (1989) 'Why the Greeks and not the Romans in Victorian Britain?', in *Rediscovering Hellenism: The Hellenic Inheritance and the English Imagination*, ed. G. W. Clarke, Cambridge: 61–81.

Turner, J. (1975) 'Social comparison and social identity: some prospects for inter-group behaviour', *European Journal of Social Psychology* 5: 5–34.

Turner, T. (1980) 'The social skin', in *Not Work Alone: A Cross-Cultural View of Activities Superfluous to Survival*, ed. J. Cherfas *et al.*, Beverley Hills: 112–40.

Turner, T. S. (1977) 'Transformation, hierarchy and transcendence: a reformulation of van Gennep's model of the structure of *rites de passage*', in *Secular Ritual*, ed. S. F. Moore and B. G. Myerhoff, Assen and Amsterdam: 53–70.

Turner, V. (1977) 'Variations on a theme of liminality', in *Secular Ritual*, ed. S. F. Moore and B. G. Myerhoff, Assen and Amsterdam: 36–52.

Turner, V., and Bruner, E. (eds.) (1986) *The Anthropology of Experience*, Urbana, Ill.

Turnure, J. H. (1965) 'Etruscan ritual armour: two examples in bronze', *AJA* 69: 39–48.

Tyrrell, W. B. (1984) *Amazons: A Study in Athenian Mythmaking*, Baltimore.

Tyrrell, W. B., and Brown, F. S. (1991) *Athenian Myths and Institutions: Words in Action*, Oxford.

Ucko, P. J., Tringham, R., and Dimbleby, G. W. (eds.) (1972) *Man, Settlement and Urbanism*, London.

V. Freytag gen. Löringhoff, B. (1990) *CSE Bundesrepublik Deutschland*, vol. III, Munich.

Vance, J. E. (1990) *The Continuing City: Urban Morphology in Western Civilization*, Baltimore and London.

Vanzetti, A. (2002) 'Some current approaches to protohistoric centralisaton and urbanisation in Italy', in *New Developments in Italian Landscape Archaeology*, BAR International Series 1091, ed. P. Attema *et al.*, Oxford: 36–51.

Vernant, J.-P. (1980) *Myth and Society in Ancient Greece*, Brighton.

(1981) 'Death with two faces', in *Mortality and Immortality: The Anthropology and Archaeology of Death*, ed. S. C. Humphreys and H. King, London: 285–91.

(1983) *Myth and Thought Among the Greeks*, London.

(1990) *Figures, idoles, masques*, Paris.

(1968) *Problèmes de la guerre en Grèce ancienne*, Paris.

(1991) *Mortals and Immortals: Collected Essays by Froma I. Zeitlin*, Princeton.

Versnel, H. S. (1990) 'What's sauce for the goose is sauce for the gander', in *Approaches to Greek Myth*, ed. L. Edmunds, Baltimore: 23–90.

Vickers, M. (1985–6) 'Imaginary Etruscans: changing perceptions of Etruria since the fifteenth century', *Hephaistos* 7–8: 153–68.

Vidal-Naquet, P. (1986) *The Black Hunter: Forms of Thought and Forms of Society in the Greek World*, trans. A. Szegedly-Maszak, Baltimore and London.

Vidén, A. (1986) 'Architettura domestica: Acquarossa', in *Architettura etrusca nel Viterbese: Ricerche svedesi a San Giovenale e Acquarossa, 1956–1986*, ed. C. Nylander, Rome: 50–6.

Villa D'Amelio, P. (1963) 'San Giuliano: scavi e scoperte nella necropoli dal 1957 al 1959', *NSA*: 1–76.

Vinattieri, M. N. (1957) 'Il sepolcreto vetuloniese di Poggio alla Guardia ed il problema di "rispostogli"', *SE* 15: 329–65.

Vitali, D. (1985) 'L'acropoli di Marzabotto', in *Santuari d'Etruria*, ed. G. Colonna, Milan: 88–92.

Voutsaki, S. (1993) 'Society and Culture in the Mycenean World: An Analysis of Mortuary Practices in the Argolid, Thessaly and the Dodecanese', unpublished PhD thesis, University of Cambridge.

Wagstaff, J. M. (1987a) 'Introduction', in *Landscape and Culture: Geological and Archaeological Perspectives*, ed. J. M. Wagstaff, Oxford.

(1987b) 'The new archaeology and geography', in *Landscape and Culture: Geological and Archaeological Perspectives*, ed. J. M. Wagstaff. Oxford: 26–36.

(ed.) (1987) *Landscape and Culture: Geological and Archaeological Perspectives*, Oxford.

Walberg, G. (1988) 'The tomb of the Baron reconsidered', *SE* 56: 51–9.

Walde, D., and Willows, N. D. (eds.) (1991) *The Archaeology of Gender: Proceedings of the 22nd Annual Chacmool Conference, Calgary*, Calgary.

Walker, L. (1985a) 'Doganella – Kalousion: un esperimento di ricognizione urbana', in *La romanizzazione dell'Etruria: il territorio di Vulci*, ed. A. Carandini, Milan: 114–15.

(1985b) 'The site at Doganella in the Albegna Valley: spatial patterns in an Etruscan landscape', in *Papers in Italian Archaeology*, vol. IV: *The Cambridge Conference*, Part 3: *Patterns in Prehistory*, BAR International Series 245, ed. C. A. T. Malone and S. K. F. Stoddart, Oxford: 243–54.

Wall, D. D. (1994) *The Archaeology of Gender: Separating the Spheres in Urban America*, New York.

Wallace-Hadrill, A. (1994) *Houses and Society in Pompeii and Herculaneum*, Princeton.

Walters, H. B. (1896) *Catalogue of the Vases in the British Museum*, vol. IV, London.

Ward-Perkins, J. B. (1955) 'Early Roman towns in Italy', *Town Planning Review* 26: 127–54.

(1958) 'The early development of Roman town planning', in *Acta Congressus Madvigiani: Proceedings of the Second International Congress of Classical Studies*, vol. IV, ed. B. Schweitzer: 109–29.

(1959) 'Excavations beside the north-west gate at Veii 1957–1958', *PBSR* 27: 38–79.

(1961) 'Veii: the historical topography of the ancient city', *PBSR* 29: 1–119.

(1962) 'Etruscan engineering', in *Hommages à Albert Grenier*, Collection Latomus 58, ed. M. Renard: 1636–43.

(1968) (with Kahane, A., and Murray-Threipland, L.) 'The Ager Veientanus north and east of Veii', *PBSR* 36: 1–218.

(1970) 'Città e *pagus*: Considerazioni sull'organizzazione primitiva della città nell'Italia centrale', in *Studi sulla città antica: Atti del convegno di studi sulla città etrusca e italica preromana*, ed. G. A. Mansuelli and R. Zangheri, Bologna: 293–7.

(1974) *Cities of Ancient Greece and Italy: Planning in Classical Antiquity*, New York.

Ward-Perkins, J. B., and Falconi Amorelli, M. T. (1970) 'Veio (Isola Farnese): continuazione degli scavi nella necropoli villanoviana in località Quattro Fontanili', *NSA* 24: 178–329.

Warner, R., and Szubka, T. (eds.) (1994) *The Mind–Body Problem*, Oxford.

Waterhouse, A. (1993) *Boundaries of the City: The Architecture of Western Urbanism*, Toronto, Buffalo and London.

Webb, M. (1990) *The City Square*, London.

Weber, M. (1958) *The City*, New York.

Weber-Lehmann, C. (1986) 'The Archaic period', in *Etruscan Painting*, ed. S. Steingräber, New York: 44–53.

Webster, D. (1975) 'Warfare and the evolution of the state: a reconsideration', *American Antiquity* 40.4: 464–70.

Webster, T. B. L. (1958) *From Mycenae to Homer*, London.

Wees, H. van (1992) *Status Warriors: War, Violence and Society in Homer and History*, Amsterdam.

Weinstock, S. (1946) 'Martianus Capella and the cosmic system of the Etruscans', *JRS* 36: 101–29.

(1951) "*Libri Fvlgvrales*", *PBSR* 19: 122–53.

Weiss, K. M. (1972) 'On the systematic bias in skeletal sexing', *American Journal of Physical Anthropology* 37: 239–50.

Welch, K. (1994) 'The Roman arena in late-republican Italy: a new interpretation', *JRA* 7: 59–80.

Wells, P. S. (1984) *Farms, Villages and Cities: Commerce and Urban Origins in Late Prehistoric Europe*, Ithaca and London.

(1995) 'Identities, material culture and change: "Celts" and "Germans" in late Iron-Age Europe', *Journal of European Archaeology* 3: 169–85.

(1998) 'Identity and material culture in the later prehistory of Central Europe', *Journal of Archaeological Research* 6: 239–98.

Wendt, L., *et al.* (1994) *Acquarossa*, vol. VII: *Trial Trenches, Tomb and Surface Finds*, AIRRS 4.38.7, Stockholm.

West, M. L. (1971) *Early Greek Philosophy and the Orient*, Oxford.

(1988) 'The rise of the Greek epic', *JHS* 108: 151–72.

Wheatley, P. (1972) 'The concept of urbanism', *Man, Settlement and Urbanism*, ed. P. J. Ucko *et al.*, London: 601–37.

Whelan, M. K. (1991) 'Gender and archaeology: mortuary studies and the search for the origins of gender differentiation', in *The Archaeology of Gender: Proceedings of the 22nd Annual Chacmool Conference, Calgary*, ed. D. Walde and N. D. Willows, Calgary: 358–65.

Whitehouse, R. (1977) *The First Cities*, Oxford.

(1991) 'Ritual knowledge, secrecy and power in a small state society', in *Papers of the Fourth Conference of Italian Archaeology*, Part 1, ed. E. Herring *et al.*, London: 195–206.

(ed.) (1998) *Gender and Italian Archaeology: Challenging the Stereotypes*, London.

Whitelaw, T. M. (1983) 'The settlement of Fournou Korifi, Myrtos, and aspects of early Minoan social organisation', in *Minoan Society: Proceedings of the Cambridge Colloquium 1981*, ed. O. Krzyszkowska and L. Nixon, Bristol: 323–45.

(1994) 'Order without architecture: functional, social and symbolic dimensions in hunter-gatherer settlement organisation', in *Architecture and Order: Approaches to Social Space*, ed. M. Parker Pearson and C. Richards, London and New York: 217–43.

Whitley, J. (1987) 'Art history, archaeology and idealism: the German tradition', in *Archaeology as Long Term History*, ed. I. Hodder, Cambridge: 9–15.

(1991) *Style and Society in Dark Age Greece: The Changing Face of a Pre-literate Society 1100–700 BC*, Cambridge.

(1997) 'Beazley as theorist', *Antiquity* 71: 40–7.

Whittaker, C. R. (1974) 'The western Phoenicians: colonisation and annihilation', *PCPS* 200: 58–79.

Wicker, N. L., and Arnold, B. (eds.) (1999) *From the Ground Up: Beyond Gender Theory in Archaeology. Proceedings of the Fifth Gender and Archaeology Conference, University of Wisconsin-Milwaukee, October 1998*, BAR International Series 812, Oxford.

Wieselgren, T. (1969) *Luni sul Mignone*, vol. II/1: *The Iron Age Settlement on the Acropolis*, AIRRS 4.27.2.1.

Wiessner, P. (1983) 'Style and social information in Kalahari San projectile points', *American Antiquity* 49.2: 253–76.

(1988) 'Style or isochrestic variation? A reply to Sackett', *American Antiquity* 50.1: 160–6.

(1989) 'Style and changing relations between the individual and society', in *The Meanings of Things: Material Culture and Symbolic Expression*, ed. I. Hodder, London: 56–63.

(1990) 'Is there a unity to style?', in *The Uses of Style in Archaeology*, ed. M. W. Conkey and C. A. Hastorf, Cambridge: 105–14.

Wikander, C. (1988) *Acquarossa*, vol. I: *The Painted Architectural Terracottas*, Part 2: *Typological and Decorative Analysis*. Stockholm, *AIRRS* 4.38.1.2.

(1993) 'Acquarossa: campagna di scavo 1991', *ORom* 19: 91–5.

(2001) 'From huts to houses: the problem of architectural decoration', in *From Huts to Houses: Transformations of Ancient Societies. Proceedings of an International Seminar Organised by the Norwegian and Swedish Institutes in Rome, 21–24 September 1997*, ed. J. R. Brandt and L. Karlsson, Stockholm: 269–72.

Wikander, C., and Wikander, Ö. (1990) 'The early monumental complex at Aquarossa: a preliminary report', *ORom* 18: 189–205.

Wikander, Ö. (1981) 'Architectural terracottas from San Giovenale', *ORom* 13: 69–89.

Wilkins, J. B. (ed.) (1996) *Approaches to the Study of Ritual: Italy and the Ancient Mediterranean*, London.

Williams, D. J. (1988) 'The late-archaic class of eye cup', in *Ancient Greek and Related Pottery*, ed. J. Cristiansen and T. Melander, Copenhagen: 674–83.

Williams, J. D. (1986) 'Greek potters and their descendants in Campana and Southern Italy', in *Italian Iron-age Artefacts in the British Museum*, ed. J. Swaddling, London: 295–304.

Willis, P. (1990) *Common Culture: Symbolic Work at Play in the Everyday Cultures of the Young*, Milton Keynes.

Wilson, E. (1985) *Adorned in Dreams: Fashion and Modernity*, London.

(1991) *The Sphinx and the City: Urban Life, the Control of Disorder, and Women*, London.

Wiman, I. M. B. (1990) *Malstria-Malena: Metals and Motifs in Etruscan Craft*, Studies in Mediterranean Archaeology 91, Göteborg.

(1992) 'The adornment of Malavisch in a three-parted disc group mirror in Lund', *Medelhavsmuseet Bulletin* 26–7: 90–102.

(1998) 'Further studies of metals and motifs on Etruscan mirrors', *Etruscan Studies* 5: 109–27.

Winkler, J. J. (1981) 'Gardens of nymphs: public and private in Sappho's Lyrics', *Women's Studies* 8: 67–91.

(1990a) *The Constraints of Desire: The Anthropology of Sex and Gender in Ancient Greece*, London and New York.

(1990b) 'The *ephebes*' song: *tragoidia* and *polis*', in *Nothing to Do with Dionysos? Athenian Drama in Its Social Context*, ed. J. J. Winkler *et al.*, Princeton: 20–62.

Winkler, J. J., and Zeitlin, F. I. (eds.) (1990) *Nothing to do with Dionysos? Athenian Drama in its Social Context*, Princeton.

Winter, F. E. (1971) *Greek Fortifications*, London.

Winther, H. C. (1997) 'Princely tombs of the orientalizing period in Etruria and Latium Vetus', in *Urbanization in the Mediterranean in the 9th to 6th Centuries BC*, Acta Hyperborea 7, ed. H. Damgaard Andersen *et al.*, Copenhagen: 432–46.

Wiseman, T. P. (1995) *Remus: A Roman Myth*, Cambridge.

(1996) 'What do we know about early Rome?', *JRA* 9: 310–15.

Wobst, H. M. (1977) 'Stylistic behaviour and information exchange', in *For the Director: Research Essays in Honour of James B. Griffin*, ed. C. E. Cleland, Museum of Anthropology Paper 61, Ann Arbor: 317–42.

(1997) 'Towards an "appropriate metrology" of human action in archaeology', in *Time, Process and Structure Transformation in Archaeology*, ed. S. van der Leeuw and J. McGlade, London: 426–48.

(1990) 'Agency in (spite of) material culture', in *Agency in Archaeology*, ed. M.-A. Dobres and J. Robb, London: 40–50.

Woodhead, A. G. (1962) *The Greeks in the West*, London.

Woolf, G. (1994) 'Power and the spread of writing in the West', in *Literacy and Power in the Ancient World*, ed. A. K. Bowman and G. Woolf, Cambridge: 84–98.

(1996) 'Monumental writing and the expansion of Roman society in the early empire', *JRS* 86: 22–39.

(1998) *Becoming Roman: The Origins of Provincial Civilization in Gaul*, Cambridge.

Wright, J. C. (1994) 'The spatial configuration of belief: the archaeology of Mycenaean religion', in *Placing the Gods: Sanctuaries and Sacred Space in Ancient Greece*, ed. S. E. Alcock and R. Osborne, Oxford: 37–78.

Wycherley, R. E. (1949) *How the Greeks Built Cities*, London.

Wyke, M. (1994) 'Woman in the mirror: the rhetoric of adornment in the Roman world', in *Women in Ancient Societies: An Illusion of the Night*, ed. L. J. Archer *et al.*, London: 134–51.

Wylie, A. (1991) 'Gender theory and the archaeological record: why is there no archaeology of gender?', in *Engendering Archaeology: Women and Prehistory*, ed. J. M. Gero and M. W. Conkey, Oxford: 31–54.

Yates, T. (1991) '*Habitus* and social space: some suggestions about meaning in the Saami (Lapp) tent *ca.* 1700–1900', in *The Meanings of Things: Material Culture and Symbolic Expression*, ed. I. Hodder, London: 249–62.

Yentsch, A. (1991) 'The symbolic divisions of pottery: sex-related attributes of English and Anglo-American households', in *The Archaeology of Inequality*, ed. R. H. McGuire and R. Paynter, Oxford: 192–230.

Zamarchi Grassi, P. (ed.) (1995) *Castiglion Fiorentino: Un nuovo centro etrusco*, Cortona.

Zevi, F. (1990) 'Il foro', in *La Grande Roma dei Tarquini*, ed. M. Cristofani, Rome: 47–52.

Zifferero, A. (1991a) 'Forme di possesso della terra e tumuli orientalizzanti nell'Italia centrale tirrenica', in *Papers of the Fourth Conference of Italian Archaeology*, vol. I, *The Archaeology of Power*, Part 1, ed. E. Herring, R. Whitehouse and J. Wilkins, London: 107–34.

    (1991b) 'Miniere e metallurgia estrattiva in Etruria meridionale: per una lettura critica di alcuni dati archeologici e minerari', *SE* 57: 201–41.

    (1995) 'Economia, divinità e frontiera: sul ruolo di alcuni santuari di confine in Etruria meridionale', *Ostraka* 4: 333–50.

    (ed.) (1997) *L'architettura funeraria a Populonia tra IX e VI secolo a.C.: Atti del convegno, Castello di Populonia, 30–31 ottobre 1997*, Florence.

    (2002a) 'Some remarks on the production and interpretation of pre-Roman pottery in the middle Tyrrhenian area', in *New Developments in Italian Landscape Archaeology*, BAR International Series 1091, ed. P. Attema *et al.*, Oxford: 180–4.

    (2002b) 'The geography of ritual landscape in complex societies', in *New Developments in Italian Landscape Archaeology*, BAR International Series 1091, ed. P. Attema *et al.*, Oxford: 246–65.

No author (1881) 'Cerveteri', *NSA*: 166–7.

    (1883) 'Montefiascone', *NSA*: 434.

    (1884) 'Vergato', *NSA*: 21–2.

    (1886) 'Civitella d'Arna', *NSA*: 287.

    (1887a) 'Orvieto: nuovi Scavi in Contrada Cannicella', *NSA*: 90–1.

    (1887b) 'Perugia: tombe etrusche scoperte nel cimitero', with notes from E. Brizio and G. F. Gamurrini, *NSA*: 391–8.

    (1889) 'Orvieto: nuove scoperte della necropoli volsiniese in Contrada Cannicella', *NSA*: 59–60.

    (1892) 'Bolsena', *NSA*: 154.

Index